WARRINGTON CAMPUS

LIBRARY

Telephone: 01925 534284

This book is to be returned on or before the
last date stamped below. Overdue charges
will be incurred by the late return of books.

UNIVERSITY
COLLEGE CHESTER
WARRINGTON CAMPUS

The Feminist Reader

Essays in Gender and the Politics of Literary Criticism

Second Edition

Edited by Catherine Belsey and Jane Moore

First edition 1989

Reprinted 5 times

Second edition 1997

Published 1997 by
MACMILLAN PRESS LTD
Houndmills, Basingstoke, Hampshire RG21 6XS
and London
Companies and representatives
throughout the world

ISBN 0–333–66493–0 hardcover
ISBN 0–333–66494–9 paperback

A catalogue record for this book is available
from the British Library.

This book is printed on paper suitable for recycling and
made from fully managed and sustained forest sources.

10   9   8   7   6   5   4   3   2
06   05   04   03   02   01   00

Printed in Great Britain by
Creative Print and Design (Wales), Ebbw Vale

TO OUR PARENTS

Contents

Preface

The aim of the second edition of this anthology is to make available to the feminist reader a collection of essays which does full justice to the range and diversity, as well as to the eloquence and the challenge of recent feminist critical theory and practice. The idea of the book arose directly from our experience of teaching feminist criticism. Existing anthologies, though excellent in many ways, seemed to us to be composed on too narrow a basis to display the differences within feminism and the debates which were the evidence of its continuing vitality. More recent collections cover a wider range, but without the focus and commentary that we hope students find helpful.

The anthology begins at the point a great many feminist readers start from, a feeling of outrage at the patriarchal nature of the canon and the relative exclusion of women from literary history. It goes on to consider the implications of this. Is writing by women necessarily feminist? What kind of literary history would serve the needs of feminism? Is there a women's language? What is the relation between racial politics and the politics of gender, or between gender and the body?

The essays, in other words, either implicitly or explicitly, enter into a kind of dialogue with each other, enlisting the reader in a developing debate. The diversity of feminism thus appears as the effect of a continuing discussion, and not simply as a range of distinct and static points of view.

Some of the available positions are difficult to grasp, at least in the first instance, because of their unfamiliarity. We have done our best to make them accessible without intruding between the reader and the essays themselves. The Introduction offers an updated map of the field of feminist critical theory. In addition, before the author's Notes on each essay we have offered a Summary of the essay's main propositions. We also supply a Glossary of terms which may be unfamiliar to readers not already acquainted with poststructuralist varieties of feminism. And finally, we offer annotated Suggestions for Further Reading, in an expanded bibliography which sets out to be selective rather than comprehensive. The project of all this is to facilitate discussion of the questions the essays raise, the issues which seem to us to matter to the feminist reader.

No feminist critic ever works alone. We are grateful to friends, colleagues and students who have shared our feminist commitment and discussed questions of criticism with us. The contributors have been a pleasure to work with. And we should like to thank in particular Margaret Bartley, Andrew Belsey, Moira Eminton, Chris Evans, Kate McGowan, Susan Moore, Beverley Tarquini and Chris Weedon for their help and support.

Catherine Belsey
Jane Moore

Acknowledgements

The editors and publishers wish to thank the following for permission to use copyright material:

Gillian Beer, for 'Representing Women Re-presenting the Past', by permission of the author; Helénè Cixous for 'Sorties: Out and Out: Attacks/Ways Out/Forays' from Helénè Cixous and Catherine Clément, *The Newly Born Woman*, trans. Betsy Wing (1986) pp. 63–4, 83–8, 91–7. Copyright © in original French language 1975 by Union Générale d'Editions, Paris. English translation copyright © 1986 by the University of Minnesota, by perrnission of I. B. Tauris & Co and the University of Minnesota Press; Rosalind Coward, for 'The True Story of How I Became My Own Person' from *Female Desire: Women's Sexuality Today* (1984), pp. 175–86, by permission of Grafton Books, a division of HarperCollins Publishers; Diane Elam, for extracts from 'Feminism and the Postmodern: Theory's Romance' from *Romancing the Postmodern* (1992), pp. 143–9,153–66, 174, by permission of Routledge; Shoshana Felman, for 'Women and Madness: the Critical Phallacy', *Diacritics* (Winter 1975), 2–10, by permission of The Johns Hopkins University Press; Majorie Garber, for 'Cross-dressing, Gender and Representation: Elvis Presley', extracts from 'The Transvestite Continuum: Liberace–Valentino–Elvis' in *Vested Interests: Cross-Dressing and Cultural Anxiety*, ed. Marjorie Garber (1992), pp. 353–7, 359, 363–74, by permission of Routledge, New York; Luce Irigaray, for 'The Looking Glass, from the Other Side' from *This Sex Which Is Not One*, trans. Catherine Porter with Carolyn Burke, (1985), pp. 9–22. Copyright © 1985 by Cornell University, by permission of Cornell University Press; Mary Jacobus, for 'The Difference of View' from *Women Writing and Writing About Women* (1979), pp. 10–21 by permission of Croom Helm; Julia Kristeva, for an extract from 'Women's Time', trans. Alice Jardine and Harry Blake, *Signs*, 7 (1981), 18–35, by permission of The University of Chicago Press; Toril Moi, for 'Feminist, Female, Feminine' extracts from 'Feminist Literary Crticism' from *Modern Literary Theory*, ed. Anne Jefferson and David Robey (1986) pp. 204–21, by permission of B. T. Batsford Ltd and Barnes & Noble Books; Toni Morrison, for 'Disturbing Nurses and the Kindness of Sharks' from *Playing in the Dark* (1992), Harvard University Press, pp. 63–91. Copyright © 1992 by Toni Morrison, by permission of International Creative Management, Inc. on behalf of the author; Line Pouchard, for 'Queer Desire in *The Well of Loneliness*', by permission of the author; Dale Spender, for extracts from 'Women and Literary History' from *Mothers of the Novel*, Routledge and Kegan Paul (1986) pp. 115–18, 138–44, by permission of the author; Gayatri Chakravorty Spivak, for extracts from 'Three Women's Texts and a Critique of Imperialism', *Critical Inquiry*, 12 (1985) 243–7, 247–51, 252–61, by permission of the author.

Every effort has been made to trace the copyright holders but if any have been inadvertently overlooked the publishers will be pleased to make the necessary arrangement at the first opportunity.

1

Introduction: The Story So Far

Catherine Belsey and Jane Moore

The feminist reader is enlisted in the process of changing the gender relations which prevail in our society, and she regards the practice of reading as one of the sites in the struggle for change.

For the feminist reader there is no innocent or neutral approach to literature: all interpretation is political. Specific ways of reading inevitably militate for or against the process of change. To interpret a work is always to address, whether explicitly or implicitly, certain kinds of issues about what it says. The feminist reader might ask, among other questions, how the text represents women, what it says about gender relations, how it defines sexual difference. (A few texts, of course, do not depict any women at all, and say nothing about gender relations, and from a feminist point of view that too signifies.) A criticism which ignores these issues implies that they do not matter.

A feminist does not necessarily read in order to praise or to blame, to judge or to censor. More commonly she sets out to assess how the text invites its readers, as members of a specific culture, to understand what it means to be a woman or a man, and so encourages them to reaffirm or to challenge existing cultural norms.

Feminist criticism has in a sense no beginnings. When in the seventeenth century Esther Sowernam and Bathsua Makin pointed out that many classical texts identified powerful deities and influential muses as women, they were reading from a feminist perspective. When Mary Wollstonecraft at the end of the eighteenth century argued that sentimental novels encouraged women to see themselves as helpless and silly, she was practising a form of feminist criticism. Indeed, Wollstonecraft contributed to a feminist anthology of sorts called *The Female Reader*.[1] Two of the most distinguished feminist readers of the twentieth century were Virginia Woolf in *A Room of One's Own* and Simone de Beauvoir in *The Second Sex*.

Nevertheless, the politics of gender entered a new phase in the late 1960s, and since that time feminist criticism has been developed, debated, institutionalised and diversified as never before. In 1970 three revolutionary books appeared within a few months of each other. Germaine Greer's *The Female Eunuch*, Kate Millett's *Sexual Politics* and

1

Patriarchal Attitudes by Eva Figes were all bestsellers. They were witty, eloquent, wide-ranging and polemical, and they caught and crystallised a moment when the challenges of the sixties to a range of existing authorities had given a new impetus to the politics of liberation. These three works, and others like them, did much to define an agenda for a new, self-conscious phase of feminist reading.

It is a striking feature of all three books that when they discuss literature they refuse to isolate it from the culture of which it forms a part. Indeed, they are not primarily works of literary criticism at all in the conventional sense of that term. Figes considers the Brontës and George Eliot in the context of the restricted range of possibilities for women in the nineteenth century. Greer analyses Shakespeare's plays to find in them a depiction of love and marriage new in the sixteenth century, when romantic love became the basis of marriage as partnership, and the nuclear family emerged as the main unit of a developing consumerism. Millett's denunciation of the Lawrentian idealisation of the phallus – unforgettably entertaining, and probably unsurpassed, however much more complex feminist criticism has since become – is part of a generalised analysis of sexual power relations in a range of texts, not all of them fictional. Millett herself draws attention to the nature of her book as 'something of an anomaly, a hybrid, possibly a new mutation altogether'.[2] Greer makes no apology for discussing literature alongside popular culture: she simply points to the parallels between D. H. Lawrence and Barbara Cartland, and leaves it at that.

The challenge to traditional literary criticism was in this respect extremely radical. 'Art' was no longer a cover for politics; 'literature' ceased to be a special category, a repository of timeless truths concerning an eternal human nature; and 'great authors' could get it wrong. The works on the syllabus, it appeared, were not necessarily neutral, not simply depictions of reality, but interpretations of the world, and some of them presented women in trivialising or degrading ways. Writing was a cultural rather than a purely individual phenomenon, and the social context of literature was more than an explanatory 'background'. Fiction, it seemed, both manifested and influenced the ways in which societies understood themselves and the world. Literature was in this sense profoundly historical.

History itself has always been important to feminism, because it is history which provides us with evidence that things have changed. And if they have changed in the past, they do not have to stay as they are now. 'Nature', on the other hand, has long been one of the most powerful weapons in the war against change. If women are passive, helpless and subservient by nature, then feminism is already a lost cause: we shall inevitably revert to type as soon as the present moment of rebellion comes to an end. If men have always been more rational, more judicious, more authoritative, patriarchy is a fact of nature, and women might as well lie back and enjoy it. But feminist history shows some cultures as more patriarchical than others. Greer traces the emerging tyranny of the nuclear family; Figes sees male domination increasing from the Middle Ages onwards, reaching its highest point in the Victorian period, when women were most enthusiastically idealised and most thoroughly subordinated.

And feminism too has its history. Millett records the development of women's resistance to patriarchy during the epoch of their deepest oppression. The official inauguration of the Women's Movement in America took place in 1848. The degree and the effectiveness of patriarchal control seem to have varied from one historical moment to another.

It follows that gender relations have more to do with custom than with nature. 'Women', as Eva Figes puts it, 'have been largely man-made'.[3] Feminist cultural history emphasises the ways in which social convention has tended to operate on behalf of the dominant group, and norms of femininity have worked in the interests of men.

It comes as something of a shock to encounter 'he' as the generalised pronoun in these books published in 1970, though even at that stage a certain unease was beginning to be evident about what feminists have since called he-man language. Germaine Greer drew attention to the wide range of abusive terms applicable solely to women. Figes exploited the ambiguity of 'man'. But when, ten years later, Dale Spender published *Man Made Language*, the title drew explicit attention to the patriarchal implications of the supposedly gender-neutral term. The human race, it implied, was male, and if women were included, it was on condition that, linguistically at least, they were neither seen nor heard.

By this time a good deal of work had been done on language from a feminist point of view, and feminists were becoming aware that it was only women who were likely to chatter, gossip, tittle-tattle, whine, nag or bitch. On the other hand, only men could be virile and potent: there were no female equivalents for these terms of praise. Powerful creatures that they are, men conventionally perform the sexual act, while women are merely involved in sexual relationships. Men, but not women, are entitled to be aggressive or, better, abrasive, and women who protest about it are inclined to be shrill or, worse, strident. But then none of this should surprise us, in view of the asymmetries that have developed between masters and mistresses, wizards and witches, governors and governesses, knights and dames. In each case the word for women has negative meanings or connotations, while the male term consistently implies authority.

As Spender points out, these binary oppositions, in which one pole is privileged over the other, are 'fundamental premises in an order based on the supremacy of one group over another'.[4] Language does not merely name male superiority: it produces it. The tendency of words to seem transparent, to appear simply to label a pre-existing reality, indicated to feminists the crucial role of language in the construction of a world picture which legitimates the existing patriarchal order. Meanings, it became clear, are cultural, and are learned, though we learn them so young that they seem to be there by nature.

It was a common theme of feminists of the early seventies that the patriarchy they denounced was reinforced by psychoanalysis. Freud, they maintained, was an arch-misogynist, and the role of the psychoanalytic institution was to reinstate within the patriarchal order women whose symptoms showed evidence of rebellion against it. Kate Millett's account is the most detailed, and probably the hardest to resist. In her analysis Freud, who evidently felt threatened by them, set out to disarm the feminists by invoking the concept of penis-envy. The little girl, he argued, glimpsing the penis of the little boy, instantly recognises her own inadequacy. As she matures, she becomes reconciled to her inevitable condition of inferiority, and learns to replace the desire for a penis with the wish for a baby. Motherhood is thus 'really' a manifestation of the desire to be a man. If, on the other hand, the little girl fails to mature adequately, she continues to pursue masculine aims: she seeks independence, competes with men and becomes a feminist – or a neurotic. In either case, it is well known that women in general are prone to feelings of insecurity and jealousy; they have a reduced sense of justice, a less developed commitment to moral principles than men; and they are more commonly motivated by feelings than by reason. In his early work Freud made some allowances for the role of culture in what he observed, but as time went on he attributed it increasingly to nature.

Millett engagingly ridicules all this and, temporarily at least, renders Freud quite as unreadable, as impossible for feminists as Lawrence. But the position did not long go uncontested. In 1974 Juliet Mitchell published *Psychoanalysis and Feminism*, arguing that Freud's pessimistic account of women was indeed a description of a particular culture, and not an interpretation of a universal human nature. Only the structures psychoanalysis identifies, and not their content, are in Mitchell's reading universal. What is radical for feminism in Freud is the theory of undifferentiated infant sexuality: the initial object of desire for little girls as well as little boys is the mother. The Oedipus complex represents the entry into a specific culture and thus into the gender roles defined by that culture. Psychoanalysis, Mitchell urges, explains how we acquire sexual identity by repressing desires which are culturally unacceptable; it does not require us to believe that sexual identity is synonymous with anatomy.

Mitchell's reading of Freud owes something to the work of Jacques

Lacan, who reread Freud in the light of Saussure's account of the nature of language. Jacqueline Rose, who has worked with Juliet Mitchell, also draws on Lacan to take Mitchell's position a stage further. Rose argues that psychoanalysis is indispensable to feminism, on the basis that it provides a theory of sexual identity as culturally enjoined and constantly resisted. The complexity of undifferentiated sexual desire is repressed when the child learns to identify itself as either masculine or feminine. Anatomy is not the source of sexual difference, but its reductive *figure*, its representation. But for these reasons the identification required by culture can never be complete. What is radical in Freud is the concept of the unconscious, that 'other scene', as Lacan calls it, which challenges and resists the cultural norms imposed on it. Femininity is never achieved; the unconscious refuses to submit to what Lacan calls the symbolic order, the discipline of language and culture. At this ultimate level, in other words, we reject the paternal Law, the symbolic order of a patriarchal society.

> Feminism's affinity with psychoanalysis rests above all, I would argue, with this recognition that there is a resistance to identity at the very heart of psychic life. Viewed in this way, psychoanalysis . . . becomes one of the few places in our culture where it is recognised as more than a fact of individual pathology that most women do not painlessly slip into their roles as women, if indeed they do at all.[5]

And Rose goes on in the same volume to bring psychoanalysis and feminism to bear on George Eliot and *Hamlet*.

The disagreement about psychoanalysis within feminism has tended to be perceived as a conflict over the *truth* of Freud's texts. One side or the other, it was assumed, must have got it wrong, failed to grasp the key meanings of his writings or distorted his views. But there is no need to understand the debate in this way. Even in this very simplified summary of representative positions, it is possible to see that Millett on the one hand, and Mitchell and Rose on the other, are implicitly asking different questions about psychoanalysis. Millett asks, 'how has psychoanalysis contributed to the oppression of women?' Mitchell and Rose ask, 'how could psychoanalysis be read as an explanation of the oppression of women?' The different questions elicit different answers. Millett looks for evidence of patriarchal assumptions, and finds penis-envy. Mitchell and Rose look for explanatory terms, and find undifferentiated infant sexuality and unconscious resistance.

Meanwhile, in *The Enigma of Woman* Sarah Kofman offers a psychoanalytic reading of Freud's own work to show that the theory of penis-envy is not necessary to psychoanalysis. There are in the Freudian texts alternative accounts of woman as mysterious, aloof and self-contained. But the founder of psychoanalysis, Kofman argues, could not bear to leave the riddle of woman unsolved. The idea of penis-envy permits Freud to master the enigma of woman, thereby fulfilling his own desire to immobilise and thus kill the elusive eternal feminine.

Freud's texts are increasingly misogynistic; psychoanalysis can be appropriated in the interests of feminism. These statements are not contradictory. The debate throws into relief something that feminists had known all along in practice, if not in theory. The texts of psychoanalysis, like all writings, and like culture itself, are plural: different approaches produce different readings. The practice of interpretation is not neutral, but takes place from a specific perspective. In this instance, one approach is not more feminist than the other. The distinction is that Millett is more concerned with the way patriarchy victimises women, while Mitchell, Rose and Kofman are concerned with evidence that the victims of patriarchy are in a position to strike back.

In a similar way, a second current of feminist literary criticism grew up alongside and in response to the analysis of patriarchal culture. This was concerned with women's writing, and specifically with writing as a mode of resistance. Kate Millett, denouncing patriarchy, necessarily attended most carefully to writing by men. In what Elaine Showalter inventively terms 'gynocritics', the study of woman as writer, women are invited to speak for themselves, even if they continue to do so from within a patriarchal culture.[6] Showalter's eminently readable and excellently documented book, *A Literature of Their Own*, published in 1977, is perhaps the most influential of the accounts of women's writing in its difference from men's. Showalter identifies a female subculture in which fiction by women constitutes a record of their experience. She defines three separate but overlapping phases, 'feminine', 'feminist' and 'female'. In the first of these, from the 1840s to 1880, women wrote mainly in imitation of masculine models, but with distinctively feminine concerns; in the second phase, which lasted until 1920, they formulated specifically feminist protests and demands; and in the third, from 1920 to the present, women's writing moves increasingly towards self-discovery, the exploration of an inner space of female experience.

Though she takes Freud for granted, Showalter explicitly repudiates literary theory. In *The Madwoman in the Attic* (1979), their expansive analysis of Victorian women's writing, Sandra Gilbert and Susan Gubar present women's resistance to social and literary constraint in terms of a theory of the anxiety of patriarchal influence. Appropriating for feminism Harold Bloom's model of the writer struggling to overthrow the domination of a strong literary father, Gilbert and Gubar trace in women's writing the inscription of tension, self-doubt, renunciation and, above all, rage against the society which confines them.

Paradoxically, however, it was Ellen Moers's *Literary Women*, published in 1976, apparently less scholarly and more popular than either

Showalter's book or Gilbert and Gubar's, which in the event broke most radically with the assumptions of conventional criticism. Moers reinstates the by now traditional feminist interest in literature as an aspect of the whole culture. *Literary Women* is a contribution to cultural history in its analysis of the way that the exclusion of women from so many aspects of social and political life was precisely what propelled them into a form of utterance requiring no formal professional training and no special equipment. It was possible for women to write – in the middle of the night if necessary – and by this means to make money, especially to make the capital sums which would render them marriageable. Not simply a lonely struggle against patriarchy, women's writing in the eighteenth and nineteenth centuries also appears in *Literary Women* as one of patriarchy's unintended consequences. The evidence is presented in snatches of biography, but the mode of reading in *Literary Women*, though sometimes artlessly biographical, is often compelled by the nature of the material it confronts to break with the assumption that writing is a simple transcription of experience. In discussing the love poetry of so many nineteenth-century virgin poets, Moers takes into account the degree to which poetry is a form of fiction. And her analysis of Ann Radcliffe's Gothic fantasies, travel stories about capable heroines, and thus feminine equivalents of the contemporary picaresque tradition, implicitly acknowledges the degree to which fiction is the effect not only of experience but of other fiction. Perhaps inadvertently, but none the less effectively, *Literary Women* throws into relief the limited explanatory power of traditional literary history.[7]

Gynocritics also has the effect of challenging conventional critical value judgments. It has drawn attention to the work of a great many women writers whose work has been forgotten or suppressed, among them Mary Brunton, who made Jane Austen nervous because she was so clever. 'Who,' asks Ellen Moers ironically, 'wants to associate the great Jane Austen, companion of Shakespeare, with someone named Mary Brunton? Who wants to read or indeed can find a copy of *Self-Control* (1810) by that lady . . .?'[8] Within ten years of the question, however, Mary Brunton and a number of her contemporaries were to become available in paperback in the series *Mothers of the Novel*, edited by Dale Spender.

These different modes of feminist criticism, the denunciation of patriarchy on the one hand, and the study of women's writing on the other, have often been presented as rival approaches, each competing to be more politically correct than the other. It is not necessary to see them in this way, but it might be helpful to point out that each has (inevitably) its limitations, and that these limitations have specific political implications. The early denunciations of patriarchy, for instance, tended to retreat from the most radical aspects of their own analysis into an insistence that the patriarchal account of life was false, a distortion of the truth about women. Of course, in some instances this has been the case: motherhood is not inevitably a serene experience; housework is not necessarily fulfilling; clitoral orgasm is not immature. But in general the insistence that a political practice, the subordination of women, is based on falsehood, seems to imply that there is a truth about women which is outside culture, outside language and meaning, a question of nature. What was radical, however, about the work of Millett, Greer and Figes was precisely their break with the myth of a known and knowable nature that could be invoked in defence of specific political practices. Meanwhile, the construction of a feminine subculture, a form of writing which is essentially different from men's, paradoxically shares something of the same difficulty. It too takes culture for nature. The danger here is that the emphasis on difference tends either to have the effect of leaving things exactly as they are, with women eternally confined to a separate sphere, or to lead to a politics of separatism, which despairs of changing patriarchy and settles instead for an alternative space on the edges of it.

If feminist analysis was to continue to develop, therefore, it was necessary to confront in theory the implications of the radical discoveries that had been made in practice. In *Feminist Practice and Poststructuralist Theory* Chris Weedon makes a lucid and persuasive case for the feminist appropriation of recent (mainly French) theories of language and culture. These theories enable us to analyse both the injustices of patriarchy and women's resistance to them, while at the same time identifying specific pressure points for change.

In poststructuralist theory meanings are cultural and learned, but they are also unfixed, sliding, plural. They are therefore a matter for political debate. Culture itself is the limit of our knowledge; there is no available truth outside culture with which we can challenge injustice. But culture is also contradictory, the location of resistances as well as oppression, and it is therefore ultimately unstable. It too is in consequence a site of political struggle.

One result of feminism's engagement with poststructuralist theory was the emergence of forms of cultural history that analysed a range of signifying practices. In 1984 Rosalind Coward published *Female Desire*, which identified not only fiction, but food, snapshots, advertisements and fashion as locations of contemporary constructions of femininity. A year later Rachel Bowlby's book *Just Looking* traced the cultural formation of women's stereotypical obsession with shopping back to the development of department stores in the nineteenth century. Both books implicitly argue that a feminist politics needs to analyse the cultural construction of femininity, past and present, if it is to be able to identify the possibilities for future change. And in their focus on desire, which encircles the lives of feminist and non-feminist women alike, each theorises the process by which women are enlisted as gendered subjects. 'To be a woman',

Coward writes, 'is to be constantly addressed, to be constantly scrutinized, to have our desire constantly courted – in the kitchen, on the streets, in the world of fashion, in films and fiction.'[9] Put like this, it becomes apparent that women are the destination of desire: its subjects, not its origin. Desire and femininity are thus thrown into relief as historically- and culturally-specific constructions; and if there is nothing natural or universal about the meanings of femininity prevailing at any one moment, it follows that those meanings can be challenged. While it is unlikely, however, that a poststructuralist account of the cultural production of gender and desire can bring about the end of patriarchy alone, poststructuralism's understanding of sexual difference does at least release feminists from the tyranny of biological imperatives and allow the possibility of a future where the old hierarchies no longer structure relations of gender.

From the beginning, poststructuralist accounts of gender aimed at denaturalising all the cultural and aesthetic assumptions about sexuality. Of course, it is not only women who are enlisted as subjects of patriarchal values but men too, and one noticeable feature of poststructuralist criticism of the 1980s was the growing involvement of male theorists in issues of gender. An example is Stephen Heath's book *The Sexual Fix*, published in 1982, which analyses discourses of sexology in novels, magazines and sex manuals to show that there is nothing outside culture to hold sexual meanings in place. Heath discovers evidence of patriarchal stereotypes in writing by both men and women, thereby suggesting that the biological sex of an author provides no 'natural' foundation or guarantor of sexual meanings. The assertion that representations of sexuality are in no way synonymous with an author's sex simultaneously calls into question the popular feminist belief that women write differently from men.

For many feminists, however, poststructuralism's refusal to endorse an essentialist understanding of gender identity raised unsettling questions about the implications of the theory for a feminist politics, especially when viewed in the light of men's interest in the project. Rosi Braidotti, who contributed to an anthology of mainly American essays entitled *Men in Feminism*, published in 1987, maintains that most male analysis of gender is written without any awareness either of the practical issues at stake in feminist politics or of feminism's commitment to social change. Other contributors to the debate argue that poststructuralism's interrogation of the integrity of biological difference results in a slippage of sexual boundaries which necessarily loses something of the specificity of the category 'Woman'. This in turn entails the danger of reinstating, however implicitly, the ostensibly universal masculine pronoun and of ensuring men's continued dominance in the world of theory. That most of the powerful poststructuralist theorists are indeed men (Barthes, Derrida,

Foucault, Lacan, Lyotard) has added to the prevalent feminist suspicion that, as a genre, theory tends to support patriarchal interests.

Meanwhile, in her influential book *Gender Trouble*, first published in 1990, the American theorist Judith Butler accuses one of the most controversial male theorists, Jacques Lacan, of subsuming the specificity of Woman under a masculine Symbolic. On Butler's reading, Lacanian theory ultimately authorises patriarchy by privileging the Phallus.

In France, however, where theory in general has been more widely accepted, a generation of feminists schooled in Freud and Lacan have retained the language of psychoanalysis but reversed its sexual hierarchy. While psychoanalysis conventionally marginalises woman to the place of the 'other', the French feminists Luce Irigaray and Hélène Cixous revalue that pejorative label and celebrate woman's difference from man at all levels, psychic, physical and intellectual. Thus, in place of masculine reason and its restraining laws, French feminism promotes feminine irrationality and sexual anarchy. In her mystical, lyrical prose, the very antithesis of patriarchal prescriptions for good style, Cixous writes appreciatively of witches, hysterics, and homosexuals. These are the victims of patriarchy but also its most dangerous rebels, the ones who refuse patriarchal imperatives, the poetic spirits that cannot be tamed.

It is not a question, though, of attributing such rebelliousness to nature. Femininity is the criterion which Cixous uses to define 'otherness', and femininity is not grounded in anatomy. On the contrary, it is situated in language and in culture. The difficulty, then, is not with individual men or women but with patriarchy. It is patriarchy that imposes male privilege, that prescribes heterosexuality and strives to repress the disruptive excess of alternative sexualities, of unconscious resistance, play and creativity. But, Cixous insists, there have always been exceptions: 'those uncertain, poetic persons . . . Men or women: beings who are complex, mobile, open', who inscribe rebellion in the very act of writing.[10]

And it is in writing that Cixous herself performs resistance. *Ecriture féminine*, which embraces both 'female' and 'feminine', is suffused with metaphors of the body that link the extravagance of feminine sexuality to a writing whose opulent lyricism and blatant disrespect for 'common sense' breaks all patriarchal codes. Luce Irigaray, whose work is often discussed alongside that of Cixous, offers a similarly opaque and poetic language of insurrection. Again breaking all the rules for 'proper' style, the writing that she calls 'womanspeak' is written by and from the female body. Closely attentive to the implications of Freudian and Lacanian theory for understanding femininity, Irigaray looks at psychoanalysis from the 'other side', and finds a repressed female psycho-sexual economy that at once resists and disrupts phallocentricism's specular certainties.

Given that the project of French feminist writing is to displace old patriarchal truths, to rewrite their narratives and re-vision the role of language itself, it is difficult to assess its implications for a practical feminist politics. Womanspeak and *écriture féminine* prefigure a space beyond patriarchy, one that is in many senses utopian, because it cannot be accommodated within current social, economic and sexual structures. In this respect, they are neither historically nuanced, nationally differentiated, nor class-conscious languages. And, like the psychoanalytic theories they draw on, *écriture féminine* and womanspeak run the risk of constructing a universal model of femininity.

Nonetheless, French feminism has been remarkably influential in Britain and America. Indeed, it is possible, as Mary Jacobus shows here in 'The Difference of View', to bring psychoanalytic approaches to sexuality and writing within a historical framework. Jacobus uses Freud to bring out the unconscious meanings in women's novels, thereby displaying their ideological constitution. Gaps and silences, questions and hesitations, such as the famous 'awkward break' that Virginia Woolf detects in *Jane Eyre*, indicate what Jacobus calls the 'fictionality' of the text's sexual ideology: 'By a breach of fictional decorum, writing enacts protest as well as articulating it . . . the disruption reveals what the novel cannot say within its legitimate confines, and hence reveals its fictionality.'[11]

Jacobus's later work assiduously endeavours to persuade feminist readers to analyse the textual constitution of femininity and to forego any essentialist return to the author in the act of literary criticism. In place of the liberal-humanist question: "'Is there a woman in this text?'" Jacobus urges us to ask: "'*Is there a text in this woman?*'"[12] For some schools of feminist criticism, however, it is not enough to practise textual analysis: it is equally important to focus on the individuality of authors, and to do so with the aim of establishing traditions of women's writing which are neither heterosexual, white nor Western. In the context of identity politics, the figure of the author endorses the distinctiveness of particular beliefs, and both lesbian and black critics have called on writers to establish the uniqueness of their aesthetic and cultural values.

Adrienne Rich's influential essay 'Compulsory Heterosexuality and Lesbian Existence', first published in 1980, thus criticises heterosexual feminists for assuming that their beliefs represent those of women in general. The following year Bonnie Zimmerman also identified the absence of lesbian ideas and authors from 'mainstream' feminist anthologies and biographies. Her tellingly entitled essay, 'What Has Never Been: An Overview of Lesbian Feminist Criticism', pushes for the development of a canon of lesbian texts but it also urges lesbian critics to develop 'a greater specificity, historically and culturally', thereby avoiding the assumption of universal experience.[13]

Indeed, one of the radical consequences of constructing a lesbian tradition has been precisely to call into question the existence of universal sexual norms and experiences. Subsequent theorists such as Teresa de Lauretis, Eve Sedgwick and Judith Butler have used the term queer in order to problematise further the status of lesbian and gay identities. As Line Pouchard points out in her essay here, queer dislodges essentialist understandings of sexuality that propose a unified model of subjectivity based on biology. More than this, queer implies a sexuality or sexualities that confuse the old distinctions, male/female, gay/lesbian, and even gay/straight. Performances of sexuality, cross-dressing, transvestism and drag, produce queer sexualities that contest the possibility of legitimising identity in terms of sexual preference, individual destiny or biological truth.

Queer theory makes it impossible to speak of a discrete, unified, body of lesbian theory. There isn't just one lesbian approach and even the appellation lesbian is insufficient to do justice to the diversity of the debates. Moreover, to place queer theory within a linear chronology is similarly misleading and is in danger of reducing the complexity of feminism's histories. As early as 1929 Joan Riviere brought out the queerness of sexuality in her essay 'Womanliness as a Masquerade', which explicitly challenges the existence of an essential femininity. In this respect, the history of feminism does not chart the progression towards a moment of truth, or liberation. Certainly there have been generations of feminism but those generational spaces do not constitute a linear narrative. On the contrary, they tell of advances and retreats, triumphs and setbacks, that confuse any teleological organisation.

This does not mean, however, that historical moments are unmarked by peculiar blindnesses. In the 1970s, the high point of North American and European feminism, it was apparent to African-American women that white, Western theories of sexual difference did not recognise distinctions of colour or race or nationality. Drawing on their experience of being rendered doubly invisible within American culture, a generation of black women activists, autobiographers, critics and novelists aimed to distinguish the difference of their history and art. In 1977 Barbara Smith's ground-breaking essay, 'Toward a Black Feminist Criticism', called for the construction of black female traditions to counter the cultural dominance of white, heterosexual and male values. Since then, black feminist writers have established their own canons of literature and criticism. Barbara Christian, for example, published *Black Women Novelists* in 1980 and *Black Feminist Criticism* in 1985. In consequence, other histories have been told, not only those of black women writers but also the (largely unacknowledged) history of white feminism's racism. Angela Davis's monumental work *Women, Race and Class*, published in 1981, made public the prevalence of racism in America's early anti-slavery and women's rights campaigns. In common with black women's writing of the period, *Women, Race and Class* is at once a scholarly, polemical and deeply personal book, which implicitly and explicitly draws attention to the racial and cultural politics of style. Weaving personal anecdote with textual analysis and cultural history to the point of inseparability, Davis, Smith and Christian show in practice, in their own style, the importance of authorial biography for a black feminist politics. But their work also indicates that an emphasis on the cultural location and racial specificity of the author does not necessarily spell retreat into a liberal-humanist understanding of that self as the sole source of meaning. Toni Morrison's eloquent essays in literary criticism, for example, pointedly invoke biographical material alongside the intertextuality of meaning precisely in order to expose and explain the impact of a culture's racial values on the literary imagination.

By 1987, when Gayatri Spivak published *In Other Worlds: Essays in Cultural Politics*, the work of non-Western and African-American women had begun to be recognised by the white literary establishment. And theory too, although not dominant, had been brought onto the agenda of many feminist and literary critics. Indeed, Spivak was responsible for presenting Jacques Derrida's work to Anglophone readers: she translated and introduced his book *Of Grammatology* in 1976. It is no surprise, then, that her own literary criticism marks a rapprochement between feminist literary theory, postcolonial concerns and poststructuralist criticism.

The essays collected in *In Other Worlds* expose the national and cultural partiality of Western feminism's insistence on the centrality of the question 'Who am I?' and propose, instead, a set of further questions: 'not merely who am I? but who is the other woman? How am I naming her? How does she name me?'[14] Naming, Spivak shows, is a never a neutral activity, and she shares the project of postcolonial feminism in general of directing attention to the appropriating and colonising gestures of language.

Spivak's analysis of how subjects are colonised by modes of address, how they are enlisted within discourses of national identity, or alternatively, excluded from them, is part of a larger body of postcolonial feminisms that are acutely attuned to discourses of power and bear witness to both the powerful appeal of poststructuralist theories of subjectivity, language, meaning, and the need to beware of the complicity of these theories with the agendas of sexual and national imperialism. That tension, however, is not an unproductive one. Noticeably, a common concern of postcolonial work of the 1990s is the intersection of 'first-world' and 'third-world' feminisms. Laura E. Donaldson's book, *Decolonizing Feminisms: Race, Gender and Empire-Building*, published in 1992, and Jenny Sharpe's study, *Allegories of Empire: The Figure of Woman in the Colonial Text*, which appeared a year later, explore relations of difference and reciprocity between contemporary theories of textual interpretation and postcolonial reading practices.

Feminist theories, and the patriarchal knowledges they contest, have been in constant battle over Truth. Postmodern theory, which has emerged as a new current in feminist thought, is not concerned, however, with laying claim to the truth of what it means to be a woman or a man, gay or straight, black or white. Rather, postmodernism calls into question the very possibility of absolute knowledge or universal meaning, and in doing so it radically exposes the political interests that are at stake in invoking metaphysical categories such as Nature, Reason, Science, Justice to legitimate the 'truth' of a culture, of gender, race or language.

In the history of patriarchal knowledge woman has figured as a metaphor for non-truth, non-knowledge, everything, in other words, that falls outside the confines of 'male reason'. Yet, as Alice Jardine has argued in her book *Gynesis*, published in 1987, the marginalisation of woman to the perimeter of patriarchal meanings simultaneously produces a space from which to counter the 'truth' of patriarchal accounts of the world, including that of sexual identity itself. This space is also akin to that which Julia Kristeva aligns with a third phase of feminism, a phase identified in her essay here as one that represents a radically sceptical attitude to sexual truth, a questioning of any notion of a universal or essential sexual identity.

To the degree that postmodernism implies a fundamental questioning of the 'great truths' of Western patriarchy, it is compatible with a feminist politics of change. For if it is the linguistic culture, not nature, that constitutes the range of meanings available in any one time or place, then it follows that there is no single truth, no absolute knowledge, which would hold all others in place. This does not mean that we are free simply to create new meanings (on the contrary, we are the subjects of language and culture) but it does imply that the meanings a culture subscribes to work on behalf of specific political interests.

And yet it is precisely postmodernism's incredulity towards the truth of sexuality that simultaneously brings it into conflict with feminism's interest in identity politics. Certainly, as Alice Jardine has argued, when feminism participates in the Enlightenment project of establishing the truth of woman, it is radically incompatible with postmodernism. Indeed, a number of theorists have maintained that in so far as feminism depends upon a relatively stable and unified model of female subjectivity, postmodernism's refusal to ground meaning in any pre-cultural or transcendent truth inevitably entails a revision (even a destruction) of feminism itself.

But from its conception feminism has continually been under revision. The postmodern movement testifies to the wide diversity of feminist theories, each pointing towards different possible futures and allowing the feminist reader to peruse a range of narratives other than the male stories told so far.

Postmodernity releases us from the naturalisation of patriarchal values. If we are all in a sense cross-dressed, if 'femininity' is no more than masquerade, and gender a performance negotiated with a sexed body, there is no theoretical limit to the possibilities for change. Already twentieth-century feminism has severely undermined traditional misogynist assumptions and masculinist language. Feminist modes of reading have transformed the institutional practices of literary criticism and cultural studies, propelling them out towards work on sexuality, desire and the instability of identity. It is imaginable – though perhaps no more than that – that feminist reading may one day give way to a mode of analysis that acknowledges and celebrates a plurality of differences.

Now read on . . .

2

Women and Literary History

Dale Spender

I have no reason to suspect that my own university education was peculiarly biased or limited. On the contrary, it appears to have been fairly representative. Yet in the guise of presenting me with an overview of the literary heritage of the English-speaking world, my education provided me with a grossly inaccurate and distorted view of the history of letters. For my introduction to the 'greats' was (with the exception of the famous five women novelists) an introduction to the great men. Even in the study of the novel where women were conceded to have a place, I was led to believe that all the initial formative writing had been the province of men. So along with other graduates of 'Eng. Lit.' departments I left university with the well-cultivated impression that men had created the novel and that there were no women novelists (or none of note) before Jane Austen.[1]

There was no reason for me to be suspicious about what I was being taught. I was a student in a reputable university being tutored by experts who referred me to the literary scholars who, without qualification, asserted the ascendancy of men. For example, the authoritative treatise on the early novel was by Ian Watt and was entitled *The Rise of the Novel: Studies in Defoe, Richardson and Fielding* (1957) and it opened with the bald statement that the novel was begun by Defoe, Richardson and Fielding, and that it was the genius of these three men that had created the new form. Had it even occurred to me to be dubious about the frequency with which I was asked to accept men's good opinion of men, by what right could I have questioned the scholarship and authority of such established and sanctioned critics?

Besides, what contrary evidence was available? No matter where I looked around me, I encountered almost exclusively the publications of men. Like Virginia Woolf in the British Museum (*A Room of One's Own*, 1928) I too found that the library catalogue and shelves were filled with books predominantly authored by men. And in the bookshops a steady stream of new and attractively packaged editions of early male novelists helped to reinforce the belief that it was only men who had participated in the initial production of this genre. I neither stumbled across fascinating 'old' editions of women's novels on the library shelves nor found interesting republications when browsing through bookshops. As far as I knew both the old and the new were representative of the books that had been published, and as there were virtually no women among them, it had to be because women had not written books.

So I had no difficulty accepting the statements of Ian Watt: men were to be congratulated for the birth of the novel. Women – or more precisely, one woman – entered only *after* men had ushered the novel into the world: Jane Austen, writes Ian Watt in 'A Note' at the end of *The Rise of the Novel*, provided a steady and guiding influence for this new form but neither she, nor any other woman, had helped to bring it into existence. In this book in which Fanny Burney is mentioned on only three occasions (and in less than three lines) he does say that 'Jane Austen was the heir of Fanny Burney',[2] but as this is the only cursory reference, the impression remains that when it comes to women novelists there was no one to speak of, before Jane Austen.

It does not, of course, strain the limits of credibility to believe that for women, Jane Austen started it all. Her novels reveal such a great talent that it is possible to accept that she was capable of bringing forth – in fully fledged form and without benefit of female 'models' – those superb novels which to my mind still stand as one of the high points of achievement in English fiction. But if it is possible to accept this version of women's literary history, I have discovered since that it is exceedingly unwise. For to see Jane Austen as a starting point is to be dreadfully deceived. Any portrayal of her which represents her as an originator and not as an inheritor of women's literary traditions is one which has strayed far from the facts of women's fiction writing. And when Jane Austen is seen to *inherit* a literary tradition this has ramifications not just for the history of women novelists but for the history of novelists in general.

For more than a century before Jane Austen surreptitiously took up her pen, women, in ever increasing numbers and with spectacular success, had been trying their hand at fiction. And not just the few women already referred to either, although obviously the Duchess of Newcastle, Aphra Behn and Delarivière Manley had played an important part, and Eliza Haywood, 'a woman of genius', had helped to conceive the possibilities and realities of fiction. And not just the 'refreshing' Fanny Burney or the 'worthy' Maria Edgeworth who are sometimes briefly acknowledged in passing for their 'historic interest'. (Maria Edgeworth is not mentioned in Ian Watt's *The Rise of the Novel*.) But a whole gallery of women: women from different backgrounds, different regions, and with different concerns, who all published well-acclaimed novels by the end of the 1700s.

That such women and their writing exist raises numerous questions about the traditions of women: this also raises questions about the traditions of men!

Without doubt the novel came into its own during the eighteenth century; the publication figures in themselves tell a story of sure and steady growth: 'The annual production of works of fiction, which had averaged only about seven in the years between 1700 to 1740, rose to an average of about twenty in the three decades following 1740 and this output was doubled in the period from 1770 to 1800', writes Ian Watt.[3] About two thousand novels in all, by the end of the century. And the distinct impression that they were written mainly by men.

Now, it's not possible to make definitive statements about how many of these two thousand novels were written by women, and how many by men. In quite a few cases, the sex of the author remains unknown – particularly because of the penchant for anonymous publications, a practice, it must be noted, which was more likely to tempt (particularly modest) women rather than men. But even if the 'sex unknown' authors are subtracted from the list of novelists of the 1700s, the number of women novelists and their works which remain is little short of astonishing, given that we have been led to believe that women played no part in these productions. As a result of a little detective work and a great deal of perseverance, I have been able to find one hundred good women novelists of the eighteenth century and together they were responsible for almost six hundred novels.

This means that even by the most conservative standards women would have to be granted a half-share in the production of fiction in the 1700s. And yet they have *all* 'disappeared'. It must be noted that this is not a reference to the occasional obscure woman writer who has slipped through the net of literary standards, not the 'one-off' achievement that has unfortunately been lost, not the eclipsing of one woman of genius like Eliza Haywood. This is at least half the literary output in fiction over a century; it is six hundred novels which in their own time were accorded merit.

And if since the eighteenth century it has become a well-established fact that women did not write novels during the 1700s, or that women did not write good novels, this was a fact which was *not* known at the time. For it was then widely appreciated that women wrote novels, and wrote them well. So firmly entrenched was this belief that it affords a most unusual and interesting chapter in the history of letters. While ever since it has been men who have been seen as the more significant and better novelists – to the extent that on occasion women have tried to increase their chances of publication by pretending to be men – it was not unknown during the eighteenth century for men to masquerade as female authors in the attempt to obtain some of the higher status (and greater chances of publication) which went with being a woman writer.

So frequent had this practice become that as early as June 1770 the *Gentleman's Magazine* thought it proper to conduct its own investigations as to the sex of authors, in the interest of being able to provide its readers with information on whether the latest production from a supposedly female pen was indeed genuine. For as the reviewer commented, 'among other literary frauds it has long been common for authors to affect the stile and character of ladies' (page 273). Which means that eighteenth-century readers knew something that twentieth-century ones do not: namely that in the beginning, and for quite a long time thereafter, the novel was seen as the female forte.

In 1773 the *Monthly Review* stated that when it came to fiction the field was filled by ladies, and well into the nineteenth century it was conceded that not only were women novelists plentiful, but that they were good.

Yet by the twentieth century when Ian Watt comes to outline the rise of the novel, women are no longer held in high esteem. He does – in passing – acknowledge that *the majority of eighteenth-century novels were written by women*, but how very damning is this faint and only praise.

How is it that we have come to lose this knowledge about many good women novelists? How have we come to lose it so completely that its one-time existence does not even register, so we are blissfully unaware of what has been lost? So that we do not even appreciate the significance of the single sentence that once women wrote (and published) reams? For so thoroughly have early women novelists been edited out of the literary records and removed from consciousness, their absence does not even ordinarily prompt comment, let alone concern.

And it is not because they were all no good that these hundred women novelists and their six hundred novels have been consigned to oblivion. For when the pronouncements of the literary establishment are perused for the case against the worth of these women writers, a curious omission comes to light. *There is no case against them.* If these many novels have been evaluated, the findings are not contained in the official literary records. And when the worth of women writers is not being based on any consideration of their writing, the only conclusion which can be drawn is that their worth is being determined by their sex.

That the writing of women does not count because it is written by women is the distinct impression given by Ian Watt. While his assertions about the quality of male novelists are based on a detailed examination of their writing, it is clear that he thinks the stand he takes on the absence of quality in women's writing does not even call for substantiation. He devotes three hundred pages to his assessment of male novelists and restricts his assessment of females to a single sentence: 'The majority of eighteenth-century novels were actually written by women.'[4] With no further discussion of the women, no entry to them in the index, and no explanation for his failure to discuss 'the majority' of novels of the eighteenth century, Ian Watt indicates that it is not necessary to examine the writing of women to know it is of no account.

Perhaps Ian Watt offers no evidence for the simple reason that it does not support his beliefs.

In the eighteenth century it was not known that women writers did not count. Quite the reverse. Charlotte Lennox, Mary Wollstonecraft, Fanny Burney, Elizabeth Inchbald, Mary Hays, Amelia Opie and Maria Edgeworth were not just 'actually' the majority, they were the *esteemed* majority. They were highly praised by readers and reviewers alike. They were valued by some of the best educated and most distinguished persons – of both sexes. And if today they do not count among the scholars and critics this was not how it was in their own day, when their writing was read and studied, when their efforts were consistently applauded, when they enjoyed extensive and positive reviews, when they were congratulated on their contribution to literature. (One way of rediscovering these women novelists is to go through the review sections of the literary periodicals of the day.)

Strange that those who read the novels then should have found them so good when today the verdict is that they are so bad they do not warrant examination. This is a most interesting additional insight. Now when we are presented with an exclusively male literary tradition – and this is how the early novel is presented – we must bear in mind that this is not because women did not write, could not get published, or went unacclaimed. Women qualified on all these counts. It was only later that they were disqualified.

How do we explain this transition from prominence to negation? What does it mean when women who were esteemed in their own lifetime are later denied and dismissed? It could be the rationale of an 'individual case' when earlier this century attempts were made to prove that Aphra Behn did not even exist, but such an explanation will not suffice when we are confronted with one hundred women whose work appears to have been systematically denied. Could it be that there is pattern and purpose in this treatment of women?

Germaine Greer certainly thinks so. She has referred to the 'phenomenon of the transience of female literary fame', and not just in relation to the novel. It is her contention that there have always been good women writers, in every area and every era, and that they always disappear. Since the days of Aphra Behn, she states, there have been 'women who have enjoyed dazzling literary prestige during their own lifetimes, only to vanish without trace from the records of posterity'.[5]

Once acclaimed, but now denied. This is the problem of women writers and it is one which almost every woman critic of the past few decades has addressed. Although in some circles it may be in order to 'accept' the disappearance of women writers as just a strange and random quirk of literary history, such an explanation has no place among women critics who have noted that the same fate does not await men. Of course many male writers have fallen by the wayside with the passage of time – but not *all* of them, not one hundred of them over a century. And not those who were widely acclaimed in their own day. Enough men are retained to allow for an uninterrupted tradition of men writers. The same is not true for women.

In the eighteenth century women wrote in much the same (if not greater) numbers than men, with much the same (if not more) success than men, and attained much the same (if not more) status than men. Yet not only has this achievement of women been edited out of literary history, but a false version has been substituted in its place. A distorted version which makes no mention of women's former greatness, but which presents the birth of the novel solely in terms of men. So Daniel Defoe's *Robinson Crusoe* (1720) is transformed into the first novel; Samuel Richardson's *Pamela* (1740) becomes a turning point in the development of the novel and is celebrated; Henry Fielding, Lawrence Sterne and Tobias Smollett are accorded the status of proud parents of this new form. And all this with little or no regard for 'the facts of life'.

How is such a falsified version of events to be explained? And is it a practice of the past or one that persists in the present? For if the denial of women's literary achievement continues to this day, what fate awaits some of the current women writers who enjoy considerable literary acclaim? They too could be consigned to oblivion so that future generations would neither know nor suspect that there has been an 'explosion' in women's writing over the last few years. To those who are yet to come could be bequeathed the legacy of Norman Mailer, Anthony Burgess, Graham Greene and it could be as though Fay Weldon, Alison Lurie, Edna O'Brien, Erica Jong, Marilyn French, Anita Brookner, Mary Gordon, Margaret Drabble and so many more – never existed.

A range of explanations has been offered for the transience of female literary fame. At one end of the spectrum are rationalisations that as literature became increasingly institutionalised during the eighteenth and nineteenth centuries, the decision-making powers were concentrated in the hands of men who not surprisingly found the good and the great among their fellow men. While the novel was in a state of flux – as it was in the earlier part of the eighteenth century – while there was much new activity and little form to follow, women had been able to find a place in literature – as had Aphra Behn in the ferment which accompanied an earlier literary upheaval during the Restoration; but once things settled down, once patterns and experts and credentials were established, the traditional relationship of the sexes reasserted itself, and the dominance of men as critics and writers soon became the reality of the literary world.

Such an account is plausible. It posits a male-dominated society and presumes a male-dominated literary tradition as a result. It is based on the premise that when women and men are equal, they will have literary traditions in which women and men are equally represented.

But there are women critics, past and present, who have gone further than this explanation of men finding in favour of their own sex; further even than arguing that men find fault with women. They have introduced the argument that in a male-dominated society, women are denied the right to their own creative resources and that these resources are taken by men to augment their own. And such a conceptualisation provides a very different framework for interpretations of the treatment of women writers.

It suggests that the men of letters are not blind to the achievements of women but instead of according them validity in their own right, men take from women what they want and leave the rest – which they determine to be of no value – to fade from view. So men writers and critics can deny women's creativity and appropriate women's efforts, claiming women's achievement as their own. So Eliza Haywood can be reduced in stature to a mere copier, her contributions appropriated by her male colleagues, and in the eyes of the critics her achievement is denied and becomes the property of the men.

This explanation is plausible when applied not just to Eliza Haywood, but to all the women novelists of the eighteenth century. It is not just that Walter Allen or Ian Watt neglect to include the women writers, but that they deny the way the men profited from the women's work. The end result is that the reputation of men is built at the expense of women and, in the words of Matilda Joslyn Gage, this is nothing other than the *theft* of women's creativity.

Men 'steal the fruits of women's creative labour,' declared Matilda Joslyn Gage,[6] and according to some contemporary women critics men continue to engage in such illicit literary practice. Hilary Simpson has pointed to the extent to which D. H. Lawrence, for example, appropriated the creative resources of women and passed them off as his own: and she has also noted that within the literary establishment there has been no accusation of foul play.

Without acknowledgement of his sources, D. H. Lawrence 'solicited notes and reminiscences from Jessie (Burrows), from his wife Frieda, from Mabel Dodge Luhan and others . . . he also took over women's manuscripts and rewrote them, as in the cases of Helen Corke and Mollie Skinner . . .'.[7] If one such distinguished man of letters could feel that it was in order to take these creative contributions to enhance his own achievement, then the possibility can be admitted that a collective of men of letters could act in the same way, and take the contributions of the early women novelists to enhance their own claims.

If F. Scott Fitzgerald could take the creative resources of Zelda Fitzgerald's diaries as his own property and build his novels upon them, if he could see *her* creativity as the raw material for *his* work – and if the law upheld his right to do this and prevented Zelda from publishing her own work (which it did) – then the practice of men stealing women's creativity is hardly outrageous or unknown. It is accepted practice and as such its widespread presence should be expected.[8]

Were these but isolated examples, the evidence in support of Matilda Joslyn Gage's thesis of theft would not be so strong: but Samuel Richardson, Thomas Hardy and William Wordsworth are among other great writers known to have similar propensities for taking the writing of women and using it for their own ends. Further investigations in this area might even yield more examples of men at this work. Perhaps behind the dedications or ritual brief acknowledgements to 'the skills of the wife' there lie more examples of women's intellectual and creative resources being appropriated by men to lend substance to their own claims to fame. Marion Glastonbury certainly thinks so.[9] With these examples in mind - and more to follow – it seems reasonable to suggest that it could have become routine for literary men to perceive women's work as available for their own use. And unless challenged why should they not continue with this arrangement?

However, whether the men of letters have overlooked women's writing, or whether they have exploited it, what can be stated unequivocally is that they have in effect suppressed the traditions of writing women. And the question that arises is – does this matter? Does it really matter to past, present, future generations of women – and men – that the early women writers have been removed from the literary heritage so it is as if they never existed? Is it not a little short of fanatical to dig up all these lost women and to confront the seemingly benign men of letters with an accusation which borders on being a charge of malign conspiracy? What possible difference can it make to writers, readers, or the world in general to know that contrary to what we've been led to believe, women as well as men (and even more significantly than men) participated in the conception and development of the new genre, the novel?

The answer depends on the role and importance that is attached to tradition. On the one hand it won't make an immediate and tangible difference to insist on the acknowledgement of women's literary contributions – or to challenge the massive censoring exercise that has been undertaken by men. It won't lead to direct improvements in women's poverty or bring a dramatic end to world wars. But on the other hand, the reinstatement of women's meanings and achievements within the culture could make a very big difference: Virginia Woolf thought that in the long run it would even make a difference to women's poverty and to the prospects of war.

No one can quantify but few would want to totally repudiate the influence that the cultural heritage of the past has on the attitudes and values of the present. And when that heritage of the past blatantly mistreats and devalues half of humanity why should it not be assumed that this predisposes the society which possesses such a heritage to mistreat and devalue human beings?

When, for example, the literary traditions represent the views and values of one small select group of men who agree that those who are not in their own image are not worthy of recognition – or that they are available for exploitation – then the divisions of good and bad, rich and poor, dominant and subordinate, are readily constructed. And the implications of such divisions extend far beyond the confines of the woman writer; they affect women, men, the whole society. This was the stand taken by Virginia Woolf in *A Room of One's Own* (1928) where she made the connections between women's cultural poverty and women's material poverty; it was the stand she took in *Three Guineas* (1938) where she linked the male domination of the cultural heritage with exploitation, violence and war.

She associated the injustice of the suppression of women's meanings with social injustice on a grand scale and she insisted that it was imperative – for the sake of society and the survival of the species – that women's *different* meanings should be reinstated in literary (and other cultural) traditions. Part of Virginia Woolf's argument was based on the premise that *one* world view – the view of men who exercised power – was simply not enough to provide full understanding about the way the world worked. It was too limited: too much was left out. It was the very perspective of those who did *not* exercise power, over whom power was exercised, and who were defined as alien, other, and unworthy of recognition, that was needed for a full view of the world, she insisted. It was her fundamentally simple assertion that women could see much that men – because of their position – could not; that women could see in men precisely what men could not see in themselves; it was this that led her to argue that the meanings forged by women, and represented in their writing, should be included in the cultural heritage. Only then would it provide a fair and reliable basis for making sense of the world.

This is the argument of many women: that in the broadest possible sense, the knowledge of women's contribution could make a significant difference to the judgments and practices of the whole society. Women, whose philosophies are as far apart as Dora Russell's, Elizabeth Robins's, Kate Millett's and Adrienne Rich's have nonetheless agreed on the central point that male dominance means women's silence and that society can no longer afford to neither hear nor heed the voice of half of humanity.[10] These women – and many others as well – have insisted that while women are kept out of the cultural traditions we have a heritage which is comprised of nothing other than political propaganda, in which the powerful decree their world view as the *only* world view, and in which those who differ from the powerful are censored, suppressed, outlawed. To reclaim and revalue the women writers men have removed is, in this framework, to do more than challenge a biased version of literary history: it is to take a political stand and to challenge the propaganda of a dictatorship.

Whether or not one subscribes to the theory that women should seize and control their own creative resources, or concedes the sweeping claim that the reinstatement of women in the literary traditions will lead to a better society, it seems safe to assert that the establishment of the existence and extent of the cultural heritage of women could make a big difference to women. A big difference to the image of women and to the reality of female achievements. While the catalogues, the library shelves, the bookshops, the reviews, the courses of study, all help to suggest that women are without a literary tradition, the belief in female inferiority is surely sustained. And it erodes women's confidence; it undermines the woman writer; it produces doubts. If women were indeed without a great literary tradition, much could be said for the advisability of inventing one, for the positive influence it could provide for women and women's literary endeavours. Such is the power of a tradition.

3

The True Story of How I Became My Own Person

Rosalind Coward

Fiction is a passionate pleasure in many women's lives, far more so than it appears to be for men. Women, it seems, are addicted to fiction. As novelist Rachel Billington put it, 'Women read fiction. Women need fiction. Men do too but only the discerning. They read good novels. Women, even those with brains like razors, never lose that longing for the Big One, the big emotional high' (*Guardian*, 5 October 1981). And not only do women consume fiction, but novel writing is one of the few areas of the arts where women are recognised as equal to men.

It is not just novels in general that women consume. Recently a new genre of novel has appeared aimed at a specifically female audience and usually written by women. These are not just the novels of a publishing house like Mills and Boon specialising in romantic fiction for women; there are also more recent publishing ventures like Virago, committed to printing and reprinting books by women which are aimed at a female audience. Virago director Carmen Callil explained the commercial success of Virago as satisfying women's demand for women-centred fiction: 'We have shown there is a real public demand. We are looking for things in books which are central to women's experience' (*Guardian*, 26 January 1981).

The production of such novels where women's experiences are at the forefront and which are aimed at a specifically female readership is not, however, confined to the feminist press. The success for commercial publishers of novels like *Kinflicks, Original Sins, The Women's Room, The Bleeding Heart, Fear of Flying* and *The Woman Warrior* can hardly be overlooked. They have all at one time or another been hailed as 'the number one international best-seller'. And the success of women writers, appealing with their women-orientated fiction to women, means that commercial publishers are looking out for more. Women *are* the fiction market. 'An English male writer in America was recently asked to use only his initials in order to disguise his unfashionable sex' (Billington, *Guardian*, op. cit.). What then is the history of these women-centred novels? What form of pleasure do they offer women and why have they become so popular now?

Women-centred novels are by no means a new phenomenon. Indeed, novels like *Pamela* and *Clarissa* are usually seen as the precursors of the modern novel and they had the lives of individual women at the centre of the narrative.[1] The novel as we know it today emerged as a distinct form of entertainment in the eighteenth century. It was to be enjoyed in private, and at its heart was a narrative following the life of one individual. The novel, as an entertainment form, almost certainly emerged because the pleasures and interests which it offered corresponded to distinct historical conditions. Some think that the life and experiences of individuals came to the forefront in these stories at the same time as the values of the new bourgeoisie came to dominate social beliefs. The values of economic competitiveness and individualism, for instance – both crucial to the early novel – came into their own in this period.[2]

In the cases where a heroine occupied the position of central consciousness, the novel was invariably preoccupied with questions of sexual morality, and especially marriage. In fact novels increasingly featured the movement towards marriage as the centrally significant event of the narrative. Marriage was the point where the narrative was resolved and often concluded. *How* that point was reached, of course, was all-important and varied enormously between writers. For Jane Austen, the movement towards marriage was invariably also a movement towards an intellectual apprehension of social values. For all the women protagonists in Jane Austen's novels, marriage represents the establishment of certain social values. In *Emma*, the sentimental lesson in the protagonist's appreciation of her love for Mr Knightley is also an intellectual lesson where her impulsive behaviour is criticised. In *Mansfield Park*, the marriage of Fanny represents the triumph of the established order of the house Mansfield Park, upheld in the face of disintegration through new sexual, moral and economic forces.

Even though the progress and forms of the novels are quite different, it is still worth making some general points about marriage as a central narrative device. In most novels of this early period there is a crucial moment for the individual, embodied in the choices around marriage. For the individual heroine, it is a moment where *significant events may happen*, after which her choices and identity are lost for ever.

By the nineteenth century this narrative had become quite rigid, even though this is, of course, remembered as the period where the novel reached its greatest expression. In *Shirley*, Charlotte Brontë can write of her protagonist: 'Caroline was just eighteen years old and at eighteen the true narrative of life has yet to be commenced' – more accurate would be, 'the true narrative of the novel of this period'. For what is implicit is that the novel can justify this concentration on the consciousness of the heroine only around these moments of social and sexual decision. It is interesting to reflect that the consciousness of the heroine and her eventual marriage are dominant themes in the popular literature of the nineteenth century.

In retrospect, it is not so difficult to see why the 'heroine', her particular qualities and the decisions she took about marriage were so important for that period. One aspect shows this clearly. The female protagonists of the nineteenth-century novel are profoundly silent. Their characters express sensitivity and inner feelings. Their looks, as the saying goes, 'speak volumes'. Thus the same Caroline in *Shirley* speaks only through her appearance: 'her face expressive and gentle; her eyes were handsome, gifted at times with a winning beam that stole into the heart with a language that spoke to the affection.'

The female protagonists invariably hold the position of understanding; silently feeling, they naturally perceive and uphold what is truly valuable. As in Elizabeth Gaskell's *North and South*, the female protagonist in *Shirley* represents the soft and understanding aspects of humanity.

Women, then, were represented as somehow outside social relations. In both *Shirley* and *North and South*, the women are in some way untainted by the harsh world of economic competition which their lovers inhabit; they represent the realm of pure feeling. Indeed the heroines of this period do not even speak their desire and their love; they blush and their eyes are downcast. Theirs is a silent sexuality expressed again from the body, physically but without a voice.

Small wonder that women writers of this period had such difficulty with their female protagonists. Silent and subdued heroines didn't always suit the aspirations of women writers, who sometimes produced 'strange' atypical heroines such as Lucy in Charlotte Brontë's *Villette*. Lucy clearly experiences violent, if not pressing, sexual desire but cannot express it. The novel, for that matter, cannot speak it explicitly either, except in terms of what would now be taken to be a nervous breakdown, and through the strange identification Lucy feels with a neurotic, religious and sexually repressed teacher. *Villette*'s themes of derangement, fantasy and hallucination are typical and recur in other women's novels of the period. Derangement and hallucination are responses to the burden of inferiority placed on the heroine by the novel form, responses to the speaking silence of the female figure. Nor is it surprising to find women writers who followed this route and expressed this burden through their writings now rediscovered as the precursors of contemporary feminist writers.

In the nineteenth century, then, the consciousness of the heroine was treated in a recognisable format. Her choices were for a brief moment before marriage of crucial importance, socially and sexually. Yet she is the silent woman, necessarily so because she is outside the cruelty and viciousness of the economic order. In retrospect we can now see how this novel form in fact corresponded to certain definite social ideologies. The marriage of this heroine whose sentiment and sensibilities put her above the economy provided a sort of validation of the social structure. Her love was somehow untainted and contributed very forcefully to the ideology which was able to separate the public, economic realm from the domestic. The domestic sphere could then be represented as the realm of pure feeling – borne by the woman – where men's true identity could be expressed. Novelistic conventions contributed to the rigid separation between the public economic sphere and the private domestic sphere. The ideology promoted within the novels allowed individuals to live at ease with their consciences; it enabled them to believe that in loving a woman, a man expressed his true goodness. The ideology of the domestic sphere and the love of a good woman allowed people to treat their homes as if the economic world did not exist and as if individuals were not implicated in the injustice of this world.

This narrative structure dealing centrally with the heroine's marriage arose at a definite historical period and had distinct social reasons for existing. But in spite of historical changes, this kind of narrative still exists. Interestingly, though, it has moved to the margins, and is dismissed by the critics as pulp fiction. Pleasurable though this form of novel may be, it is a frozen and repetitive form, unable to lay claim to being serious literature because it no longer deals with the main problems of contemporary life. Contemporary romantic fiction is repetitive and predictable – speechless and pure heroine with a masterful and cruel lover whose better self is expressed in his love of the heroine. But it is no longer a form able to explore central social problems.

The *mainstream* of popular fiction, however, appears to have completely inverted the values of the Victorian novel. If Victorian heroines spoke only through their eyes and their central nervous systems, contemporary women protagonists are positively garrulous about their intimate personal histories. Everything must and can be told. '"You must not tell anyone," my mother said, "what I am about to tell you,"' opens *The Woman Warrior*, and then proceeds to tell it all.[3] Contemporary woman-centred fiction is characterised by this; above all, the female protagonist has become the speaking sex.

If sexual desire rendered the Victorian heroine mad, it now appears to be a vital component of 'the number one international best-seller'. So much so, that 'women-centred' novels have become almost synonymous with the so-called sexual revolution. More than anything, the sexual revolution is presented as the transformation of women's relation to sex:

Liberating the libido. Getting sex straight was an essential first step along the noisy road to liberation; writing about it could be the next leap forward. Books by women surveying sex, and novels by women

whose heroines savour sex, are selling like hotdogs in America –
beating men into second place and turning authoresses into
millionairesses at the drop of a hardsell dustjacket.

Sunday Times Colour Supplement

These novels are often seen by the writers themselves as relating to
feminism, although many feminists have received them with suspicion.
Sometimes consciousness-raising is used as a narrative device, as in *Loose
Change* and *The Women's Room*; often the encounter with feminism and the
discovery of how general the individual's experience as a woman actually
is, is a vital element of the narrative. But regardless of this political
commitment, the commercial world has recognised these novels as a
genre of sexual writing, showing that women can write about sex as well
as if not better than men.

What then are we to think about these novels? What needs do they
appear to satisfy? How did they arise and can they, as is sometimes
claimed, 'change lives' and contribute to a more progressive
understanding of women's sexuality?

One point which is immediately striking is that these novels have
followed the general pattern in fiction towards sexual confession. The
confessional novel has become more and more dominant in
contemporary fiction, both male and female. Increasingly the novel's
structure has been based on the voice of the protagonist describing the
significant events in his or her life. Since the turn of the century this
stream of consciousness writing has been widespread. But recently, the
consciousness has been more and more preoccupied with talking about
sex. Sexual confessions moved to the mainstream in the 1950s and 60s
with writers like J. D. Salinger, Kingsley Amis, Henry Miller and Philip
Roth. These novels exhibit interesting similarities with Victorian
pornography which took the form of detailed pseudo-autobiographical
accounts of sexual encounters.[4] But it wasn't until the late 1960s that this
kind of writing became virtually synonymous with women writers and
sexual revolution.

Where the sexual confessions – both male and female – differ from their
pornographic and romantic precedents is in the fact that the narrative has
expanded to encompass a much wider span of significant moments. If the
narrative of life was just beginning at eighteen for Charlotte Brontë's
heroines, the contemporary heroine has met the crucial determinants of
her life in the 'formative' encounters of childhood and adolescence.
Childhood has become a period permeated with sexual meanings,
foretastes and crucial moments in the development of sexual identity.

It is appropriate, too, that with this concentration on childhood should
have come a peculiarly regressive form of writing. This form is the
written equivalent of the family album. It has generated a convention

where humorous sketches are delivered. 'Here's Aunt Emily. She married Uncle Morgan who ran off with the post-lady. They lived down White Bay Creek, and used to take in drifters.' Then follows the anecdote, the vignette to show just what type of person Uncle Morgan was. This often has the effect of reducing the characters to the bare bones of their particular eccentricity. And this form of writing is one of the reasons why many reviewers can't make up their minds whether they are dealing with a 'riproaring, hilarious' novel or something actually quite serious. Lisa Alther's *Kinflicks* is a novel which has met this fate. *Kinflicks* embodies a real tension in trying to make serious points about women's experience in a form which is basically 'playing for laughs'. I call this style of writing regressive because it arises from an ideology of how children are supposed to see the world. The central protagonist is shown making sense of the world as a child makes sense of its world: children, it is believed, work out their world slowly, only through enquiry, eaves-dropping, prying and looking into the closets of their immediate family. The child in this ideology is a sort of miniature detective, working out its genealogy, with a quick eye for the missing links.

This ideology also postulates that the child sees its world as essentially eccentric. All children, after all, believe that their family is more bizarre than the next one. And the ideology assumes that the child's view of its parents is extended to the whole world. The world is bizarre and eccentric, full of haphazard events, and occurrences which have no apparent causal connection. These novels about women's lives frequently attempt a re-creation of this childish world of eccentricities, anecdotes, and the sense of haphazard happenings.

Of course, this view of the world is a version of how reality is to the child. The lack of causal explanations, the haphazard events and inexplicable eccentricities are visions which, if they ever existed, are rarely carried into the adult world. In the adult world, a sense of the causal connection between things has been profoundly and irreversibly formed by that early history. In the adult world, strong feelings about how things happened are usually present. The adult blames and feels guilt, feels dependent on some people and rejects others, in short has taken up a place. This place is conditioned no doubt by infantile experiences, but these experiences are now interpreted in the light of the adult personality. How indeed could a writer produce a 'true' narrative, in the sense of an objective account of events, not yet coloured by emotional dramas?

Yet these novels make their claim to a 'higher degree of realism' than their romantic predecessors precisely by attempting to produce an objective sequence of events and re-create a childish consciousness which does not see and does not evaluate the connections between people's actions. When it comes down to it, of course, even within this ideology the novels are making clear choices about what events are picked out as the most significant. In these novels where women's experience is highlighted, it has become a standing joke that we are to expect the first period, first kiss, first (fumbled) intercourse, first (disastrous) marriage, lesbian affair and usually lonely resolution. The end product is normally that the protagonist feels she has 'become her own person'. This disingenuous construction of an adolescent world derives precisely from the novel's attempt to create a higher realism. The complex family history and interrelations, the anecdotes presented as if passed from generation to generation, the eccentric view of the world, are all practices aimed at creating the sense of the autobiographical. This is something which is often reinforced by the way in which the central characters, as in *The Women's Room* (Marilyn French) or *Sita* (Kate Millett), are themselves writers or novelists.

It is no coincidence that high on the best-seller lists alongside these 'novels that change lives' are the sexual autobiographies of so-called personalities – Mandy Rice Davies, Joan Collins and Fiona Richmond – who also employ these confessional tactics: family genealogy, school days, first sexual encounters, then the hard stuff of adult sexual experience. Women-centred novels represent a fictionalised version of our culture's contemporary obsession with autobiography and with intimate revelations.

Certain points can be made about the confessional forms of writing and their preoccupation with sexuality. I have hinted that this telling all does not in fact bear witness to a radical break with our 'repressed' past. What used to be the structure of written pornography has now appeared in the mainstream merged with the traditions of the novelistic, derived from the heyday of the Victorian novel. In fact, it has been suggested elsewhere that this obsessive talking about sexuality represents a continuation of certain practices relating to the control of sexuality. Sexuality in fact has never been repressed as the vision of the Victorians would have it. For several centuries now, sexuality has been at the heart of a number of discourses, and since the last century has been made more and more important. In the Victorian period, these discourses were directed towards the prohibition of certain sexual practices, such as masturbation or female 'promiscuity'. We can see this negative aim in the educational and medical writings of the Victorian era. But however negative and controlling these discourses were, they all had sexuality as the central object of concern. In contemporary society there has been a shift rather than a liberation in the treatment of sexuality; now the discourses are directed at making sex explicit rather than denying it.

In countries where the Catholic Church had a powerful presence the confessional seems to have influenced the form taken by these social and scientific discourses on sex. Like church confessionals, they simultaneously enquire into sexuality and command that all be revealed in its most minute and detailed ramifications. This detailed pursuit of the tiniest pleasures in sexuality was, of course, a method of control. Owning up to the pleasures of the flesh, the subject accepted the control of the Church, which was seen as having the key to the soul, bestowing forgiveness and absolution. Scientific discourses also 'listen' to sexuality *and* take sexuality to be the true expression of innermost identity. Hence pseudo-medical disciplines like sexology developed, classifying individuals according to their constitutional and sexual predisposition, anxious to fix and describe a whole classificatory system of sexualities. Michel Foucault, in *The History of Sexuality*, described the way in which power can be exercised through concern with sexuality. The identity of the subject is found within these discourses, which multiply the areas and possibilities for sexual pleasure only to control, classify and subject.

These ideas are useful because they indicate how the centrality of sexuality in novels, either coyly in romantic fiction or explicitly in confession of sexual experiences, has definite correspondences with the wider social organisation of sexuality. We have to treat with suspicion the whole notion of sexual revolution which these novels are said to represent because there has been no such violent change from repression to freedom. Even the most apparently open and explicit detailing of sex can be an expression of sex in a way which means it is structured by very definite social movements and relates to the structures of power in society at large.

Within the novel, the 'confession' has appeared overdetermined by traditions specific to the novel. In particular it has been influenced by the importance of narrative which organises a series of events or experiences as significant and progressing towards a meaningful conclusion. This space of time, or narrative, is one in which the central character or characters undergo a series of experiences which radically affect their lives or transform their attitudes. The effect of this structure is to create a distinct ideology of knowledge and indeed life – that experience brings knowledge and possibly wisdom.

But where novels focusing on women's lives are concerned, a distinctive variant has occurred. Knowledge or understanding has been focused exclusively on sexual experience – love, marriage, divorce or just sexual encounters. This has the effect of reproducing the ideology where (albeit now disillusioned) women are viewed in relation to their sexual history. Women again defined through their sexuality, are the sex to be interrogated and understood. Becoming my own person or woman is in the grain of the sexual; it is how a woman deals with her sexuality. Novels with male characters may well also concentrate obsessively on sex. But what the sex means is different. For men, sexual encounters represent access to power, a series of encounters and experiences which build up a sense of the individual's power in having control over women's bodies. Sexual experience in women's novels represents access to knowledge, rather than power. Sexual experience becomes the way in which a woman finds out about herself.

There's a danger that such structures reproduce the Victorian ideology that sexuality is somehow outside social relations. The idea that a woman could become her own person just through sexual experience and the discovery of sexual needs and dislikes again establishes sexual relations as somehow separate from social structures. The emphasis on sex as knowledge may well obscure the fact that sex is implicated in society as a whole, that sex has consequences and that there are always other people to consider in a sexual experience. Questions of social responsibility and not hurting other people are no less important to women critical of conventional morality. Yet there's a danger that sexual experience has been represented as an end in itself, as if other social decisions and work experiences didn't affect us as much.

It is hardly surprising that women have been represented as having a crucial role in the 'sexual revolution'. Sexology, psychology, psychoanalysis, films, pornography all ask the question, 'What is women's sexuality?' At a period when a society represents itself as shaking off the mysteries of our repressed past it is women who are represented as being at the centre of this transformation.

This society chooses to represent women as responsible for the sexual revolution: sexual repression was overthrown as soon as women were clear about wanting and needing sex as much as men. In fact, women have realised that greater freedom of opportunity for sexual intercourse does not of itself bring about changes in men's attitudes towards women, or changes in how the sexes relate to one another. Men, in short, have remained in their position of privilege, often contemptuous of women, who therefore did not gain from a discovery of their sexual personalities in the ways represented.

But does this invalidate these novels and their spoken commitment to changing the position of women? I think not. Because like feminism itself, these novels probably transcend their origins in wider social movements. It is not sufficient to suggest that because women have been shot to the fore as the speaking sex they simply reproduce the values which have made women the group whose sexuality is interrogated. For as with the Victorian heroine, the current preoccupation with women's sexual experiences corresponds to a general social concern with women's social position and how it will be resolved. Women's social position and possibilities have changed radically in the last fifty years; conceptions of what is possible and what is desirable have been greatly changed and such changes represent upheavals to some of the most dearly held ideologies and beliefs of this society. It would suit society to reduce women to being *the* sex – the talking, the experiencing sex – because again this would pose little threat to the idea of the experiential individual at the heart of this society. But because women have always been confined to this realm, albeit in different ways over different historical periods, any investigation of this construction has the potential for exposing it *as construction*. Thus even those novels which appear to correspond to most widely held sexual ideologies often attempt more interesting things. For the autobiographical voice of these contemporary women-centred novels often appeals to a collectivity. I am, but I am a representative of all women. The history of my oppression is the history of all women's oppression.

And beyond the format are those writers who have begun to deconstruct the whole notion of identity, at the same time challenging the conventions of the novel. Writers like Doris Lessing or Fay Weldon both occasionally disrupt the conventions of a central narrative voice or character, and their writing becomes a myriad of historical, social and sexual concerns which do not belong to any individual subjectivity. And both Doris Lessing and Angela Carter explore the fantastic and the erotic in ways that do not appeal to any realistic identification with a self-discovering heroine on the way to her own personhood. Nor is it surprising to find reinstated other earlier novelists who also stretch the reader's understanding beyond the conventions of a sexual self-discovery. Some of Rosamond Lehmann's novels, for instance, appear to explore the whole basis of fiction, creating a narrative which can never be validated, where the hopes and fantasies of the individual protagonists are validated and the objective narrative rendered fictional.

The term 'women-centred' novels covers a multitude of sins. But at the heart of this multi-faceted phenomenon is one dominant convention, a type of narrative which corresponds to existing (and therefore problematic) ways of defining women through their sexual personhood. Because the whole issue of women's sexuality and changes in structures of living are crucial to our experiences now, these novels are sometimes able to explore the question of how female identity has been constructed and how this relates to society as a whole. Often, though, the convention itself pulls the novels back into banal repetitions, asserting a world without fantasy where women struggle on, often grim, brutalised and victimised. I'm not sure that becoming my own person is sufficient compensation for such a world.

4

disturbing nurses and the kindness of sharks

Toni Morrison

But there was
a special hell besides
where black women lie waiting
for a boy –

William Carlos Williams from 'Adam'

Race has become metaphorical – a way of referring to and disguising forces, events, classes, and expressions of social decay and economic division far more threatening to the body politic than biological 'race' ever was. Expensively kept, economically unsound, a spurious and useless political asset in election campaigns, racism is as healthy today as it was during the Enlightenment. It seems that it has a utility far beyond economy, beyond the sequestering of classes from one another, and has assumed a metaphorical life so completely embedded in daily discourse that it is perhaps more necessary and more on display than ever before.

I am prepared to be corrected on this point insofar as it misrepresents the shelf life of racism in social and political behaviour. But I remain convinced that the metaphorical and metaphysical uses of race occupy definitive places in American literature, in the 'national' character, and ought to be a major concern of the literary scholarship that tries to know it.

In this essay I wish to observe and trace the transformation of American Africanism from its simplistic, though menacing, purposes of establishing hierarchic difference to its surrogate properties as self-reflexive meditations on the loss of difference, to its lush and fully blossomed existence in the rhetoric of dread and desire.

My suggestion that Africanism has come to have a metaphysical necessity should in no way be understood to imply that it has lost its ideological utility. There is still much ill-gotten gain to reap from rationalising power grabs and clutches with inferences of inferiority and the ranking of differences. There is still much national solace in continuing dreams of democratic egalitarianism available by hiding class conflict, rage, and impotence in figurations of race. And there is quite a lot of juice to be extracted from plummy reminiscences of 'individualism' and 'freedom' if the tree upon which such fruit hangs is a black population forced to serve as freedom's polar opposite: individualism is foregrounded (and believed in) when its background is stereotypified, enforced dependency. Freedom (to move, to earn, to learn, to be allied with a powerful centre, to narrate the world) can be relished more deeply in a cheek-by-jowl existence with the bound and unfree, the economically oppressed, the marginalised, the silenced. The ideological dependence on racialism is intact and, like its metaphysical existence, offers in historical, political, and literary discourse a safe route into meditations on morality and ethics; a way of examining the mind–body dichotomy; a way of thinking about justice; a way of contemplating the modern world.

Surely, it will be said, white America has considered questions of morality and ethics, the supremacy of mind and the vulnerability of body, the blessings and liabilities of progress and modernity, without reference to the situation of its black population. After all, it will be argued, where does one find a fulsome record that such a referent was part of these deliberations? My answer to these questions is another: where is it not?

In what public discourse does the reference to black people not exist? It exists in every one of this nation's mightiest struggles. The presence of black people is not only a major referent in the framing of the Constitution, it is also in the battle over enfranchising unpropertied citizens, women, the illiterate. It is there in the construction of a free and public school system; the balancing of representation in legislative bodies; jurisprudence and legal definitions of justice. It is there in theological discourse; the memoranda of banking houses; the concept of manifest destiny and the pre-eminent narrative that accompanies (if it does not precede) the initiation of every immigrant into the community of American citizens. The presence of black people is inherent, along with gender and family ties, in the earliest lesson every child is taught regarding his or her distinctiveness. Africanism is inextricable from the definition of Americanness – from its origins on through its integrated or disintegrating twentieth-century self.

The literature of the United States, like its history, represents commentary on the transformations of biological, ideological, and metaphysical concepts of racial difference. But the literature has an additional concern and subject matter: the private imagination interacting with the external world it inhabits. Literature redistributes and mutates in figurative language the social conventions of Africanism. In minstrelsy, a layer of blackness applied to a white face released it from law. Just as entertainers, through or by association with blackface, could render permissible topics that otherwise would have been taboo, so American writers were able to employ an imagined Africanist persona to articulate and imaginatively act out the forbidden in American culture.

Encoded or explicit, indirect or overt, the linguistic responses to an Africanist presence complicate texts, sometimes contradicting them entirely. A writer's response to American Africanism often provides a subtext that either sabotages the surface text's expressed intentions or escapes them through a language that mystifies what it cannot bring itself to articulate but still attempts to register. Linguistic responses to Africanism serve the text by further problematising its matter with resonances and luminations. They can serve as allegorical fodder for the contemplation of Eden, expulsion, and the availability of grace. They provide paradox, ambiguity; they strategise omissions, repetitions, disruptions, polarities, reifications, violence. In other words, they give the text a deeper, richer, more complex life than the sanitised one commonly presented to us.

In his book on Faulkner, James Snead comments that racial divisions 'show their flaws best in written form':

> Racism might be considered a normative recipe for domination created by speakers using rhetorical tactics. The characteristic figures of racial division repeat on the level of phoneme, sentence, and story: (1) The fear of merging, or loss of identity through synergistic union with the other, leads to the wish to use racial purification as a separating strategy against difference; (2) Marking, or supplying physically significant (usually visual) characteristics with internal value equivalents, sharpening, by visual antithesis, their conceptual utility; (3) Spatial and conceptual separation, often facilitated through unequal verbal substitutions that tend to omit and distance a subordinate class from realms of value and esteem; (4) Repetition, or pleonastic reinforcement of these antitheses in writing, story telling, or hearsay; (5) Invective and threat, exemplified in random and unpredictable violence to punish real or imagined crimes; (6) Omission and concealment of the process by a sort of paralepsis that claims discrimination to be self-evidently valid and natural.

'Faulkner' he goes on to say, 'counters these social figures with literary devices of his own.'[1]

Following Snead's helpful categories, it may be useful to list some of the common linguistic strategies employed in fiction to engage the serious consequences of blacks.

I. Economy of stereotype. This allows the writer a quick and easy image without the responsibility of specificity, accuracy, or even narratively useful description.

2. Metonymic displacement. This promises much but delivers little and counts on the reader's complicity in the dismissal. Colour coding and

other physical traits become metonyms that displace rather than signify the Africanist character.

3. Metaphysical condensation. This allows the writer to transform social and historical differences into universal differences. Collapsing persons into animals prevents human contact and exchange; equating speech with grunts or other animal sounds closes off the possibility of communication.

4. Fetishisation. This is especially useful in evoking erotic fears or desires and establishing fixed and major difference where difference does not exist or is minimal. Blood, for example, is a pervasive fetish: black blood, white blood, the purity of blood; the purity of white female sexuality, the pollution of African blood and sex. Fetishisation is a strategy often used to assert the categorical absolutism of civilisation and savagery.

5. Dehistoricising allegory. This produces foreclosure rather than disclosure. If difference is made so vast that the civilising process becomes indefinite – taking place across an unspecified infinite amount of time – history, as a process of becoming, is excluded from the literary encounter. Flannery O'Connor's 'The Artificial Nigger' makes this point with reference to Mr Head's triumphantly racist views in that brilliant story. Carson McCullers deploys allegory among her characters in *The Heart Is a Lonely Hunter*, to mourn the inevitability of closure and the fruitlessness of monologue. Melville uses allegorical formations – the white whale, the racially mixed crew, the black–white pairings of male couples, the questing, questioning white male captain who confronts impenetrable whiteness – to investigate and analyse hierarchic difference. Poe deploys allegorical mechanisms in *Pym* not to confront and explore, as Melville does, but to evade and simultaneously register the cul de sac, the estrangement, the non-sequitur that is entailed in racial difference. William Styron opens and closes *The Confessions of Nat Turner* with the sealed white structure that serves as an allegorical figuration of the defeat of the enterprise he is engaged in: penetration of the black–white barrier.

6. Patterns of explosive, disjointed, repetitive language. These indicate a loss of control in the text that is attributed to the objects of its attention rather than to the text's own dynamics.

I have gone on at some length about these linguistic strategies because I want to make use of them in a specific connection.

My interest in Ernest Hemingway becomes heightened when I consider how much apart his work is from African-Americans. That is, he has no need, desire, or awareness of them either as readers of his work or as people existing anywhere other than in his imaginative (and imaginatively lived) world. I find, therefore, his use of African-Americans much more artless and unselfconscious than Poe's, for example, where social unease required the servile black bodies in his work.

Hemingway's work could be described as innocent of nineteenth-century ideological agenda as well as free of what may be called recent, postmodernist sensitivity. With this in mind, a look at how Hemingway's fiction is affected by an Africanist presence – when it makes the writing belie itself, contradict itself, or depend on that presence for attempts at resolution – can be taken by way of a 'pure' case to test some of the propositions I have been advancing.

I begin with the novel said by many to be intentionally political, *To Have and Have Not* (published in 1937). Harry Morgan, the central figure, seems to represent the classic American hero: a solitary man battling a government that would limit his freedom and his individuality. He is romantically and sentimentally respectful of the nature he destroys for a living (deep-sea fishing) – competent, street-wise, knowing, and impatient with those who are not. He is virile, risk-taking, risk-loving, and so righteous and guiltless in his evaluation of himself that it seems a shame to question or challenge it. Before I do challenge it, I want to examine how Hemingway shows the reader that Harry is knowing, virile, free, brave, and moral.

Only ten pages into the novel we encounter the Africanist presence. Harry includes a 'nigger' in his crew, a man who, throughout all of part one, has no name. His appearance is signalled by the sentence, 'Just then this nigger we had getting bait comes down the dock'.[2] The black man is not only nameless for five chapters, he is not even hired, just someone 'we had getting bait' – a kind of trained response, not an agent possessing a job. His inclusion on the voyage, objected to by the white client, Johnson, is defended by Harry on the basis of the black man's skill: he 'put on a nice bait and he was fast'.[3] The rest of the time, we are told, this nameless man sleeps and reads the papers.

Something very curious happens to this namelessness when, in part two, the author shifts voices. Part one is told in the first person, and whenever Harry thinks about this black man he thinks 'nigger'. In part two, where Hemingway uses the third-person point of view in narrating and representing Harry's speech, two formulations of the black man occur: he both remains nameless and stereotyped and becomes named and personalised.

Harry *says* 'Wesley' when speaking to the black man in direct dialogue; Hemingway *writes* 'nigger' when as narrator he refers to him. Needless to report, this black man is never identified as one (except in his own mind). Part two reserves and repeats the word 'man' for Harry. The spatial and conceptual difference is marked by the shortcut that the term 'nigger' allows, with all of its colour and caste implications. The term occupies a territory between man and animal and thus withholds specificity even while marking it. This black character either does not speak (as a 'nigger' he is silent) or speaks in very legislated and manipulated ways (as a 'Wesley' his speech serves Harry's needs). Enforcing the silence of the 'nigger' proves problematic in this action-narrative and requires of Hemingway some strenuous measures.

In part one, at a crucial moment during the fishing expedition, which has disappointed both the captain and his customer, the boat moves into promising waters. Harry is coaching Johnson; the black man is at the wheel. Earlier Harry assured us that the black man does nothing aside from cutting bait but read and sleep. But Hemingway realises that Harry cannot be in two critical places at the same time, instructing the incompetent Johnson and guiding the vessel. It is important to remember that there is another person aboard, an alcoholic named Eddy, who is too unreliable to be given the responsibility of steering but who is given manhood and speech and a physical description. Eddy is white, and we know he is because nobody says so. Now, with Harry taking care of his customer and Eddy in a pleasant stupor, there is only the black man to tend the wheel.

When the sign heralding the promising waters arrives – the sighting of flying fish beyond the prow of the boat – the crewman facing forward ought to be the first to see them. In fact he is. The problem is how to acknowledge that first sighting and continue the muzzling of this 'nigger' who, so far, has not said one word. The solution is a strangely awkward, oddly constructed sentence: 'The nigger was still taking her out and I looked and saw he had seen a patch of flying fish burst out ahead.'[4] ' Saw he had seen' is improbable in syntax, sense, and tense but, like other choices available to Hemingway, it is risked to avoid a speaking black. The problem this writer gives himself, then, is to say how one sees that someone else has already seen.

A better, certainly more graceful choice would be to have the black man cry out at the sighting. But the logic of the narrative's discrimination prevents a verbal initiative of importance to Harry's business coming from this nameless, sexless, nationless Africanist presence. It is the powerful one, the authoritative one, who sees. The power of looking is Harry's; the passive powerlessness is the black man's, though he himself does not speak of it. Silencing him, refusing him the opportunity of one important word, forces the author to abandon his search for transparency in the narrative act and to set up a curiously silent mate–captain relationship.

What would have been the cost, I wonder, of humanising, genderising, this character at the opening of the novel? For one thing, Harry would be positioned – set off, defined – very differently. He would have to be compared to a helpless alcoholic, a contemptible customer, and an individualised crew member with, at least by implication, an independent life. Harry would lack the juxtaposition and association with a vague presence suggesting sexual excitement, a possible threat to his virility and competence, violence under wraps. He would, finally, lack the complementarity of a figure who can be assumed to be in some way bound, fixed, unfree, and serviceable.

The proximity to violence is stressed at once in the novel, before the black crewman's entrance, by the shooting outside the café. The Cubans in this scene are separated not by nationality (all the people born in Cuba are Cubans) but as black and not black, Cubans and blacks. In this slaughter the blacks are singled out as the most gratuitously violent and savage. Hemingway writes:

> The nigger with the Tommy gun got his face almost into the street and gave the back of the wagon a burst from underneath and sure enough one came down . . . at ten feet the nigger shot him in the belly with the Tommy gun, with what must have been the last shot . . . old Pancho sat down hard and went over forwards. He was trying to come up, still holding onto the Luger, only he couldn't get his head up, when the nigger took the shotgun that was lying against the wheel of the car by the chauffeur and blew the side of his head off. Some nigger.[5]

In part two, Harry and the black crewman do engage in dialogue, and the black man talks a great deal. The serviceability of the black man's speech, however, is transparent. What he says and when he says it are plotted to win admiration for Harry. Wesley's speech is restricted to grumbles and complaints and apologies for weakness. We hear the grumbles, the groans, the weakness as Wesley's responses to his gunshot wounds for three pages before we learn that Harry is also shot, and much worse than Wesley is. By contrast, Harry has not only not mentioned his own pain, he has taken Wesley's whining with compassion and done the difficult work of steering and tossing the contraband overboard in swift, stoic gestures of manliness. Information about Harry's more serious pain is deferred while we listen to Wesley:

> 'I'm shot . . .'
> 'You're just scared.'
> 'No, sir. I'm shot. And I'm hurting bad. I've been throbbing all night.' . . .
> 'I hurt,' the nigger said. 'I hurt worse all the time.'
> 'I'm sorry, Wesley,' the man said. 'But I got to steer.'
> 'You treat a man no better than a dog,' the nigger said. He was getting ugly now. But the man was still sorry for him.[6]

Finally, our patience and Harry's exhausted, we get this exchange: '"Who the hell's shot worse?" he asked him. "You or me?" "You're shot worse," the nigger said.'[7]

The choice and positioning of the naming process ('nigger', 'Wesley', and, once, 'negro') may seem arbitrary and confusing, but in fact it is carefully structured. Harry, in dialogue with a helpmate, cannot say 'nigger' without offending the reader (if not the helpmate) – and losing his claim to compassionate behaviour – so he uses a name. No such responsibility is taken on, however, by the legislating narrator, who always uses the generic and degrading term: 'The nigger blubbered with his face against a sack. The man went on slowly lifting the sacked packages of liquor and dropping them over the side.'[8] Once Wesley has apologised, recognised, and accepted his inferiority, Harry can and does use 'nigger', along with the proper name, in direct dialogue – in familiar camaraderie: '"Mr Harry," said the nigger, "I'm sorry I couldn't help dump that stuff." "Hell," said Harry, "ain't no nigger any good when he's shot. You're a all right nigger, Wesley."'[9]

I mentioned two main categories of speech for the black man: grumbles and apology. But there is a third. Throughout the exchange, while the two men are suffering – one stoically, one whimperingly – the black man criticises the white man in lapses between his whining and his terror. They are interesting lapses because they limn another Harry – a figure of antihuman negation and doom. Such lapses occur over and over again in Hemingway's fiction. Accusations of inhumanity, used as prophecies of doom, are repeatedly placed in the mouths of the blacks who people his work. 'Ain't a man's life worth more than a load of liquor?' Wesley asks Harry.[10] 'Why don't people be honest and decent and make a decent honest living? . . .'[11] You don't care what happens to a man . . . You ain't hardly human.'[12] '"You ain't human,"' the nigger said "You ain't got human feelings."'[13]

The serviceability of the Africanist presence I have been describing becomes even more pronounced when Hemingway begins to describe male and female relationships. In this same novel, the last voice we hear is that of Harry's devoted wife, Marie, listing and celebrating the virtues, the virility and bravery, of her husband, who is now dead. The elements of her reverie can be schematically organised as follows: (1) virile, good, brave Harry; (2) racist views of Cuba; (3) black sexual invasion thwarted; (4) reification of whiteness.

Marie recalls him fondly as 'snotty and strong and quick, and like some kind of expensive animal. It would always get me to just watch him move.'[14] Immediately following this encomium to sexuality and power and revered (expensive) brutality, she meditates on her hatred of Cubans (the Cubans killed Harry) and says they are 'bad luck for Conchs' and 'bad luck for anybody. They got too many niggers there too.'[15] This judgment is followed by her recollection of a trip she and Harry took to Havana when she was twenty-six years old. Harry had a lot of money then and while they walked in the park a 'nigger' (as opposed to a Cuban, though the black man she is referring to is both black and Cuban) 'said something'[16] to Marie. Harry smacked him and threw his straw hat into the street where a taxi ran over it.

Marie remembers laughing so hard it made her belly ache. With nothing but a paragraph indention between them, the next reverie is a further association of Harry with sexuality, power, and protection. 'That was the first time I ever made my hair blonde.'[17] The two anecdotes are connected in time and place and, significantly, by colour as sexual coding. We do not know what the black man said, but the horror is that he said anything at all. It is enough that he spoke, claimed an intimacy perhaps, but certainly claimed a view and inserted his sexual self into their space and their consciousness. By initiating the remark, he was a speaking, therefore aggressive, presence. In Marie's recollection, sexuality, violence, class, and the retribution of an impartial machine are fused into an all-purpose black man.

The couple, Marie and Harry, is young and in love with obviously enough money to feel and be powerful in Cuba. Into that Eden comes the violating black male making impertinent remarks. The disrespect, with its sexual overtones, is punished at once by Harry's violence. He smacks the black man. Further, he picks up the fallen straw hat, violating the black man's property, just as the black man had sullied Harry's property – his wife. When the taxi, inhuman, onrushing, impartial machine, runs over the hat, it is as if the universe were rushing to participate in and validate Harry's response. It is this underscoring that makes Marie laugh – along with her obvious comfort in and adulation of this 'strong and quick' husband of hers.

What follows in the beauty parlour is positioned as connected with and dependent on the episode of black invasion of privacy and intimation of sexuality from which Marie must be protected. The urgency to establish difference – a difference within the sexual context – is commanding. Marie tells us how she is transformed from black to white, from dark to blonde. It is a painful and difficult process that turns out to be well worth the pain in its sexual, protective, differentiating payout: 'They were working on it all afternoon and it was naturally so dark they didn't want to do it . . . but I kept telling them to see if they couldn't make it a little lighter . . . and all I'd say was, just see if you can't make it a little lighter.'[18]

When the bleaching and perming are done, Marie's satisfaction is decidedly sensual, if not explicitly sexual: 'when I put my hand and touched it, and I couldn't believe it was me and I was so excited I was choked with it . . . I was so excited feeling all funny inside, sort of faint like.'[19] It is a genuine transformation. Marie becomes a self she can hardly believe, golden and soft and silky.

Her own sensual reaction to her whitening is echoed by Harry, who sees her and says, 'Jesus, Marie, you're beautiful.'[20] And when she wants to hear more about her beauty, he tells her not to talk – just 'Let's go to the hotel.'[21] This enhanced sexuality comes on the heels of a sexual intrusion by a black man.

What would have been the consequence if the insult to Marie had come from a white man? Would the bleaching have followed? If so, would it have been in such lush and sexually heightened language? What does establishing a difference from darkness to lightness accomplish for the concept of a self as sexually alive and potent? Or so powerful and coherent in the world?

These tourists in Havana meet a native of that city and have a privileged status because they are white. But to assure us that this status is both deserved and, by implication, potently generative, they encounter a molesting, physically inferior black male (his inferiority is designated by the fact that Harry does not use his fists, but slaps him) who represents the outlaw sexuality that, by comparison, spurs the narrative on to contemplation of a superior, legal, white counterpart.

Here we see Africanism used as a fundamental fictional technique by which to establish character. Within a milieu that threatens the dissolution of all distinctions of value – the milieu of the working poor, the unemployed, sinister Chinese, terrorist Cubans, violent but cowardly blacks, upper-class castrati, female predators – Harry and Marie (an ex-prostitute) gain potency, a generative sexuality. They solicit our admiration by the comparison that is struck between their claims to fully embodied humanity and a discredited Africanism. The voice of the text is complicit in these formulations: Africanism becomes not only a means of displaying authority but, in fact, constitutes its source.

The strategies that employ and distribute Africanism in *To Have and Have Not* become more sophisticated in the other work by Ernest Hemingway I will discuss here. In the posthumously published *The Garden of Eden* ideological Africanism is extended metaphorically to function as a systematic articulation, through an Africanist discursive practice and an Africanist mythology, of an entire aesthetics. Africanism – the fetishising of colour, the transference to blackness of the power of illicit sexuality, chaos, madness, impropriety, anarchy, strangeness, and helpless, hapless desire – provides a formidable field for a novel that works out the terms and maps a complete, if never formalised, aesthetics. Before describing this aesthetic field, I would like to mention one of the author's special concerns.

Hemingway's romantic attachment to a nurse is well documented in the fiction, in criticism, in biographical data, and more recently in the published recollection of the original nurse herself. The wounded soldier and the nurse is a familiar story and contains elements reliably poignant. To be in a difficult, even life-threatening position and to have someone dedicated to helping you, paid to help you, is soothing. And if you are bent on dramatic gestures of self-reliance, eager to prove that you can go it alone (without complaining), a nurse who chooses or is paid to take care of you does not violate your view of yourself as a brave, silent sufferer. Needfulness does not enter the picture; asking for help is always out of the question, and the benefits that derive from the attentive, expert care do not incur emotional debt.

Some of the other women in Hemingway's fiction who become objects of desire have the characteristics of nurses without the professional status. They are essentially the good wives or the good lovers, ministering, thoughtful, never needing to be told what the loved man needs. Such perfect nurses are rare, though important because they serve as a reference toward which the prose yearns. More common are the women who abandon or have difficulty sustaining their nursing abilities: women who destroy the silent sufferer, hurt him instead of nurturing him.

But in the exclusively male world that Hemingway usually prefers to inhabit, it would be missing something not to notice that there are nurse figures in the masculine domain as well. These characters are just as dedicated, thoughtful, and ministering of the narrator's needs as the few female nurses are. Some of these male nurses are explicitly, forthrightly tender helpers – with nothing to gain from their care but the most minimal wage or the pleasure of a satisfied patient. Other male nurses serve the narrator reluctantly, sullenly, but are excessively generous in the manner in which they serve the text. Cooperative or sullen, they are Tontos all, whose role is to do everything possible to serve the Lone Ranger without disturbing his indulgent delusion that he is indeed alone.

The reference is pertinent here, for not only is the Hemingway Ranger invariably accompanied but his Tontos, his nursemen, are almost always black. From the African bearers who tote the white man's burden in the hunting grounds of Africa, to the bait cutters aboard fishing boats, to loyal companions of decaying boxers, to ministering bartenders – the array of enabling black nursemen is impressive.

Along with their enabling properties are some disabling ones. They say – once their rank and status are signalled by the narrator and accepted by the black man – extraordinary things. Sam, the black man in 'The Killers', tells Nick that 'little boys always know what they want to do', scorning and dismissing what Nick takes on as his responsibility, commenting with derision on Nick's manhood.[22] Wesley tells Harry Morgan, 'You ain't hardly human'.[23] Bearers tell Francis Macomber that the lion is alive, and the buffalo too.[24] Bugs in 'The Battler' is described as a 'gentle-voiced, crazy black man'.[25] According to Kenneth Lynn, Bugs 'mothers' Ad, the ex-fighter deformed by his profession, 'cooking him delicious fried ham and egg sandwiches and referring to him with unfailing politeness as Mister Francis. But the solicitous Negro is also a sadist, as the worn black leather on the blackjack he carries silently testifies. Master as well as slave, destroyer as well as caretaker, this black man is another of Hemingway's dark mother figures.'[26] Although this critic uses the label 'mother', he is extrapolating not the biological relationship but the caretaking, nursing characteristic inherent in the term. When Ad gets unmanageable, Bugs smashes him with his blackjack. (Remember the slave Jupiter in Poe's 'Gold-Bug' who has similar leave to whip his master.) Bugs has also been given the gift of prophecy: 'He says he's never been crazy,' Ad tells Bugs. Bugs replies, 'He's got a lot coming to him.'[27] Lynn notes that, in the late 1950s, Hemingway would reveal to a friend 'an astonishing touchiness about these ominous words, as though he considered them to be a prophecy fulfilled'.

No matter if they are loyal or resistant nurses, nourishing *and* bashing the master's body, these black men articulate the narrator's doom and gainsay the protagonist-narrator's construction of himself. They modify his self-image; they violate the nurse's primary function of providing balm. In short, they disturb, in subtle and forceful ways, the narrator's construction of reality. We are left, as readers, wondering what to make of such prophecies, these slips of the pen, these clear and covert disturbances. And to wonder, as well, why they are placed so frequently in the mouths of black men.

It is as if the nurse were quite out of control. The other side of nursing, the opposite of the helping, healing hand, is the figure of destruction – the devouring predator whose inhuman and indifferent impulses pose immediate danger. Never still, always hungry, these figures are nevertheless seductive, elusive, and theatrical in their combination of power and deceit, love and death.

The devouring properties are given to women like Mrs Macomber, women who slaughter their mates rather than see them in control and strongly independent. Hemingway describes the wife in 'The Snows of Kilimanjaro' as 'this kindly caretaker and destroyer of his talent'.[28] The black male nurses may verbalise destruction and doom, deny and contradict manliness, introduce and represent antagonism, but the Africanist codes keep them bound to their nursing function. The female nurses – as wives and lovers with caretaking as their primary role – give voice to and complete acts of destruction. They are predators, sharks, unnatural women who combine the signs of a nurse with those of the shark. This combination brings us back for a moment to *To Have and Have Not*.

During a passionate scene of lovemaking, when even the stump of Harry's arm is in sexual play, Marie asks her husband:

> 'Listen, did you ever do it with a nigger wench?'
> 'Sure.'
> 'What's it like?'
> 'Like nurse shark.'[29]

This extraordinary remark is saved and savoured for Hemingway's description of a black female. The strong notion here is that of a black female as the furthest thing from human, so far away as to be not even mammal but fish. The figure evokes a predatory, devouring eroticism and signals the antithesis to femininity, to nurturing, to nursing, to replenishment. In short, Harry's words mark something so brutal, contrary, and alien in its figuration that it does not belong to its own species and cannot be spoken of in language, in metaphor or metonym, evocative of anything resembling the woman to whom Harry is speaking – his wife Marie. The kindness he has done Marie is palpable. His projection of black female sexuality has provided her with solace, for which she is properly grateful. She responds to the kindness and giggles, 'You're funny'.[30]

It would be irresponsible and unjustified to invest Hemingway with the thoughts of his characters. It is Harry who thinks a black woman is like a nurse shark, not Hemingway. An author is not personally accountable for the acts of his fictive creatures, although he is responsible for them. And there is no evidence I know of to persuade me that Hemingway shared Harry's views. In point of fact there is strong evidence to suggest the opposite.

In *The Garden of Eden* Catherine, the wife of the narrator/protagonist David Bourne, spends all her days tanning, and clearly requires this darkening process for complex reasons other than cosmetic. Early in the novel, David interrogates her about what appears to him, and to us, an obsession with the aesthetics of her body:

> 'Why do you want to be so dark?'
> 'I don't know. Why do you want anything? Right now it's the thing that I want most. That we don't have I mean. Doesn't it make you excited to have me getting so dark?'
> 'Uh-huh. I love it.'
> 'Did you think I could ever be this dark?'
> 'No, because you're blonde.'
> 'I can because I'm lion colour and they can go dark. But I want every part of me dark and it's getting that way and you'll be darker than an Indian and that takes us further away from other people. You see why it's important.'[31]

Catherine well understands the association of blackness with strangeness, with taboo – understands also that blackness is something one can 'have' or appropriate; it's the one thing they lack, she tells him. Whiteness here is a deficiency. She comprehends how this acquisition of blackness 'others' them and creates an ineffable bond between them – unifying them within the estrangement. When this lack is overcome, it is taken to be an assertion. The effect is heightened by Catherine's accompanying obsession with blonding her hair. Both of these colouring gestures – blackening up and whiting out – are codes Catherine imposes on David (inscribes on his body and places in his mind) to secure the sibling-twin emphasis that produces further sexual excitement.

The couple is not content with the brother–sister relationship; they require the further accent of twins, which the colour coding, like the offprint of a negative, achieves. (This excitement of brother–sister incest is also the story the black man Bugs in 'The Battler' tells Nick to explain why Ad went crazy: Ad's marriage dissolved after rumours that his wife was his sister.)

That story, acted out by a blacked-up couple in *The Garden of Eden*, is marked and stressed in its forbiddenness. Its voluptuous illegality is enforced by the associations constantly made between darkness and desire, darkness and irrationality, darkness and the thrill of evil. 'Devil things', 'night things', are Hemingway's descriptions of David and Catherine's appetites, and 'Devil' becomes Catherine's nickname. 'Just look at me', she says, after they have both had bleaching and haircuts, 'That's how you are . . . And we're damned now. I was and now you are. Look at me and see how much you like it.'[32]

The remarkable and overt signs of brother–sister incest and of cross-gender have occupied most of the published criticism of this novel. Unremarked is the Africanist field in which the drama is played out. Echoing Marie's tryst in the beauty parlour compelled by the spectre of black sexuality she has just encountered, Catherine persuades herself that, while she needs regular hair whitening, she no longer needs tanning. 'I don't really wear it,' she says. 'It's me. I really am this dark. The sun just develops it.'[33]

Catherine is both black and white, both male and female, and descends into madness once Marita appears, the 'real' nurse, with dedicated, normal nursing functions. And it should be noted that Marita is naturally dark, with skin like the Javanese, a woman given to David by Catherine as a healing balm. The figurative gift that Harry gives Marie is analysed and reformulated here: Catherine the shark gives David a dark nurse as an act of kindness. Her own nursing capabilities – her breasts – she calls her dowry. What is new and powerful and *hers* is the bleached white male-cut hair. It is a change Hemingway describes as 'dark magic'.

'When we go to Africa I want to be your African girl too,' Catherine tells him.[34] While we are not sure of exactly what this means to her, we are sure of what Africa means to him. Its availability as a blank, empty space into which he asserts himself, an uncreated void ready, waiting, and offering itself up for his artistic imagination, his work, his fiction, is unmistakable.

At the heart of *The Garden of Eden* is 'Eden': the story David is writing about his adventures in Africa. It is a tale replete with male bonding, a father–son relationship, and even the elephant they track is loyal to his male companion. This fictional, Africanised Eden is sullied by the surrounding events of the larger Catherine–David Africanist Eden. Africa, imagined as innocent and under white control, is the inner story; Africanism, imagined as evil, chaotic, impenetrable, is the outer story.

The inner story Catherine despises and eventually destroys. She thinks it boring, irrelevant. David ought to be writing about her instead. The reader is made to understand and be repelled by her selfish narcissism. But in fact she is right. At least Hemingway thinks she is, for the story we are reading and the one he has written *is* about her. The African story David is struggling to write (and is able to write when Marita, the authentic dark nurse, takes over) is an old, familiar myth, Africa-as-Eden before and after its fall, where, as in 'The Snows of Kilimanjaro', one goes to 'work the fat off [one's] soul'.[35]

That story, which Catherine burns up, has value as a cherished masculine enclave of white domination and slaughter, complete with African servants who share David's 'guilt and knowledge'. But the narrative that encloses it, the blacked-up, Africanist one, comments thoroughly on an aestheticised blackness and a mythologised one. Both are fantastic. Both are pulled from fields of desire and need. Both are enabled by the discursive Africanism at the author's disposal.

I wish to close by saying that these deliberations are not about a particular author's attitudes toward race. That is another matter. Studies in American Africanism, in my view, should be investigations of the ways in which a non-white, Africanist presence and personae have been constructed – invented – in the United States, and of the literary uses this fabricated presence has served. In no way do I mean investigation of what might be called racist or non-racist literature, and I take no position, nor do I encourage one, on the quality of a work based on the attitudes of an author or whatever representations are made of some group. Such judgments can and are being formed, of course. Recent critical scholarship on Ezra Pound, Céline, T. S. Eliot, and Paul de Man comes to mind. But such concerns are not the intent of this exercise (although they fall within its reach). My project is an effort to avert the critical gaze from the racial object to the racial subject; from the described and imagined to the describers and imaginers; from the serving to the served.

Ernest Hemingway, who wrote so compellingly about what it was to be a white male American, could not help folding into his enterprise of American fiction its Africanist properties. But it would be a pity if the criticism of that literature continued to shellac those texts, immobilising their complexities and power and luminations just below its tight, reflecting surface. All of us, readers and writers, are bereft when criticism remains too polite or too fearful to notice a disrupting darkness before its eyes.

5

Queer Desire in *The Well of Loneliness*

Line Pouchard

Radclyffe Hall's *The Well of Loneliness*[1] narrates the childhood, education and coming out of a young woman who gradually becomes aware of her attraction to other members of the same sex in a claustrophobic and repressive family environment. The novel was written for a mainstream readership and its appearance was highly publicised in the contemporary media. *The Well of Loneliness* was subjected to an obscenity trial and withdrawn from publication in England six weeks after it was issued in 1928. The trial provoked instant attention and prompted public debates on lesbianism, an issue until that time discussed only within a moral and religious rhetoric of sin.[2] Paradoxically, censorship afforded the book long-lasting fame and gave it an underground aura reinforced by the publication of the novel in France and America: copies were smuggled into England until it was finally published there in 1948. For many readers, *The Well of Loneliness* still epitomises 'the lesbian novel', and through the years since its publication it has in turn been praised and condemned for its monolithic representation of a lesbian's life and sexuality. As an indicator of the novel's continuing popularity, it was reprinted ten times between 1982 and 1994.

The Well illustrates the ambiguities, struggles and pain involved in constructing and asserting a 'lesbian's identity', and living through 'lesbian experiences' in a predominantly heterosexual culture and in the face of a world replete with lesbophobic discourse and actions. Despite the deceptively straightforward narrative techniques, the novel questions with varying degrees of self-reflexivity the appropriation of gender models in the narrative of its characters' lives. The mise-en-scène of the protagonist's emerging sexual, emotional and erotic desire for other women enacts a confrontation with gender roles traditionally enforced in her world. Performances of same-sex desire occur within the frameworks of sex/gender roles which attempt to fix the characters in stable, recognisable 'sexual identities', while, I will argue, other narrative features undermine these identities.

In *The Well*, the mother–daughter relationship features importantly, with the biological mother acting as a negative – heterosexual, phallic – blueprint in her daughter's coming out, and a friendly older woman playing the role of surrogate mother and companion. The mother plays a crucial part in her daughter's recognition that society does not look kindly upon love relationships between members of the same sex. The aristocratic Stephen Gordon exiles herself from Morton, family estate and metaphoric Garden of Eden, when Lady Anna, her mother, confronts Stephen with her love for Angela, a neighbour's wife. Leaving paradise for self-imposed exile, Stephen 'quite suddenly found her manhood' (p. 205). In the absence of Sir Philip, Stephen's dead father, Lady Anna tries to enforce compulsory heterosexuality upon her daughter and impose upon her the clear marks of a gender she rejects. The mother acts as the guardian of a rigid distinction between the sexes based upon biological, socio-cultural and religious factors. As she fails in her enterprise of normalising and assimilating her daughter into her own social group and class, her daughter's exile follows. Stephen Gordon embarks on a quixotic quest for a stable 'invert' identity and for the community of 'those like her' (p. 378).

QUEER THEORY AND THE CONSTRUCTION OF THE SUBJECT

The essentialist reliance upon sexual and gendered identities has been thoroughly exposed by Judith Butler, who demonstrates that these identities are not stable and immutable even within patriarchal culture.[3] Medically documented cases of hermaphrodites and transvestism like that of Herculine Barbin, a nineteenth-century hermaphrodite whose diaries have been scrutinised by Foucault, challenge the possibility of assigning fixed sexes and stable genders to form identities.[4] Working at the crossroads between psychoanalysis and political critique in order to shift the epistemology of writing about sexuality, Butler shows that, even for Foucault, the cultural assignation of gender is always an inscription on the surface of bodies.

Many feminist analyses based on metaphors of the body are rooted in an essentialism by which 'the body' becomes a monolithic, impervious, fixed and almost natural guarantor of sexual meanings.[5] But, according to Butler, bodies do not pre-exist discourses about them; they support the limits of the social constructs of sexuality with their surfaces and boundaries which guarantee a separation between an inner and an outer world. Sexual acts of same-sex desire which question the integrity of bodily boundaries expose this separation constitutive of identity as unstable and permeable. The appearance of cross-dressed bodies playing with the visible ornaments of gender displaces the inner/outer boundary of the body and exposes the illusion of coherence and unified origin in constructions of gender.[6] Gender is not synonymous with sexual acts; it inscribes its own culturally prescribed meanings and effects upon bodies, rather than being dictated by their demands.

Butler's description of sexual acts and gender-poses in terms of performance underlines the imitative aspects of socio-cultural constructions of gender. A discrete and differentiated repetition of these acts ensures the re-enactment and re-experiencing of meanings in the public as well as private domains. Gender becomes a temporally defined identity 'instituted in an exterior space through a stylised repetition of these acts'.[7] In addition, performance emphasises the possibility of a parody of gender roles, and the postmodern parody of a lack of origin and parody of the parodic.[8] A stable gender identity and a fixed sexual preference no longer provide adequate models to account for the construction and effects of sex/gender roles; rather, reversing the terms of the description but not mirroring it, the performances of bodily acts confer sexual identifications which may proceed from the choice of love objects, may stem from sexual acts, may embody a type of discourse, and may also strike a series of poses. The various terms describing identity positions and gender roles in lesbian acts reflect both a departure from the categories imposed by compulsory heterosexuality and a parodic recuperation of these categories: in drag, butch/femme acts, queens' and girls' performances, erotic interplay emerges within the distance between the poses which question in their multiple deployment the very existence of a gendered referent. It is this erotic interplay in the construction of the gendered subjects, Stephen Gordon and her lovers, that I will try to trace in *The Well*.

THE CONSTRUCTION OF GENDER CATEGORIES IN *THE WELL OF LONELINESS*

The Well attempts to create in Stephen Gordon and her lovers textbook examples illustrating the categories of 'inversion', as they were defined by late nineteenth- and early twentieth-century sexologists such as Krafft-Ebing and Havelock Ellis. Ellis, who wrote the introduction to the first edition of *The Well*, proposed to classify lesbians according to a hierarchy in which could be found 'the congenital invert' at one end, and the 'misguided heterosexual woman' at the other. In a problematic middle category, from his own avowal, stood the 'woman who responds to true inverts'. Whereas only true inversion is innate, permanent, and characteristic of sterile women, the other two types exemplify temporary, acquired behaviour. At the time, these medico-psychological categories represented a significant progress from earlier accounts of homosexuality because they presented it as a natural defect for which the subject should incur no blame.

The novel sets out to defend as natural the 'inversion' it invokes to account for lesbianism in accordance with these theories, but contradicts its own project in a number of ways. The narrative only partially succeeds in its attempt to fix Stephen and Mary within the rigidly prescribed categories of the 'invert' and the 'truly feminine' respectively. The internal logic of these rigid distinctions leads Stephen to sacrifice Mary on the altar of heterosexuality and sends Stephen off to become the prophet of 'her kind', a Christ-like figure who will redeem 'inverts', as Ellis called lesbians, from the scorn of the world by her writing. The novel introduces elements questioning nature as the very basis of 'inversion', and physical characteristics as the foundation of a stable sexuality.

Stephen Gordon's appearance as a child follows the physical characteristics described by Ellis for the 'true invert': her body is that of a boy, 'narrow-hipped', 'flat-chested', 'broad-shouldered', and 'with the lanky wiry flanks of a greyhound' (p. 33). Her little seven-year-old fingers are 'curiously strong and efficient' like her father's, which greatly displeases her mother when she takes her arm to cross the street (p. 30). According to Ellis, the lover was to be a rather plain girl, although she could have a good figure, but not a face to attract men. Mary, Stephen's lover, is an orphan of low-class origin, thus compensating by lack of birth for pretty looks, a significant detail in a novel where class is an indispensable element for distinguishing sex/gender roles. *The Well* is governed by naturalistic and rigid definitions of these roles, and the description of the characters who form those categories conforms either to the heterosexual model or to the model of congenital inversion. In the narrative, Stephen's innate 'inversion' proposed by Ellis' theories is reinforced by Stephen's education. It is Stephen's father who, desiring a son, christens his daughter with a boy's name, and encourages every masculine pursuit in the little girl's education, in spite of her mother's warnings. Greatly encouraged by her father, Stephen indulges in the manly physical pleasures of sports, learns fencing, rides horses astride, plays with dumb-bells, goes hunting and later studies the Classics. All this leads to asocial behaviour in the child, who cannot relate to other children, and gets into a fist fight with a boy during a social call.

Rather than reinforcing the hypothesis of a congenital trait, however, in practice the description of Stephen's education stresses that she has been raised following the gender roles appropriate to males in her social class and epoch. The emphasis on boys' activities shows the degree to which her gender is actually constructed rather than biologically determined, and unless the reader grants some power of divination to Stephen's father before her birth, the girl's identification with boys from the days of her youthful cross-dressing as young Nelson may be read as nothing more than a child's eagerness to please a parent.

Although the novel sets out to define 'inversion' as part of nature, it emphasises the unnatural character of her mother's reaction to her strange daughter. Stephen's relationship to her mother displays more ambiguities than the unquestioning, reciprocated love she enjoys with her father. From the start Lady Anna feels a discomfort with her own child. Even during the pre-Oedipal phase, no bond is established between mother and daughter, except through the intercession of the father, who shows his wife how to love the baby's tiny fingers. Much more than the tomboy's education, Lady Anna's dislike of her daughter allows the novel to play within the framework of 'inversion' as inborn rather than acquired. The instant dislike of the mother for a child who adores her is inexplicable and presented as unnatural by the essentialist claims of the naturalness of motherly love and mother–child relationship. The rhetoric of 'Nature' which sustains the genealogy of families at Morton, and therefore guarantees a natural separation of genders, also establishes the category of 'inverts'. However, *The Well* does not resolve the contradiction that, in its 'natural' state as Garden of Eden, Morton has no room for both Lady Anna and her daughter, although the two are equally part of 'Nature'. Lady Anna, described as 'a mother of sons' (p. 8), who expected to give her beloved husband a boy, produces a baby girl whom she dislikes at once, even as she breast-feeds her. The mother expresses an 'unnatural' antipathy for her daughter, which she attributes to the fact that Stephen is a girl and with which she torments herself and the daughter to the point of cruelty. Within the naturalistic world of the novel, even the Great Malvern hills are 'full-bosomed, courageous, great green-girdled mothers of splendid sons' (p. 8). Since it deprives the estate of a rightful heir, giving birth to a daughter as first-born is much more than a simple accident: it is a betrayal of Nature itself. The later revelation to Lady Anna of Stephen's love for Angela, a neighbour's wife, keeps mother and daughter together within the domain of the 'unnatural': it is no longer the mother whose feelings for Stephen are contrary to nature but Stephen 'who is unnatural' (p. 203).

Moreover, heterosexual marriage based on an antithesis between masculinity and femininity is seen as the only source of happiness. The mother plays a significant role as model in the unsuccessful enforcement of traditional gender roles. Lady Anna as a young girl was 'difficult to win but when won, all-fulfilling', and the mother's virginal body 'betokened happy promise – the archetype of the very perfect woman'. She sits in her drawing-room doing needlework all day, and she despises all forms of intellectual pursuit for women. Leaving it to her husband to make decisions concerning Stephen's education, she plays a primary role only in her daughter's emotional and social development, first as an object of admiration, then as a will to oppose. The narrative emphasises the parents' love as a model and great source of joy for the child with the repetitions of 'perfect', 'one', 'oneness', 'symbol of perfect fulfilment', though this fantasised heterosexual ideal becomes shadowed by Stephen's emerging sexual identity. Intelligible only to her father, who keeps a copy of Krafft-Ebing's treatise on sexuality in his library, homosexuality is by contrast to the parents' happiness shown in an unfavourable light, in spite of the novel's agenda to speak up in its favour. Stephen's failed love affairs and her decision at the end of the book to redeem her peers with her writer's pen never achieve or even promise the solid happiness described for the parents' heterosexual couple. In spite of the narrative's efforts to describe a 'third gender', as Ellis described 'inverts', and in spite of the fact that social prejudice is officially the cause of Stephen's distress, its terms remain very rooted within the frame of compulsory heterosexuality for which there can be no happiness nor fulfilment outside heterosexual marriage.

Nevertheless, I would like to propose two ways of reading the novel which may open the debate to a more qualified analysis. One traces the recurrences of the word 'queer' in *The Well*, with the purpose of showing that its frequent use makes audible a distancing tone in a narrative otherwise so eloquently serious and devoid of humour. The other examines Stephen's loves, especially her affair with Mary, for the circulation of desire within the couple and its implications for gender roles.

THE INSISTENT QUESTIONING OF QUEER

The word 'queer' repeatedly appears in *The Well*. The *Oxford English Dictionary* notes that 'queer' is of 'doubtful' and 'obscure origin', with few examples recorded prior to 1700. In the sense of 'odd, peculiar, eccentric in appearance and character, of questionable character, suspicious, dubious', the *OED* quotes various examples since 1508. Another sense given is 'not in a normal condition', and even 'drunk' in slang. The third meaning, 'queer' as 'homosexual', usually male, is a word of American origin, which is quoted for the first time in 1922 in *Practical Value of Scientific Study of Juvenile Delinquents by the Children's Bureau*, US Department of Labor. A fourth section under 'queer' lists an adjective meaning 'bad, worthless', especially in relation to counterfeit money. The overwhelmingly negative connotations of 'queer' run parallel to its uncertain etymology and its early registered use in criminal records. As deconstruction has shown, the various connotations of a word disseminate into one another, making it impossible to separate these connotations when the word is used, regardless of the intention of the user. Thus, 'queer' meaning 'odd' and 'suspicious' endows the meaning 'homosexual' with its negative connotations and 'queer' as 'homosexual' invades phrases containing the adjective.

In a Foucaultian strategy of re-appropriation of the power of naming, the pejorative meaning of 'queer' as 'homosexual' has become for some gays and lesbians a political and theoretical label designed to challenge the bourgeois pre-eminence of a binary heterosexual/homosexual order, in which identities are based on sex, rather than viewed as a series of discrete performances.[9] Incorporating lesbians under the term 'queer' risks the danger that lesbian writings and concerns will become invisible once again, erased by unquestioned assimilation under one universalising label, even in discussions of homosexuality, so that other lesbians reject 'queer' as an unsuitable label. For my purposes here, let it suffice to trace some occurrences of 'queer' in *The Well*, with the aim of producing an example of queer reading. The project is to deflate the demands of sex/gender as an ordering principle of sexual identity, and expose sex/gender roles as signifiers without a signified.

With uncanny over-determination, *The Well of Loneliness* uses 'queer' to describe at one point or other most characters in the book, whether the situation implies a sexual context or not, and whether or not the word seems appropriate to the description. In *The Well*, even nature is 'queer' at times. First, as one might expect, Stephen and her two lovers are 'queer'. In the words of the beloved maid Collins and the cook, Stephen is 'a queer child' (p. 16) and 'a queer fish' (pp. 20–1), and for others, 'queer and absurd'(p. 73), 'a queer-looking girl' (p. 160), and 'a queer guest' (p. 138). The narrative combines Stephen's first awareness of Angela's attractiveness with a romantic image of nature: 'she was like some queer flower that had grown up in darkness' (p. 130). Stephen's lover, Mary, has a 'queer voice' (pp. 444–5) and 'laughs a queer, little joyless laugh' (p. 381). Puddle, Stephen's teacher and a closet lesbian, who acts as a surrogate mother and protective companion for Stephen when she is exiled from Morton, enters the scene as 'this queer little woman . . . who was going to become a fixture' (p. 65). Queerness pervades every aspect, emotion, and experience of the 'invert's' life in *The Well*. When a male friend talks to Stephen about her relationship with Mary, she experiences 'a queer sense of relief' (p. 350) in consequence of being open with at least one person. Even Stephen's debuts as a writer are queer: she shows her father some of her 'queer compositions' (p. 78). With such an abundance of queerness, it is difficult for a modern reader of *The Well* not to read 'queer' as connoting a parodic view of sexuality, in spite of the novel's monolithic style.

Pursuing further the play of double-entendre upon the accumulation of 'queer', the reader finds an excess of incongruous pairing operating along the axis of queerness, as if the novel could not stop pairing women together. The sexual connotations of 'queer' lend the over-abundance of queer pairs a parodistic quality which seemingly escapes the didactic project of the novel. For instance, when Stephen and Mary get involved in the lesbian community in post-war Paris, the narrative describes at length several lesbian couples and single women of varied class and national origin socialising in bars, and at salons. At Christmas time, Wanda, one of the lesbians in the group, goes with Stephen to the Sacre-Coeur, the important Catholic church in Montmartre. At prayer, Stephen experiences 'queer, unbidden thoughts' in which she asks Christ for an answer to 'the riddle . . . of existence' (p. 382). This religious experience, announcing the novel's final conversion, is contiguous in the time of narration with Stephen reproaching herself for not sending her car to Mademoiselle Duphot, her old French teacher, to drive both her and Wanda to the Midnight Mass.

In Stephen's mind, Mademoiselle Duphot, in her penultimate appearance in the novel, is associated with Wanda thanks to their common religious fervour: 'how queer, she and Wanda'. A sexual connotation appears when the reader recalls Stephen's pre-war discovery of Paris's back alleys and visits to Mademoiselle Duphot: 'oh, the lure of the Passage Choiseul, the queer, rather gawky attraction of it'. The incongruous juxtaposition of Wanda, young Polish painter, drunk most of the time, with Mademoiselle Duphot, old, frail, innocent and greedy for cakes, undermines the frenzy of pairing that the novel has indulged in. As the reader cannot take the pair formed by Wanda and Mademoiselle Duphot as a serious possibility, queer here signals a parodic repetition of performance in the narration of *The Well*. Gender roles repeated at length in performances multiplying their poses condition repeated performances of pairing in the narrative.

'Queer' applied to other characters undermines their relentless heterosexuality, and thus deconstructs the rigid separations between sex/gender roles that the narrative attempts to establish. But before we examine this in Stephen's parents and her love for her mother, a small detour through the animal kingdom will be useful in order to point out the limits of the naturalistic model in *The Well*. The novel presents Stephen's immediate acceptance by animals at Morton as a sign that 'inverts' belong to the same natural order as they do: animals ignore the outer disguises of gender but recognise expressions of 'true' gender, that Stephen is in fact a man, despite the outer appearance of her woman's body. However, the tropes of naturalism also belong to a 'queer' representational framework: nature itself is described as 'queer'. 'The queer, pungent smell' of dog-daisies (p. 28) and the 'queer light slanting over the hills' (p. 31) accompany Stephen's pleasure in nature during excursions around the estate with her mother. The beauty of nature in the late afternoon light brings 'a queer feeling' to the child who is close to tears (p. 32). Stephen's rapport with dogs and horses is 'naturally skilful and fearless' (p. 36) but animals participate in the queerness of nature. Thus, nature, a founding principle of homo- and heterosexual order in the novel, appears to erase the distinctions it is intended to establish. The parody of distinct and essentialist sexes and genders introduced by 'queer' reaches its climax when a fixed sex/gender role is attributed to a dog. At a time when the adult Stephen retreats to work on her novel, Mary is left alone in the company of her dog. The dog misses Stephen, particularly the male companionship available to 'him' during their solitary walks. The dog's longing for Stephen stems from a 'male instinct', equated to 'the instinct that displays itself in club windows and in other places of male congregation' (p. 344). The dog, which is given a human cultural construction in order to justify an essentialist, nature-based and God-given sexual order, longs 'for that queer, intangible something about her that appealed to the canine manhood in him' (p. 345). The parody of gender roles performed by the attribution of 'manhood' to a dog re-inscribes itself within the narrative through the agency of queer.

Yet, nothing in the narrative indicates that this episode, like many others, is offered with any intention of self-mockery. Rather, the *reader's* understanding of queer with its multiple connotations reveals the parodic performance of the text. Thanks to the engagement of the critic with queerness and the attempt at queer reading, biological nature as a producer of sexual difference is exposed as a grotesque caricature. When Stephen and the dog recognise that they possess manhood (the reader remembers that Stephen found hers when leaving Morton) the knowledge that neither Stephen nor the dog are men cannot be discarded. Both Stephen and the dog refer to manhood as if by instinct and the parallel between the two is less than flattering for lesbians. The narrative posits some original, natural manhood, the one possessed by men, which may be imitated, but not duplicated or performed. Stephen's imitations of manhood, except perhaps her heroic actions during the war, remain flawed and inferior to originals because they are only imitations and lack the biological referent available to men. Stephen is forbidden the recognition and privileges which accompany manhood in her social class. In her thoughts, actions, and cross-dressing, she constantly tries to approximate what her instinct depicts as manhood, and she is constantly reproached for 'trying to ape what [she is] not' (p. 173).

'Aping' and not being 'real' are constant dangers and fears for Stephen: she uses the degrading term 'aping' to condemn other 'inverts', as she has been taunted with it in her childhood and adolescence. Within the naturalistic framework of the narrative, Stephen's actions become repeated imitations without an origin; therefore she can never really achieve 'true manhood'. For her and for many others like her, the only way to identify with manhood is through the tragedy of the soul and spirit of a man, trapped in a woman's body, aping real men. The interplay of performances which deploy for us her possible sexual identifications, performances made visible through our reading of queer, is not available to the protagonist and other characters in the novel as terms of analysis. The narrative is caught within its own frame of reference and cannot escape its specifications.

THE POSES OF SEXUAL DIFFERENCE

Stephen's sexuality appears best when it stands in opposition to or in conjunction with other types of sexuality rather than in a void by itself. The focus on the dynamic relationship within a pair questions the bipolar assignation of gender roles as masculine and feminine. It is this univocal reliance upon sexual difference as founding sexual identities, a single mode of representing sexual practice and what Teresa De Lauretis calls 'sexual indifference', which renders *The Well* in some ways so dated for a modern reader.[10] In the context of a strict separation of genders, Stephen's 'inversion' is most sharply contrasted with her parents' heterosexuality, but the discourse of queer re-inscribes itself within this heterosexuality. Young Stephen's acts of desire seem locked within an Oedipal triangle which alternatively pairs her off against the father and the mother, thus justifying the homo/heterosexual dichotomy. Loving and sharing interests with the father to the point of making Lady Anna jealous, Stephen is paired in a heterosexual couple. Resembling him and loving her mother in his admiring and protective manner, Stephen gets caught up in the tropes of 'unnaturalness'.

The parents, these archetypes of 'perfect', 'happy' heterosexuality are themselves described as 'queer', and, for Lady Anna, this queerness is related to motherhood. In addition to being a gentleman, a hunter, a lover, Sir Philip is described as 'a queer mixture', 'part sportsman, part student' (p. 22). Although Lady Anna is never described as 'queer', from Stephen's point of view, the pre-sexual time before marriage is for both parents a queer time: 'how queer it seemed there had been a time when her father had actually not known her mother' (p. 83). The mother's virginal body is queer before penetration, and the Biblical image of sexual knowing ensures that the father's unidirectional phallic power establishes heterosexual relations. Lady Anna re-enters the discourse of queer when her baby girl is born ten years into the marriage. The child raises in her a 'queer antagonism that amounted almost to anger' (p. 11), actually the first occurrence of the word in the novel. The child is pleasing enough but the close resemblance to her father first elicits the antagonism. Later it is the very admiration, close to worship, that the girl feels in the presence of her mother's beauty, which makes her particularly disgusting to her mother. Lady Anna dislikes the love she sees in the young Stephen's eyes because it resembles too much that of her husband: young Stephen's love does not spring out of her 'self' as the narrative would have it at times, but it is learnt by imitation of her father's love for her mother.

The impossibility of representing women's desire in language, independently of the masculine representations of desire and the phallic system of the logos, is articulated in the narrative by what Puddle, Stephen's governess, calls 'a conspiracy of silence'. Stephen's queer desire for queer love objects lacks the means of its expression in language. Having guessed Stephen's 'real nature', Puddle refrains from discussing it with the girl and remains silent in spite of her own past sufferings. Lady Anna cannot talk to her husband of her aversion to her child, nor can Stephen mention to her mother her love for Collins, nor can Sir Philip share with his wife and daughter his medical insights into 'her nature'. Breaking 'the conspiracy of silence' certainly was a significant aspect of the book, and one which still justifies reading and teaching it.

The couple formed by Stephen and Mary proves the most fruitful pairing in *The Well*, since during this period, Stephen seems to be most prolific as a novelist. It contains the prototype of its modern equivalent, the butch–femme duo. The narrative describes Mary as a fundamentally heterosexual woman whom Stephen may easily push into the consoling arms of the first man she puts into the courtyard for this very purpose, but a closer scrutiny of Mary's character reveals other aspects of her sexuality. Reneging on her earlier resolution that men are 'selfish, arrogant, possessive' (p. 302), Stephen designs to protect Mary from a life among 'the miserable army' of lesbians (p. 393) by affording her the rewards of heterosexual life, such as a family, society's approval, a home among her people with a husband. The novel stresses the social reasons why heterosexuality is the only available route to happiness. This point, which dictates the narrative closure, is crucial to the politics of the novel and the plea for social acceptance of lesbianism. Barred from visiting Morton and Lady Massey, Mary is particularly desolate. The lesbians in Paris afford her little social comfort, as they are all outcasts. In marked contrast with Stephen's affair with Angela, which fails because of the latter's moral inferiority, Mary's and Stephen's love is crunched largely because of society's reproof.

Mary's characterisation seems to conform to Ellis's middle category of 'women who respond to true inverts', but the closure of the plot leaves open the question of whom the 'invert' loves, and who loves the 'invert'. In her femme incarnation, Mary performs with conviction and commitment as Stephen's lover, but her homosexuality is understood to be accidental and temporary. If lesbianism is an essence, as the novel purports, there is a contradiction. The category of femme prises open the naturalisation of homosexuality and points forward to Butler's performance theory. Esther Newton, in her fundamental essay 'The Mythic Mannish Lesbian', makes a distinction between Stephen and

Mary, 'forgettable and inconsistent character' whose 'real story has yet to be told'.[11] Mary, although she assumes the traditional 'feminine' role in the couple, taking care of Stephen's house and papers (p. 300), also expresses sexual desire for Stephen while they live together. The narrative implies that Stephen's sexual desire is masculine, the mark of an active, outgoing character, but Mary's desire is not feminised as only receptive and passive. It is Mary who requests and elicits a first kiss after staying in Stephen's study late at night instead of going to bed as she is told (p. 301). Mary demands that they have sexual relations for the first time, while they are on holiday in Orotava, and her sexual desire for her beloved is so strong that she threatens to leave if she does not get sex, an event described with the single memorable phrase: ' . . . and that night they were not divided' (p. 316).

Adopting Stephen's point of view, the narrative insists that Mary does not know what she is doing. Her admiration, gratitude and worship for Stephen bespeak 'something far more fundamental of which she herself was unconscious' (p. 300). Her youthful ardour and faith seem cruel to Stephen, who hesitates to 'drag through the maze of passion' (p. 303) an innocent child 'ignorant of life'. But nothing suggests that Mary's love is timid, foolish or childish. Her passion is as thoughtful as it is constant. Mary's desire, called 'feminine' but exhibiting characteristics described as 'masculine' for other characters, questions the novel's assignation of gender in the couple. Even in most contemporary representational contexts, Teresa de Lauretis points out that Stephen's desire would continue to stand for lesbian desire, and Mary's homosexuality might remain invisible 'unless she enters the frame of vision as or with a lesbian in male body drag'.[12] In the butch–femme couple, drag functions as a catalyst exposing gender roles as signifiers available to play with. Drag performances call attention to the inscription of desire within a pair through the parodic imitation of gender roles, an imitation which points to itself and its poses rather than to a fixed referent. Sue-Ellen Case has argued that the playful re-appropriation of gender roles in the 'dynamic duo' of the butch–femme couple contains the possibility of reclaiming 'the agency to change ideology'.[13] Despite a closure which depends on Mary re-entering into the heterosexual sphere she seemingly left by mistake, the repeated performance of desiring the mannish Stephen casts her, at least during the length of their affair, outside the constraints of heterosexual roles and in the ambiguous role of femme. Although the constant conflation of Stephen's point of view and the narrative voice clearly implies that Mary will go on to embrace heterosexual marriage, the descriptions of her desire and her wilful actions upon this desire call into question the ending of the novel.

The Mary–Stephen pair defies the sex/gender classifications imposed upon it by the narrative, which develops around a circulation of desire escaping the rigid control of its best didactic intentions. The assignation of this desire to define bipolar (masculine–feminine) sexual identities in the couple formed by the two women fails to produce the strict categories of 'inversion' that the novel depends upon. Although the pair has been translated into the more contemporary butch–femme dyad, the narrative's seriousness in establishing genuine, traditional gender roles, even for lesbians, makes uneasy the adoption of these terms, as such lack of distance erases the self-conscious, parodic play with the trappings of gender upon which a 'butch–femme aesthetic' thrives.[14] The militant project of denouncing ostracism is based upon naturalistic claims that the 'invert' should not be punished any more than anyone born with a congenital defect, because she is born that way. The novel's hypothesis is threatened by the very elements of its development, because the 'invert' is not an invert by herself, but she is caught in queer desire which resists straightforward assimilation into theoretical categories. The main character's torments and victories are best illustrated in the love relationships she participates in: Stephen Gordon is not mannish on her own, nor is she in love without an object of love like Mary or Angela, who may enter into a relationship with her.

Even the love objects who refuse to enter into a pairing with Stephen, such as the maid Collins, and her own mother, help define her position. Stephen's play with drag and masculine attire never occurs within a void. The little girl dressing up as young Nelson with such pleasure and excitement does it in order to parade in front of the beloved maid; the young woman who refuses to wear dresses does so in opposition to her mother's wishes. The same young woman who has come of age and rushes to her father's tailor to order new suits, neckties and shoes is eagerly anticipating her first official visit to Angela's Grange after their first encounter. Angela's and Mary's feminine appearances reinforce Stephen's by contrast, and in *The Well*, the gendered, socially and culturally determined items that are clothes become both expressions of a naturalistic inner self and the a posteriori justification of sexual identity. Clothes become the extension of the human body and the expression of an inner nature, as for Stephen, even her physical body both displays and covers her gender position: strength and muscles denote maleness in a female body. But the self-conscious, parodic play of imitation found in contemporary drag is absent from character construction, in a way that prevents an easy translation of Stephen and her lovers into the butch–femme representational frame. The playful act of the butch–femme duo stands a long way from the born invert of Ellis's category.

Reading lesbian fiction and accounting for lesbian theatre performances have contributed a great deal to the enrichment of literature. By securing substantial visibility in the arts and in academic discourse, 'lesbian' productions have enforced recognition for themselves. This recognition has in turn obliged feminists to take account of such claims and alter their methods of analysis. But as with the rights obtained by minority groups, and indeed with feminism itself within patriarchy, the advantages are never secured and always remain in danger of being eradicated or simply forgotten. Only practice may ensure continuous visibility.

6

The Difference of View

Mary Jacobus

For George Eliot, as for her heroines (wrote Virginia Woolf),

> the burden and the complexity of womanhood were not enough; she
> must reach beyond the sanctuary and pluck for herself the strange
> bright fruits of art and knowledge. Clasping them as few women have
> ever clasped them, she would not renounce her own inheritance – *the
> difference of view, the difference of standard . . .* [1]

The terms here are worth lingering on; they bring to light a hidden
problem as well as articulating an obvious one. The problem explicitly
located is, in one way or another, the theme of many of the essays
included in this book – or rather, their question: that is, the nature of
women's access to culture and their entry into literary discourse. The
demand for education ('the strange bright fruits of art and knowledge')
provides the emancipatory thrust of much nineteenth- and twentieth-
century feminism, and goes back to Mary Wollstonecraft's attempt to
appropriate the language of Enlightenment Reason for her own sex in *The
Rights of Woman.* But this access to a male-dominated culture may equally
be felt to bring with it alienation, repression, division – a silencing of the
'feminine', a loss of women's inheritance. The problem, then, is not
George Eliot's alone; it is that of women's writing (and of feminist literary
criticism) itself. To propose a difference of view, a difference of standard
– to begin to ask what the difference might be – is to call in question the
very terms which constitute that difference.

The terms used by Virginia Woolf, therefore, also uncover something of
the rift experienced by women writers in a patriarchal society, where
language itself may re-inscribe the structures by which they are
oppressed. Reaching beyond the sanctuary, transgressing the boundaries
of womanhood (womanhood: the sacred hearth, at once home, womb and
tomb; something is being stilled into silence, for the burden of
womanhood is also the burden of the mystery) – the movement becomes
an exit from the sacred into the profane. In this scheme, woman as silent
bearer of ideology (virgin, wife, mother) is the *necessary* sacrifice to male
secularity, worldliness, and tampering with forbidden knowledge. She is

the term by which patriarchy creates a reserve of purity and silence in the materiality of its traffic with the world and its noisy discourse. Feminised, the Faustian hero becomes a militant adventuress, Eve, plucking 'the strange bright fruits' that bring both knowledge and unhappiness. The archetypal gesture installs George Eliot in a specifically Judaeo-Christian drama, that of sin and death; the fall is from innocence (mindlessness?) into mortality. It's not surprising, therefore, that Virginia Woolf should end her essay with what amounts to a funeral oration. For her, George Eliot was literally worn into the grave by the battle with 'sex and health and convention' which attended her quest for 'more knowledge and more freedom'.

In this traditional drama, a lively sense of sin is matched with a weighty sense of ancient female suffering and hopeless desire; but George Eliot's heroines, Virginia Woolf tells us, no longer suffer in silence:

> The ancient consciousness of woman, charged with suffering and sensibility, and for so many ages dumb, seems in them to have brimmed and overflowed and uttered a demand for something – they scarcely know what – for something that is perhaps incompatible with the facts of human existence.[2]

(That notion of dumbness and utterance, of demand for an impossible desire, forms a recurrent motif in both women's writing and feminist literary criticism.) What is striking here is the association of ancient suffering and modern desire with women's inheritance, as if they were almost synonymous. This is elegy, not affirmation. Elegy which, in Virginia Woolf's case, one might justifiably link with the death of a mother or mothering step-sister. Our mothers were killed by the burden and the complexity of womanhood; or, like George Eliot, died in giving birth to their writing (as Dorothea rests in an unvisited tomb in order that 'George Eliot' may write her epitaph). Such, at any rate, seems to be the melancholy inference. It's surely significant that for at least one woman looking back at another, the price of combining womanhood and writing seemed so high – that the transgression of writing seemed to bring with it mortal consequences; the sacrifice not only of happiness, but of life itself.

Contemporary feminist criticism is more likely to stress pleasure than suffering – the freeing of repressed female desire; *jouissance* and *'la mère qui jouit'* (no longer barred from sexual pleasure) as against the burden of womanhood. Recent French writing about women and literature, marked as it is by the conjunction of neo-Freudian psychoanalysis and structuralism, has particularly tended to diagnose the repression of women's desire by representation itself, and by the order of language as instated by the Law of the Father: the symbolic order, predicated on lack and castration.[3] In this theoretical scheme, femininity itself –

heterogeneity, otherness – becomes the repressed term by which discourse is made possible. The feminine takes its place with the absence, silence, or incoherence that discourse represses; in what Julia Kristeva would call the semiotic, the pre-Oedipal phase of rhythmic, onomatopoeic babble which precedes the symbolic but remains inscribed in those pleasurable and rupturing aspects of language identified particularly with *avant-garde* literary practice. But here again, there's a problem for feminist criticism. Women's access to discourse involves submission to phallocentricity, to the masculine and the symbolic: refusal, on the other hand, risks re-inscribing the feminine as a yet more marginal madness or nonsense. When we speak (as feminist writers and theorists often do) of the need for a special language for women, what then do we mean?

Not, surely, a refusal of language itself; nor a return to a specifically feminine linguistic domain which in fact marks the place of women's oppression and confinement. Rather, a process that is played out within language, across boundaries. The dream of a language freed from the Freudian notion of castration, by which female difference is defined as lack rather than otherness, is at first sight essentially theoretical, millennial and Utopian. Its usefulness lies in allying feminism and the *avant-garde* in a common political challenge to the very discourse which makes them possible; the terms of language itself, as well as the terms of psychoanalysis and of literary criticism, are called in question – subverted from within. Woman and artist, the feminine and the *avant-garde*, are elided in the privileged zone of contemporary intellectual and aesthetic concern: writing. Such a move has the advantage of freeing off the 'feminine' from the religion-bound, ultimately conservative and doom-ridden concept of difference-as-opposition which underlies Virginia Woolf's reading of the 'case' of George Eliot. *Difference* is redefined, not as male versus female – not as biologically constituted – but as a multiplicity, joyousness and heterogeneity which is that of textuality itself. Writing, the production of meaning, becomes the site both of challenge and otherness; rather than (as in more traditional approaches) simply yielding the themes and representation of female oppression. *Difference*, in fact, becomes a traversal of the boundaries inscribed in Virginia Woolf's terms, but a traversal that exposes these very boundaries for what they are – the product of phallocentric discourse and of women's relation to patriarchal culture. Though necessarily working within 'male' discourse, women's writing (in this scheme) would work ceaselessly to deconstruct it: to write what cannot be written.

So much for one formulation of the question: what is the nature (the difference) of women's writing? Another way to pose the question is to explore the extent to which patriarchal representation, by contrast, 'silences' women – the extent to which *woman* or *womanhood*, considered not as an image but as a sign, becomes the site of both contradiction and repression. For D. H. Lawrence, woman is 'the unutterable which man must forever continue to try to utter'; she achieves womanhood at the point where she is silenced (like Sue Bridehead) and installed within the sanctuary.[4] If writing is a transgression punishable by death, being written about, by however loving a Father, can also prove fatal. Take the disquieting way in which Hardy, in a famous scene from *Tess of the D'Urbervilles*, reveals the sign *woman* to be a rich source of mythic confusion, ideological contradiction, and erotic fascination:

> She was yawning, and he saw the red interior of her mouth as if it had been a snake's. She had stretched one arm so high above her coiled-up cable of hair that he could see its satin delicacy above the sunburn; her face was flushed with sleep, and her eyelids hung heavy over their pupils. The brim-fulness of her nature breathed from her. It was a moment when a woman's soul is more incarnate than at any other time; when the most spiritual beauty bespeaks itself flesh; and sex takes the outside place in the presentation. (ch. XXVII)

Sex having taken the outside place in the presentation, it's not surprising that within a short space Tess should become, first feline, and then Eve. The language of incarnation (body and soul, presence and absence) signals an underlying structure which comes near to collapse before the threat of female sexuality. Though Hardy seems to be salvaging Tess's body for spirituality (the vessel is brim-full), the yawning mouth opens up a split in the very terms he uses. The incarnate state of Tess's soul appears to be as close to sleep – to unconsciousness – as is compatible with going about her work. At the same time, the snake-mouth marks the point of (desired) entry to an interior which is offered to us as simply yet more body (she is all red inside, *not* all soul). Fascination with this unknown, unrepresentable, interiorised sexuality is surely at the centre of male fantasies of seduction and engulfment. No wonder that Hardy goes on to make Tess, not the object of male gaze, but the mirror in which the male is reflected ('*she* regarded *him* as Eve at her second waking might have regarded Adam'; my italics): otherness is domesticated, made safe, through narcissism – the female mouth can't utter, only receive and confirm the male.

Tess's silence, like her purity, makes female desire dumb; places her on the side of unconsciousness and, finally, death. 'Shut up already' might be the hidden message which a feminist critique uncovers. But to stop at such readings (or at exposing the reproduction of sexist ideology by male critics) is to take only the first step towards uttering an alternative. Utterance, though, brings the problem home for women writers (as for feminist critics). The options polarise along familiar lines: appropriation or separatism. Can women adapt traditionally male-dominated modes of writing and analysis to the articulation of female oppression and desire? Or should we rather reject tools that may simply re-inscribe our marginality and deny the specificity of our experience, instead forging others of our own? – reverting, perhaps, to the traditionally feminine in order to revalidate its forms (formlessness?) and preoccupations – rediscovering subjectivity; the language of feeling; ourselves. The risks on either side are illuminatingly played out in the writing of feminism's founding mother herself: Mary Wollstonecraft. *The Rights of Woman*, in claiming sense for women rather than sensibility, pays a price that is reflected in its own prose. Putting herself outside the confines of a despised femininity, aligning herself with 'sense', Mary Wollstonecraft also eschews 'pretty feminine phrases' as a male conspiracy designed to soften female slavery. Linguistic pleasure (literary language) is placed on the side of the feminine; banned, like female desire:

> I shall disdain to cull my phrases or polish my style. I aim at being useful, and sincerity will render me unaffected; for, wishing rather to persuade by the force of my arguments than dazzle by the elegance of my language, I shall not waste my time in rounding periods, or in fabricating the turgid bombast of artificial feelings, which, coming from the head, never reach the heart. I shall be employed about things, not words! and, anxious to render my sex more respectable members of society, I shall try to avoid that flowery diction which has slided from essays into novels, and from novels into familiar letters and conversations. ('Author's Introduction')

A swagger of busy self-presentation makes this as much the creation of an alienated persona as it is a feminist preface to *Lyrical Ballads*. A plain-speaking utilitarian speaks not so much *for* women, or *as* a woman, but *against* them – over their dead bodies, and over (having attempted to cast it out) the body of the text too: 'I shall be employed about things, not words!'

Speaking both for and as a woman (rather than 'like' a woman): this is the problem of women's writing. For the feminist critic, the problem may resolve itself as one of style. For Mary Wollstonecraft, the solution lay in fiction that gave her access not only (paradoxically) to her own situation as a woman, but to literarity. *The Wrongs of Woman* inverts both the title and the assumptions of her earlier essay in order to show how, if 'sense' excludes women, 'sensibility' confines them – yet offers a radical challenge to patriarchy; a challenge which it must repress. (When the heroine pleads her own case in a court of law, the judge alludes to 'the fallacy of letting women plead their feelings . . . What virtuous woman thought of her feelings?', thereby exposing the double-bind.) The prison of sensibility is created by patriarchy to contain women; thus they experience desire without Law, language without power. Marginalised, the language of feeling can only ally itself with insanity – an insanity which, displaced into writing, produces a moment of imaginative and linguistic excess over-brimming the container of fiction, and swamping the distinction between author and character:

> What is the view of the fallen column, the mouldering arch, of the most exquisite workmanship, when compared with this living memento of the fragility, the instability, of reason, and the wild luxuriancy of noxious passions? Enthusiasm turned adrift, like some rich stream overflowing its banks, rushes forward with destructive velocity, inspiring a sublime concentration of thought. *Thus thought Maria* – These are the ravages over which humanity must ever mournfully ponder . . . It is not over the decaying productions of the mind, embodied with the happiest art, we grieve most bitterly. The view of what has been done by man, produces a melancholy, yet aggrandizing, sense of what remains to be achieved by human intellect; but a mental convulsion, which, like the devastation of an earthquake, throws all the elements of thought and imagination into confusion, makes contemplation giddy, and we fearfully ask on what ground we ourselves stand.[5]

This is what it means for women to be on the side of madness as well as silence. Like the rich stream overflowing its banks, a wash of desire throws all the elements of thought and imagination into confusion. By contrast with the ruins of (male) cultural imperialism, the earthquake is feminised; demands 'on what ground we ourselves stand'; opens on to a feminist sublime where all foundations are called in question.

Mary Wollstonecraft's concern in this passage for 'words', not 'things', makes it a crucial moment for both women's writing and feminist literary criticism. A mental convulsion breaches the impasse between undifferentiated disappearance into a 'male' text and the prison of sensibility. Rejecting the essentialism that keeps women subjected as well as subjective, it also rejects mastery and dominance. Madness imagined as revolution, or the articulation of Utopian desire ('a demand for something – they scarcely know what'), represent gestures past the impasse played out by Mary Wollstonecraft's prose. In writing, such gestures may release possibilities repressed by a dominant ideology or its discourse. The transgression of literary boundaries – moments when structures are shaken, when language refuses to lie down meekly, or the marginal is brought into sudden focus, or intelligibility itself refused – reveal not only the conditions of possibility within which women's writing exists, but what it would be like to revolutionise them. In the same way, the moment of desire (the moment when the writer most clearly installs herself in her writing) becomes a refusal of mastery, an opting for openness and possibility, which can in itself make women's writing a challenge to the literary structures it must necessarily inhabit.

'Thus thought Maria' – the container overflowed by authorial Enthusiasm – has its analogue in a famous 'awkward break' noticed by Virginia Woolf. Her example is Charlotte Brontë's intrusion into *Jane Eyre* with what *A Room of One's Own* rightly identifies as a protest against the confinement of the nineteenth-century woman writer:

> It is in vain to say human beings ought to be satisfied with tranquillity: they must have action; and they will make it if they cannot find it . . . Women are supposed to be very calm generally: but women feel just as men feel; they need exercise for their faculties, and a field for their efforts as much as their brothers do; they suffer from too rigid a restraint, too absolute a stagnation, precisely as men would suffer . . . It is thoughtless to condemn them, or laugh at them, if they seek to do more or learn more than custom has pronounced necessary for their sex.
> *When thus alone, I not unfrequently heard Grace Poole's laugh . . .* [6]

('That is an awkward break, I thought', comments Virginia Woolf.) The author herself has burst the bounds of 'too rigid a restraint' – making action if she cannot find it. By a breach of fictional decorum, writing enacts protest as well as articulating it. It is not simply that the excess of energy disrupts the text; it is that the disruption reveals what the novel cannot say within its legitimate confines, and hence reveals its fictionality. The unacceptable text gets the blue pencil from Virginia Woolf ('the woman who wrote those pages . . . will write in a rage where she should write calmly . . . She will write of herself where she should write of her characters. She is at war with her lot'); but it also opens up a rift in her own seamless web. What she herself cannot say without loss of calmness (rage has been banned in the interests of literature) is uttered instead by another woman writer. The overflow in *Jane Eyre* washes into *A Room of One's Own*. This oblique recuperation of feminist energy has implications for feminist criticism as well as for fiction; might, in fact, be said to characterise the practice of the feminist critic, for whom the relation between author and text (her own text) is equally charged. Editing into her writing the outburst edited out of Charlotte Brontë's, Virginia Woolf creates a point of instability which unsettles her own urbane and polished decorum. The rift exposes the fiction of authorial control and objectivity, revealing other possible fictions, other kinds of writing; exposes, for a moment, its own terms.

The slippage here is both seductive and threatening. Seductive, because passion is involved; threatening, because the structures on which both fiction and criticism depend are seen to be built on words alone. And perhaps the correction of authorial transgression – the domestication of authorial desire – may be necessary in the interests of writing itself. Take a significant moment of self-censorship like that which closes the 'Finale' of *Middlemarch*. George Eliot's compassionately magisterial verdict on the 'determining acts' of Dorothea's life ('the mixed result of young and noble impulse struggling amidst the conditions of an imperfect social state, in which great feelings will often take the aspect of error, and great faith the aspect of illusion') cancels what had originally been 'an awkward break' in the final pages of the first edition:

> They were the mixed results of young and noble impulse struggling under prosaic conditions. Among the many remarks passed on her mistakes, it was never said in the neighbourhood of Middlemarch that such mistakes could not have happened if the society into which she was born had not smiled on . . . modes of education which make a woman's knowledge another name for motley ignorance – on rules of conduct which are in flat contradiction with its own loudly-asserted beliefs. While this is the social air in which mortals begin to breathe, there will be collisions such as those in Dorothea's life, where great feelings will take the aspect of error, and great faith the aspect of illusion.[7]

Authorial indignation risks turning the neighbourhood of Middlemarch into 'social air', uncovering fiction as polemic. Whether the cancellation springs from loss of nerve or aesthetic judgement, it makes George Eliot (so to speak) the heir of Virginia Woolf as well as Charlotte Brontë. In doing so, it opens up the possibility of the author's dissolution into her own text; the closing sentences of the novel point beyond the 'Finale' to their own writing – to the full nature that has its strength broken by being diverted into channels whose effect is incalculably diffusive:

> Her finely-touched spirit had still its fine issues, though they were not widely visible. Her full nature, like that river of which Cyrus broke the strength, spent itself in channels which had no great name on the earth. But the effect of her being on those around her was incalculably diffusive: for the growing good of the world is partly dependent on unhistoric acts; and that things are not so ill with you and me as they might have been, is half owing to the number who lived faithfully a hidden life, and rest in unvisited tombs. ('Finale')

Earlier, George Eliot has referred to Casaubon's turgid scholarship as 'minor monumental productions'; monuments to dead languages. By contrast with this sterile imperialism (Casaubon *versus* the world), we have the unhistoric acts that make for growing good. Though a new St Theresa will find no conventual life to reform, a new Antigone no Creon to oppose with self-immolation ('the medium in which their ardent deeds took shape is forever gone'), still, the writer may find another 'medium' of her own for ardent deeds. Dorothea's hidden life and entombment make her a silent reformer, an unremembered protester; but her silence and anonymity are the sacrifice which allows 'George Eliot' speech and name.

If the gain seems marginal, this may be because writing is itself marginal, unhistoric; if diffusive, incalculably so. But the possibility glimpsed at the end of *Middlemarch* – that of Enthusiasm overflowing into ink – points to the quietly subversive power of writing, its power to destabilise the ground on which we stand. In *A Room of One's Own*, Virginia Woolf dissolves 'truth' (the withheld 'nugget of truth') into 'the lies that flow from my pen'; the subject of women and writing becomes a fiction: 'I propose, making use of all the liberties and licences of a novelist, to tell you the story . . .'[8] As hard fact dissolves into fluid fiction, so the authorial 'I' becomes 'only a convenient term for somebody who has no real being'; many 'I's', many Marys ('Mary Beton, Mary Seton, Mary Carmichael' and I) – a plurality contrasted to the unified 'I' which falls as a dominating phallic shadow across the male page, like Casaubon's monumental egotism. And as the subject ('I') is dissolved into writing, so boundaries themselves are called into question; rendered, not *terra firma*, but fiction too. Once returned to its proper medium (the Cam), the thought-fish which swims through *A Room of One's Own* 'as it darted and sank, and flashed hither and thither, set up such a wash and tumult of ideas that it was impossible to sit still'. The story becomes the narrative of its own inception, then of the arrest of verbal energy – this darting, flashing, linguistic play – by the figure of a man, representative of the Law, of the phallic 'I' that bars and bounds:

> It was thus that I found myself walking with extreme rapidity across a grass plot. Instantly a man's figure rose to intercept me. Nor did I at first understand that the gesticulations of a curious-looking object, in a cut-away coat and evening shirt, were aimed at me. His face expressed horror and indignation. Instinct rather than reason came to my help; he was a Beadle; I was a woman. This was the turf; there was the path. Only the Fellows and Scholars are allowed here; the gravel is the place for me. Such thoughts are the work of a moment. As I regained the path the arms of the Beadle sank, his face assumed its usual repose . . .[9]

The protest against male exclusiveness is obvious enough; so is the comical reduction of an educational institution to a grass plot and a clockwork beadle. Acquiescing in the terms of her trespass, Virginia Woolf yet shows, with pleasurable obliqueness (via her short cut), that these terms are arbitrary – a matter of cut-away coats and gravel paths.

Virginia Woolf's satire, in delineating the confines within which women must walk ('This was the turf; there was the path') traverses and exposes them. The story she tells is in fact that of her own oblique relation, as a woman writer, to the dominant culture and to patriarchal institutions (she labels them Oxbridge, the educational system which inscribes her marginality). At once within this culture and outside it, the woman writer experiences not only exclusion, but an internalised split. Elsewhere in *A Room of One's Own* she puts it like this:

> if one is a woman one is often surprised by a sudden splitting off of consciousness, say in walking down Whitehall, when from being the natural inheritor of that civilisation, she becomes, on the contrary, outside of it, alien and critical.[10]

'Alien and critical' – the stance glimpsed behind the urbane and playful style of *A Room of One's Own*. Though Virginia Woolf never fails to remind us that the matter of inheritance is absolutely a matter of access to power, property and education, an experienced division forms part of that inheritance too. To recognise both the split and the means by which it is constituted, to challenge its terms while necessarily working within them – that is the hidden narrative of the trespass on the grass. But what about that elusive thought-fish? For Virginia Woolf, rage drove it into hiding; the rage that for her distorts Charlotte Brontë's fiction ('She will write in a rage where she should write calmly'). It is in this light, perhaps, that we should re-read her famous remarks about androgyny – not as a naïve attempt to transcend the determinants of gender and culture (though it is that), not as a Romantic enshrining of Shakespearian creativity (though it is that too), but rather as a harmonising gesture, a simultaneous enactment of desire and repression by which the split is closed with an essentially Utopian vision of undivided consciousness. The repressive male/female opposition which 'interferes with the unity of the mind' gives way to a mind paradoxically conceived of not as one, but as heterogeneous, open to the play of difference: 'resonant and porous . . . it transmits emotion without impediment . . . it is naturally creative, incandescent, and undivided.'[11] That's as good a description as one could wish, not of the mind, but of Virginia Woolf's own prose – and of the play of difference perpetually enacted within writing.

The gesture towards androgyny is millennial, like all dreams of another language or mode of being; but its effect is to remove the area of debate (and the trespass) from biological determination to the field of signs; from gender to representation ('words' not 'things'). And in holding open other possibilities – otherness itself – such writing posits 'the difference of view' as a matter of rewriting. 'A woman writing thinks back through her mother'; thinking back through the mother becomes at once recuperation and revision. The rediscovery of a female literary tradition need not mean a return to specifically 'female' (that is, potentially confining) domains, any more than the feminist colonising of Marxist, psychoanalytic, or poststructuralist modes of thought necessarily means a loss of that alien and critical relation which is one aspect of women's inheritance. Rather, they involve a recognition that all attempts to inscribe female difference within writing are a matter of inscribing women within fictions of one kind or another (whether literary, critical, or psychoanalytic); and hence, that what is at stake for both women writing and writing about women is the rewriting of these fictions – the work of revision which makes 'the difference of view' a question rather than an answer, and a question to be asked not simply of women, but of writing too.

7

Representing Women: Re-presenting the Past

Gillian Beer

This essay was originally a lecture addressed to a group whose views and assumptions I largely share; its function was to make us look critically at some of those assumptions. In preparing it as an essay I have not tried to erase the traces of its first form, since much of the energy of my counter-assertions works out from this communal starting point. Our shared position affirms the value of women's studies, the importance of theory in giving us a purchase on literary and political practice, and the need to recognise ways in which the past is appropriated and re-written to justify the present. In the argument of the essay itself my emphasis falls on literary history, on the need to recognise the *difference* of past writing and past concerns instead of converting them into our current categories. Rather than seeking always the 'relevance' of past writing to our present reading, we may need to learn lost reading skills which bring to light elements in the text not apparent to our current training. I argue also the necessity within women's studies to analyse writing by men alongside that by women. All these elements are concentrated on bringing to our notice the 'presentism' and the fixed gender assumptions that may lurk still in some of our critical practice. In giving the paper, I was, of course, *there*: in my body, as a woman, with a woman's voice. The absence of any but a nominal presence of writer in writing must shift some of the balances within the argument, and I have tried to take account of that in my presentation. Though I'm still sorry I can't be there to argue with the reader.

We favour currently the word 'representation' because it sustains a needed distance between experience and formulation. It recognises the fictive in our understanding. It allows a gap between how we see things and how, potentially, they might be. It acknowledges the extent to which ideologies harden into objects and so sustain themselves as real presences in the world. The objects may be books, pictures, films, advertisements, fashion. Their encoding of assumptions and desires reinforces as natural and permanent what may be temporary and learnt. So representations rapidly shift from being secondary to being primary in their truth-claims.

This speedy shift to claiming authority we can all observe, in others' practice and our own. Representations rapidly become representatives – those empowered to speak on behalf of their constituency: the authentic voices of a group. That is where the trouble starts when the claim is representing women: speaking on behalf of women – speaking on behalf of who? Are we offering and receiving formulations of an abiding group; offering accounts of a person, or a group of people, conceived as stable?

One thing needs to be clear, then, as I start to de-stabilise my title. *I* am not a representative woman representing all women: I am not speaking on behalf of all of us, or occupying the space of those who differ from me. The demand that as women we claim women as our constituency may rapidly move from desirable solidarity to tokenism. So the woman finds herself there *in place of* a wide range of other women, uttering wise saws on their behalf, creating the uniformity of universals all over again. As Gayatri Spivak puts it, woman is not one instrument added to the orchestra. But, the refusal that I am offering also takes us into a contradiction that persists in representation. Though I resist the role of representative, to others I may represent women – or a particular type of woman – and certainly I *am* a woman, at home in my body, liking much of the condition, and closely sharing with other women, concerned with the theoretical consequences – and the practical ones – of my gender. We women are a body of people and share bodily features. Go too far along that road and we find biologism, with its emphasis on bodily characteristics, particularly those of reproduction, as the essential characterisation of all women. We need to prevent metaphor settling into assumption, the fate of Cixous's famous 'writing in milk'.[1] As much recent gender theory (Chodorow, Dinnerstein, etc.) has emphasised, that body, those bodies, have been produced culturally as well as physiologically.[2] They are then *recognised* culturally and those recognitions are further internalised. These embodied recognitions have ricocheted back and forth as description between men and women, forming psychic conditions over time within which we live, write, and expect.[3]

If we are to understand the processes of gender formation within a culture, and if we are to understand the shiftiness with which cultures have laid claim to the formulations of their predecessors in order to naturalise their own perceptions, we need to study how things have changed. This requires the reading of men's and women's writing side by side. *How* things have changed is likely to challenge any notion of a sustained arc of progress in representing women; it will challenge also the notion of a stable archetypal order. Clutter, inertia, scurry: the hoped for and longed for, long delayed but informing the present – these are more often the motions we shall discover in reading through the writing of past periods.

To assert in our theory that men have dominated discourse and yet to pretend in our practice as students and teachers that women's writing is autonomous, by studying only genetically female authors, becomes sentimental. Moreover, it leads to theoretical confusion because it expunges economic, epistemic, shared historical conditions of writing and makes it impossible to *measure* difference. To read Joyce, and Lawrence, and Woolf alongside, for example, does not collapse difference: it specifies it; it takes us some way into understanding the complex relationships between modernism and feminism, as well as between male and female non-combatants' experience of the First World War (all were non-combatants, of course). Moreover, if gender is a largely cultural product it is risky to read women's representations of women, even, as if the gender of the writer makes them thereby automatically authoritative. Such an assumption is to simplify our understanding both of the writing and of our own internalisation of past gender constructions.

In the eighteenth century, particularly, the mere naming of authors as female may in any case lead us into a crasser kind of error. Many men then wrote as women. John Cleland commented, as Halsband reminds us, 'in reviewing a novel entitled *The School for Husbands. Written by a Lady*:

> "As ladies are generally acknowledged to be superior to our sex in all works of imagination and fancy, we doubt not this is deemed a sufficient reason for placing their names in the title-page of many a dull, lifeless story which contains not one single female idea, but has been hammered out of the brainless head of a Grubstreet hireling."'

In this novel, he continues, many of the scenes convince him of 'the *femality* of its Author'.[4]

The crux here is that what has made the fraud desirable is the ascription of *imagination* to women as a specifically female, rather than a human power – and then thereby its peripheralisation on to the edge of power patterns. Qualities, however fine, which are prescribed exclusively to one gender become falsified. Evelyn Fox Keller has recently shown how the metaphoric representation of men's activities in science has narrowed the methodological range of scientific practice. As women we may like many qualities exclusively prescribed for us in the past (insight, nurturing, empathy) and prefer them to those exclusively represented as men's (dominance, go-getting, genius), but we should cast an extremely sceptical eye on the grounds of that preference, and not naturalise it. As Mary Hays pointed out towards the end of the eighteenth century, men have valued 'women's' virtues, such as prudence, patience, wisdom, when they prove convenient to themselves.

Prudence being one of those rare medicines which affect by sympathy, and this being likewise one of those cases, where the husbands have no objections to the wives acting as principals, nor to their receiving all the honors and emoluments of office; even if death should crown their martyrdom, as has been sometimes known to happen. Dear, generous creatures![5]

Literary history will always be an expression of now: current needs, dreads, preoccupations. The cultural conditions within which we receive the texts will shape the attention we first bring to them. We shall read as readers in 1987 or 1988, or, with luck, 1998, but we need not do so helplessly, merely hauling, without noticing, our own cultural baggage. That is likely to happen if we read past texts solely for their grateful 'relevance' to our expectations and to those of our circumstances that we happen to have noticed. The encounter with the otherness of earlier literature can allow us also to recognise and challenge our own assumptions, and those of the society in which we live.[6] To do so we must take care not to fall into the trap of assuming the evolutionist model of literary development, so often taken for granted, in which texts are praised for their 'almost modern awareness' or for 'being ahead of their time'. This presentist mode of argument takes *now* as the source of authority, the only real place.

We can nudge and de-stabilise the word 'representation' in another usable way. It can mean also re-presenting: making past writing a part of our present, making present what is absent. Not bringing it up to date, with the suggestion of the past aspiring to become our present – improved, refurbished, in the hoteliers' discourse – but re-presenting. This means engaging with the *difference* of the past in our present and so making us aware of the trajectory of our arrival and of the insouciance of the past – their neglectfulness of our prized positions and our assumptions. We can use this awareness, if we will, to reinforce and gratify our sense of our own correctness, 'an almost modern understanding' – but that won't get us far. Rather, the study of past writing within the conditions of its production disturbs that autocratic emphasis on the self and the present, as if they were stable entities. It makes us aware too of how far that view continues despite postmodernism.

The problem with the concept of relevance is that it assumes an autonomous and coherent subject. The present, the self, is conceived as absolute; all else as yielding relativistically to it and unacceptable unless it yields (in both senses). The incorrectness of this once fashionable position has become dramatically manifest with its adoption by the present government: 'relevance' now requires that everything be honed to a meagre utilitarianism. Applied science is to be advantaged over fundamental enquiry with the absurd assumption that applications can be reliably foreseen and that usefulness alone justifies enquiry. Relevance assumes fixity – it is not self-questioning and does not incorporate change.

The connection with the representation of women is not far to seek. Unless we believe in fixed entities – man and woman – we need to be alert to the processes of gender formation and gender change. We cannot construe this in isolation from other elements within a culture, and, moreover, we shall better discover our own fixing assumptions if we value the *unlikeness* of the past. For 'relevance' is not the same as the analysis of internalised history.

The formation of gender, and its condensation in the literature of the time, is not cut loose from economics, or architecture, or class, or, come to that, animal care. No one of these is the single source of authority either: there is no sole source of oppression, though there are dominant forms of it in class, race, and gender power-structures. In the literature of the past we are presented with immensely detailed interconnecting systems: power and pleasure caught into representations so particular as to be irreplaceable. So the informing of the text with our learnt awareness of historical conditions is not a matter simply of providing 'context' or 'background'. Instead it is more exactly in-forming, instantiation – a coming to know again those beliefs, dreads, unscrutinised expectations which may differ from our own but which may also bear upon them.

The task of the literary historian is to receive the same fullness of resource from past texts as from present: to respect their difference, to revive those shifty significations which do not pay court to our concerns but are full of the meaning of that past present. The text fights back: but it can do so with meaning for us only if we read it with enough awareness of the submerged controversies and desires which are *not* concerned with us. The past is past only to us. When it was present, it was/is the present. So, re-presenting literature representing women in a way that is concerned with something other than our own design and story is a challenge which 'relevance' bypasses. We are not at work on a supine or docile text which we can colonise with our meaning or meanings. Instead we have difficult inter-action. Symptomatic reading should not be concerned only to read *through* texts. Why do we so value gaps and contradiction? Is it because it allows us to exercise a kind of social control, to represent ourselves as outside history, like those late nineteenth-century doctors who described their patients and yet exempted themselves from the processes of disease and decay they described? Our necessary search for gaps, lacunae, as analytical tools may have the effect of privileging and defending us. The inquisitorial reading of past literature for correctness and error casts *us* as the inquisitors: we identify with authority and externality.

We can never become past readers: learning the conditions of the past brings them to light. It dramatises what could remain unscrutinised for first readers. We can re-learn lost skills, though. Readers have not all become cleverer since Henry James – only cleverer at reading Henry James. We need different skills for reading Richardson and Wollstonecraft, and different ones again for reading Chrétien de Troyes and Christine de Pisan. We need, always, double reading; or perhaps multiple reading is a better expression – since binarism is another of the hidden metaphors within which we function. The numerology of the culture has replaced the magic of seven, and of three, with the magic of two, with its fixing polarities: what Cixous calls its 'hierarchised oppositions', night/day, law/nature, woman/man, private/public, etc.[7] We need a reading which acknowledges that we start now, from here; but which re-awakens the dormant signification of past literature to its first readers. Such reading seeks intense meaning embedded in semantics, plot, formal and generic properties, conditions of production. These have been overlaid by the sequent pasts and by our present concerns which cannot be obliterated, but we need to explore both likeness and *difference*. Such reading gives room to both scepticism and immersion.

When we were setting up the Cambridge course called 'The Literary Representation of Women' six years ago we wanted to test some of the views then prevalent which seemed close to essentialism and presentism.[8] Among these was the implication that feminism was a product primarily of the past twenty years or so, that there had been a steady arc of progress in women's production and in the recognition of women writers. We wanted to discover whether certain formulations of 'womanhood' persisted irremovably, or whether the cultural inflection of the fourteenth, the seventeenth, the eighteenth centuries would show us real diversity. We wanted, moreover, to understand how men and women construed their gender-identities and their relations in conditions very different from our own. We knew that we would read *now* with all the necessary, and sometimes beloved, baggage of our own cultural responses. But we wanted more than that single reading. So everybody who takes the paper specialises in one or two earlier genre/period complexes: Medieval Poetry; Jacobean Drama; Eighteenth-Century Novel. The second part of the paper concentrates on theoretical issues.

This communal work has made us aware of how sceptically we must survey the virtues and strengths ascribed to women in different periods. In much recent work, such as that of Simon Barker and Patrick Wright, on the re-presentment of past history and literature to justify the present (the Falklands, the Gloriana/Thatcher years, the raising of the Elizabethan ship, the *Mary Rose*) the emphasis has been on the corralling of sixteenth- and seventeenth-century stories.[9] For the representation of women eighteenth-century writing offers a fruitful field, but here it is not so easy to hold a single ideological focus pointed right. Instead, ideas such as the 'natural' powers of women, their enhanced sensibility and imagination, their earth-mother status, are among the myths employed among the left. Our thinking is often at the mercy of our communal metaphors, and though we may develop a sharp eye for those favoured by people with a different ideology from ourselves, we need to remain alert to our own and not allow them to bed down into our consciousness so far that they become determining. This process of persistent recognition involves also an understanding of the changing import of images.

Things mean differently at different historical moments, and different things need to be asserted at different times. This is both obvious and often ignored, so that one may come across critics accusing George Eliot of capitulating to male values when she claims the power of generalisation for women, without noting that the power of generalisation was denied by men to women at the period when she was writing and that, typically, she generalises out from the woman's position. So, Antigone can become the type of the human revolutionary for her, not only of the female sufferer. She can claim centrality for the experience of women.[10]

The problem of the relation between the centre and the periphery has remained in the favoured discourse of feminism and the left. The danger is that we may begin to welcome positions ascribed to us, and then find ourselves unable to move from them. Proper resistance leads to the 'oppositional mode', to alternative readings and to a celebration of the periphery. The list of inhabitants of the periphery becomes a carnivalesque group – the mad, the poor, women and workers – who are idealised as outside the power centre.[11] Such idealisation of the 'deviant mode' leaves its inhabitants powerless and may perpetuate exclusion. Even words like imagination and sensibility may prove synonyms for powerlessness if too easily invoked. The claimed homology of 'women' and 'nature' may equally prove a trap, since nature is so socialised a category.

Just as sociology may be said to be the study of institutionalisation as well as institutions, literary criticism can undertake the study of naturalisation as well as nature. The identification of women with nature has sometimes empowered women but also acts as a restricting metaphor.[12] It has been adopted by women themselves without always sufficient analysis of its implications. The words *nature* and *natural* are perhaps the most artful in the language. They soak up ideology like a sponge. When we hear the word *naturally* in our own or other's discourse we should raise our antennae. Argument has already been prejudged in that word. Communality is being lined up behind the speaker. The identification of woman with nature has prolonged the idea of separate spheres and has tended to figure woman as the object: an object of pursuit, enquiry, knowing. The pursuit is one which represents man as pursuing, even, as experimenter, entering and rupturing. In *A Room of One 's Own* Woolf chose as her image for future female friendship two young women scientists who work in the same lab.[13] She thereby challenged the identification of science as male which she elsewhere identified: 'Science, it would seem, is not sexless; she is a man, a father, and infected too.' The ordinariness of the image of women lab-workers to us is a measure of real change: Woolf's point was that the woman scientist would no longer be exceptional; the lab would become both a humdrum workplace and a site where women could work together. She does not see nature as woman's ally or avatar: 'Nature was called in; Nature it was claimed who is not only omniscient but unchanging, had made the brain of woman of the wrong shape or size.'[14] Woolf here brings out the ideological constituents in the authority of 'Nature', or what George Eliot had her heroine Armgart scornfully describe as 'the theory called Nature'.

One of the most important apparent freedoms that literature offers us is that of crossing gender in our reading experience, disturbing the categories within which society regularises our activities. Is this a specious freedom? In the second part of this paper I want to look at two works which bring into question the reader's and the writer's activity in crossing gender: *Moll Flanders* (1722) and *Orlando* (1928). These works also bring to the surface the problems of historical record – *Moll Flanders* is purported ghosted autobiography, *Orlando* the purported biography of an impossible life. *Moll Flanders*, moreover, is not just a distant eighteenth-century novel by a concealed male author about a mercantile woman prostitute. It is, by means of the social internalisation of literary texts, still partly constitutive of responses – diverse as they may be – to figures like Cynthia Payne. And, in a softened form (Molly instead of Moll), the generic name of the loose woman is incorporated into Joyce's *Ulysses*, shaping our responses by means of half-received reminiscence. *Orlando* is both a response to the exclusion of women from the national records and a joke about the pompous exaggeration of difference within patriarchal society. What's so distinguished about having a penis? Can we give or take a few genitalia and remain much the same? asks the work. Perhaps, if our class position doesn't shift, might be the answer it suggests. Both books – though in very different ways – raise questions about the identification of woman with nature, as well as about the 'nature of woman' argument.

This is not new, entirely. We find Catherine Macaulay, the eighteenth-century historian, heading a chapter in her 'Letters on Education': 'No characteristic Difference in Sex':

The great difference that is observable in the characters of the sexes, Hortensia, as they display themselves in the scenes of social life, has given rise to much false speculation on the natural qualities of the female mind. – For though the doctrine of innate ideas, and innate affections, are in a great measure exploded by the learned, yet few persons reason so closely and so accurately on abstract subjects as, through a long chain of deductions, to bring forth a conclusion which in no respect militates with their premises.

. . . It is from such causes that the notion of a sexual difference in the human character has, with a very few exceptions, universally prevailed from the earliest times, and the pride of one sex, and the ignorance and vanity of the other, have helped to support an opinion which a close observation of Nature, and a more accurate way of reasoning, would disprove.

. . . It must be confessed, that the virtues of the males among the human species, though mixed and blended with a variety of vices and errors, have displayed a bolder and a more consistent picture of excellence than female nature has hitherto done.[15]

She emphasises *correcting women* – but we need to enquire sceptically about 'women's virtues and perfections' as well as 'vices and foibles'.

One thing that became clearer through our joint study is that all strong works can be read along at least two, often contradictory, ideological pathways, and usually more: signs point in more than one direction. With this in mind, it seems useful to compare two works of very different periods of production, both of which tease out issues of gender and its construction: one a pseudo-autobiography written by a male writer in the person of a woman, and with no indication in the early editions of the actual author's name; the other, a re-writing of social history in the form of biography – a biography of the landed classes in England, both male and female. Both works concern themselves with 'history' in the sense of enacted event, and with historiography: the ideological forms within whose patterns we represent events.

Defoe was one of Woolf's most admired writers, though that is not the connection I most wish to discuss. In *Moll Flanders*, and in *Roxana*, Defoe recorded meta-lives which challenged, even while they fawned upon, the ideal possibilities of lives for women imagined by his society. Defoe can be read as a form of soft porn, particularly in *Roxana*, setting up the woman as commodity for the consumption of a male reader. Or he can, with equal justification, be seen as a proto-feminist, disturbing the genre of the rogue's tale to show the woman as capable of her own transactions, engaging in her own trading activities, and surviving.[16] Ideas of 'the natural' are brought under scrutiny and shifted both in Defoe and in Woolf's novels. Luce Irigaray argues in 'When the goods get together' that 'the trade that organises patriarchal society takes place exclusively among men. Women, signs, goods, currency, all pass from one man to another or – so it is said – suffer the penalty of relapsing into the incestuous and exclusively endogamous ties that could paralyse all commerce. The workforce, products, even those of mother-earth, would thus be the object of transactions among men only.'[17] In *Capital* Marx had argued along the same lines: 'Commodities cannot themselves go to market and perform exchanges in their own right.' In this passage, quoted by Irigaray, Marx alludes to women among his list of commodities, though it is not only of women he is speaking when he remarks that 'commodities are things, and therefore lack the power to resist man. If they are unwilling, he can use force; in other words, he can take possession of them.'[18]

In Defoe's writing the women are not merely vessels or mediums. They use their bodies as their capital; they go to market, making men the medium of their survival. Moreover, the first person narrative places Moll at the centre of discourse, as she is the source of trade. She 'utters' in the early as well as in our latter sense: that is, she offers goods for sale as well as speaks. Utterance in trade requires a buyer; utterance in language requires a listener, or reader. The silenced speech of Defoe's book draws our attention to Moll as a source of event and interpretation, and one which the reader finds hard to work against. Moll names everything but herself. The name 'Moll Flanders' is, she insists, not her own. Moll is the generic name for a whore; Flanders a well-known hotbed of venereal disease. Moll has been named by society, but she insists at the outset that this is a fictional name and she keeps her own name secret. The first-person form gives us also a promise throughout our reading of the work that Moll will survive it. Moll is a survivor. At seventy she returns to England, with wealth four pages long, and a husband younger than she by two years. She fulfils more than one kind of fantasy for the reader, and gratifies women and men together and diversely. She is wooed past menopause, always clean (neither she nor any of her associates suffers venereal disease). She is improbably intact at the end of her buffeted life story. She has become, as she wished to be in the book's first scene, 'a gentlewoman', and we have realised the full equivocality of the means she has innocently announced as a child: 'by my fingers' ends.'

Moll is bonny in old age. She is independent and successful. She may seem to be a cheering model for beset female readers. But that sanguine view of her can also be read another way: Moll is an Aunt Sally. She shows that women are tough. The concealed message here is: do what you will to them, they survive. Poverty, sexual ill-usage, depression, imprisonment: they can take it all. So it is not salaciousness which may mislead male readers of this representative woman (there is remarkably little of that in the penning of her adventures). It is *optimism*, the book's licence to conceive women as impermeable.

But there are further ways in which the work constructs its reader. We never read major works of literature simply in our own person, without constraint or re-ordering. The text re-shapes our responses by means of its multiple systems, of genre, of syntax, of semantics, of exclusions, of historical reference. In the case of *Moll Flanders* the genre element is particularly important and has to be re-learnt by present-day readers. This is a deviant text – not in a judgmental but in a generic sense. It is part of an already established tradition of rogue's stories, which allow to the reader the frisson of licensed ill-doing and the safety of the character's bad end. These outlaw tales can bring to the surface the wrongs of society. The characters are also held within an ellipse which allows their views to be voiced but simultaneously disowned. It is one mode in which radical opinions can declare themselves, but it risks a final acquiescence.

The Counterfeit Lady Unveiled (1673), an earlier rogue's story, by Francis Kirkman, explores the theme of women as false traders, able by means of their sexuality to cozen men and to be socially mobile. Kirkman's heroine is disposed of and made to exemplify various follies by the insistent 'I' of the male narrator. One of her first follies was her desire to be a lady, into which she was led by her reading of '*Cassandra*, *Cleopatra*, and the rest of those romances'. (*Cassandra*, it is worth noting, is La Calprenède's romance from which Defoe drew the name and figure of Roxana). The third-person narrator judges harshly the spirited cozening of society by Mary Carleton, known as 'The German Princess'. The book relishes and dismisses her wit. In a striking passage at the end, one of her female friends, referred to as a 'witty baggage', upbraids men: 'talking of the frailness of human nature, and that these crimes, which men would slip through and make nothing of, were accounted highly criminal with women; but before the great tribunal in heaven, men and women should then have equal justice, adding that it was an unworthy action in men to come only to behold that poor soul there as a wonder, when indeed she was more like a looking glass. "Yes, indeed," replied the prisoner. "I am very like a looking glass wherein you may all see your own frailties."'[19]

Like Mary Carleton, Moll Flanders internalises and reflects the values of her society. She would be a gentlewoman. Defoe, unlike Kirkman, is loyal to and sustains throughout the work her sense of her *self* as valuable. But this value can find expression only in the terms of success offered by her society. She thus becomes a critique of the values of that society, as well as a successful tradeswoman within it. She begins with her body only as her capital and by good husbandry (in both senses) concludes her life, after her transportation, back home in England with her Lancashire husband. Having earlier in the book cozened each other, they are thus absolved from the cheats of marketing into a true affection buoyed up (and magically verified) by wealth: 'Why, who says I was deceived when I married a wife in Lancashire? I think I have married a fortune, and a very good fortune too,' says he. Fortune as riches and good-fortune and as happiness vouch for each other, and they end their lives in a comfortable state of 'sincere penitence for the wicked lives we have lived' – instead of at Tyburn like the counterfeit lady.[20]

The first person here allows the reader to participate in Moll's disasters and triumphs with the confidence of survival. There is almost no mirroring in this book: inner and outer are not set sharply off from each other. Moll's inner life is blandly available to our gaze, not critically distinguished from the outside 'real' world. This is particularly the case with Moll's self-justifying fantasies. She peoples the world with careless, feckless, and thoughtless women who justify her proceedings, as when she taps on the window of a house in Greenwich, seeking a possibly careless housewife who has left her rings unattended, to whom she plans to say that she has seen two rough-looking men. When the housewife does not appear, Moll pockets the rings. Likewise, she rebukes the careless maidservant who has wandered off to talk to her young man, thus leaving Moll to rob and to be tempted to murder the little girl left in the nurse's charge. Both maidservant and boyfriend are Moll's fantasies, but as we read we hardly observe that. The robustness and the lack of challenge in Moll's address to the reader relies on the absence of doubles, mirrors, speaking likenesses. Within Moll Flanders we are presented with a single sign system in which Moll acts out her needs. Only in Newgate does Defoe introduce images from without her experience: 'like the waters in the cavities and hollows of mountains, which petrify and turn into stone whatever they are suffered to drop upon, so the continual conversing with such a crew of hell hounds as I was had the same common operation upon me as upon other people. I degenerated into stone.'[21]

Of course, in the Preface we have been assured that this coherence and cleanliness of language (the thing that establishes Moll Flanders as romance rather than as record is her mealy-mouthedness) is the product of an intervening censorship by a (male) author, 'an author must be hard put to it to wrap it up so clean as not to give room, especially for vicious readers, to turn it to his disadvantage.' He has dressed her fit to be seen, 'no immodest turns in the new dressing up of this story', cleaned up the language, and leaves a tantalising doubt about the degree of her repentance. Like the unknown true name of Moll Flanders her unrecorded natural language lies behind the censored written text, titillating the 'vicious reader'.[22] Here, instead of doubling or mirroring within first person, there is an obscured further source which gives the reader a lazy and pleasurable licence to imagine that she was worse than is here recorded but to enjoy her presence as it is in writing. She is never 'unveiled' in the Kirkman punitive sense, never exposed – and *that* (rather than its cleaned up language) is why *Moll Flanders*, despite its account of whoring and cozening, is not a pornographic text. The reader is not salaciously entangled in the punishing of Moll; she is not there as an object of trade and transaction, but as a tradeswoman, generating barter and exchange and labour. Moll is no 'earth-mother', or, in Irigaray's phrase, 'mother-earth'. She disposes of her children scrupulously but dispassionately. But then trade is for Defoe another form of Nature: 'Nothing obeys the course of Nature more exactly than trade.' Moll turns out to be another, less familiar, representation of nature, here presented as the active principle of interchange, not of nurture.[23]

Moll Flanders may have been received by its first readers as fact, but more probably as in that shameless borderland between event and hope which awakens us, without much pain, to the way things are now: which brings to our notice that they are other than they are represented in the work. Virginia Woolf takes further this shameless and alerting ratification of desire in *Orlando*. Orlando, whose name combines, in throw-away style, gold and land, is the deathless aristocrat. S/he has lived as man and as woman. S/he has by-passed the male-dominated inheritance laws, contriving to preserve her estate in her own right and to bear a son to continue it. In this, s/he is a painfully teasing contrary to Vita Sackville-West, Woolf's lover and friend, who managed to move freely across gender boundaries, dressing sometimes as a man, loving women and her husband, but who could not inherit the family estate, Knole, because she was a woman. Sackville-West suffered intensely the loss of the house in which she had grown up. Woolf re-endows her with it in this fantasy, though at the work's end the house collapses into dust leaving Orlando as a free spirit in the present day of 1928.

Orlando, by being in every way the exception, draws attention to women's disadvantage. Woolf is particularly concerned and angrily amused by their absence from the *historical record*, and in *Orlando* she is responding to the assumption of then new social historians, most notably G. M. Trevelyan's *History of England* (1926), that women can be subsumed under men's concerns.[24] Of Trevelyan's 723 pages, only seven include discussion of the position of women, other than women monarchs. In *A Room of One's Own* (1929) Woolf speaks of the lack of 'facts' about past woman: 'History scarcely mentions her'; and she quotes Trevelyan's chapter headings to show his categorical mis-understanding of 'social' history. In *A Room* she speaks of the possibility of 'a supplement to history', 'calling it, of course, by some inconspicuous name so that women might figure there without impropriety'. But in *Orlando* she offers something bolder: a transformation of history. Instead of her-story, she plays with the interacting power-structures of class, gender, and representation. The pseudo-biographer of Orlando is flummoxed because none of the ordinary narrative categories work for this hero/ine. Woolf herself writes a history of the land as language, parodying with loving *élan* the diversity of writing from the Elizabethans to the present moment. She writes about English landscape in the style of Ruskin, and about Pope in the spirit of Lady Mary Wortley Montague. Her hyperbole is all her own. This blowing up and exploding of the taken-for-granted allows her, through linguistic pleasure, to bring to the surface our false associations. The absurd song-and-dance of reticence and neo-classical personification (Our Lady of Purity, of Chastity and of Modesty)[25] which accompanies the moment when Orlando changes sex makes us have to notice how little embarrassment we ordinarily feel, as readers, in inhabiting the fictional persons of women and of men, how freely we move between them. She de-natures our assumptions about gender, about nature and the natural, and brings to light the collusion that pretends that inheritance through the male line is 'natural law'. All this is possible because she presents the work simultaneously as biography and as fantasy, jarring categories which call attention to masked contradictions.

Both Defoe and Woolf challenge their societies' gender-assumptions, but they challenge also some other assumptions: that autobiography is the space especially inhabited by women writers, that the male writer representing a woman is salacious, that 'nature' has remained a constant concept, and constantly in alliance with women. In order to read them fully we need to respond to their generic shaping and to the different weight they give to apparently familiar concepts, such as trade and the market, class and nurture. Radical reading is not a reading that simply assimilates past texts to our concerns but rather an activity that tests and de-natures our assumptions in the light of the strange languages and desires of past writing.

8

Sorties: Out and Out: Attacks/Ways Out/Forays

Hélène Cixous

Where is she?
Activity/Passivity
Sun/Moon
Culture/Nature
Day/Night

Father/Mother
Head/Heart
Intelligible/Palpable
Logos/Pathos.
Form, convex, step, advance, semen, progress.
Matter, concave, ground – where steps are taken, holding- and dumping-
ground.
<u>Man</u>
Woman

    Always the same metaphor: we follow it, it carries us, beneath all its
figures, wherever discourse is organised. If we read or speak, the same
thread or double braid is leading us throughout literature, philosophy,
criticism, centuries of representation and reflection.
Thought has always worked through opposition.
Speaking/Writing
Parole/Ecriture
High/Low

    Through dual, hierarchical oppositions. Superior/Inferior. Myths,
legends, books. Philosophical systems. Everywhere (where) ordering
intervenes, where a law organises what is thinkable by oppositions (dual,
irreconcilable; or sublatable, dialectical). And all these pairs of
oppositions are *couples*. Does that mean something? Is the fact that
Logocentrism subjects thought – all concepts, codes and values – to a
binary system, related to 'the' couple, man/woman?

Nature/History

Nature/Art
Nature/Mind
Passion/Action

Theory of culture, theory of society, symbolic systems in general – art, religion, family, language – it is all developed while bringing the same schemes to light. And the movement whereby each opposition is set up to make sense is the movement through which the couple is destroyed. A universal battlefield. Each time, a war is let loose. Death is always at work.
Father/son   Relations of authority, privilege, force.
The Word/Writing   Relations: opposition, conflict, sublation, return.
Master/slave   Violence. Repression.
   We see that 'victory' always comes down to the same thing: things get hierarchical. Organisation by hierarchy makes all conceptual organisation subject to man. Male privilege, shown in the opposition between *activity* and *passivity*, which he uses to sustain himself. Traditionally, the question of sexual difference is treated by coupling it with the opposition: activity/passivity.

THE MASCULINE FUTURE

There are some exceptions. There have always been those uncertain, poetic persons who have not let themselves be reduced to dummies programmed by pitiless repression of the homosexual element. Men or women: beings who are complex, mobile, open. Accepting the other sex as a component makes them much richer, more various, stronger, and – to the extent that they are mobile – very fragile. It is only in this condition that we invent. Thinkers, artists, those who create new values, 'philosophers' in the mad Nietzschean manner, inventors and wreckers of concepts and forms, those who change life cannot help but be stirred by anomalies – complementary or contradictory. That doesn't mean that you have to be homosexual to create. But it does mean that there is no invention possible, whether it be philosophical or poetic, without there being in the inventing subject an abundance of the other, of variety: separate-people, thought-/people, whole populations issuing from the unconscious, and in each suddenly animated desert, the springing up of selves one didn't know – our women, our monsters, our jackals, our Arabs, our aliases, our frights. That there is no invention of any other I, no poetry, no fiction without a certain homosexuality (the I/play of bisexuality) acting as a crystallisation of my ultrasubjectivities.[1] I is this exuberant, gay, personal matter, masculine, feminine or other where I enchants, I agonises me. And in the concert of personalisations called I, at the same time that a certain homosexuality is repressed, symbolically, substitutively, it comes through by various signs, conduct-character, behaviour-acts. And it is even more clearly seen in writing.

Thus, what is inscribed under Jean Genêt's name, in the movement of a text that divides itself, pulls itself to pieces, dismembers itself, regroups, remembers itself, is a proliferating, maternal femininity. A phantasmic meld of men, males, gentlemen, monarchs, princes, orphans, flowers, mothers, breasts gravitates about a wonderful 'sun of energy' – love, – that bombards and disintegrates these ephemeral amorous anomalies so that they can be recomposed in other bodies for new passions.

She is bisexual:

What I propose here leads directly to a reconsideration of *bisexuality*. To reassert the value of bisexuality,[2] hence to snatch it from the fate classically reserved for it in which it is conceptualised as 'neuter' because, as such, it would aim at warding off castration. Therefore, I shall distinguish between two bisexualities, two opposite ways of imagining the possibility and practice of bisexuality.

(1) Bisexuality as a fantasy of a complete being, which replaces the fear of castration and veils sexual difference insofar as this is perceived as the mark of a mythical separation – the trace, therefore, of a dangerous and painful ability to be cut. Ovid's Hermaphrodite, less bisexual than asexual, not made up of two genders but of two halves. Hence, a fantasy of unity. Two within one, and not even two wholes.

(2) To this bisexuality that melts together and effaces, wishing to avert castration, I oppose the *other bisexuality*, the one with which every subject, who is not shut up inside the spurious Phallocentric Performing Theatre, sets up his or her erotic universe. Bisexuality – that is to say the location within oneself of the presence of both sexes, evident and insistent in different ways according to the individual, the nonexclusion of difference or of a sex, and starting with this 'permission' one gives oneself, the multiplication of the effects of desire's inscription on every part of the body and the other body.

For historical reasons, at the present time it is woman who benefits from and opens up within this bisexuality beside itself, which does not annihilate differences but cheers them on, pursues them, adds more: in a certain way *woman is bisexual* – man having been trained to aim for glorious phallic monosexuality. By insisting on the primacy of the phallus and implementing it, phallocratic ideology has produced more than one victim. As a woman, I could be obsessed by the sceptre's great shadow, and they told me: adore it, that thing you don't wield.

But at the same time, man has been given the grotesque and unenviable fate of being reduced to a single idol with clay balls. And terrified of homosexuality, as Freud and his followers remark. Why does man fear *being* a woman? Why this refusal (*Ablehnung*) of femininity? The question that stumps Freud. The 'bare rock' of castration. For Freud, the repressed is not the other sex defeated by the dominant sex, as his friend Fliess (to whom Freud owes the theory of bisexuality) believed; what is repressed is leaning toward one's own sex.

Psychoanalysis is formed on the basis of woman and has repressed (not all that successfully) the femininity of masculine sexuality, and now the account it gives is hard to disprove.

We women, the derangers, know it only too well. But nothing compels us to deposit our lives in these lack-banks; to think that the subject is constituted as the last stage in a drama of bruising rehearsals; to endlessly bail out the father's religion. Because we don't desire it. We don't go round and round the supreme hole. We have no *woman's* reason to pay allegiance to the negative. What is feminine (the poets suspected it) affirms: . . . and yes I said yes I will Yes, says Molly (in her rapture), carrying *Ulysses* with her in the direction of a new writing; I said yes, I will Yes.

To say that woman is somehow bisexual is an apparently paradoxical way of displacing and reviving the question of difference. And therefore of writing as 'feminine' or 'masculine'.

I will say: today, writing is woman's. That is not a provocation, it means that woman admits there is an other. In her becoming-woman, she has not erased the bisexuality latent in the girl as in the boy. Femininity and bisexuality go together in a combination that varies according to the individual, spreading the intensity of its force differently and (depending on the moments of their history) privileging one component or another. It is much harder for man to let the other come through him. Writing is the passageway, the entrance, the exit, the dwelling place of the other in me – the other that I am and am not, that I don't know how to be, but that I feel passing, that makes me live – that tears me apart, disturbs me, changes me, who? – a feminine one, a masculine one, some? – several, some unknown, which is indeed what gives me the desire to know and from which all life soars. This peopling gives neither rest nor security, always disturbs the relationship to 'reality,' produces an uncertainty that gets in the way of the subject's socialisation. It is distressing, it wears you out; and for men this permeability, this nonexclusion is a threat, something intolerable.

In the past, when carried to a rather spectacular degree, it was called 'possession'. Being possessed is not desirable for a masculine imaginary, which would interpret it as passivity – a dangerous feminine position. It is true that a certain receptivity is 'feminine'. One can, of course, as History has always done, exploit feminine reception through alienation. A woman, by her opening up, is open to being 'possessed', which is to say, dispossessed of herself.

But I am speaking here of femininity as keeping alive the other that is confided to her, that visits her, that she can love as other. The loving to be other, another, without its necessarily going the rout of abasing what is same, herself.

As for passivity, in excess, it is partly bound up with death. But there is a nonclosure that is not submission but confidence and comprehension; that is not an opportunity for destruction but for wonderful expansion.

Through the same opening that is her danger, she comes out of herself to go to the other, a traveller in unexplored places; she does not refuse, she approaches, not to do away with the space between, but to see it, to experience what she is not, what she is, what she can be.

Writing is working; being worked; questioning (in) the between (letting oneself be questioned) of same *and of* other without which nothing lives; undoing death's work by willing the togetherness of one-another, infinitely charged with a ceaseless exchange of one with another – not knowing one another and beginning again only from what is more distant, from self, from other, from the other within. A course that multiplies transformations by the thousands.

And that is not done without danger, without pain, without loss – of moments of self, of consciousness, of persons one has been, goes beyond, leaves. It doesn't happen without expense – of sense, time, direction.

But is that specifically feminine? It is men who have inscribed, described, theorised the paradoxical logic of an economy without reserve. This is not contradictory; it brings us back to asking about their femininity. Rare are the men able to venture onto the brink where writing, freed from law, unencumbered by moderation, exceeds phallic authority, and where the subjectivity inscribing its effects becomes feminine

Where does difference come through in writing? If there is difference it is in the manner of spending, of valorising the appropriated, of thinking what is not-the-same. In general, it is in the manner of thinking any 'return,' the relationship of capitalisation, if this word 'return' (*rapport*) is understood in its sense of 'revenue'.

Today, still, the masculine return to the selfsame is narrower and more restricted than femininity's. It all happens as if man were more directly threatened in his being by the nonselfsame than woman. Ordinarily, this is exactly the cultural product described by psychoanalysis: someone who still has something to lose. And in the development of desire, of exchange, he is the en-grossing party: loss and expense are stuck in the commercial deal that always turns the gift into a gift-that-takes. The gift brings in a return. Loss, at the end of a curved line, is turned into its opposite and comes back to him as profit.

But does woman escape this law of return? Can one speak of another spending? Really, there is no 'free' gift. You never give something for nothing. But all the difference lies in the why and how of the gift, in the values that the gesture of giving affirms, causes to circulate; in the type of profit the giver draws from the gift and the use to which he or she puts it. Why, how, is there this difference?

When one gives, what does one give oneself?

What does he want in return – the traditional man? And she? At first what *he* wants, whether on the level of cultural or of personal exchanges, whether it is a question of capital or of affectivity (or of love, of *jouissance*) – is that he gain more masculinity: plus-value of virility, authority, power, money, or pleasure, all of which reinforce his phallocentric narcissism at the same time. Moreover, that is what society is made for – how it is made; and men can hardly get out of it. An unenviable fate they've made for themselves. A man is always proving something; he has to 'show off', show up the others. Masculine profit is almost always mixed up with a success that is socially defined.

How does she give? What are her dealings with saving or squandering, reserve, life, death? She too gives *for*. She too, with open hands, gives herself – pleasure, happiness, increased value, enhanced self-image. But she doesn't try to 'recover her expenses'. She is able not to return to herself, never settling down, pouring out, going everywhere to the other. She does not flee extremes; she is not the being-of-the-end (the goal), but she is how-far-being-reaches.

If there is a self proper to woman, paradoxically it is her capacity to depropriate herself without self-interest: endless body, without 'end,' without principal 'parts'; if she is a whole, it is a whole made up of parts that are wholes, not simple, partial objects but varied entirety, moving and boundless change, a cosmos where eros never stops travelling, vast astral space. She doesn't revolve around a sun that is more star than the stars.

That doesn't mean that she is undifferentiated magma; it means that she doesn't create a monarchy of her body or her desire. Let masculine sexuality gravitate around the penis, engendering this centralised body (political anatomy) under the party dictatorship. Woman does not perform on herself this regionalisation that profits the couple head-sex, that only inscribes itself within frontiers. Her libido is cosmic, just as her unconscious is worldwide: her writing also can only go on and on, without ever inscribing or distinguishing contours, daring these dizzying passages in other, fleeting and passionate dwellings within him, within the hims and hers whom she inhabits just long enough to watch them, as close as possible to the unconscious from the moment they arise; to love them, as close as possible to instinctual drives, and then, further, all filled with these brief identifying hugs and kisses, she goes and goes on infinitely. She alone dares and wants to know from within where she, the one excluded, has never ceased to hear what-comes-before-language reverberating. She lets the other tongue of a thousand tongues speak – the tongue, sound without barrier or death. She refuses life nothing. Her tongue doesn't hold back but holds forth, doesn't keep in but keeps on enabling. Where the wonder of being several and turmoil is expressed, she does not protect herself against these unknown feminines; she surprises herself at seeing, being, pleasuring in her gift of changeability. I am spacious singing Flesh: onto which is grafted no one knows which I – which masculine or feminine, more or less human but above all living, because changing I.

I see her 'begin'. That can be written – these beginnings that never stop getting her up – can and must be written. Neither black on white nor white on black, not in this clash between paper and sign that en-graves itself there, not in this opposition of colours that stand out against each other. This is how it is:

There is a ground, it is her ground – childhood flesh, shining blood – or background, depth. A white depth, a core, unforgettable, forgotten, and this ground, covered by an infinite number of strata, layers, sheets of paper – is her sun (*sol . . . soleil*). And nothing can put it out. Feminine light doesn't come from above, doesn't fall, doesn't strike, doesn't go through. It radiates, it is a slow, sweet, difficult, absolutely unstoppable, painful rising that reaches and impregnates lands, that filters, that wells up, that finally tears open, wets and spreads apart what is dull and thick, the stolid, the volumes. Fighting off opacity from deep within. This light doesn't plant, it spawns. And I see that she looks very closely with this light and she sees the veins and nerves of matter. Which he has no need of.

Her rising: is not erection. But diffusion. Not the shaft. The vessel. Let her write! And her text knows in seeking itself that it is more than flesh and blood, dough kneading itself, rising, uprising openly with resounding, perfumed ingredients, a turbulent compound of flying colours, leafy spaces, and rivers flowing to the sea we feed.

Writing femininity transformation:

And there is a link between the economy of femininity – the open, extravagant subjectivity, that relationship to the other in which the gift doesn't calculate its influence – and the possibility of love; and a link today between this 'libido of the other' and writing.

At the present time, defining a feminine practice of writing is impossible with an impossibility that will continue; for this practice will never be able to be *theorised*, enclosed, coded, which does not mean it does not exist. But it will always exceed the discourse governing the phallocentric system; it takes place and will take place somewhere other than in the territories subordinated to philosophical–theoretical domination. It will not let itself think except through subjects that break automatic functions, border runners never subjugated by any authority. But one can begin to speak. Begin to point out some effects, some elements of unconscious drives, some relations of the feminine imaginary to the real, to writing.

What I have to say about it is also only a beginning, because right from the start these features affect me powerfully.

First I sense femininity in writing by: a privilege of *voice*: *writing and voice* are entwined and interwoven and writing's continuity/voice's rhythm take each other's breath away through interchanging, make the text gasp or form it out of suspenses and silences, make it lose its voice or rend it with cries.

In a way, feminine writing never stops reverberating from the wrench that the acquisition of speech, speaking out loud, is for her – 'acquisition' that is experienced more as tearing away, dizzying flight and flinging oneself, diving. Listen to woman speak in a gathering (if she is not painfully out of breath): she doesn't 'speak', she throws her trembling body into the air, she lets herself go, she flies, she goes completely into her voice, she vitally defends the 'logic' of her discourse with her body; her flesh speaks true. She exposes herself. Really she makes what she thinks materialise carnally, she conveys meaning with her body. She *inscribes* what she is saying because she does not deny unconscious drives the unmanageable part they play in speech.

Her discourse, even when 'theoretical' or political, is never simple or linear or 'objectivised', universalised; she involves her story in history.

Every woman has known the torture of beginning to speak aloud, heart beating as if to break, occasionally falling into loss of language, ground and language slipping out from under her, because for woman speaking – even just opening her mouth – in public is something rash, a transgression.

A double anguish, for even if she transgresses, her word almost always falls on the deaf, masculine ear, which can only hear language that speaks in the masculine.

We are not culturally accustomed to speaking, throwing signs out toward a scene, employing the suitable rhetoric. Also, it is not where we find our pleasure: indeed, one pays a certain price for the use of a discourse. The logic of communication requires an economy both of signs – of signifiers – and of subjectivity. The orator is asked to unwind a thin thread, dry and taut. We like uneasiness, questioning. There is waste in what we say. We need that waste. To write is always to make allowances for superabundance and uselessness while slashing the exchange value that keeps the spoken word on its track. That is why writing is good, letting the tongue try itself out – as one attempts a caress, taking the time a phrase or a thought needs to make oneself loved, to make oneself reverberate.

It is in writing, from woman and toward woman, and in accepting the challenge of the discourse controlled by the phallus, that woman will affirm woman somewhere other than in silence, the place reserved for her in and through the symbolic. May she get out of booby-trapped silence! And not have the margin or the harem foisted on her as her domain!

In feminine speech, as in writing, there never stops reverberating something that, having once passed through us, having imperceptibly and deeply touched us, still has the power to affect us – song, the first music of the voice of love, which every woman keeps alive.

The Voice sings from a time before law, before the symbolic took one's breath away and reappropriated it into language under its authority of separation. The deepest, the oldest, the loveliest Visitation. Within each woman the first, nameless love is singing.

In woman there is always, more or less, something of 'the mother' repairing and feeding, resisting separation, a force that does not let itself be cut off but that runs codes ragged. The relationship to childhood (the child she was, she is, she acts and makes and starts anew, and unties at the place where, as a same she even others herself), is no more cut off than is the relationship to the 'mother', *as it consists of* delights and violences. Text, my body: traversed by lilting flows; listen to me, it is not a captivating, clinging 'mother'; it is the equivoice that, touching you, affects you, pushes you away from your breast to come to language, that summons *your* strength; it is the rhyth-me that laughs you; the one intimately addressed who makes all metaphors, all body(?) – bodies(?) – possible and desirable, who is no more describable than god, soul, or the other; the part of you that puts space between yourself and pushes you to inscribe your woman's style in language. Voice: milk that could go on forever. Found again. The lost mother/bitter-lost. Eternity: is voice mixed with milk.

Not the origin: she doesn't go back there. A boy's journey is the return to the native land, the *Heimweh* Freud speaks of, the nostalgia that makes man a being who tends to come back to the point of departure to appropriate it for himself and to die there. A girl's journey is farther – to the unknown, to invent.

How come this privileged relationship with voice? Because no woman piles up as many defences against instinctual drives as a man does. You don't prop things up, you don't brick things up the way he does, you don't withdraw from pleasure so 'prudently'. Even if phallic mystification has contaminated good relations in general, woman is never far from the 'mother' (I do not mean the role but the 'mother' as no-name and as source of goods). There is always at least a little good mother milk left in her. She writes with white ink.

Voice! That, too, is launching forth and effusion without return. Exclamation, cry, breathlessness, yell, cough, vomit, music. Voice leaves. Voice loses. She leaves. She loses. And that is how she writes, as one throws a voice – forward, into the void. She goes away, she goes forward, doesn't turn back to look at her tracks. Pays no attention to herself.

Running breakneck. Contrary to the self-absorbed, masculine narcissism, making sure of its image, of being seen, of seeing itself, of assembling its glories, of pocketing itself again. The reductive look, the always divided look returning, the mirror economy; he needs to love himself. But she launches forth; she seeks to love. Moreover, this is what Valéry sensed, marking his Young Fate in search of herself with ambiguity, masculine in her jealousy of herself: 'seeing herself see herself', the motto of all phallocentric speculation/specularisation, the motto of every Teste; and feminine in the frantic descent deeper deeper to where a voice that doesn't know itself is lost in the sea's churning.

Voice-cry. Agony – the spoken 'word' exploded, blown to bits by suffering and anger, demolishing discourse: this is how she has always been heard before, ever since the time when masculine society began to push her offstage, expulsing her, plundering her. Ever since Medea, ever since Electra.

Voice: unfastening, fracas. Fire! She shoots, she shoots away. Break. From their bodies where they have been buried, shut up and at the same time forbidden to take pleasure. Women have almost everything to write about femininity: about their sexuality, that is to say, about the infinite and mobile complexity of their becoming erotic, about the lightning ignitions of such a minuscule-vast region of their body, not about destiny but about the adventure of such an urge, the voyages, crossing, advances, sudden and slow awakenings, discoveries of a formerly timid region that is just now springing up. Woman's body with a thousand and one fiery hearths, when – shattering censorship and yokes – she lets it articulate the proliferation of meanings that runs through it in every direction. It is going to take much more than language for him to make the ancient maternal tongue sound in only one groove.

We have turned away from our bodies. Shamefully we have been taught to be unaware of them, to lash them with stupid modesty; we've been tricked into a fool's bargain: each one is to love the other sex. I'll give you your body and you will give me mine. But which men give women the body that they blindly hand over to him? Why so few texts? Because there are still so few women winning back their bodies. Woman must write her body, must make up the unimpeded tongue that bursts partitions, classes, and rhetorics, orders and codes, must inundate, run through, go beyond the discourse with its last reserves, including the one of laughing off the word 'silence' that has to be said, the one that, aiming for the impossible, stops dead before the word 'impossible' and writes it as 'end'.

In body/Still more: woman is body more than man is. Because he is invited to social success, to sublimation. More body hence more writing. For a long time, still bodily, within her body she has answered the harassment, the familial conjugal venture of domestication, the repeated attempts to castrate her. Woman, who has run her tongue ten thousand times seven times around her mouth before not speaking, either dies of it or knows her tongue and her mouth better than anyone. Now, I-woman am going to blow up the Law: a possible and inescapable explosion from now on; let it happen, right now, in language.

When '*The* Repressed' of their culture and their society come back, it is an explosive return, which is *absolutely* shattering, staggering, overturning, with a force never let loose before, on the scale of the most tremendous repressions: for at the end of the Age of the Phallus, women will have been either wiped out or heated to the highest, most violent, white-hot fire. Throughout their deafening dumb history, they have lived in dreams, embodied but still deadly silent, in silences, in voiceless rebellions.

And with what force in their fragility: 'fragility,' a vulnerability to match their matchless intensity. Women have not sublimated. Fortunately. They have saved their skins and their energy. They haven't worked at planning the impass of futureless lives. They have furiously inhabited these sumptuous bodies. Those wonderful hysterics, who subjected Freud to so many voluptuous moments too shameful to mention, bombarding his mosaic statue/law of Moses with their carnal, passionate body-words, haunting him with their inaudible thundering denunciations, were more than just naked beneath their seven veils of modesty – they were dazzling. In a single word of the body they inscribed the endless vertigo of a history loosed like an arrow from all men's history, from biblicocapitalist society. Following these yesterday's victims of torture, who anticipate the new women, no intersubjective relationship will ever be the same. It is you, Dora, you, who cannot be tamed, the poetic body, the true 'mistress' of the Signifier. Before tomorrow your effectiveness will be seen to work – when your words will no longer be retracted, pointed against your own breast, but will write themselves against the other and against men's grammar. Men must not have that place for their own any more than they have us for their own.

If woman has always functioned 'within' man's discourse, a signifier referring always to the opposing signifier that annihilates its particular energy, puts down or stifles its very different sounds, now it is time for her to displace this 'within', explode it, overturn it, grab it, make it hers, take it in, take it into her woman's mouth, bite its tongue with her woman's teeth, make up her own tongue to get inside of it. And you will see how easily she will well up, from this 'within' where she was hidden and dormant, to the lips where her foams will overflow.

It is not a question of appropriating their instruments, their concepts, their places for oneself or of wishing oneself in their position of mastery. Our knowing that there is a danger of identification does not mean we should give in. Leave that to the worriers, to masculine anxiety and its obsessional relationship to workings they must control – knowing 'how it runs' in order to 'make it run'. Not taking possession to internalise or manipulate but to shoot through and smash the walls.

Feminine strength is such that while running away with syntax, breaking the famous line (just a tiny little thread, so they say) that serves men as a substitute cord, without which they can't have any fun (*jouir*), to make sure the old mother really is always behind them watching them play phallus, she goes to the impossible where she plays the other, for love, without dying of it.

De-propriation, depersonalisation, because she, exasperating, immoderate, and contradictory, destroys laws, the 'natural' order. She lifts the bar separating the present from the future, breaking the rigid law of individuation. Nietzsche, in *The Birth of Tragedy*, said that this is the privilege of divinatory, magical forces. What happens to the subject, to the personal pronoun, to its possessives when, suddenly, gaily daring her metamorphoses (because from her within – for a long time her world, she is in a pervasive relationship of desire with every being) she makes another way of knowing circulate? Another way of producing, of communicating, where each one is always far more than one, where her power of identification puts the same to rout. – And with the same traversing, dispersing gesture with which she becomes a feminine other, a masculine other, she breaks with explanation, interpretation, and all the authorities pinpointing localisation. She forgets. She proceeds by leaps and bounds. She flies/steals.

To fly/steal is woman's gesture, to steal into language to make it fly. We have all learned flight/theft, the art with many techniques, for all the centuries we have only had access to having by stealing/flying; we have lived in a flight/theft, stealing/flying, finding the close, concealed ways-through of desire. It's not just luck if the word 'voler' volleys between the 'vol' of theft and the 'vol' of flight, pleasuring in each and routing the sense police. It is not just luck: woman partakes of bird and burglar, just as the burglar partakes of woman and bird: hesheits pass, hesheits fly by, hesheits pleasure in scrambling spatial order, disorienting it, moving furniture, things, and values around, breaking in, emptying structures, turning the selfsame, the proper upside down.

What woman has not stolen? Who has not dreamed, savoured, or done the thing that jams sociality? Who has not dropped a few red herrings, mocked her way around the separating bar, inscribed what makes a difference with her body, punched holes in the system of couples and positions, and with a transgression screwed up whatever is successive, chain-linked, the fence of circumfusion?

A feminine text cannot not be more than subversive: if it writes itself it is in volcanic heaving of the old 'real' property crust. In ceaseless displacement. She must write herself because, when the time comes for her liberation, it is the invention of a *new, insurgent* writing that will allow her to put the breaks and indispensable changes into effect in her history. At first, individually, on two inseparable levels: – woman, writing herself, will go back to this body that has been worse than confiscated, a body replaced with a disturbing stranger, sick or dead, who so often is a bad influence, the cause and place of inhibitions. By censuring the body, breath and speech are censored at the same time.

To write – the act that will 'realise' the un-censored relationship of woman to her sexuality, to her woman-being giving her back access to her own forces; that will return her goods, her pleasures, her organs, her vast bodily territories kept under seal; that will tear her out of the superegoed, over-Mosesed structure where the same position of guilt is always reserved for her (guilty of everything, every time: of having desires, of not having any; of being frigid, of being 'too' hot; of not being both at once; of being too much of a mother and not enough; of nurturing and of not nurturing . . .). Write yourself: your body must make itself heard. Then the huge resources of the unconscious will burst out. Finally the inexhaustible feminine imaginary is going to be deployed. Without gold or black dollars, our naphtha will spread values over the world, un-quoted values that will change the rules of the old game.

9

Feminist, Female, Feminine

Toril Moi

What is the meaning of the word 'feminist' in 'feminist literary criticism'? Over the past decade, feminists have used the terms 'feminist', 'female' and 'feminine' in a multitude of different ways. One of the main points of this essay, however, is to urge that only a clear understanding of the differences between them can show what the crucial political and theoretical issues of contemporary feminist criticism really are. Initially, I will suggest that we distinguish between 'feminism' as a political position, 'femaleness' as a matter of biology and 'femininity' as a set of culturally defined characteristics.

FEMINIST

The words 'feminist' or 'feminism' are political labels indicating support for the aims of the new women's movement which emerged in the late 1960s. 'Feminist criticism', then, is a specific kind of political discourse: a critical and theoretical practice committed to the struggle against patriarchy and sexism, not simply a concern for gender in literature, at least not if the latter is presented as no more than another interesting critical approach on a par with a concern for sea-imagery or metaphors of war in medieval poetry. It is my view that, provided they are compatible with her politics, a feminist critic can use whichever methods or theories she likes. There are, of course, different political views within the feminist camp. My point here is not to try to unify or totalise these differences, but simply to insist that recognisable feminist criticism and theory must in some way be relevant to the study of the social, institutional and personal power relations between the sexes: what Kate Millett in her epochal study called *sexual politics*. For Millett, the 'essence of politics is power', and the task of feminist critics and theorists is to expose the way in which male dominance over females (which constitutes her simple and versatile definition of 'patriarchy') constitutes 'perhaps the most pervasive ideology of our culture and provides its most fundamental concept of power'.[1]

In keeping with Millett's approach, feminists have politicised existing critical methods (in much the same sort of way that Marxists have), and it is on this basis that feminist criticism has grown to become a new branch of literary studies. Feminists therefore find themselves in a position roughly similar to that of other radical critics: speaking from their marginalised positions on the outskirts of the academic establishment, they strive to make explicit the politics of the so-called 'neutral' or 'objective' works of their colleagues, as well as to act as cultural *critics* in the widest sense of the word. Like socialists, feminists can in a sense afford to be tolerantly pluralistic in their choice of literary methods and theories, precisely because any approach that can be successfully appropriated to their political ends must be welcome.

A key word here is *appropriation* in the sense of creative *transformation*. Given the feminist insistence on the dominant and all-pervasive nature of patriarchal power so far in history, feminists have to be pluralists: there is no pure feminist or female space from which we can speak. All ideas, including feminist ones, are in this sense 'contaminated' by patriarchal ideology. There is thus no reason to hide the fact that Mary Wollstonecraft was inspired by the male-dominated ideas of the French Revolution, or that Simone de Beauvoir was deeply influenced by Sartre's phallocentric categories when she wrote *The Second Sex*. Nor is it necessary to refuse to recognise John Stuart Mill's efforts to analyse the oppression of women simply because he was a male liberal. The point is not the origins of an idea (no provenance is pure), but the use to which it is put and the effects it can produce. What matters is therefore not so much whether a particular theory was formulated by a man or a woman, but whether its effects can be characterised as sexist or feminist in a given situation.

In this specific context, then, the fact that there are no purely female intellectual traditions available to us is not as depressing as it might have been. What is important is whether we can produce a recognisable feminist impact through our specific use (appropriation) of available material. This emphasis on the productive transformation of other thinkers' material in a way simply restates what creative thinkers and writers have always done: nobody thinks well in a vacuum, nor does anybody ever live in one. Feminists nevertheless often accuse male intellectuals of 'stealing' women's ideas, as for instance the title of one of Dale Spender's many books, *Women of Ideas and What Men Have Done to Them*, makes clear.[2] But can we accuse men of 'stealing' women's ideas if we at the same time argue vociferously for the feminist appropriation of *everybody's* ideas? Spender's book examines cases of clear intellectual dishonesty: men presenting women's ideas as their own without any kind of acknowledgement of their borrowing which must be said to constitute an obvious example of the widespread patriarchal effort to silence women. Feminists appropriating traditional thought explicitly discuss the assumptions and strategies of the material they want to use or transform:

there can be no question of recommending silent appropriation of other theories. (Many feminists object to the idea that thoughts should be considered anybody's personal property. Although I agree with this view, it remains important to criticise the presentation of impulses received from others *as one's own*: this practice can only reinforce the ideology of intellectual property.) As politically motivated critics, feminists will try to make the political context and implications of their work explicit, precisely in order to counter the tacit acceptance of patriarchal power politics which is so often presented as intellectual 'neutrality' or 'objectivity'.

The problem with Spender's approach is that it casts women as eternal victims of male ploys. While it is true that many women have been victimised intellectually, emotionally and physically by men, it is also true that some have managed efficiently to counter male power. Stressing our right, aggressively if necessary, to appropriate other people's ideas for our own political purposes, we may avoid a defeatist analysis of the situation of intellectually and culturally active women. As examples of this task of cultural transformation, we can point to the many women who have started the massive task of turning Freudian psychoanalysis into a source of truly feminist analyses of sexual difference and the construction of gender in patriarchal society, Hélène Cixous and Luce Irigaray who have put the philosophy of Jacques Derrida to illuminating feminist use, and Sandra Gilbert and Susan Gubar who have thoroughly rewritten the literary theory of Harold Bloom.[3]

FEMALE

If feminist criticism is characterised by its *political* commitment to the struggle against all forms of patriarchy and sexism, it follows that the very fact of being *female* does not necessarily guarantee a feminist approach. As a political discourse feminist criticism takes its *raison d'être* from outside criticism itself. It is a truism, but it still needs to be said that not all books written by women on women writers exemplify anti-patriarchal commitment. This is particularly true for many early (pre-1960s) works on women writers, which often indulge in precisely the kind of patriarchal stereotyping feminists want to combat. A female tradition in literature or criticism is not necessarily a feminist one.

In her incisive essay 'Are Women's Novels Feminist Novels?' Rosalind Coward discusses the general confusion of *feminist* with *female* writing, both within the women's movement and in publishing and the other media. 'It is just not possible to say that woman-centred writings have any necessary relationship to feminism', Coward argues. 'The Mills and Boon romantic novels are written by, read by, marketed for, and are all about women. Yet nothing could be further from the aims of feminism than these fantasies based on sexual, racial, and class submission which so frequently characterise these novels.'[4] Behind the frequent confusion of feminist with female texts is a complex web of assumptions. It is, for example, often assumed that the very fact of describing experience typical of women is a feminist act. On the one hand this is obviously true: since patriarchy has always tried to silence and repress women and women's experience, rendering them visible is clearly an important anti-patriarchal strategy. On the other hand, however, women's experience can be made visible in alienating, deluded or degrading ways: the Mills and Boon accounts of female love or Anita Bryant's praise of heterosexual love and motherhood are not *per se* emancipatory reading for women. The mistaken belief in *experience* as the essence of feminist politics, stems from the early emphasis on consciousness-raising (c-r) as the main political base of the new women's movement. The point is that consciousness-raising, founded as it is on the notion of 'representative experience', cannot in itself ground a politics, since any experience is open to conflicting political interpretations.[5] It would seem that many feminists today have realised this. Rosalind Coward even argues that c-r groups are no longer central to the women's movement: 'For the most part, consciousness-raising no longer forms the heart of feminism; small groups which do still have a central place in feminist politics are now often either campaigning groups or study groups.'[6]

To believe that common female experience in itself gives rise to a feminist analysis of women's situation, is to be at once politically naïve and theoretically unaware. The fact of having the same experience as somebody else in no way guarantees a common political front: the millions of soldiers who suffered in the trenches during the First World War did not all turn pacifist – or socialist or militarist – afterwards. Unfortunately, the experience of childbirth or period pains is neither common to all women nor particularly apt to inspire a deep desire for political liberation: if it did, women would long since have changed the face of the earth. Although crucially shaped by its anti-patriarchal emphasis on female experience, feminism as a political theory cannot be reduced to a reflection or a product of that experience. The Marxist view of the necessary dialectical relationship between theory and practice also applies to the relationship between female experience and feminist politics.

The fact that so many feminist critics have chosen to write about female authors, then, is a crucial political choice, but not a definition of feminist criticism. It is not its object, but its political perspective which gives feminist criticism its (relative) unity. Feminist critics, then, may well deal with books written by men, as they have done from the late 60s to the present day. Kate Millett, in her pioneering *Sexual Politics*, reveals the fundamental sexism of male writers such as Norman Mailer, Henry Miller and D. H. Lawrence; Mary Ellmann in *Thinking About Women* wittily discusses the sexist habits of male literary critics, and Penny Boumelha analyses the sexual ideology of Thomas Hardy in her *Thomas Hardy and Women*, just to mention a few.[7]

A final problem raised by the distinction between feminist and female is the question of whether men can be feminists or feminist critics. If feminists do not have to work exclusively on female authors, perhaps they do not need to *be* females, either? In principle, the answer to this question is surely yes: men can be feminists – but they can't be women, just as whites can be anti-racist, but not black. Under patriarchy men will always speak from a different *position* than women, and their political strategies must take this into account. In practice, therefore, the would-be male feminist critic ought to ask himself whether he as a male is really doing feminism a service in our present situation by muscling in on the one cultural and intellectual space women have created for themselves within 'his' male-dominated discipline.

FEMININE

If the confusion of *female* with *feminist* is fraught with political pitfalls, this is no less true of the consequences of the collapse of *feminine* into *female*. Among many feminists it has long been established usage to make 'feminine' (and 'masculine') represent *social constructs* (patterns of sexuality and behaviour imposed by cultural and social norms), and to reserve 'female' and 'male' for the purely biological aspects of sexual difference. Thus 'feminine' represents nurture, and 'female' nature in this usage. 'Femininity' is a cultural construct: one isn't born a woman, one becomes one, as Simone de Beauvoir puts it. Seen in this perspective, patriarchal oppression consists of imposing certain social standards of femininity on all biological women, in order precisely to make us believe that the chosen standards for 'femininity' are *natural*. Thus a woman who refuses to conform can be labelled both *unfeminine* and *unnatural*. It is in the patriarchal interest that these two terms (femininity and femaleness) stay thoroughly confused. Patriarchy, in other words, wants us to believe that there is such a thing as an essence of femaleness, called femininity. Feminists, on the contrary, have to disentangle this confusion, and must therefore always insist that though women undoubtedly are *female*, this in no way guarantees that they will be *feminine*. This is equally true whether one defines femininity in the old patriarchal ways or in a new feminist way. Essentialism (the belief in a given female nature) in the end always plays into the hands of those who want women to conform to predefined patterns of femininity. In this context *biologism* is the belief that such an essence is biologically given. It is not less *essentialist*, however, to hold that there is a historically or socially given female essence.

But if, as suggested, we define *feminism* as a political position and *femaleness* as a matter of biology, we are still confronted with the problem of how to define *femininity*. 'A set of culturally defined characteristics' or a 'cultural construct' may sound irritatingly vague to many. It would seem that any content could be poured into this container; it does not read like a 'proper' definition. The question is, however, whether it is desirable for feminists to try to fix the meaning of femininity at all. Patriarchy has developed a whole series of 'feminine' characteristics (sweetness, modesty, subservience, humility, etc.). Should feminists then really try to develop another set of 'feminine' virtues, however desirable? And even if we did want to define femininity normatively, would it then not just become a part of the metaphysical binary oppositions Hélène Cixous rightly criticises? There is also a danger of turning a positive, feminist definition of femininity into a definition of femaleness, and thereby falling back into another patriarchal trap. Gratifying though it is to be told that women really are strong, integrated, peace-loving, nurturing and creative beings, this plethora of new virtues is no less essentialist than the old ones, and no less oppressive to all those women who do not want to play the role of Earth Mother. It is after all patriarchy, not feminism, which has always believed in a true female/feminine nature: the biologism and essentialism which lurk behind the desire to bestow feminine virtues on all female bodies necessarily plays into the hands of the patriarchs.

THE DECONSTRUCTION OF BINARY OPPOSITIONS

So far, we have looked at the terms female – feminine – feminist in relation only to each other. It is, however, equally important to be aware of the political and theoretical implications of assuming that they enter into automatic and static binary oppositions, such as female/male or feminine/masculine.

The case of *feminist* or *feminism*, however, would seem to be somewhat different. The relationship between words like feminism, sexism and patriarchy would seem to be more complex than in the case of female/male or feminine/masculine, possibly because of the political nature of these terms. I am therefore not assuming that the following discussion of the ideology of binary oppositions necessarily goes for sexist/feminist or patriarchal/feminist as well, since there seems to be no automatic homology with 'pairs' such as male/female or masculine/feminine.

Hélène Cixous has contributed a valuable discussion of the

consequences of what she calls 'death-dealing binary thought'. Under the heading 'Where is she?', Cixous lines up a list of binary oppositions [see pp. 91–2 above]. Corresponding as they do to the underlying opposition Man/Woman, these binary oppositions are heavily imbricated in the patriarchal value system: each opposition can be analysed as a hierarchy where the 'feminine' side is always seen as the negative, powerless instance. The biological opposition male/female, in other words, is used to construct a series of negative 'feminine' values which then are imposed on and confused with the 'female'. For Cixous, who at this point is heavily indebted to Jacques Derrida's work, Western philosophy and literary thought is and has always been caught up in this endless series of hierarchical binary oppositions, which always in the end come back to the fundamental 'couple' of male/female. Her examples show that it does not much matter which 'couple' one chooses to highlight: the hidden male/female opposition with its inevitable positive/negative evaluation can always be traced as the underlying paradigm.

In a typical move, Cixous then goes on to locate *death* at work in this kind of thought. For one of the terms to acquire meaning, she claims, it must destroy the other. The 'couple' cannot be left intact: it becomes a general battlefield where the struggle for signifying supremacy is forever re-enacted. In the end, victory is equated with activity and defeat with passivity; under patriarchy, the male is always the victor. Cixous passionately denounces such an equation of femininity with passivity and death as leaving no positive space for woman: 'Either woman is passive or she does not exist'.[8] Broadly inspired by the thinking and intellectual strategies of Jacques Derrida, her whole theoretical project can in one sense be summed up as the effort to undo this logocentric ideology: to proclaim woman as the source of life, power and energy and to hail the advent of a new, feminine language which ceaselessly subverts these patriarchal binary schemes where logocentrism colludes with phallocentrism in an effort to oppress and silence women. (*Phallocentrism* denotes a system that privileges the phallus as the symbol or source of power. The conjuncture of logocentrism and phallocentrism is often called, after Derrida, *phallogocentrism*.) This project is itself fraught with dangers: although more aware of the problems involved, Cixous often finds herself in great trouble when she tries to distinguish her concept of a *feminine* writing from the idea of a *female* writing. After an heroic struggle against the dangers of biologism, it is probably fair to say that Cixous's theories of an *écriture féminine* in the end fall back into a form of biological essentialism.[9]

But Cixous's 'deconstruction' of the feminine/masculine opposition remains valuable for feminists. If her analysis is correct, for a feminist to continue advocating binary thought, implicitly or explicitly, would seem to be tantamount to remaining inside patriarchal metaphysics. The idea of a unified *female* opposition pitting itself against a *male* front would thus not be a possible feminist strategy for the defeat of patriarchy: on the contrary, it would shore up the very system it seeks to undo. Against any binary scheme of thought, Cixous sets multiple, heterogeneous *difference*. In so doing, she is deeply influenced by the French philosopher Jacques Derrida's concept of difference, or, more correctly, differance. For Derrida, meaning (signification) is not produced in the static closure of the binary opposition. Rather it is achieved through the 'play of the signifier'.[10] To enclose maleness and femaleness in an exclusive opposition to each other, Cixous argues, is thus precisely to force them to enter into the death-dealing power struggle she locates within the binary opposition. Following this logic, the feminist task *par excellence* becomes the deconstruction of patriarchal metaphysics (the belief in an inherent, present meaning in the sign). If, as Derrida has argued, we are still living under the reign of metaphysics, it is impossible to produce new concepts untainted by the metaphysics of presence. To propose a new definition of femininity is therefore necessarily to fall back into the metaphysical trap.

FEMININITY AS MARGINALITY

But doesn't all this theory leave feminists in a kind of double impasse? Is it really possible to remain in the realm of deconstruction when Derrida himself acknowledges that we still live in a 'metaphysical' intellectual space? And how can we continue our political struggle if we first have to deconstruct our own basic assumption of an opposition between male power and female submission? One way of answering these questions is to look at the French-Bulgarian linguist and psychoanalyst Julia Kristeva's considerations on the question of femininity. Flatly refusing to define 'femininity', she prefers to see it as a *position*. If femininity then can be said to have a definition at all in Kristevan terms, it is simply as 'that which is marginalised by the patriarchal symbolic order'. This relational 'definition' is as shifting as the various forms of patriarchy itself, and allows her to argue that men can also be constructed as marginal to the symbolic order, as her analyses of male avant-garde artists (Joyce, Céline, Artaud, Mallarmé, Lautréamont) have shown.[11]

Kristeva's emphasis on femininity as a patriarchal construct enables feminists to counter all forms of biologistic attacks from the defenders of phallocentrism. To posit all women as necessarily feminine and all men as necessarily masculine, is precisely the move which enables the patriarchal powers to define, not femininity, but all *women* as marginal to the symbolic order and to society. If, as Cixous has shown, femininity is defined as lack, negativity, absence of meaning, irrationality, chaos, darkness – in short, as non-Being – Kristeva's emphasis on marginality allows us to view this repression of the feminine in terms of *positionality* rather than of essences. What is perceived as marginal at any given time depends on the position one occupies. A brief example will illustrate this shift from essence to position: if patriarchy sees women as occupying a marginal position within the symbolic order, then it can construe them as the *limit* or border-line of that order. From a phallocentric point of view, women will then come to represent the necessary frontier between man and chaos, but because of their very marginality they will also always seem to recede into and merge with the chaos of the outside. Women seen as the limit of the symbolic order will in other words share in the disconcerting properties of *all* frontiers: they will be neither inside nor outside, neither known nor unknown. It is this position which has enabled male culture sometimes to vilify women as representing darkness and chaos, to view them as Lilith or the Whore of Babylon, and sometimes to elevate them as the representatives of a higher and purer nature, to venerate them as Virgins and Mothers of God. In the first instance the borderline is seen as part of the chaotic wilderness outside, and in the second it is seen as an inherent part of the inside: the part which protects and shields the symbolic order from the imaginary chaos. Needless to say, neither position corresponds to any essential truth of woman, much as the patriarchal powers would like us to believe that they did.[12]

Such a positional perspective on the meaning of femininity would seem to be the only way of escaping the dangers of biologism (conflation with femaleness). But it does not answer our basic political questions. For if we now have deconstructed the *female* out of existence, it would seem that the very foundations of the feminist struggle have disappeared. In her article 'Women's Time', Kristeva advocates a deconstructive approach to sexual difference. The feminist struggle, she argues, must be seen historically and politically as a three-tiered one, which can be schematically summarised as follows:

(1) Women demand equal access to the symbolic order. Liberal feminism. Equality.
(2) Women reject the male symbolic order in the name of difference. Radical feminism. Femininity extolled.
(3) Women reject the dichotomy between masculine and feminine as metaphysical. (This is Kristeva's own position.)

The third position is one that has deconstructed the opposition between masculinity and femininity, and therefore necessarily challenges the very notion of identity. Kristeva writes:

In this third attitude, which I strongly advocate – which I imagine? – the very dichotomy man/woman as an opposition between two rival entities may be understood as belonging to *metaphysics*. What can 'identity', even 'sexual identity', mean in a new theoretical and scientific space where the very notion of identity is challenged? [see below, pp. 214–15]

The relationship between these three positions requires some comments. Elsewhere in her article Kristeva clearly states that she sees them as simultaneous and non-exclusive positions in contemporary feminism, rather than as a feminist version of Hegel's philosophy of history. To advocate position 3 as exclusive of the first two is to lose touch with the political reality of feminism. We still need to claim our place in human society as equals, not as subordinate members, and we still need to emphasise that difference between male and female experience of the world. But that difference is shaped by the patriarchal structures feminists are opposing; and to remain faithful to it, is to play the patriarchal game. Nevertheless, as long as patriarchy is dominant, it still remains *politically* essential for feminists to defend women *as* women in order to counteract the patriarchal oppression that precisely despises women as women. But an 'undeconstructed' form of 'stage 2' feminism, unaware of the metaphysical nature of gender identities, runs the risk of becoming an inverted form of sexism. It does so by uncritically taking over the very metaphysical categories set up by patriarchy in order to keep women in their places, despite attempts to attach new feminist values to these old categories. An adoption of Kristeva's 'deconstructed' form of feminism therefore in one sense leaves everything as it was – our positions in the political struggle have not changed; but in another sense, it radically transforms our awareness of the nature of that struggle. A feminist appropriation of deconstruction is therefore both possible and politically productive as long as it does not lead us to repress the necessity of incorporating Kristeva's two first stages into our perspective.

FEMALE CRITICISM AND FEMININE THEORY

Against this background, the field of feminist criticism and theory today could helpfully be divided into two main categories: 'female' criticism and 'feminine' theory. 'Female' criticism, which *per se* only means criticism which in some way focuses on women, may then be analysed according to whether it is feminist or not, whether it takes female to mean feminist, or whether it conflates female with feminine. The apolitical study of female authors is obviously not in itself feminist: it could very well just be an approach which reduces women to the status of interesting scientific objects on a par with insects or nuclear particles. It is nevertheless important to stress that in a male-dominated context an interest in women writers must objectively be considered a support for the feminist project of making women visible. This would of course not be true for obviously sexist research on women. It is in other words possible to be a 'female' critic without necessarily being a feminist one.

The great majority of American feminist critics nevertheless write from an explicitly feminist position. The emphasis in the United States has been on 'gynocritics', or the study of women writers. Elaine Showalter's *A Literature of Their Own* and Sandra Gilbert and Susan Gubar's *The Madwoman in the Attic* are the most accomplished examples of this genre within feminist criticism.[13] In the context of this essay, Gilbert and Gubar's monumental study furnishes an instructive example of the consequences of the confusion not only of femaleness with femininity, but also of this amalgamated femaleness/femininity with feminism. In their investigation of typical motifs and patterns among nineteenth-century women writers, they persistently use the adjective *female*, discussing for instance the 'female tradition in literature', 'female writing', 'female creativity' or 'female anger', just to mention a few. One of their central arguments is that nineteenth-century women writers chose to express their own female anger in a series of duplicitous textual strategies whereby both the angel and the monster, the sweet heroine and the raging madwoman, are aspects of the author's self-image, as well as elements of her treacherous anti-patriarchal strategies. This is an extremely seductive theory, and strikingly productive, for instance when applied to the works of Charlotte Brontë, who of course created the eponymous madwoman in the first place. But if we unravel the probable meanings of the word *female* in Gilbert and Gubar's text, we find that this theory of 'female creativity' rests on the assumption that *female* authors always experience anti-patriarchal rage in their hearts and that this *feminist* anger will create a typically *feminine* pattern of writing, where a shrewd strategy of disguise is used to make the message from the marginalised group acceptable to the patriarchal powers. This feminine pattern, however, is not available to male authors, but common to all *female* writers. The patriarchal strategy of collapsing the feminine into the female can here be seen at work: the *écriture féminine* emerging from this kind of argument is more than tinged with biologism. Gilbert and Gubar's account homogenises all female creative utterances into *feminist* self-expression: a strategy which singularly fails to account for the ways in which women can come to take up a masculine subject position – that is to say, become solid defenders of the patriarchal status quo.

'Feminine' theory in its simplest definition would mean theories concerned with the construction of femininity. From a feminist perspective the problem with this kind of thought is that it is particularly prone to attacks of biologism and often unwittingly turns into theories about female essences instead. At the same time, even the most determinedly 'constructionist' of theories may very well not be feminist ones. The works of Sigmund Freud for example offer a splendid illustration of a theory formation which, while in no way feminist, provides a crucial foundation for a non-essentialist analysis of sexual difference. The alternative, a theory of essential female qualities, would, as we have seen, simply play the patriarchal game. Although psychoanalysis still needs to be creatively transformed for feminist purposes, the fact remains that feminism needs a non-essentialist theory of human sexuality and desire in order to understand the power relations between the sexes.

Much French feminist theory, as well as various feminist rereadings of psychoanalysis, may be considered 'feminine theories' in this sense. But there is a paradox involved in my arguments here. Many French feminists, for example, would strongly take issue with my attempt to define 'femininity' at all. If they reject labels and names and 'isms' in particular – even 'feminism' and 'sexism' – it is because they see such labelling activity as betraying a phallogocentric drive to stabilise, organise and rationalise our conceptual universe. They argue that it is masculine rationality that has always privileged reason, order, unity and lucidity, and that it has done so by silencing and excluding the irrationality, chaos and fragmentation that has come to represent femininity. My own view is that such conceptual terms are at once politically crucial and ultimately metaphysical; it is necessary at once to deconstruct the opposition between traditionally 'masculine' and traditionally 'feminine' values *and* to confront the full political force and reality of such categories. We must aim for a society in which we have ceased to categorise logic, conceptualisation and rationality as 'masculine', not for one from which these virtues have been expelled altogether as 'unfeminine'.

To sum up this presentation of feminist literary theory today, we can now define as *female*, writing by women, bearing in mind that this label does not say anything at all about the nature of that writing; as *feminist*, writing which takes a discernible anti-patriarchal and anti-sexist position; and as *feminine*, writing which seems to be marginalised (repressed, silenced) by the ruling social/linguistic order. The latter does not (*pace* Kristeva) entail any specific *political* position (no clear-cut feminism), although it does not exclude it either. Thus some feminists, such as Hélène Cixous, have tried to produce 'feminine' writing, and others (Simone de Beauvoir) have not. The problem with the 'feminine' label so far has been its tendency to privilege and/or overlap with existing forms of literary modernism and avant-gardism. This, I think, is only one possible way of being marginal in relation to the dominant order (in this case in relation to the traditional representational or realist forms of writing). 'Marginality' cannot or should not *only* be a matter of form.

Perhaps the most important point in all this is to realise that these three 'labels' are not essences. They are categories we as readers or critics operate. *We* produce texts as marginal by situating them in relation to other, dominant structures; we choose to read early texts by women as pre-feminist work; we decide to work on 'female' texts. The definitions proposed here are intended to be open for debate, not to put an end to it, although they are also supposed to say something about the terrain on which the debate might fruitfully be staged: politics, biology and marginality would seem to be key issues here. There is not, unfortunately, such a thing as an intrinsically feminist text: given the right historical and social context, all texts can be recuperated by the ruling powers – or appropriated by the feminist opposition. As Julia Kristeva might have argued, all forms of language are sites of struggle. As feminist critics our task is to prevent the patriarchs from getting away with their habitual trick of silencing the opposition. It is up to us to make the struggle over the meaning of the sign – the meaning of the text – an explicit and inevitable item on the cultural agenda.

10

Women and Madness: the Critical Phallacy

Shoshana Felman

Silence gives the proper grace to women.
> Sophocles, *Ajax*

Dalila: In argument with men a woman ever
            Goes by the worse, whatever be her cause.
Samson: For want of words, no doubt, or
            lack of breath!
> Milton, *Samson Agonistes*

I   WOMAN AS MADNESS

Is it by chance that hysteria (significantly derived, as is well known, from the Greek word for 'uterus') was originally conceived as an exclusively *female* complaint, as the lot and *prerogative* of women? And is it by chance that even today, between women and madness, sociological statistics establish a privileged relation and a definite correlation? 'Women,' writes Phyllis Chesler, in her book *Women and Madness*, 'Women more than men, and in greater numbers than their existence in the general population would predict, are involved in "careers" as psychiatric patients.'[1] How is this sociological fact to be analysed and interpreted? What is the nature of the relationship it implies between women and madness? Supported by extensive documentation, Phyllis Chesler proposes a confrontation between objective data and the subjective testimony of women: laced with the voices of women speaking in the first person – literary excerpts from the novels and autobiographies of women writers, and word-for-word interviews with female psychiatric patients – the book derives and disputes a 'female psychology' conditioned by an oppressive and patriarchal male culture. 'It is clear that for a woman to be healthy she must "adjust" to and accept the behavioural norms for her sex even though these kinds of behaviour are generally regarded as less socially desirable [. . .] The ethic of mental health is masculine in our culture.'[2] 'The *sine qua non* of "feminine" identity in patriarchal society is the

117

violation of the incest taboo, i.e. the initial and continued "preference" for Daddy, followed by the approved falling in love and/or marrying of powerful father figures.'[3] From her initial family upbringing throughout her subsequent development, the social role assigned to the woman is that of *serving* an image, authoritative and central, of man: a woman is first and foremost a daughter/a mother/a wife. 'What we consider "madness", whether it appears in women or in men, is either the acting out of the devalued female role or the total or partial rejection of one's sex-role stereotype.'[4]

In contrast to the critical tendency currently in fashion in Europe, through which a certain French circle has allied itself philosophically with the controversial indictments of the English 'anti-psychiatry' movement, Phyllis Chesler, although protesting in turn against psychiatry as such, in no way seeks to bestow upon madness the romanticised glamour of political protest and of social and cultural contestation: 'It has never been my intention to romanticise madness, or to confuse it with political or cultural revolution.'[5] Depressed and terrified women are not about to seize the means of production and reproduction: quite the opposite of rebellion, madness is the impasse confronting those whom cultural conditioning has deprived of the very means of protest or self-affirmation. Far from being a form of contestation, 'mental illness' is a *request for help*, a manifestation both of cultural impotence and of political castration. This socially defined help-needing and help-seeking behaviour is itself part of female conditioning, ideologically inherent in the behavioural pattern and in the dependent and helpless role assigned to the woman as such.

It is not the material, social, and psychological female condition, but rather the very *status of womanhood* in Western *theoretical* discourse which concerns Luce Irigaray in her book, *Speculum de l'autre femme*.[6] In contrast to Phyllis Chesler, Luce Irigaray interrogates not the empirical voice of women and their subjective testimony, but the key theoretical writings of men – fundamental texts in philosophy and in psychoanalysis – which, in one way or another, involve the concept of femininity. Her study focuses on the text of Freud's (fictive) lecture entitled 'On Femininity' and on the feminine metaphors in Plato's myth of the Cave. A psychoanalyst herself, Luce Irigaray adopts the traditional feminist critique of the male-centred orientation and of the anti-feminine bias in psychoanalytical theory; but her elaboration and consolidation of these classical feminist arguments is derived from the current philosophical methods of thinking developed in France by Jacques Derrida and others in their attempt to work out a general critical 'deconstruction' of Western metaphysics. According to Derrida's radicalisation of the Nietzschean and Heideggerian critiques of traditional philosophy, Western metaphysics is based on the totalitarian principle of so-called 'logocentrism', that is, on the repressive predominance of 'logos' over 'writing', on the privileged status of the present and the consequent valorisation of presence. This *presence-to- itself* of a *centre* (given the name of Origin, God, Truth, Being, or Reason) centralises the world through the authority of its self-presence and subordinates to itself, in an agonistic, hierarchical manner, all the other cognisable elements of the same epistemological (or ontological) system. Thus, the metaphysical logic of dichotomous oppositions which dominates philosophical thought (Presence/Absence, Being/ Nothingness, Truth/Error, Same/Other, Identity/Difference, etc.) is, in fact, a subtle mechanism of hierarchisation which assures the unique valorisation of the 'positive' pole (that is, of a *single* term) and, consequently, the repressive subordination of all 'negativity', the mastery of difference as such. It is by thus examining the mere illusion of duality and the repressive way in which the polarity Masculine/Feminine functions in Western thought so as to privilege a unique term, that Luce Irigaray proceeds to develop her critical argument. Theoretically subordinated to the concept of masculinity, the woman is viewed by the man as *his* opposite, that is to say, as *his* other, the negative of the positive, and not, in her own right, different, other, otherness itself. Throughout the Platonic metaphors which will come to dominate Western discourse and to act as a vehicle for meaning, Luce Irigaray points out a latent design to exclude the woman from the production of speech, since the woman, and the other as such, are philosophically subjugated to the logical principle of Identity – Identity being conceived as a solely *masculine* sameness, apprehended as *male* self-presence and consciousness-to-itself. The possibility of a thought which would neither spring from nor return to this masculine Sameness is simply unthinkable. Plato's text thus establishes the repressive systematisation of the logic of identity: the privilege of 'oneness', of the reproduction of likeness, of the repetition of sameness, of literal meaning, analogy, symmetry, dichotomous oppositions, teleological projects.

Freud, who for the first time freed thought from a certain conception of the present and of presence-to-oneself, whose notions of deferred action, of the unconscious, of the death instinct and of the repetition compulsion radically undermine the classical logic of identity, remains, nevertheless, himself a prisoner of philosophy when he determines the nature of sexual difference in function of the a priori of sameness, that is, of the male phallus. Female sexuality is thus described as an absence (of the masculine presence), as lack, incompleteness, deficiency, envy with respect to the only sexuality in which value resides. This symmetrical conception of otherness is a theoretical blindness to the woman's actual Difference, which is currently asserting itself, and asserting precisely its claim to a new kind of logic and a new type of theoretical reasoning.

A question could be raised: if 'the woman' is precisely the other of any conceivable Western theoretical locus of speech, how can the woman as such be speaking in this book? Who is speaking here, and who is asserting the otherness of the woman? If, as Luce Irigaray suggests, the woman's silence, or the repression of her capacity to speak, are constitutive of philosophy and of theoretical discourse as such, from what theoretical locus is Luce Irigaray herself speaking in order to develop her own theoretical discourse about the woman's exclusion? Is she speaking the language of men, or the silence of women? Is she speaking as a woman, or *in place of* the (silent) woman, *for* the woman, *in the name of* the woman? Is it enough to *be* a woman in order to *speak* as a woman? Is 'speaking as a woman' a fact determined by some biological *condition* or by a strategic, theoretical *position*, by anatomy[7] or by culture? What if 'speaking as a woman' were not a simple 'natural' fact, could not be taken for granted? With the increasing number of women and men alike who are currently choosing to share in the rising fortune of female misfortune, it has become all too easy to be a speaker *'for* women'. But what does 'speaking *for* women' imply? What is 'to speak *in the name of* the woman'? What, in a general manner, does 'speech in the name of' mean? Is it not a precise repetition of the oppressive gesture of *representation*, by means of which, throughout the history of logos, man has reduced the woman to the status of a silent and subordinate object, to something inherently *spoken for*? To 'speak in the name of,' to 'speak *for*', could thus mean, once again, to appropriate and to silence. This important theoretical question about the status of its own discourse and its own 'representation' of women, with which any feminist thought has to cope, is not thought out by Luce Irigaray, and thus remains the blind spot of her critical undertaking.

In a sense, the difficulty involved in any feminist enterprise is illustrated by the complementarity, but also by the incompatibility, of the two feminist studies which we have just examined: the works of Phyllis Chesler and Luce Irigaray. The interest of Chesler's book, its overwhelming persuasive power as an outstanding clinical document, lies in the fact that it *does not* speak *for* women: it lets women speak for themselves. Phyllis Chesler accomplishes thus the first symbolical step of the feminist revolution: she *gives voice* to the woman. But she can only do so in a pragmatic, empirical way. As a result, the book's theoretical contribution, although substantial, does not go beyond the classical feminist thought concerning the socio-sexual victimisation of women. On the other side of the coin, Irigaray's book has the merit of perceiving the problem on a theoretical level, of trying to think the feminist question through to its logical ends, reminding us that women's oppression exists not only in the material, practical organisation of economic, social, medical, and political structures, but also in the very foundations of logos, reasoning, and articulation – in the subtle linguistic procedures and in the logical processes through which meaning itself is produced. It is not clear, however, that statement and utterance here coincide so as to establish actual feminine difference, not only on the thematic, but also on the rhetorical level: although the otherness of the woman is here fully assumed as the subject of the statement, it is not certain whether that otherness can be taken for granted as positively occupying the unthought-out, problematical locus *from which* the statement is being *uttered*.

In the current attempt at a radical questioning and a general 'deconstruction' of the whole range of cultural codes, feminism encounters the major theoretical challenge of all contemporary thought. The problem, in fact, is common to the revaluation of madness as well as to the contention of women: how can one speak from the place of the other? How can the woman be thought about outside of the Masculine/Feminine framework, *other* than as opposed to man, without being subordinated to a primordial masculine model? How can madness, in a similar way, be conceived outside of its dichotomous opposition to sanity, without being subjugated to reason? How can difference as such be thought out as *non-subordinate* to identity? In other words, how can thought break away from the logic of polar oppositions?

In the light of these theoretical challenges, and in keeping with the feminist questioning of psychoanalytical and philosophical discourse, it could be instructive to examine the ideological effects of the very production of meaning in the language of literature and in its critical exegesis. We therefore propose here to undertake a reading of a text by Balzac which deals with the woman as well as with madness and to examine the way in which this text, and its portrayal of feminine madness, has been traditionally perceived and commented upon. The text – entitled *Adieu* – is a short story first published in 1830, and later included by Balzac in the volume of *Philosophical Studies* of the *Comédie humaine*.[8]

II   THE REALISTIC INVISIBLE

The story is divided into three parts. The first describes a mysterious domain into which have inadvertently wandered two lost hunters: Philippe de Sucy, a former colonel, and his friend d'Albon, a magistrate. Anxious to find out where they are, they turn to two women, the only human beings in the vicinity, but their questions meet only silence: one of the women, Geneviève, turns out to be a deaf-mute, and the other, an aphasic madwoman whose entire vocabulary consists of the word 'adieu'. On hearing this word, Philippe faints, recognising in the madwoman his former mistress, Countess Stéphanie de Vandières, who had accompanied him to Russia during the Napoleonic Wars but whom he has not seen again since their separation on the banks of the Berezina River and whose trace he has ever since been unable to recover.

The second part is a flashback to the war episode. Among the collapsing masses of the retreating French army, Stéphanie and Philippe are fighting against unbearable cold, inhuman exhaustion and debilitating hunger, in the midst of the snowy plains. Philippe heroically shields Stéphanie in the hope of crossing the Berezina and of thus reaching and having her reach the safety of the other side, free from the Russian threat. But when it turns out that only two places are left on the life raft, Philippe leaves them to Stéphanie and her husband, the Count of Vandières, sacrificing himself for the latter. The Count, however, never reaches the other side: in a violent jolt during the crossing, he is swept overboard and killed. Stéphanie cries out to Philippe, 'Adieu!': it is to be her last lucid word before she loses her reason. For two years thereafter, she continues to be dragged along by the army, the plaything of wretched riff-raff. Mad and cast off like an animal, she is discovered one day after the end of the war by her uncle, an elderly doctor, who takes her in and sees to her needs.

The third part describes the combined efforts of the two men – the doctor having been joined by Philippe – to save and to cure Stéphanie. Stéphanie, on seeing Philippe, fails to recognise him: her continuous repetition of the word 'adieu' implies no understanding and bears no relation to conscious memory. At the sight of the 'stranger' (Philippe), she runs away like a frightened animal. Following the advice of the doctor, Philippe learns how to 'tame' Stéphanie by giving her sugar cubes, thus accustoming her to his presence. Philippe still hopes that Stéphanie will some day recognise him. Driven to despair, however, by the long wait, Philippe decides to hasten Stéphanie's recognition of him by subjecting her to a psycho-drama designed to restore her memory: he artificially creates a replica of the Russian plains and of the Berezina River; using peasants disguised as soldiers, he theoretically reconstructs and replays before the madwoman's eyes the exact scene of their wartime separation. Stéphanie is thus indeed cured: overwhelmed, she recognises Philippe, smiles to him, repeats once again 'adieu'; but at that very instant she dies.

A current pocket edition of this amazing story (published by Gallimard in the 'Folio' collection) ensures, in two different ways, its critical presentation: the text is preceded and followed by pedagogical commentary – a Preface by Pierre Gascan and a 'Notice' by Philippe Berthier – which are supposed to 'explain' it and 'situate' its importance. It is striking that, of the three chapters which constitute this short story – the discovery of the madwoman in the mysterious domain, the war scene, and the scene of the cure – *both* commentators discuss only one: the chapter depicting the war. The main plot, which consists of the story of a woman's madness (episodes I and III), is somehow completely neglected in favour of the subplot (episode II), a historical narrative whose function is to describe the events which preceded and occasioned the madness. The 'explication' thus excludes two things: the madness and the woman. Viewed through the eyes of the two academic critics, *Adieu* becomes a story about the suffering of men in which the real protagonists are none but 'the soldiers of the Grand Army'. The Preface indeed makes a great point of praising Balzac for 'the realism, unprecedented in the history of literature, with which the war is here depicted':[9] 'by showing us, in *Adieu*, the soldiers of the Grand Army haggard, half dead with hunger and cold, draped in rags, surging toward the pontoon bridge thrown across the Berezina, he [Balzac] deals with the myth of military grandeur [. . .] a blow whose repercussions extend well beyond the post-Napoleonic era.'[10] This supposedly 'objective' reading of what is called Balzac's 'realism' in fact screens out and disguises an ideological pattern of textual amputations and cuts, in which only a *third* of the text is brought to the reader's attention. 'Indeed,' concedes the Preface's author, 'these scenes do not take up much room in [. . .] *Adieu*, where most of the action occurs subsequent to the historic events which they symbolise. *But they suffice* to give the war its true countenance.'[11] As for the author of the 'Notice', he does not even seek to justify the arbitrary, disproportionate cuts underlying his 'explication' – by putting forward a *truth* 'which suffices': 'the *true* countenance of the war.' In line with the academic tradition of 'selected passages', he proposes, simply and 'innocently', literally to *cut up* the text, to *extract* the second chapter, and truly materialise the operation of ideological extirpation with a serene pedagogical confidence: 'the second chapter, *which can be isolated from the work* as was the story of Goguelat from the *Country Doctor* (cf. our edition of this novel in Folio) marks the appearance in Balzac's work of the theme of the wartime disappearance of an officer who comes back many years later.'[12] The story is here explicitly summed up as being exclusively that of a man: that of 'the wartime disappearance of an officer who comes back many years later.' It is, therefore, by no means surprising to see the author of the 'Notice' taken aback by the fact – to him incomprehensible – that in its second version this text could have been, as he puts it, 'oddly entitled' *A Woman's Duty*.[13] Evident in an abandoned title, but in the text neither seen nor heard, the woman does not belong to the realm of the 'explicable'; her claim to commentary is solely an inexplicable piece of knowledge, an unusable article of erudition.

It is just in this manner that the institution of literary criticism pronounces its expert, professional discourse, without even noticing the conspicuousness of its flagrant misogyny. To the *sociological* sexism of the educational system corresponds, in this case, the naïve, though by no means innocent, sexism of the exegetical system of *literary analysis*, of the academic and pedagogical fabrication of 'literary' and critical discourse.

By guiding the reader, through the extirpation of 'explicable' facts, to the 'correct' perception, to the literal 'proper', so-called 'objective' level of textual interpretation, academic criticism conditions the very norms of 'legibility'. Madness and women, however, turn out to be the two outcasts of the establishment of readability. An ideological conditioning of literary and critical discourse, a political orientation of reading thus affirms itself, not so much through the negative treatment of women as through their total neglect, their pure and simple *omission*. This critical oversight, which appears as a *systematic* blindness to significant facts, functions as a censorship mechanism, as a symbolic eradication of women from the world of literature. It is therefore essential to examine the theoretical presuppositions which permit and sanction this kind of blindness.

We have seen that what is invoked so as to authorise the arbitrariness of the curtailment of the text is the critical concept of Balzac's 'realism': the realism of war, 'unprecedented' – as the Preface puts it – 'in the history of literature'. In the context of this manly realism, the woman is relegated to non-existence, since she is said to partake of the 'unreal': 'Beside the Berezina [. . .] Stéphanie's carriage, blocked among hordes of French soldiers savage with hunger and shock, becomes the *unwonted, almost unreal element* in which the whole absurdity of the situation bursts out.'[14] What, then, is this 'realism' the critic here ascribes to Balzac, if not the assumption, not shared by the text, that what happens to men is more important, and/or more 'real', than what happens to women? A subtle boundary line, which gives itself as a 'natural frontier', is thus traced, in the critical vocabulary, between the realm of the 'real' and that of the 'unreal', between the category of 'realism' and that of the so-called 'supernatural':

> While *Colonel Chabert* contains no *supernatural* elements [. . .] *Adieu* allots a great deal of space to psychic phenomena, with Stéphanie's madness, and even to parapsychic phenomena, with her death [. . .] It is noteworthy [. . .] that Balzac's short stories [. . .] devote infinitely more space to the *supernatural*, to the presence of the *invisible* [. . .] than do his novels. [. . .] In these four stories where it exists side by side with the most striking *realism, the marvellous* is in fact only represented by the *state of semi-unreality* which the main characters attain through the horror of their ordeal. We here come across [. . .] the romantic conception of the transfiguring power of suffering.[15]

The 'supernatural', as everyone knows, cannot be rationally explained and hence should not detain us and does not call for *thought*. Flattened out and banalised into the 'edifying conclusion'[16] of the beneficent power of suffering, Stéphanie's madness is *not problematic*, does not deserve to detain us, since it is but a 'state of semi-unreality'. Realism thus postulates a conception of 'nature' and of 'reality' which seeks to establish itself, tautologically, as 'natural' and as 'real'. Nothing, indeed, is less neutral than this apparent neutrality; nothing is less 'natural' than this frontier which is supposed to separate 'the real' from 'the unreal' and which in fact delimits only the inside and the outside of an ideological circle: an inside which is *inclusive* of 'reason' and men, i.e., 'reality' and 'nature'; and an outside which is *exclusive* of madness and women, i.e., the 'supernatural' and the 'unreal'. And since the supernatural is linked, as the critic would have it, to 'the presence of the invisible',[17] it comes as no surprise to find the woman predestined to be, precisely, *the realistic invisible*, that which realism as such is inherently unable to see.

> It is the whole field of a problematic, which defines and structures the invisible as its definite outside – excluded from the domain of visibility and defined as excluded by the existence and the structure of the problematic field itself.[. . .] The invisible is defined by the visible as its invisible, its prohibited sight [. . .]. To see this invisible [. . .] requires something quite different from a sharp or attentive eye, it takes an *educated eye*, a revised, renewed way of looking, itself produced by the effect of a 'change of terrain' reflected back upon the act of seeing.[18]

With a 'revised' way of looking, 'educated' by the 'change of terrain' brought about by the feminist interrogation, let us now attempt to re-read Balzac's text and to reinterpret its relation to the woman as well as to madness.

III 'SHE? WHO?'

From the very beginning the woman in this text stands out as a problem. The opening pages present the reader with a series of abstract questions concerning a female identity: the two lost hunters are trying to situate themselves, to ascertain the identity of the woman they have just glimpsed in the unknown place into which they have wandered: '*Where the devil are we? [. . .]/She, who? [. . .]/Where are we? What is that house? Whose is it? Who are you? Do you live here? [. . .]/But who is this lady? [. . .]/She? Who? [. . .]*'[19]

The reader, too, cannot get his/her bearings: deluged with questions, at the same time deprived systematically of information, not really knowing *who* is speaking, much less about whom, s/he is in turn as *lost* in the text as the two protagonists are in geographical space. The text thus originates in the *loss* of the very conditions of localisation and identification, in a general state of confusion from which, in an almost anonymous manner, a recurrent question emerges: 'She? Who?' The feminine pronoun preceding any proper denomination, the ambiguous question preceding any informative clarification, this preliminary inquiry takes on an abstractly emphatic and allegorical character, and seems to situate from the start the textual problematic within a systematic search for the nature of feminine identity. From the beginning, however, the question reaches a dead end: addressed to the women themselves, the query meets only silence, since both women here are deprived of the ability to speak. Addressed to others, the question obtains only distant and hypothetical answers: *'But who is this lady? [. . .]/It is presumed that she comes from Moulins [. . .]; she is said to be mad [. . .] I wouldn't guarantee you the truth of these rumours.'*[20]

The allegorical question, 'She? Who?' will thus remain unanswered. The text, nonetheless, will play out the question to its logical end, so as to show in what way it *precludes* any answer, in what way the question is set as a trap. The very *lack of the answer* will then write itself as a *different* question, through which the original question will find itself dislocated, radically shifted and transformed.

'She? Who?' The women cannot respond: mad, they do not understand the men's questions. Nor do the rational men understand the senseless words of the women. But the women, though mad, understand each other. The doctor thus interprets the friendship that seems to unite Stéphanie and the peasant Geneviève: 'Here [. . .] she has found another creature she seems to get along with. It's an idiot peasant-woman [. . .] My niece and this poor girl are in a way united by the invisible chain of their common destiny, and by the feeling that causes their madness.'[21] Understanding occurs in this text only on one side or the other of the boundary line which, separating silence from speech, distinguishes madness from reason. It is nonetheless striking that the dichotomy Reason/Madness, as well as Speech/Silence, exactly coincides in this text with the dichotomy Men/Women. Women as such are associated both with madness and with silence, whereas men are identified with prerogatives of discourse and of reason. In fact, men appear not only as the possessors, but also as the dispensers, of reason, which they can at will mete out to – or take away from – others. While Philippe and the doctor undertake to 'restore Stéphanie's reason', the magistrate, on the other hand, brags: 'If you should ever bring a suit to court, *I would make you lose it, even if reason were a hundred per cent on your side.* '[22] The three men in the story in fact symbolically represent – by virtue of their professions: magistrate, doctor, soldier – the power to act *upon* others' reason, in the name of the law, of health or of force.

With respect to the woman's madness, man's reason reacts by trying to *appropriate* it: in the first place, by claiming to 'understand' it, but with an external understanding which reduces the madwoman to a spectacle, to an *object* which can be *known* and *possessed*. 'Go on, Sir, leave her alone,' the doctor recommends to Philippe, 'I know how to live with the dear little creature; I *understand* her madness, I *spy upon* her gestures, I am in on her secrets.'[23] To 'spy on' in order to 'know'; to 'tame' in order to 'cure': such are the methods used by masculine reason so as to *objectify* feminine madness, thereby mastering it. If the madwoman is throughout the story seen as and compared to an animal, this pervasive metaphor tells us less about Stéphanie's delirium than about the logic of her therapists. For the object is precisely to capture the animal and to tame it. Thus we see the symbolic import of the initial hunting scene. A metaphorical parody of the episode of war and of its martial logic ('"Come on, deputy, forward! Double time! Speed up [. . .] march over the ruts [. . .] Come on, march! [. . .] If you sit down, you're lost,"'[24] the opening scene of the hunt already symbolically prefigures Philippe's attitude toward Stéphanie: 'Come on,' cries Philippe from the very first, not yet knowing whom he is talking about, but integrating as a matter of course the woman into his hunter's mentality, 'Come on, let's run after the white and black lady! Forward!'[25] But the hunter's chase will here be but the measure of the flight of his prey.

If masculine reason thus constitutes a scheme to capture and master, indeed, metaphorically *rape* the woman, by the same token, Stéphanie's madness is not contingent on but directly related to her femininity: consisting, precisely, in its loss. Several times Philippe, in fact, explicitly defines Stéphanie's madness as the loss of her womanhood. When the doctor advises him to tame her by feeding her pieces of sugar, Philippe sadly answers: '*When she was a woman*, she had no taste for sweets.'[26] And again, in a burst of sorrow, Philippe cries: 'I die a little more every day, every minute! My love is too great! I could bear everything if only, in her madness, she had kept some *semblance of femininity.*'[27] Madness, in other words, is precisely what makes a woman *not* a woman. But what is a 'woman'? Woman is a 'name', denied in fact to Geneviève in the same way as it is denied to Stéphanie: 'Then a *woman*, if such a *name* can be applied to the *undefinable being* who got up from under the bushes, pulled on the cow by its rope.'[28] 'Woman' is consequently a 'definable being' – chained to a 'definition' itself implying a model, a definition commanded by a *logic of resemblance*. Even in the war scene, Stéphanie had already lost her 'femininity'. '[When] all rolled around herself, *she really resembled nothing* [. . .] *Was this that charming woman, the glory of her lover, the queen of the Parisian ballrooms?* Alas! even the eyes of her most devoted friend could perceive *nothing feminine* left in that heap of linens and rags.'[29] If a 'woman' is strictly, exactly, 'what *resembles* a woman' ('she really resembled nothing [. . .] nothing feminine left'), it becomes apparent that 'femininity' is much less a 'natural' category than a rhetorical one, analogical and metaphorical: a metaphorical category which is explicitly bound, as perceived by Philippe, to a socio-sexual stereotype, to the 'definable' role of the mistress – 'the queen of the Parisian ballrooms'. Of course, the 'queen' here implies a king; the literal, *proper* meaning of metaphorical femininity, paradoxically enough, turns out to be a masculine property: the 'queen of the Parisian ballrooms', 'that charming woman', is above all *'The glory of her lover'*. 'Woman', in other words, is the exact metaphorical measure of the narcissism of man.

The Masculine thus turns out to be the universal equivalent of the opposition: Masculine/Feminine. It is insofar as Masculinity conditions Femininity as its universal equivalent, as what determines and measures its value, that the textual paradox can be created according to which the woman is 'madness', while at the same time 'madness' is the very 'absence of womanhood'. The woman is 'madness' to the extent that she is other, *different* from man. But 'madness' is the 'absence of womanhood' to the extent that 'womanhood' is what precisely resembles the Masculine universal equivalent, in the polar division of sexual roles. If so, the woman is 'madness' since the woman is *difference*; but 'madness' is 'non-woman' since madness is the *lack of resemblance*. What the narcissistic economy of the Masculine universal equivalent tries to eliminate, under the label 'madness', is nothing other than *feminine difference*.

IV THE THERAPEUTIC FALLACY

Such is the male narcissistic principle on which the system of reason, with its therapeutic ambition, is based. For, to 'restore Stéphanie's reason' signifies, precisely, to reinstate her 'femininity': to make her *recognise* man, the 'lover' whose 'glory' she ought to be. 'I'm going to the Bons-Hommes,' says Philippe, 'to see her, speak to her, *cure* her [. . .] Do you think the poor woman would be able to *hear me* and *not recover her reason*?'[30] In Philippe's mind, 'to recover her reason' becomes synonymous with 'to hear *me*'. 'The cure of the madman,' writes Michel Foucault, 'is in the reason of the other – his own reason being but the very truth of his madness.'[31] Stéphanie's cure is in Philippe's reason. The 'recovery' of her reason must thus necessarily entail an act of recognition:

> 'She doesn't recognise me,' cried the colonel in despair. Stéphanie! it's Philippe, your Philippe, Philippe!"[32]

> 'Her; not to recognise me, and to run away from me,' repeated the colonel.[33]

> 'My love,' he said, ardently kissing the countess's hands, 'I am Philippe.' 'Come,' he added, [. . .] 'Philippe is not dead, he is here, you are sitting on his lap. You are my Stéphanie, and I am your Philippe.' 'Adieu,' she said, 'adieu.'[34]

Stéphanie's recovery of her 'reason', the restoration of her femininity as well as of her identity, depends then, in Philippe's eyes, on her specular recognition of *him*, on her *reflection* of his own name and of his own identity. If the question of female identity remains in the text unanswered, it is simply because it is *never* truly asked: in the guise of asking, 'She? Who?' Philippe is in fact always asking 'I? Who?' – a false question, the answer to which he believes he knows in advance: 'It's Philippe.' The question concerning the woman is thereby transformed into the question of a guarantee for men, a question through which nothing is questioned, whose sole function is to ensure the validity of its predefined answer: 'You are *my* Stéphanie.' The use of the possessive adjective makes explicit the act of appropriation focused here on the *proper* names. But it is from Stéphanie's own mouth that Philippe must obtain his proper name, his guarantee of the propriety of his own identity, and of hers: Stéphanie = Philippe, 'You are my Stéphanie, and I am your Philippe.' In Philippe's eyes, Stéphanie is viewed above all as an object, whose role is to ensure, by an interplay of reflections, his own self-sufficiency as a 'subject', to serve as a mediator in his own specular relationship with himself. What Philippe pursues in the woman is not a face, but a mirror, which, reflecting his image, will thereby *acknowledge* his narcissistic *self-image*. 'Women', writes Virginia Woolf, 'have served all these centuries as looking-glasses possessing the magic and delicious power of reflecting the figure of man at twice its natural size.' Philippe, as it turns out, desires not *knowledge* of Stéphanie herself but her *acknowledgement* of him: his therapeutic design is to restore her not to *cognition*, but to *recognition*.

To this demand for recognition and for the restoration of identity through language, through the authority of proper names, Stéphanie opposes, in the figure of her madness, the dislocation of any transitive, communicative language, of 'propriety' as such, of any correspondence or transparency joining 'names' to 'things', the blind opacity of a lost signifier unmatched by any signified, the pure recurrent difference of a word detached from both its meaning and its context.

> 'Adieu,' she said in a soft harmonious voice, but whose melody, impatiently perceived by the expectant hunters, seemed to divulge not the slightest feeling or the least idea.[35]

> 'Adieu, adieu, adieu!' she said, without her soul's conferring any perceptible inflection upon the word.[36]

To this automatic repetition of senselessness and difference, Philippe in turn will oppose another type of repetition designed precisely to restore resemblance and identity: in order to cure Stéphanie, in order to restore to her demented, dislocated language its nominative and communicative function, he decides to *reproduce* the primal scene of the 'adieu' and thus to *re-present* theatrically the errant signifier's lost significance, its proper signified. Without her knowledge, Stéphanie will literally be forced to play herself, to return to her 'proper' role. Through the theatrical set-up, everything will end up making sense: and, with all difference thus erased, re-presentation necessarily will bring about the desired re-cognition.

> The baron [de Sucy] had, inspired by a dream, conceived a plan to restore the countess's reason. [. . .] He devoted the rest of the autumn to the preparation of this immense enterprise. A small river flowed through his park where, in the winter, it flooded an extensive marsh which resembled [. . .] the one running along the right bank of the Berezina. The village of Satou, set on a hill; added the final touch to put this scene of horror in its frame [. . .]. The colonel gathered a troop of workers to dig a canal which would represent the voracious river. [. . .] Thus aided by his memory, Philippe succeeded in copying in his park the riverbank where General Elbe had built his bridges. [. . .] The colonel assembled pieces of debris similar to what his fellow sufferers had used to construct their raft. He ravaged his park, in an effort to complete the illusion on which he pinned his last hopes. [. . .] In short, he had forgotten nothing that could reproduce the most horrible of all scenes, and he reached his goal. Toward the beginning of December, when the snow had blanketed the earth with a white coat, he recognised the Berezina. This false Russia was of such appalling truth that several of his comrades recognised the scene of their former sufferings. Monsieur de Sucy kept the secret of this tragic representation.[37]

The cure succeeds. However, so as to fulfil perfectly her 'Woman's Duty', to play her role correctly in this theatre of the identical, to recognise specularly and reflect perfectly Philippe's 'identity', Stéphanie herself must disappear: she has to *die* as *other*, as a 'subject' in her own right. The tragic outcome of the story is inevitable, inscribed as it is from the outset in the very logic of representation inherent in the therapeutic project. Stéphanie will die; Philippe will subsequently commit suicide. If, as ambiguous as it is, the cure turns out to be a murder, this murder, in its narcissistic dialectic, is necessarily suicidal,[38] since, killing Stéphanie in the very enterprise of 'saving' her,[39] it is also his own image that Philippe strikes in the mirror.

Through this paradoxical and disconcerting ending, the text subverts and dislocates the logic of representation which it has dramatised through Philippe's endeavour and his failure. Literature thus breaks away from pure representation: when transparency and meaning, 'reason' and 're-presentation' are regained, when madness ends, so does the text itself. Literature, in this way, seems to indicate its impuissance to dominate or to recuperate the madness of the signifier from which it speaks, its radical incapacity to master its own signifying repetition, to 'tame' its own linguistic difference, to 'represent' identity or truth. Like madness and unlike representation, literature can signify but not *make sense*.

Once again, it is amazing to what extent academic criticism, completely unaware of the text's irony, can remain blind to what the text says about itself. It is quite striking to observe to what extent the logic of the unsuspecting 'realistic' critic can reproduce, one after the other, all of Philippe's delusions, which the text deconstructs and puts in question. Like Philippe, the 'realistic' critic seeks representation, tries, by means of fiction, to reproduce 'the real thing', to reconstruct, minutely and exhaustively, the exact historical Berezina scene. Like Philippe, the 'realistic' critic is haunted by an obsession with proper names – identity and reference – sharing the same nostalgia for a transparent, transitive, communicative language, where everything possesses, unequivocally, a single meaning which can be consequently mastered and made clear, where each name 'represents' a thing, where each signifier, properly and adequately, corresponds both to a signified and to a referent. On the critical as well as on the literary stage, the same attempt is played out to appropriate the signifier and to reduce its differential repetition; we see the same endeavour to do away with difference, the same policing of identities, the same design of mastery, of *sense-control*. For the 'realistic' critic, as for Philippe, the readable is designed as a stimulus not for knowledge and cognition, but for acknowledgement and *re-cognition*, not for the *production* of a question, but for the *reproduction* of a foreknown answer – delimited within a pre-existing, pre-defined horizon, where the 'truth' to be discovered is reduced to the natural status of a simple *given*, immediately perceptible, directly 'representable' through the totally intelligible medium of transparent language. Exactly in the same way as Philippe, the commentators of *Adieu* are in turn taken in by the illusory security of a specularly structured act of recognition. Balzac's text, which applies as much to the 'realistic' critic as to Philippe, can itself be read as a kind of preface to its own Preface, as an ironic reading of its own academic reading.

For, what Philippe *misrecognises* in his 'realistic' recognition of the Berezina is, paradoxically enough, the *real*: the real not as a convergence of reflections, as an effect of mirroring focalisation, but as a radically de-centring resistance; the real as, precisely, other, the unrepresentable as such, the ex-centric residue which the specular relationship of vision cannot embrace.

Along with the illusions of Philippe, the 'realistic' critic thus repeats, in turn, his allegorical act of murder, his obliteration of the other: the critic also, in his own way, *kills the woman*, while killing, at the same time, the question of the text and the text as a question.

But, here again, as in Philippe's case, the murder is incorporated in an enterprise which can be seen as 'therapeutic'. For in obliterating difference, in erasing from the text the disconcerting and ex-centric features of a woman's madness, the critic seeks to 'normalise' the text, to banish and eradicate all trace of violence and anguish, of scandal or insanity, making the text a reassuring, closed retreat whose balance no upheaval can upset, where no convulsion is of any consequence. 'To drive these phantoms firmly back into their epoch, to close it upon them, by means of a historical narrative, this seems to have been the writer's intent.'[40] By reducing the story to a recognition scheme, familiar, snug and canny, the critic, like Philippe, 'cures' the text, precisely of that which in it is incurably and radically uncanny.

From this paradoxical encounter between literature's critical irony and the uncritical naïvety of its critics, from this confrontation in which Balzac's text itself seems to be an ironic reading of its own future reading, the question arises: how *should* we read? How can a reading lead to something other than recognition, 'normalisation' and 'cure'? How can the critical project, in other words, be detached from the therapeutic projection?

This crucial theoretical question, which undermines the foundations of traditional thought and whose importance the feminist writings have helped to bring out, pinpoints at the same time the difficulty of the woman's position in today's critical discourse. If, in our culture, the woman is by definition associated with madness, her problem is how to break out of this (cultural) imposition of madness *without* taking up the critical and therapeutic positions of reason: how to avoid speaking both as *mad* and as *not mad*. The challenge facing the woman today is nothing less than to 're-invent' language, to *re-learn how to speak*: to speak not only against, but outside of the specular phallogocentric structure, to establish a discourse the status of which would no longer be defined by the phallacy of masculine meaning. An old saying would thereby be given new life: today more than ever, changing our minds – changing *the* mind – is a woman's prerogative.

11

Promises, Promises: the Fictional Philosophy in Mary Wollstonecraft's *Vindication of the Rights of Woman*

Jane Moore

I

This essay explores the possibility that deconstruction offers a useful mode of textual analysis both for feminist readings of past texts and relatedly, necessarily, for current feminist approaches to the politics of gender and literary criticism. I say necessarily related because how we read past representations of femininity and sexual difference has implications for understanding their present meanings. Also, I want to stress that although we always read past texts from the perspective of present-day concerns, knowledges and beliefs, there is, as Gillian Beer has noted, a significant difference between approaches which seek to convert the concerns of past texts into current categories, and those which attempt to read texts from the past in their historical difference from the present.[1]

At stake in these different approaches is the belief that meanings of femininity and sexual difference are multiple, contradictory and changing: the first way of reading fixes present meanings of sexual difference and current theoretical perspectives as the only source of authority from which to read the past, which often means judging the past; the second way of reading, which is the one I propose to adopt, foregrounds the specificity of historical meanings. This has the corresponding effect of unfixing the authority of current meanings, for to stress changes in past and present meanings is to locate the past and the present as moments in a continuous history of change. 'Now' may be the most familiar moment, but it is not any the more stable for that.

This is not meant to imply that we can somehow bypass the uncertain instabilities of the present in an effort to reach back through literary texts to an unadulterated 'true' version of the past which is untainted by the pre-conceptions of now. On the contrary, our interpretations of historical texts are always informed by present-day influences. But neither does it mean that as present-day readers we are inexorably compelled to abandon ourselves to the illusory authority of now, only that we should be alert to its imaginary effects, that is, to the way it masquerades as real. For, as Beer again notes, we will only read helplessly, 'merely hauling, without noticing, our own cultural baggage', if we 'read past texts solely for their grateful "relevance" to our expectations and to those of our circumstances that we happen to have noticed'.[2]

I have raised some of the problems and politics of reading history at the start of my paper for two reasons. The first and most obvious is that I have chosen to analyse a text from the 1790s. The second, perhaps less obvious, reason arises from the wish to use deconstructive theories in this task. By employing deconstructive textual strategies alongside a consideration of historical factors I hope to avoid the ahistoricism of certain, mainly American, deconstructors, whose inattention to the political implications of neglecting the historical limits of the texts they analyse has led Colin MacCabe to reaffirm Norman Mailer's remark that 'deconstruction–US style has been a "Reagan kind of radical theory"'; and Christopher Norris to speak of 'deconstruction on the wild side'.[3] Norris warns against a certain type of deconstructive free play which is concerned only with undoing the textual workings of the binary oppositions and metaphysical assumptions that underpin and distinguish one mode of writing, or genre, from the next. He does so on the grounds that this critical practice results in the collapse of all genre distinctions. Consequently, it becomes possible to claim, for example, that philosophy is 'simply another variety of literature, a text pervaded by the same ruses of figuration'.[4] And, by extension, it no longer makes any 'sense' for the critic to acknowledge a political preference for one discourse over another: all discourses are rendered the same, in that they are all 'pervaded by the same ruses of figuration' regardless of their different historical, cultural and sexual 'contexts'. Norris's warning against undoing all textual difference, all genre distinctions – a task which in the 1980s has perhaps become all too easy – is pertinent to an essay about feminist approaches to gender difference. For it is precisely on a recognition of genre difference that much late twentieth-century feminist theory, not to mention eighteenth-century explorations of gender difference, relies. Twentieth-century feminist criticism has identified an inextricable, though not inexorable, relationship between the taxonomy of genre and gender. This relationship occupies a privileged position in current feminist criticism's preoccupation with questioning the place from which women speak and the possibility of a specifically feminine language.

The French feminist Hélène Cixous thus begins her philosophical–poetical essay, 'Sorties', with the question 'Where is she?'[5] Cixous's essay suggests that woman's place in the history of Western thought has been at the negative pole of the series of binary oppositions which have structured that history. The examples given are 'Activity/Passivity, Sun/Moon, Culture/Nature, Day/Night, Father/ Mother, Intelligible/Palpable, Logos/Pathos'.[6] All of these 'couples' come back to 'the' couple 'Man/Woman'. They also relate to another couple, which is 'Philosophy/Literature'.

'Literature', writes Cixous, 'is under the command of the philosophical and the phallocentric.'[7] Consequently, 'Sorties' concludes that women must reject a philosophical mode of writing if they are to 'write themselves', which is to write a specifically feminine discourse, and thereby resist identification with 'the [philosophical] discourse controlled by the phallus'.[8]

II

In the eighteenth century the insistence on genre difference comes from the other side of the coin. The title of Mary Wollstonecraft's *Vindication of the Rights of Woman: with Strictures on Political and Moral Subjects*, published in 1792, immediately declares its philosophical status. The nascent feminist interests of this text result in a call to women to resist identification with dominant masculine assumptions on what it means to be a woman. This involves rejecting what the *Vindication* pinpoints as an artificial literary rhetoric of femininity and identifying instead with a philosophical rational discourse, which although controlled by the phallus is not inherently masculine.

The argument of the *Vindication* depends on maintaining a fundamental opposition between plain-speaking philosophy and fictional feminine figurality. It depends also, therefore, on the social and textual interrelation of genre and gender categories. From its beginning the *Vindication* stresses the determining influence of genre in shaping assumptions about gender; and, in line with the project to release women from false conceptions of their sex, the 'Author's Introduction' insists on discarding feminine ways of writing.

> Dismissing, then, those pretty feminine phrases, which the men condescendingly use to soften our slavish dependence, and despising that weak elegancy of mind, exquisite sensibility, and sweet docility of manners, supposed to be the sexual characteristics of the weaker vessel, I wish to show that elegance is inferior to virtue, that the first object of laudable ambition is to obtain a character as a human being, regardless of the distinction of sex, and that secondary views should be brought to this simple touchstone. (p. 82)[9]

The *Vindication*'s call to women to reject a 'secondary', because culturally constituted, femininity and instead to 'obtain a character as a human being, regardless of the distinction of sex', appears to demand the complete effacement of sexual difference. But the 'human character' referred to here is not gender-neutral: it is male, in as much as it is the qualities *attributed* to masculinity which are lauded. In writing, these qualities are manifested in a straightforward rational prose, as opposed to the 'pretty feminine phrases' which Wollstonecraft associates only with women.

Wollstonecraft's plea to women to deny the specificity of their sex may seem misplaced, not to say anti-feminist, to twentieth-century readers. Mary Jacobus, for example, declares against what she sees as the text's cold logic. And she accuses Wollstonecraft of being a 'plain-speaking utilitarian', who 'speaks not so much *for* women, or *as* a woman, but *against* them – over their dead bodies'.[10] Certainly these charges are admissible, but, I suggest, they are the result of 'judging' the *Vindication* in isolation from the culture and history of which it forms a part. Moreover, their effect is to foreclose the possibility of reading the *Vindication* positively; that is, reading it for the challenge it poses to patriarchal assumptions, and not for the ways in which it complies with them.

In order to allow the radical edge of Wollstonecraft's project to come fully into view, which is the aim of my reading, it may be useful, necessary even, to consider the *Vindication*'s historical placement. Thus, before looking at the *Vindication* more closely, I want briefly to sketch some of the dominant (male) conceptions of gender and genre difference that were in circulation at the moment of the text's production. They are all assumptions which inform the *Vindication*'s discussion of the relationship between women and language.

In the late seventeenth and eighteenth centuries the categorisation of genre was instrumental in helping to formulate and coalesce received notions of sexual difference. The position of women in relation to men was roughly analogous to the position and function of figurative language in relation to a utilitarian one. Evidence of this relationship appears in chapter 10 of John Locke's *Essay Concerning Human Understanding* (1690), as well as in the mid-eighteenth-century writings of Jean-Jacques Rousseau, and books by other later male educationalists such as John Bennett.

Locke's *Essay* sets up a series of oppositions in order both to distinguish between and to privilege the capacity of language to instruct over its ability to entertain. Wit, fancy, pleasure, delight and eloquence are differentiated from truth, knowledge, improvement and lucidity. That these are oppositions not only of genre but also of gender is revealed by the following concluding sentences:

Eloquence, like the fair sex, has too prevailing beauties in it to suffer itself ever to be spoken against. And it is in vain to find fault with those arts of deceiving wherein men find pleasure to be deceived.[11]

The implications for women of Locke's sentiments are fully spelt out in Rousseau's assertion:

A man speaks of what he knows, a woman of what pleases her; the one requires knowledge, the other taste; the principal object of a man's discourse should be what is useful, that of a woman's what is agreeable.[12]

Even towards the end of the eighteenth century, by which time the need for reforms in female education was generally accepted, Rousseau's stress on women's ornamental role in society still influenced male educational reformers. John Bennett is a case in point.[13] In volume I of his two volumes of *Letters to a Young Lady*, first published in 1789 and reprinted in 1795, Bennett argues that women's education should be restricted to less arduous intellectual pursuits than men's. For, he claims,

Whilst men, with solid judgement and a superior vigour are to combine ideas, to discriminate, and to examine a subject to the bottom, you are to give it all its brilliancy and all its charms. They provide the furniture; you dispose it with propriety. They build the house; you are to fancy, and to ornament the ceiling.[14]

It would be misleading, however, to suggest that these (male) views went uncontested. Certainly there were dissenting, mainly female, voices which countered the dominant, mainly male, ones. Along with Mary Wollstonecraft, Hannah More strongly advocated the need for a far broader system of female education. And although on other matters More spoke from the opposite end of the political spectrum to Wollstonecraft, Wollstonecraft probably would have approved of More's proposal that women's education should include reading such philosophical texts as Locke's *Essay*.[15] Also, some women's novels clearly supported a more extensive and more useful system of female education. Sarah Scott's *Millenium Hall* (1762), for example, describes a community of self-educated women living in the country, where they perform philanthropic work and read philosophical works.[16] And both Mary Hays's *Memoirs of Emma Courtney* (1796) and Mrs Opie's *Adeline Mowbray* (1804) have self-educated philosophical heroines.[17]

But at the moment of the *Vindication*'s production these voices were not dominant; indeed in some cases they hadn't even been articulated. Moreover, the 'fact' that the heroines of these women's novels are invariably self-educated suggests that, despite educational reforms, women were obliged to look beyond male-controlled pedagogic practices for their education. It also suggests, of course, that women were capable of fulfilling greater tasks than the literal and metaphoric homemaking which John Bennett prescribes.

III

To return, then, to the authorial preface of the *Vindication*, it now becomes clear why the text seeks to cement an opposition between 'pretty feminine phrases' designed to entertain, and unadorned utilitarian sentences designed to instruct, with the aim, of course, of rejecting the former.

Starting from this 'simple' conviction of difference, the text further distinguishes between primary and secondary discourses, which respectively relate to the binarism of natural/unnatural, true/false, good/bad. 'Pretty feminine phrases', a 'weak elegancy of mind', 'exquisite sensibility' and 'a sweet docility of manners', it is argued, are derivative from, or secondary to, a primordial self-evidently rational language which corresponds to a 'natural' state of being. The *Vindication* proposes that in order to return to the state where reason naturally reigns, women must throw off the artificial trappings – and tropings – of an unnatural culturally constituted femininity.

In making a distinction, however, between natural and unnatural uses of language, between a primary utilitarian language and a supplementary literarity, the *Vindication* immediately encounters the problem of its own textuality – its own wordiness: on the one hand it is argued that virtue is more natural than elegance, while on the other it is acknowledged that in order for the idea of virtue to be communicated it must be inscribed in language; and not only this, it is also hinted that meaning is itself an effect of language, including what it means to be a woman. The 'Author's Introduction' states that to be a human being one must first 'obtain a character as a human being'. In other words, one must take up a position in language. What is remarkable about the *Vindication*'s recognition of the way in which language shapes subjectivity is that it contradicts and effectively displaces the defining extra-textuality of the idea of reason, and of a 'natural' (pre-linguistic) state of being, on which the argument of that text depends. The opposition between natural and unnatural is undermined by their shared dependence for meaning on their (secondary) inscription in language, and the meaning of the word 'natural' consequently slides beyond the control of the primary/ secondary opposition.

In an attempt, then, to bring the disruptive operations of language into line, the text vigorously reasserts a distinction between proper and improper uses of language. By arguing in a manner similar to William Godwin's *Enquiry Concerning Political Justice,* not that nature, virtue, truth, and reason are constitutive of an illusory referent, or a pre-linguistic essence, but rather that the language of reason *facilitates* direct access to an external order of those ideals, the *Vindication* defuses the threat which language poses to the belief that human beings have recourse to essential, primordial and natural ideals.[18] Thus, the emphasis of the 'Author's Introduction' increasingly falls on making a difference between the perceived transparency of a rational language and the deceptiveness and obscurity of a figural one. Hence, Wollstonecraft asserts:

> I shall disdain to cull my phrases or polish my style. I aim at being useful, and sincerity will render me unaffected; for wishing rather to persuade by the force of my arguments than dazzle by the elegance of my language, I shall not waste my time in rounding periods, or in fabricating the turgid bombast of artificial feelings . . . (p. 82)

As if this commitment to an 'unaffected' transparent mode of persuasion stands in need of further reassurance Wollstonecraft goes one step further: she announces her intention to abolish not only tropes but all words:

> I shall be employed about things, not words! and, anxious to render my sex more respectable members of society, I shall try to avoid that flowery diction which has slided from essays into novels, and from novels into familiar letters and conversations. (p. 82)

Seemingly untroubled, then, by its own insights about the discursive production of meaning and the mediating agency of language, the text confidently announces its project to instruct the reader by the persuasive force of rational argument, rather than dazzle and deceive her by the elegance of its language. Correspondingly, chapter 1 sets out 'to go back to first principles in search of the most simple truths' (p. 91). It opens with a series of 'plain' questions – and answers – that enlist and instruct the reader in a peculiarly self-assured catechism, which reads as follows:

> In what does man's pre-eminence over the brute creation consist? The answer is as clear as that a half is less than the whole, in Reason.
> What acquirement exalts one being above another? Virtue, we spontaneously reply.
> For what purpose were the passions implanted? That man by struggling with them might attain a degree of knowledge denied to the brutes, whispers Experience. (p. 91)

The structure of these opening paragraphs at first sight appears to be a logical one. They offer the reader a rehearsal of the principles on which explanations and philosophical theories delivered later in the chapter will depend. It is paradoxical, then, that in order to communicate these principles, the text falls back on the tropic ruses it seeks to condemn. Transparency is re-placed by analogy and metaphor: reason is 'clear' only by analogy, while 'experience' 'whispers' to us as a personification.

Moreover, as the chapter continues, the already metaphoric language in which these 'plain' questions and answers are delivered very quickly runs out of control, thereby displacing the transparency earlier promised.

The 'first principles' outlined in the opening paragraphs become increasingly blurred at the edges by the 'dazzling' imagery of the rest of the chapter. Even by the second page it is evident that utilitarian prose has fallen victim to the wordiness of the language it is forced to communicate in: the obviousness, or transparency, of 'simple' truths is clouded by a continuous bodily metaphor of health and disease, beauty and deformity, which structures not only this chapter but all the succeeding ones. Thus, 'vice skulks with all its native deformity' and is 'rotten at the core' (p. 92). Aristocratic, monarchical and priestly powers constitute the 'pestilential vapour' (p. 96) which hovers over society; while tyranny in all forms is a 'baneful lurking gangrene', a contagion spread by the unnatural state of the 'indolent puppet of court', who is the 'luxurious monster' and the 'fastidious sensualist' (p. 99). These metaphors culminate in the final potent image of the 'pestiferous purple' which sums up all that 'renders the progress of civilisation a curse, and warps the understanding' (p. 99).

Consequently, by the end of the chapter all that the reader can be certain of, all that she can glean from her instruction is that the transparent language and forceful reasoning promised earlier have become lost in a mist of words; and that, ironically, the text has reproduced the dazzling images and eloquent phrases it set out to avoid.

How, then, are we to interpret the apparent absence of clear, rational argument in a chapter which aims to deliver precisely that? What is the epistemological status of a text that formally offers itself as a (philosophical) treatise 'on female rights and manners' (p. 79), but which leaves the reader to wander unguided through the web of intertextual, often literary, allusions and sudden long digressions which comprise it? As one critic notes, another characteristic feature of this text is its hopelessly long sentences, imitative of the eighteenth-century rounded prose rejected by the 'Author's Introduction', where the reader comes panting to the end, a little unsure of what the subject was.[19] Moreover, what are we to make of the paradox that it is in the text's tropic supplementarity, and not in a forceful and rigorous 'philosophical' argument, that reason, or at least examples that help us to understand what the text means by reason, is found?[20] How, finally, should we approach the contradiction that the text reproduces what it most fears: metaphoricity, fictionality and, by extension, femininity, whereas reason – the effect of plain words – which is what the text most desires, constantly eludes it?

Not only is the light of reason eclipsed by metaphor, it is also displaced by the text's own rhetoric of temporality. This is indicated in the following assertion:

> Rousseau exerts himself to prove that all *was* right originally: a crowd of authors that all is now right: and I, that all will *be* right. (p. 95)

Thus, there is produced the contradiction that the text wishes to rationally state the case for moving towards a society based on the principles of reason and sexual equality to the non-rational, because contemporary, female reader. This is an anachronism that haunts the *Vindication* throughout and returns with full force at its close, where it is stated:

> That women at present are by ignorance rendered foolish or vicious is, I think, not to be disputed; and that the most salutary effects tending to improve mankind might be expected from a REVOLUTION in female manners, appears, at least, with a face of probability, to rise out of the observation. (p. 317)

Exactly like those 'silly' novels (p. 308) which the Vindication reproves because they 'are only addressed to the imagination' (p. 307), and because they entice women with improbable fantasies worked up in 'stale tales' and 'meretricious scenes' (p. 306), the *Vindication* itself can *only* address the imagination, since the possibility of women taking up a rational subject position in a language devoid of metaphor is deferred beyond the discursive limits of the present text.[21]

IV

Twentieth-century critics have shown a remarkable consistency in their approach to the contradictions I have outlined. They have unfailingly 'failed' the *Vindication* for its lack of a coherent argument, clear reasoning and a logical structure. Ralph Wardle's criticism of the text's 'lack of organisation', and of Wollstonecraft's inability to resist 'far-fetched metaphors which served only to cloud her meaning' is representative in this respect.[22] Miriam Brody is perhaps less so, for she remarks: 'It doesn't seem important any longer' to apologise for Wollstonecraft's style, 'since what she had to say was clear enough'.[23]

What is notable about the *Vindication*'s twentieth-century critics is their tendency not only to fail it, but also to fail its author. Even when critics are supportive, it is Wollstonecraft, not her text, who is implicitly critiqued. Invariably it is she, it is her temperament and her life, which critics turn to in order to account for what they perceive to be the *Vindication*'s chief 'flaw': namely, a lack of unity in content and structure. But if instead of seeking unity in Wollstonecraft's text, or more exactly her life, we focus our attention on how her text is produced from the range of meanings, beliefs and knowledges in circulation at the moment of its production, we are able to release the cultural relativity and historical instability, or disunity, of the system of differences which the text presents as self-evident and natural; for example, the difference of a philosophical from a literary rhetoric. Correspondingly, the project of interpretation shifts from a corrective position which bemoans a text's, or more often the author's failures, to one that, instead of employing the value-laden terms of success and failure, while claiming to undertake an 'objective', that is, value-free, assessment of 'good' writing, openly explores the political implications of the meanings of femininity and masculinity that are produced, and recognises that all critical practice is without objective criteria. One of the consequences of this way of reading is that culpability, especially authorial culpability, is no longer what is at issue, for the author is regarded not as the sovereign producer of meaning, but as the site where meanings converge and compete for a version of the 'truth'.

The *Vindication* may be read as a text that displays this conflict of meanings, thereby revealing their fundamental instability. Instead of attempting to unify the text's inconsistencies, or, alternatively, to mark it down because of them, I want to offer the thesis that the *Vindication* produces radical implications for an understanding of the historical construction of gendered meanings. Moreover, I propose that it does so precisely because of its inability to carry out the project of cementing an opposition between philosophical and literary uses of language, and its consequent incapacity to reason in the transparent 'unaffected' style promised by the 'Author's Introduction'. What is in question here is not whether the *Vindication* is a 'philosophical' failure, or even that it is, paradoxically, a 'literary' success; rather it is the possibility that the text radically subverts the extant binarism of genre and gender difference of the 1790s.

I have suggested that textual contradictions and uncertainties come into play in moments when the *Vindication*'s narrative oscillates between a rhetoric of 'philosophical rationalism' and a 'fictional feminine figurality'. At stake in this claim is the proposition that historical meanings are produced within a network of competing, unfixed and therefore changeable discourses. Also at stake is the historical specificity of those discourses and the meanings they produce. Eighteenth-century meanings of genre difference had precise implications for those of gender difference. For the twentieth-century critic to undo the genre differences in Wollstonecraft's text is simultaneously to collapse the gender difference inscribed in it. It is also, therefore, to side-step any consideration of the social power relations that inform those textual distinctions. This has not been my project. However, I would want to claim that we can reveal the instability of the opposition which the *Vindication* makes between fiction and philosophy. We can, for example, attend to the way in which a fictional or figural rhetoric displaces and subverts the seeming priority of philosophical argument, but in doing so we have always to be alert to the limits imposed on our interpretation of this past text by its own historical placement, and by the corresponding historical specificity of the meanings it constructs.

If this essay has privileged throughout the intertextual relationship between the *Vindication*'s literary and philosophical modes, it has done so not with the aim of collapsing these categories into one another, so that it becomes impossible to speak of literature and philosophy as such, but rather to emphasise the dialectical nature of their relationship. This relationship, then, is neither one of similitude nor one of mutual exclusivity. Each part of the opposition 'philosophy/literature' simultaneously defines and disrupts the other; the movement between them is never halted, the conflicts inscribed within it are never resolved; it is a movement which is precisely in process.

That the *Vindication* is ultimately unable to curtail and thereby contain its own textual operations of displacement and difference, with the result that it cannot produce a self-contained philosophical language, is evidenced by the constant invoking of a literary other within the text. It is also implied by the (literary) consequences of a 'Note' appended to the text. Here Wollstonecraft announces her intention to produce a second volume of the *Vindication*:

> When I began to write this work, I divided it into three parts, supposing that one volume would contain a full discussion of the arguments which seemed to me to rise naturally from a few simple principles; but fresh illustrations occurring as I advanced, I present only the first part to the public.
>
> Many subjects, however, which I have cursorily alluded to, call for further investigation, especially the laws relative to women, and the consideration of their peculiar duties. These will furnish ample matter for a second volume, which in due time will be published, to elucidate some of the sentiments, and complete many of the sketches begun in the first. (p. 90)

The promised additional volume never appeared, at least not as a philosophical treatise. What did appear – perhaps in its place – was the fiction *The Wrongs of Woman: or, Maria* which, unfinished at the time of Wollstonecraft's death, was edited by William Godwin and published posthumously in 1789.[24] As its title suggests and the authorial preface confirms, this text can be read as a fictional reworking of its predecessor's philosophical arguments. *The Wrongs of Woman* makes apparent what the *Vindication* suppresses all along: this is the impossibility of treating literature and philosophy as self-enclosed categories. *The Wrongs of Woman* is an eminently 'philosophical' fiction: its project, like that of the *Vindication* is to '[exhibit] the misery and oppression, peculiar to women, that arise out of the partial laws and customs of society'.[25] And its arguments, although inscribed in the language of fiction are no less 'philosophical' for that.

V

Why, though, should the 'flowery' prose of fiction seemingly supplant the 'unaffected' prose of philosophy as the desired and dominant language for the inscription of nascent feminist beliefs in the short but climactic years from the publication of *The Rights of Woman* in 1792 to *The Wrongs of Woman* in 1798?

Deconstructionist theory is useful in helping the critic answer this question, but only up to a point, or rather a limit. This limit is history; for, lacking a social theory, deconstruction is correspondingly unable to offer historical explanations, although it is not fundamentally incompatible with them. It can, however, offer textual ones, the value of which to any radical-minded critic I would not want to obscure.

Michael Ryan has suggested that the revolutionary potential of deconstruction consists in its overturning of some of the most treasured mainstays of bourgeois philosophy.[26] Used to analyse a text like the *Vindication*, deconstructive strategies enable the critic to question, for example, the primacy of consciousness and the self-evidence of the text's binary oppositions, philosophy/literature, nature/culture, eloquent language/elegant language and, implicitly, male/female. To question the primacy of consciousness has the effect of displacing authorial intention as the source and guarantee of meaning. This displacement produces a fundamentally unstable text whose competing discursive modes struggle for dominance. Consequently, it is the relation between discourses, rather than the discourses themselves, which is brought into the foreground, and it is the unknown, uncertain, ceaselessly changing space between them which becomes the new critical terrain. Meanings are unfixed and the status quo is shown to be never quite that: the struggle between discourses replaces the possibility of any balanced or harmonious existence, however temporary.

Similarly, recognition of the differential interconstitution of a text's seemingly self-evident binary oppositions produces a reading of the *Vindication* which focuses on the relations of struggle that operate in the margins of the difference the text has as its project to cement. For if the *Vindication*'s inability to avoid what it condemns, namely 'pretty feminine phrases', 'flowery diction', rounded sentences and artificial, because constructed, tropes indicates metaphoricity as norm rather than anomaly, then the text produces not a theory of the transparent capacity of language, nor evidence of the 'simple truths' and 'first principles' assumed to pre-exist discursively constituted meanings. Rather, it produces a theory of the differential nature of textuality and offers a 'negative affirmation' of the infinite displacement and deferral of meaning.[27] Starting with a conviction of difference, the text ends by affirming differance (in the Derridean sense of to differ and to defer).

A deconstructive analysis can, then, offer textual difference as an explanation of why the *Vindication* is unable to reconcile the conflict of its competing 'philosophical' and 'literary' languages; and why, therefore, 'part two' was never produced in the promised form of a (philosophical) treatise. But this explanation points only to the impossibility of any self-enclosed discourse or system of knowledge, which would equally explain why fictions such as *The Wrongs of Woman* contain 'philosophical' passages and produce political insights.

Thus, in order to use deconstructive strategies for readings of past texts it may be useful, necessary even, to take account of history. Recourse to the historical specificity of meanings enables us to state the difference between eighteenth- and twentieth-century attitudes to genre and gender difference. It also has the corresponding effect of removing the temptation to endlessly deconstruct oppositions beyond the defining, albeit metaphysical, framework of meanings within which we make sense of the world – past and present. Could it be, then, that by temporarily limiting deconstruction's inherent lack of finality and fleetingly halting its capacity for limitless textual free play, so that, paradoxically, this limitlessness is curtailed and held to historical account, deconstruction is rendered more politically 'responsible' and more politically 'useful'?

This is a double-edged question. On the one hand it is this limitlessness, the indefinite sliding of signification that deconstruction identifies, which offers the most potentially revolutionary analysis of textual events; yet on the other, it also offers the most potentially reactionary ones. To acknowledge, for example, the open-ended possibility of metaphoric displacement in the *Vindication* usefully undoes the text's binary opposition of philosophy/literature, as well as challenging the surety of the gendered assumptions that inform it; but it also (potentially) collapses these terms and thereby effaces their historically specific meanings and political effects.

This is unsatisfactory, at least for me, because the distinction the *Vindication* makes between philosophical and literary genres is not only a textual but also a sexual one, which had precise political effects, delimiting what women were able to do, say and write. This is evidenced in part by the shift in popularity away from philosophical texts that occurred during the 1790s.

Marilyn Butler has observed that 'during the years 1797–8 the word "philosopher" becomes a term of abuse in popular fiction, drama and journalism, connoting atheist, seducer, plotter and revolutionary'.[28] In the context of Romanticism both philosophy and philosophers were denounced on the grounds that they were unnatural. The female philosopher was especially vulnerable to this charge. Lying behind the force of satiric attacks on female philosophers was the accusation that they unnaturally confused distinctions of sex. Mary Robinson's novel *The False Friend* offers one example of the combination of derision and fear which the idea of a female philosopher occasioned in men. In this novel a man accuses a woman of shortly becoming 'a he-she philosopher'.[29] Other examples include Mrs Opie's *Adeline Mowbray*, whose heroine of that ilk is, like Wollstonecraft, dubbed a hyena because of her refusal to adhere to the conventions of her sex.[30] Perhaps the best-known caricature of militant feminist philosophy in fiction is the figure cut by the significantly named Harriot Freake in Maria Edgeworth's popular novel *Belinda* (1801).[31]

The reaction against philosophy in general and philosophising women in particular did not take place in a vacuum. Rather, it emerged as one of the effects of the conservative backlash in British politics during the 1790s, which was in part a response to the increasing violence of the French Revolution. Wollstonecraft was not the only English radical to replace an attempt at the abstract reasoning of philosophy with the specific interrogations of a fictional mode increasingly concerned with subjectivity. The shift from the *Vindication*'s optimistic detailing of things as they might be to *The Wrongs of Woman*'s more pessimistic portrayal of 'things as they are' also characterises the difference of William Godwin's *Enquiry Concerning Political Justice* (1793) from his fiction *Things As They Are: or, The Adventures of Caleb Williams* (1794).[32]

On another level this shift can be described in terms of the transition from Radicalism to Romanticism. Both of Wollstonecraft's texts are products of this transitional period in British literature; *The Wrongs of Woman* in particular displays the conflict between this period's opposing discourses of collective radicalism and individual Romanticism.

To recognise the historical shifts of the 1780s–1790s and to account for the generic shaping of Wollstonecraft's texts in the light of them is not to re-fix historical meanings, thus lending to them the authority that deconstruction usefully denies, nor is it to offer totalising solutions from the hindsight made possible by reading from the perspective of 'now'; instead, it is to read past texts in their difference from the present. It is, perhaps, consciously to look in our readings of past texts for the textual operation of what is possibly deconstruction's most radical recognition: namely, differance. To attend to difference – both historical and sexual – is to release differance. It is also the first step towards denaturalising sexual difference, thereby exposing its historical relativity and cultural constitution, and so giving us a firmer grasp on understanding our own process of gender formation.

12

Three Women's Texts and a Critique of Imperialism

Gayatri Chakravorty Spivak

It should not be possible to read nineteenth-century British literature without remembering that imperialism, understood as England's social mission, was a crucial part of the cultural representation of England to the English. The role of literature in the production of cultural representation should not be ignored. These two obvious 'facts' continue to be disregarded in the reading of nineteenth-century British literature. This itself attests to the continuing success of the imperialist project, displaced and dispersed into more modern forms.

If these 'facts' were remembered, not only in the study of British literature but in the study of the literatures of the European colonising cultures of the great age of imperialism, we would produce a narrative, in literary history, of the 'worlding' of what is now called 'the Third World'. To consider the Third World as distant cultures, exploited but with rich intact literary heritages waiting to be recovered, interpreted, and curricularised in English translation fosters the emergence of 'the Third World' as a signifier that allows us to forget that 'worlding', even as it expands the empire of the literary discipline.[1]

It seems particularly unfortunate when the emergent perspective of feminist criticism reproduces the axioms of imperialism. A basically isolationist admiration for the literature of the female subject in Europe and Anglo-America establishes the high feminist norm. It is supported and operated by an information-retrieval approach to 'Third World' literature which often employs a deliberately 'non-theoretical' methodology with self-conscious rectitude.

In this essay, I will attempt to examine the operation of the 'worlding' of what is today 'the Third World' by what has become a cult text of feminism: *Jane Eyre*.[2] I plot the novel's reach and grasp, and locate its structural motors. I read *Wide Sargasso Sea* as *Jane Eyre*'s reinscription and *Frankenstein* as an analysis – even a deconstruction – of a 'worlding' such as *Jane Eyre*'s.[3]

I need hardly mention that the object of my investigation is the printed book, not its 'author'. To make such a distinction is, of course, to ignore the lessons of deconstruction. A deconstructive critical approach would loosen the binding of the book, undo the opposition between verbal text and the bio-graphy of the named subject 'Charlotte Brontë', and see the two as each other's 'scene of writing'. In such a reading, the life that writes itself as 'my life' is as much a production in psychosocial space (other names can be found) as the book that is written by the holder of that named life – a book that is then consigned to what is most often recognised as genuinely 'social': the world of publication and distribution.[4] To touch Brontë's 'life' in such a way, however, would be too risky here. We must rather strategically take shelter in an essentialism which, not wishing to lose the important advantages won by US mainstream feminism, will continue to honour the suspect binary oppositions – book and author, individual and history – and start with an assurance of the following sort: my readings here do not seek to undermine the excellence of the individual artist. If even minimally successful, the readings will incite a degree of rage against the imperialist narrativisation of history, that it should produce so abject a script for her. I provide these assurances to allow myself some room to situate feminist individualism in its historical determination rather than simply to canonise it as feminism as such.

Sympathetic US feminists have remarked that I do not do justice to Jane Eyre's subjectivity. A word of explanation is perhaps in order. The broad strokes of my presuppositions are that what is at stake, for feminist individualism in the age of imperialism, is precisely the making of human beings, the constitution and 'interpellation' of the subject not only as individual but as 'individualist'.[5] This stake is represented on two registers: childbearing and soul making. The first is domestic-society-through-sexual-reproduction cathected as 'companionate love'; the second is the imperialist project cathected as civil-society-through-social-mission. As the female individualist, not-quite/not-male, articulates herself in shifting relationship to what is at stake, the 'native female' as such (*within* discourse, *as* a signifier) is excluded from any share in this emerging norm.[6] If we read this account from an isolationist perspective in a 'metropolitan' context, we see nothing here but the psychobiography of the militant female subject. In a reading such as mine, in contrast, the effort is to wrench oneself away from the mesmerising focus of the 'subject-constitution' of the female individualist.

To develop further the notion that my stance need not be an accusing one, I will refer to a passage from Roberto Fernández Retamar's 'Caliban'.[7] José Enrique Rodó had argued in 1900 that the model for the Latin American intellectual in relationship to Europe could be Shakespeare's Ariel.[8] In 1971 Retamar, denying the possibility of an identifiable 'Latin American Culture', recast the model as Caliban. Not surprisingly, this powerful exchange still excludes any specific consideration of the civilisations of the Maya, the Aztecs, the Incas, or the smaller nations of what is now called Latin America. Let us note carefully that, at this stage of my argument, this 'conversation' between Europe and Latin America (without a specific consideration of the political economy of the 'worlding' of the 'native') provides a sufficient thematic description of our attempt to confront the ethnocentric and reverse-ethnocentric benevolent double bind (that is, considering the 'native' as object for enthusiastic information-retrieval and thus denying its own 'worlding') that I sketched in my opening paragraphs.

In a moving passage in 'Caliban', Retamar locates both Caliban and Ariel in the postcolonial intellectual:

> There is no real Ariel–Caliban polarity: both are slaves in the hands of Prospero, the foreign magician. But Caliban is the rude and unconquerable master of the island, while Ariel, a creature of the air, although also a child of the isle, the intellectual.
>
> The deformed Caliban – enslaved, robbed of his island, and taught the language by Prospero – rebukes him thus: 'You taught me language, and my profit on't / Is, I know how to curse.' ('C', pp. 28, 11)

As we attempt to unlearn our so-called privilege as Ariel and 'seek from [a certain] Caliban the honour of a place in his rebellious and glorious ranks', we do not ask that our students and colleagues should emulate us but that they should attend to us ('C', p. 72). If, however, we are driven by a nostalgia for lost origins, we too run the risk of effacing the 'native' and stepping forth as 'the real Caliban', of forgetting that he is a name in a play, an inaccessible blankness circumscribed by an interpretable text.[9] The stagings of Caliban work alongside the narrativisation of history: claiming to *be* Caliban legitimises the very individualism that we must persistently attempt to undermine from within.

Elizabeth Fox-Genovese, in an article on history and women's history, shows us how to define the historical moment of feminism in the West in terms of female access to individualism.[10] The battle for female individualism plays itself out within the larger theatre of the establishment of meritocratic individualism, indexed in the aesthetic field by the ideology of 'the creative imagination'. Fox-Genovese's presupposition will guide us into the beautifully orchestrated opening of *Jane Eyre*.

It is a scene of the marginalisation and privatisation of the protagonist: 'There was no possibility of taking a walk that day. . . . Out-door exercise was now out of the question. I was glad of it', Brontë writes (*JE*, p. 9). The movement continues as Jane breaks the rules of the appropriate topography of withdrawal. The family at the centre withdraws into the sanctioned architectural space of the withdrawing room or drawing room; Jane inserts herself – 'I slipped in' – into the margin – 'A small breakfast room *adjoined* the drawing room' (*JE*, p. 9; my emphasis).

The manipulation of the domestic inscription of space within the upwardly mobilising currents of the eighteenth- and nineteenth-century bourgeoisie in England and France is well known. It seems fitting that the place to which Jane withdraws is not only not the withdrawing room but also not the dining room, the sanctioned place of family meals. Nor is it the library, the appropriate place for reading. The breakfast room 'contained a book-case' (*JE*, p. 9). As Rudolph Ackermann wrote in his Repository (1823), one of the many manuals of taste in circulation in nineteenth-century England, these low bookcases and stands were designed to 'contain all the books that may be desired for a sitting-room without reference to the library'.[11] Even in this already triply off-centre place, 'having drawn the red moreen curtain nearly close, I [Jane] was shrined in double retirement' (*JE*, pp. 9-10).

Here in Jane's self-marginalised uniqueness, the reader becomes her accomplice: the reader and Jane are united – both are reading. Yet Jane still preserves her odd privilege, for she continues never quite doing the proper thing in its proper place. She cares little for reading what is *meant* to be read: the 'letter-press'. *She* reads the pictures. The power of this singular hermeneutics is precisely that it can make the outside inside. 'At intervals, while turning over the leaves of my book, I studied the aspect of that winter afternoon.' Under 'the clear panes of glass', the rain no longer penetrates, 'the drear November day' is rather a one-dimensional 'aspect' to be 'studied', not decoded like the 'letter-press' but, like pictures, deciphered by the unique creative imagination of the marginal individualist (*JE*, p. 10).

Before following the track of this unique imagination, let us consider the suggestion that the progress of *Jane Eyre* can be charted through a sequential arrangement of the family/counter-family dyad. In the novel, we encounter, first, the Reeds as the legal family and Jane, the late Mr Reed's sister's daughter, as the representative of a near incestuous counter-family; second, the Brocklehursts, who run the school Jane is sent to, as the legal family and Jane, Miss Temple, and Helen Burns as a counter-family that falls short because it is only a community of women; third, Rochester and the mad Mrs Rochester as the legal family and Jane and Rochester as the illicit counter-family. Other items may be added to the thematic chain in this sequence: Rochester and Céline Varens as structurally functional counter-family; Rochester and Blanche Ingram as dissimulation of legality – and so on. It is during this sequence that Jane is moved from the counter-family to the family-in-law. In the next sequence, it is Jane who restores full family status to the as-yet-incomplete community of siblings, the Riverses. The final sequence of the book is a *community of families*, with Jane, Rochester, and their children at the centre.

In terms of the narrative energy of the novel, how is Jane moved from the place of the counter-family to the family-in-law? It is the active ideology of imperialism that provides the discursive field.

Let us consider the figure of Bertha Mason, a figure produced by the axiomatics of imperialism. Through Bertha Mason, the white Jamaican Creole, Brontë renders the human/animal frontier as acceptably indeterminate, so that a good greater than the letter of the Law can be broached. Here is the celebrated passage, given in the voice of Jane:

> In the deep shade, at the further end of the room, a figure ran backwards and forwards. What it was, whether beast or human being, one could not . . . tell: it grovelled, seemingly, on all fours; it snatched and growled like some strange wild animal: but it was covered with clothing, and a quantity of dark, grizzled hair, wild as a mane, hid its head and face. (*JE*, p. 295)

In a matching passage, given in the voice of Rochester speaking *to* Jane, Brontë presents the imperative for a shift beyond the Law as divine injunction rather than human motive. In the terms of my essay, we might say that this is the register not of mere marriage or sexual reproduction but of Europe and its not-yet-human other, of soul making. The field of imperial conquest is here inscribed as Hell:

> 'One night I had been awakened by her yells . . . it was a fiery West Indian night. . . .
> '"This life," said I at last, "is hell! – this is the air – those are the sounds of the bottomless pit! *I have a right* to deliver myself from it if I can. . . . Let me break away, and go home to God!" . . .
> 'A wind fresh from Europe blew over the ocean and rushed through the open casement: the storm broke, streamed, thundered, blazed, and the air grew pure. . . . It was true Wisdom that consoled me in that hour, and showed me the right path. . . .
> 'The sweet wind from Europe was still whispering in the refreshed leaves, and the Atlantic was thundering in glorious liberty. . . .
> '"Go," said Hope, "and live again in Europe. . . . You have done all that God and Humanity require of you."' (*JE*, pp. 310–11; my emphasis)

It is the unquestioned ideology of imperialist axiomatics, then, that conditions Jane's move from the counter-family set to the set of the family-in-law. Marxist critics such as Terry Eagleton have seen this only in terms of the ambiguous *class* position of the governess.[12] Sandra Gilbert and Susan Gubar, on the other hand, have seen Bertha Mason only in psychological terms, as Jane's dark double.[13]

I will not enter the critical debates that offer themselves here. Instead, I will develop the suggestion that nineteenth-century feminist individualism could conceive of a 'greater' project than access to the closed circle of the nuclear family. This is the project of soul making beyond 'mere' sexual reproduction. Here the native 'subject' is not almost an animal but rather the object of what might be termed the terrorism of the categorical imperative.

I am using 'Kant' in this essay as a metonym for the most flexible ethical moment in the European eighteenth century. Kant words the categorical imperative, conceived as the universal moral law given by pure reason, in this way: 'In all creation every thing one chooses and over which one has any power, may be used *merely as means*; man alone, and with him every rational creature, is an *end in himself*.' It is thus a moving displacement of Christian ethics from religion to philosophy. As Kant writes: 'With this agrees very well the possibility of such a command as: *Love God above everything, and thy neighbour as thyself*. For as a command it requires respect for a law which *commands love* and does not leave it to our own arbitrary choice to make this our principle.'[14]

The 'categorical' in Kant cannot be adequately represented in determinately grounded action. The dangerous transformative power of philosophy, however, is that its formal subtlety can be travestied in the service of the state. Such a travesty in the case of the categorical imperative can justify the imperialist project by producing the following formula: *make* the heathen into a human so that he can be treated as an end in himself.[15] This project is presented as a sort of tangent in *Jane Eyre*, a tangent that escapes the closed circle of the *narrative* conclusion. The tangent narrative is the story of St John Rivers, who is granted the important task of concluding the *text*.

At the novel's end, the *allegorical* language of Christian psycho-biography – rather than the textually constituted and seemingly *private* grammar of the creative imagination which we noted in the novel's opening – marks the inaccessibility of the imperialist project as such to the nascent 'feminist' scenario. The concluding passage of *Jane Eyre* places St John Rivers within the fold of *Pilgrim's Progress*. Eagleton pays no attention to this but accepts the novel's ideological lexicon, which establishes St John Rivers' heroism by identifying a life in Calcutta with an unquestioning choice of death. Gilbert and Gubar, by calling *Jane Eyre* 'Plain Jane's progress', see the novel as simply replacing the male protagonist with the female. They do not notice the distance between sexual reproduction and soul making, both actualised by the unquestioned idiom of imperialist presuppositions evident in the last part of *Jane Eyre*:

Firm, faithful, and devoted, full of energy, and zeal, and truth, [St. John Rivers] labours for his race. . . . His is the sternness of the warrior

Greatheart, who guards his pilgrim convoy from the onslaught of Apollyon. . . . His is the ambition of the high master-spirit[s] . . . who stand without fault before the throne of God; who share the last mighty victories of the Lamb; who are called, and chosen, and faithful. (*JE*, p. 455)

Earlier in the novel, St John Rivers himself justifies the project: 'My vocation? My great work? . . . My hopes of being numbered in the band who have merged all ambitions in the glorious one of bettering their race – of carrying knowledge into the realms of ignorance – of substituting peace for war – freedom for bondage – religion for superstition – the hope of heaven for the fear of hell?' (*JE*, p. 376). Imperialism and its territorial and subject-constituting project are a violent deconstruction of these oppositions.

When Jean Rhys, born on the Caribbean island of Dominica, read *Jane Eyre* as a child, she was moved by Bertha Mason: 'I thought I'd try to write her a life.'[16] *Wide Sargasso Sea*, the slim novel published in 1965, at the end of Rhys's long career, is that 'life'.

I have suggested that Bertha's function in *Jane Eyre* is to render indeterminate the boundary between human and animal and thereby to weaken her entitlement under the spirit if not the letter of the Law. When Rhys rewrites the scene in *Jane Eyre* where Jane hears 'a snarling, snatching sound, almost like a dog quarrelling' and then encounters a bleeding Richard Mason (*JE*, p. 210), she keeps Bertha's humanity, indeed her sanity as critic of imperialism, intact. Grace Poole, another character originally in *Jane Eyre*, describes the incident to Bertha in *Wide Sargasso Sea*: 'So you don't remember that you attacked this gentleman with a knife? . . . I didn't hear all he said except "I cannot interfere legally between yourself and your husband." It was when he said "legally" that you flew at him' (*WSS*, p. 150). In Rhys's retelling, it is the dissimulation that Bertha discerns in the word 'legally' – not an innate bestiality – that prompts her violent *reaction*.

In the figure of Antoinette, whom in *Wide Sargasso Sea* Rochester violently renames Bertha, Rhys suggests that so intimate a thing as personal and human identity might be determined by the politics of imperialism. Antoinette, as a white Creole child growing up at the time of emancipation in Jamaica, is caught between the English imperialist and the black native. In recounting Antoinette's development, Rhys reinscribes some thematics of Narcissus.

There are, noticeably, many images of mirroring in the text. I will quote one from the first section. In this passage, Tia is the little black servant girl who is Antoinette's close companion: 'We had eaten the same food, slept side by side, bathed in the same river. As I ran, I thought, I will live with Tia and I will be like her. . . . When I was close I saw the jagged stone in her hand but I did not see her throw it. . . . We stared at each other, blood on my face, tears on hers. It was as if I saw myself. Like in a looking glass' (*WSS*, p. 38).

A progressive sequence of dreams reinforces this mirror imagery. In its second occurrence, the dream is partially set in a *hortus conclusus*, or 'enclosed garden' – Rhys uses the phrase (*WSS*, p. 50) – a Romance rewriting of the Narcissus topos as the place of encounter with Love.[17] In the enclosed garden, Antoinette encounters not Love but a strange threatening voice that says merely 'in here', inviting her into a prison which masquerades as the legalisation of love (*WSS*, p. 50).

In Ovid's *Metamorphoses*, Narcissus' madness is disclosed when he recognises his other as his self: 'Iste ego sum.'[18] Rhys makes Antoinette see her *self* as her other, Brontë's Bertha. In the last section of *Wide Sargasso Sea*, Antoinette acts out *Jane Eyre's* conclusion and recognises herself as the so-called ghost in Thornfield Hall: 'I went into the hall again with the tall candle in my hand. It was then that I saw her – the ghost. The woman with streaming hair. She was surrounded by a gilt frame but I knew her' (*WSS*, p. 154). The gilt frame encloses a mirror: as Narcissus' pool reflects the selfed other, so this 'pool' reflects the othered self. Here the dream sequence ends, with an invocation of none other than Tia, the other that could not be selfed, because the fracture of imperialism rather than the Ovidian pool intervened. (I will return to this difficult point.) 'That was the third time I had my dream, and it ended. . . . I called "Tia" and jumped and woke' (*WSS*, p. 155). It is now, at the very end of the book, that Antoinette/Bertha can say: 'Now at last I know why I was brought here and what I have to do' (*WSS*, pp. 155–6). We can read this as her having been brought into the England of Brontë's novel: 'This cardboard house' – a book between cardboard covers – 'where I walk at night is not England' (*WSS*, p. 148). In this fictive England, she must play out her role, act out the transformation of her 'self' into that fictive other, set fire to the house and kill herself, so that Jane Eyre can become the feminist individualist heroine of British fiction. I must read this as an allegory of the general epistemic violence of imperialism, the construction of a self-immolating colonial subject for the glorification of the social mission of the coloniser. At least Rhys sees to it that the woman from the colonies is not sacrificed as an insane animal for her sister's consolation.

Nevertheless, *Wide Sargasso Sea* marks with uncanny clarity the limits of its own discourse in Christophine, Antoinette's black nurse. We may perhaps surmise the distance between *Jane Eyre* and *Wide Sargasso Sea* by remarking that Christophine's unfinished story is the tangent to the latter narrative, as St John Rivers' story is to the former. Christophine is not a native of Jamaica; she is from Martinique. Taxonomically, she belongs to the category of the good servant rather than that of the pure native. But within these borders, Rhys creates a powerfully suggestive figure.

Christophine is the first interpreter and named speaking subject in the text. 'The Jamaican ladies had never approved of my mother, "because she pretty like pretty self" Christophine said', we read in the book's opening paragraph (*WSS*, p. 15). I have taught this book five times, once in France, once to students who had worked on the book with the well-known Caribbean novelist Wilson Harris, and once at a prestigious institute where the majority of the students were faculty from other universities. It is part of the political argument I am making that all these students blithely stepped over this paragraph without asking or knowing what Christophine's patois, so-called incorrect English, might mean.

Christophine is, of course, a commodified person. '"She was your father's wedding present to me"' explains Antoinette's mother, '"one of his presents"' (*WSS*, p. 18). Yet Rhys assigns her some crucial functions in the text. It is Christophine who judges that black ritual practices are culture-specific and cannot be used by whites as cheap remedies for social evils, such as Rochester's lack of love for Antoinette. Most important, it is Christophine alone whom Rhys allows to offer a hard analysis of Rochester's actions, to challenge him in a face-to face encounter. The entire extended passage is worthy of comment. I quote a brief extract:

> 'She is Creole girl, and she have the sun in her. Tell the truth now. She don't come to your house in this place England they tell me about, she don't come to your beautiful house to beg you to marry with her. No, it's you come all the long way to her house – it's you beg her to marry. And she love you and she give you all she have. Now you say you don't love her and you break her up. What you do with her money, eh?' [And then Rochester, the white man, comments silently to himself] Her voice was still quiet but with a hiss in it when she said 'money.' (*WSS*, p. 130)

Her analysis is powerful enough for the white man to be afraid: 'I no longer felt dazed, tired, half hypnotised, but alert and wary, ready to defend myself' (*WSS*, p. 130).

Rhys does not, however, romanticise individual heroics on the part of the oppressed. When the Man refers to the forces of Law and Order, Christophine recognises their power. This exposure of civil inequality is emphasised by the fact that, just before the Man's successful threat, Christophine had invoked the emancipation of slaves in Jamaica by proclaiming: 'No chain gang, no tread machine, no dark jail either. This is free country and I am free woman' (*WSS*, p. 131).

As I mentioned above, Christophine is tangential to this narrative. She cannot be contained by a novel which rewrites a canonical English text within the European novelistic tradition in the interest of the white Creole rather than the native. No perspective *critical* of imperialism can turn the other into a self, because the project of imperialism has always already historically refracted what might have been the absolutely other into a domesticated other that consolidates the imperialist self.[19] The Caliban of Retamar, caught between Europe and Latin America, reflects this predicament. We can read Rhys's reinscription of Narcissus as a thematisation of the same problematic.

Of course, we cannot know Jean Rhys's feelings in the matter. We can, however, look at the scene of Christophine's inscription in the text. Immediately after the exchange between her and the Man, well before the conclusion, she is simply driven out of the story, with neither narrative nor characterological explanation or justice. '"Read and write I don't know. Other things I know." She walked away without looking back' (*WSS*, p. 133).

Indeed, if Rhys rewrites the madwoman's attack on the Man by underlining of the use of 'legality', she cannot deal with the passage that corresponds to St John Rivers' own justification of his martyrdom, for it has been displaced into the current idiom of modernisation and development. Attempts to construct the 'Third World Woman' as a signifier remind us that the hegemonic definition of literature is itself caught within the history of imperialism. A full literary reinscription cannot easily flourish in the imperialist fracture or discontinuity, covered over by an alien legal system masquerading as Law as such, an alien ideology established as only Truth, and a set of human sciences busy establishing the 'native' as self-consolidating other.

In the Indian case at least, it would be difficult to find an ideological clue to the planned epistemic violence of imperialism merely by rearranging curricula or syllabi within existing norms of literary pedagogy. For a later period of imperialism – when the constituted colonial subject has firmly taken hold – straightforward experiments of comparison can be undertaken, say, between the functionally witless India of *Mrs Dalloway*, on the one hand, and literary texts produced in India in the 1920s, on the other. But the first half of the nineteenth century resists questioning through literature or literary criticism in the narrow sense, because both are implicated in the project of producing Ariel. To reopen the fracture without succumbing to a nostalgia for lost origins, the literary critic must turn to the archives of imperial governance.

In conclusion, I shall look briefly at Mary Shelley's *Frankenstein*, a text of nascent feminism that remains cryptic, I think, simply because it does not speak the language of feminist individualism which we have come to hail as the language of high feminism within English literature. It is interesting that Barbara Johnson's brief study tries to rescue this recalcitrant text for the service of feminist autobiography.[20] Alternatively, George Levine reads *Frankenstein* in the context of the creative imagination and the nature of the hero. He sees the novel as a book about its own writing and about writing itself, a Romantic allegory of reading within which Jane Eyre as unself-conscious critic would fit quite nicely.[21]

I propose to take *Frankenstein* out of this arena and focus on it in terms of that sense of English cultural identity which I invoked at the opening of this essay. Within that focus we are obliged to admit that, although *Frankenstein* is ostensibly about the origin and evolution of man in society, it does not deploy the axiomatics of imperialism.

Let me say at once that there is plenty of incidental imperialist sentiment in *Frankenstein*. My point, within the argument of this essay, is that the discursive field of imperialism does not produce unquestioned ideological correlatives for the narrative structuring of the book. The discourse of imperialism surfaces in a curiously powerful way in Shelley's novel, and I will later discuss the moment at which it emerges.

Frankenstein is not a battleground of male and female individualism articulated in terms of sexual reproduction (family and female) and social subject-production (race and male). That binary opposition is undone in Victor Frankenstein's laboratory – an artificial womb where both projects are undertaken simultaneously, though the terms are never openly spelled out. Frankenstein's apparent antagonist is God himself as Maker of Man, but his real competitor is also woman as the maker of children. It is not just that his dream of the death of mother and bride and the actual death of his bride are associated with the visit of his monstrous homoerotic 'son' to his bed. On a much more overt level, the monster is a bodied 'corpse,' unnatural because bereft of a determinable childhood: 'No father had watched my infant days, no mother had blessed me with smiles and caresses; or if they had, all my past was now a blot, a blind vacancy in which I distinguished nothing' (*F*, pp. 57, 115). It is Frankenstein's own ambiguous and miscued understanding of the real motive for the monster's vengefulness that reveals his own competition with woman as maker:

> I created a rational creature and was bound towards him to assure, as far as was in my power, his happiness and well-being. This was my duty, but there was another still paramount to that. My duties towards the beings of my own species had greater claims to my attention because they included a greater proportion of happiness or misery. Urged by this view, I refused, and I did right in refusing, to create a companion for the first creature. (*F*, p. 206)

It is impossible not to notice the accents of transgression inflecting Frankenstein's demolition of his experiment to create the future Eve. Even in the laboratory, the woman-in-the-making is not a bodied corpse but 'a human being'. The (il)logic of the metaphor bestows on her a prior existence which Frankenstein aborts, rather than an anterior death which he re-embodies: 'The remains of the half-finished creature, whom I had destroyed, lay scattered on the floor, and I almost felt as if I had mangled the living flesh of a human being' (*F*, p. 163).

In Shelley's view, man's hubris as soul maker both usurps the place of God and attempts – vainly – to sublate woman's physiological prerogative.[22] Indeed, indulging a Freudian fantasy here, I could urge that, if to give and withhold to/from the mother a phallus is *the* male fetish, then to give and withhold to/from the man a womb might be the female fetish.[23] The icon of the sublimated womb in man is surely his productive brain, the box in the head.

In the judgment of classical psychoanalysis, the phallic mother exists only by virtue of the castration-anxious son; in *Frankenstein's* judgment, the hysteric father (Victor Frankenstein gifted with his laboratory – the womb of theoretical reason) cannot produce a daughter. Here the language of racism – the dark side of imperialism understood as social mission – combines with the hysteria of masculism into the idiom of (the withdrawal of) sexual reproduction rather than subject-constitution. The roles of masculine and feminine individualists are hence reversed and displaced. Frankenstein cannot produce a 'daughter' because 'she might become ten thousand times more malignant than her mate . . . [and because] one of the first results of those sympathies for which the demon thirsted would be children, and a race of devils would be propagated upon the earth who might make the very existence of the species of man a condition precarious and full of terror' (*F*, p. 158). This particular narrative strand also launches a thoroughgoing critique of the eighteenth-century European discourses on the origin of society through (Western Christian) man. Should I mention that, much like Jean-Jacques Rousseau's remark in his *Confessions*, Frankenstein declares himself to be 'by birth a Genevese' (*F*, p. 31)?

In this overtly didactic text, Shelley's point is that social engineering should not be based on pure, theoretical, or natural-scientific reason alone, which is her implicit critique of the utilitarian vision of an engineered society. To this end, she presents in the first part of her deliberately schematic story three characters, childhood friends, who seem to represent Kant's three-part conception of the human subject: Victor Frankenstein, the forces of theoretical reason or 'natural philosophy'; Henry Clerval, the forces of practical reason or 'the moral relations of things'; and Elizabeth Lavenza, that aesthetic judgment – 'the aerial creation of the poets' – which, according to Kant, is 'fit to be the mediating link between the realm of the natural and that of the concept of freedom . . . (which) promotes . . . *moral* feeling' (*F*, pp. 37, 36).[24]

This three-part subject does not operate harmoniously in *Frankenstein*. That Henry Clerval, associated as he is with practical reason, should have as his 'design . . . to visit India, in the belief that he had in his knowledge of its various languages, and in the views he had taken of its society, the means of materially assisting the progress of European colonisation and trade' is proof of this, as well as part of the incidental imperialist sentiment that I speak of above (*F*, pp. 151–2). I should perhaps point out that the language here is entrepreneurial rather than missionary:

> He came to the university with the design of making himself complete master of the Oriental languages, as thus he should open a field for the plan of life he had marked out for himself. Resolved to pursue no inglorious career, he turned his eyes towards the East as affording scope for his spirit of enterprise. The Persian, Arabic, and Sanskrit languages engaged his attention. (*F*, pp. 66–7)

But it is of course Victor Frankenstein, with his strange itinerary of obsession with natural philosophy, who offers the strongest demonstration that the multiple perspectives of the three-part Kantian subject cannot co-operate harmoniously. Frankenstein creates a putative human subject out of natural philosophy alone. According to his own miscued summation: 'In a fit of enthusiastic madness I created a rational creature' (*F*, p. 206). It is not at all farfetched to say that Kant's categorical imperative can most easily be mistaken for the hypothetical imperative – a command to ground in cognitive comprehension what can be apprehended only by moral will – by putting natural philosophy in the place of practical reason.

I should hasten to add here that just as readings such as this one do not necessarily accuse Charlotte Brontë the named individual of harbouring imperialist sentiments, so also they do not necessarily commend Mary Shelley the named individual for writing a successful Kantian allegory. The most I can say is that it is possible to read these texts, within the frame of imperialism and the Kantian ethical moment, in a politically useful way. Such an approach presupposes that a 'disinterested' reading attempts to render transparent the interests of the hegemonic readership. (Other 'political' readings – for instance, that the monster is the nascent working class – can also be advanced.)

Frankenstein is built in the established epistolary tradition of multiple frames. At the heart of the multiple frames, the narrative of the monster (as reported by Frankenstein to Robert Walton, who then recounts it in a letter to his sister) is of his almost learning, clandestinely, to be human. It is invariably noticed that the monster reads *Paradise Lost* as true history. What is not so often noticed is that he also reads Plutarch's *Lives*, 'the histories of the first founders of the ancient republics', which he compares to 'the patriarchal lives of my protectors' (*F*, pp. 123, 124). And his *education* comes through 'Volney's *Ruins of Empires*,' which purported to be a prefiguration of the French Revolution, published after the event and after the author had rounded off his theory with practice (*F*, p. 113). It is an attempt at an enlightened universal secular, rather than a Eurocentric Christian, history, written from the perspective of a narrator 'from below', somewhat like the attempts of Eric Wolf or Peter Worsley in our own time.[25]

This Caliban's education in (universal secular) humanity takes place through the monster's eavesdropping on the instruction of an Ariel – Safie, the Christianised 'Arabian' to whom 'a residence in Turkey was abhorrent' (*F*, p. 121). In depicting Safie, Shelley uses some commonplaces of eighteenth-century liberalism that are shared by many today: Safie's Muslim father was a victim of (bad) Christian religious prejudice and yet was himself a wily and ungrateful man not as morally refined as her (good) Christian mother. Having tasted the emancipation of woman, Safie could not go home. The confusion between 'Turk' and 'Arab' has its counterpart in present-day confusion about Turkey and Iran as 'Middle Eastern' but not 'Arab'.

Although we are a far cry here from the unexamined and covert axiomatics of imperialism in *Jane Eyre*, we will gain nothing by celebrating the time-bound pieties that Shelley, as the daughter of two anti-evangelicals, produces. It is more interesting for us that Shelley differentiates the other, works at the Caliban/Ariel distinction, and *cannot* make the monster identical with the proper recipient of these lessons. Although he had 'heard of the discovery of the American hemisphere and *wept with Safie* over the helpless fate of its original inhabitants', Safie cannot reciprocate his attachment. When she first catches sight of him, 'Safie, unable to attend to her friend [Agatha], rushed out of the cottage' (*F*, pp. 114 [my emphasis], 129).

In the taxonomy of characters, the Muslim-Christian Safie belongs with Rhys's Antoinette/Bertha. And indeed, like Christophine the good servant, the subject created by the fiat of natural philosophy is the tangential unresolved moment in *Frankenstein*. The simple suggestion that the monster is human inside but monstrous outside and only provoked into vengefulness is clearly not enough to bear the burden of so great a historical dilemma.

At one moment, in fact, Shelley's Frankenstein does try to tame the monster, to humanise him by bringing him within the circuit of the Law. He 'repair[s] to a criminal judge in the town and . . . relate[s his] history briefly but with firmness' – the first and disinterested version of the narrative of Frankenstein – 'marking the dates with accuracy and never deviating into invective or exclamation. . . . When I had concluded my narration I said, "This is the being whom I accuse and for whose seizure and punishment I call upon you to exert your whole power. It is your duty as a magistrate"' (*F*, pp. 189, 190). The sheer social reasonableness of the mundane voice of Shelley's 'Genevan magistrate' reminds us that the absolutely other cannot be selfed, that the monster has 'properties' which will not be contained by 'proper' measures:

> 'I will exert myself [he says], and if it is in my power to seize the monster, be assured that he shall suffer punishment proportionate to his crimes. But I fear, from what you have yourself described to be his properties, that this will prove impracticable; and thus, while every proper measure is pursued, you should make up your mind to disappointment.' (*F*, p. 190)

In the end, as is obvious to most readers, distinctions of human individuality themselves seem to fall away from the novel. Monster, Frankenstein, and Walton seem to become each others' relays. Frankenstein's story comes to an end in death; Walton concludes his own story within the frame of his function as letter writer. In the *narrative* conclusion, he is the natural philosopher who learns from Frankenstein's example. At the end of the *text*, the monster, having confessed his guilt toward his maker and ostensibly intending to immolate himself, is borne away on an ice raft. We do not see the conflagration of his funeral pile – the self-immolation is not consummated in the text: he too cannot be contained by the text. In terms of narrative logic, he is 'lost in darkness and distance' (*F*, p. 211) – these are the last words of the novel – into an existential temporality that is coherent with neither the territorialising individual imagination (as in the opening of *Jane Eyre*) nor the authoritative scenario of Christian psychobiography (as at the end of Brontë's work). The very relationship between sexual reproduction and social subject-production – the dynamic nineteenth-century topos of feminism-in-imperialism – remains problematic within the limits of Shelley's text and, paradoxically, constitutes its strength.

Earlier, I offered a reading of woman as womb holder in *Frankenstein*. I would now suggest that there is a framing woman in the book who is neither tangential, nor encircled, nor yet encircling. 'Mrs Saville', 'excellent Margaret', 'beloved Sister' are her address and kinship inscriptions (*F*, pp. 15, 17, 22). She is the occasion, though not the protagonist, of the novel. She is the feminine *subject* rather than the female individualist: she is the irreducible *recipient*-function of the letters that constitute *Frankenstein*. I have commented on the singular appropriative hermeneutics of the reader reading with Jane in the opening pages of *Jane Eyre*. Here the reader must read with Margaret Saville in the crucial sense that she must *intercept* the recipient-function, read the letters *as* recipient, in order for the novel to exist.[26] Margaret Saville does not respond to close the text as frame. The frame is thus simultaneously not a frame, and the monster can step 'beyond the text' and be 'lost in darkness.' Within the allegory of our reading, the place of both the English lady and the unnamable monster are left open by this great flawed text. It is satisfying for a postcolonial reader to consider this a noble resolution for a nineteenth-century English novel. This is all the more striking because, on the anecdotal level, Shelley herself abundantly 'identifies' with Victor Frankenstein.[27]

I must myself close with an idea that I cannot establish within the limits of this essay. Earlier I contended that *Wide Sargasso Sea* is necessarily bound by the reach of the European novel. I suggested that, in contradistinction, to reopen the epistemic fracture of imperialism without succumbing to nostalgia for lost origins, the critic must turn to the archives of imperialist governance. I have not turned to those archives in these pages. In my current work, by way of a modest and inexpert 'reading' of 'archives', I try to extend, outside of the reach of the European novelistic tradition, the most powerful suggestion in *Wide Sargasso Sea*: that *Jane Eyre* can be read as the orchestration and staging of the self-immolation of Bertha Mason as 'good wife'. The power of that suggestion remains unclear if we remain insufficiently knowledgeable about the history of the legal manipulation of widow-sacrifice in the entitlement of the British government in India. I would hope that an informed critique of imperialism, granted some attention from readers in the First World, will at least expand the frontiers of the politics of reading.

13

Cross-dressing, Gender and Representation: Elvis Presley

Marjorie Garber

You don't understand. It's not that there's something extra that makes a superstar. It's that there's something missing.

George Michael[1]

Madonna announced to her screaming fans: 'I want you all to know that there are only three real men on this stage – me and my two backup girls!'

Liz Smith, 'Gossip'[2]

The television show 'Saturday Night Live' once featured a mock game show called '¿Quién es mas macho?' in which contestants vied with each other to make gender distinctions. '¿Quién es mas macho?' 'Fernando Lamas or Ricardo Montalban?' In Laurie Anderson's avant-garde film, *Home of the Brave*, this became a contest to distinguish between two objects: '¿*Qué* es mas macho?' Which *thing* is more macho? Pineapple or knife? Toaster or convertible? The choices here were deliberately self-parodic; it was culture itself that was being gendered. And the joke was further perpetrated by Anderson herself, deftly deploying a special microphone, or 'audio mask' that lowered her voice to a 'male' register. She appeared live onstage in a tuxedo-like black suit and white shirt, but within the film, for one startling moment, she cross-cross-dressed to play Eve in a gold-lamé skirt. *Qué es mas macho?*

The more I have studied transvestism and its relation to representation the more I have begun to see it, oddly enough, as in many ways normative: as a condition that very frequently accompanies theatrical representation when theatrical self-awareness is greatest. Transvestite theatre from Kabuki to the Renaissance English stage to the contemporary drag show is not – or not only – a recuperative structure for the social control of sexual behaviour, but also a critique of the possibility of 'representation' itself.

In order to make such large claims for transvestism as a social and theoretical force – in order to argue, as I have, that there can be no culture without the transvestite, because the transvestite marks the entry into the Symbolic – I need to test out the *boundaries* of transvestism, to see it or read it in places other than where it is most obvious. I need to argue, in other words, for an *unconscious* of transvestism, for transvestism as a language that can be read, and double-read, like a dream, a fantasy, or a slip of the tongue. In the domain of theatre, the self-reflexive locus of much transvestite activity, I want to hypothesise what might be called 'unmarked' transvestism, to explore the possibility that some entertainers who do not overtly claim to be 'female impersonators', for example, may in fact signal their cross-gender identities onstage, and that this quality of crossing – which is fundamentally related to other kinds of boundary-crossing in their performances – can be more powerful and seductive than explicit 'female impersonation', which is often designed to confront, scandalise, titillate, or shock.

But first, let me discuss for a moment the 'normative' case and the issues it raises. One clear space in which to explore the power of transvestism as theatricality is in contemporary popular culture, specifically the pop-rock-scene, where cross-dressing, 'androgyny', and gender-bending have become almost de rigueur. David Bowie, Boy George, Kiss, Tiny Tim, Twisted Sister, Siouxie Sioux, the New York Dolls, from glam- and glitter-rock to heavy metal, from the seventies to the nineties, cross-dressing has meant deliberately and brashly – and politically – calling into question received notions of 'masculine' and 'feminine', straight and gay, girl and woman, boy and man. To give one random but suggestive example, Dee Snider, male lead singer of Twisted Sister, was voted one of the worst-dressed *women* of the year in 1984.[3]

When Boy George, in full makeup, wig, and flowing skirts, accepted a Grammy Award in 1984, he remarked to the television audience, 'Thank you, America, you've got style and taste, and you know a good drag queen when you see one.'[4] When he published a book of clothing patterns, complete with makeup instructions, it was immediately snapped up – by his *female* fans.[5] Let us agree to call Boy George (né George O'Dowd) a *marked transvestite*, a cross-dresser whose clothing seems deliberately and obviously at variance with his anatomical gender assignment.

Consider another telling instance of marked transvestism. At an event billed as 'The First Annual Female Impersonator of the Year Contest' one of the broadcast commentators was short, plain, comic actress Ruth Buzzi, former star of 'Laugh-In'. As the curvaceous, stunningly coiffed and made-up contestants in their glittering gowns emerged, on-camera, from a door prominently marked 'Men', and the camera panned back and forth between them and Buzzi, the audience was tacitly invited to speculate on the nature of 'womanhood' or 'femininity'. This may well rank as a species of producer misogyny, but it also frames a question: if 'woman' is culturally constructed, and if female impersonators are conscious constructors of artificial and artifactual femininity, how does a 'female impersonator' differ from a 'woman'? The question seems both ludicrous and offensive, but its theoretical and social implications are large and important. Female impersonators are often accused of misogyny (and regularly deny the charge), but in the female impersonator, the feminist debate about essentialism versus constructedness finds an unexpected, parodic, and unwelcome test.

Here is one drag queen's answer, describing the heyday of the London drag balls of the sixties: 'there was a definite distinction then as there is now between the drag queens, who enjoyed masquerading as women, and the sex changes [that is, transsexuals], who regarded themselves, and were regarded, as real women.'[6]

'Masquerading' versus 'real' women. It makes sense that transsexuals, who have invested so much in anatomical alteration, should insist that the ground of reality is the feminised body: the body undergoing hormone treatment to develop breasts and hips, undergoing surgery to translate the penis into a vagina. But this binarism between 'masquerading' and 'real women' has been at the centre of disputes and discussions among psychoanalytic critics, feminist film theorists, and, most recently, lesbian or self-described 'queer theorists'. Drawing on Joan Riviere's classic essay, 'Womanliness as a Masquerade' and on Lacan's revision and extension of that essay in 'The Signification of the Phallus', theorists have sought to define 'woman' as a construct that depends, for reasons social and political as well as erotic, upon masks and masquerade.

Riviere had argued not only that 'women who wish for masculinity may put on a mask of womanliness to avert anxiety and the retribution feared from men', but also that it was impossible to separate womanliness *from* masquerade:

> The reader may now ask how I define womanliness or where I draw the line between genuine womanliness and the 'masquerade'. My suggestion is not, however, that there is any such difference; whether radical or superficial, they are the same thing.[7]

The woman constructed by culture is, then, according to Riviere, already an impersonation. Womanliness *is* mimicry, *is* masquerade.

Here is Jacques Lacan, rewriting Riviere to describe 'display in the human being', not just in the woman:

> the fact that femininity finds its refuge in this mask, by virtue of the fact of the [repression] inherent in the phallic mark of desire, has the curious consequence of making *virile* display in the human being itself seem feminine.[8]

What does this mean? Is it that *all* display is feminine, because it is artifactual and displaced, a sign of anxiety and lack? Or that virile display *becomes* feminine because in being displayed it exhibits its own doubt? Or is it that the phallus is that which cannot be displayed? As we will see, the upshot of each of these three scenarios is the same.

As the Lacanian analyst Eugénie Lemoine-Luccioni explains, 'if the penis was the phallus, men would have no need of feathers or ties or medals. . . . Display [*parade*], just like the masquerade, thus betrays a flaw: no one has the phallus.'[9]

In the same essay ('The Signification of the Phallus') Lacan had talked about the relations between the sexes as governed by three terms, not two: 'to have' the phallus, which is what, in fantasy, *men* do; 'to be' the phallus, the object of desire, which is what, in fantasy, *women* do; and the intervening term, 'to seem'. This intervention, of 'seeming' (or 'appearing'), substituted for 'having', and protecting against the threat of loss, is, precisely, the place of the transvestite. So that, in psychoanalytic terms, the transvestite does represent a third space, a space of representation, even within a psychic economy in which *all* positions are fantasies. The theatrical transvestite literalises the anxiety of phallic loss. The overdetermination of phallic jokes, verbal and visual, that often accompany transvestism onstage, is a manifestation of exactly this strategy of reassurance for anxiety through artifactual over-compensation.

Lacan's suggestion about 'virile display' *seeming* feminine is a key one, because it is precisely this 'curious consequence', paradoxical as it may seem, that characterises the 'transvestite effect' in what I am calling 'unmarked transvestites'. For while it is easy to speak of the power of transvestite display in figures like David Bowie, Boy George, and Annie Lennox, these overt cross-dressers, 'marked transvestites', may in fact merely literalise something that is more powerful when masked or veiled – that is, when it remains unconscious.

I would now like to turn to three figures from popular culture in whom a certain consternation of gender is, to use a distinction from Roland Barthes, 'received' but not 'read'.[10] ('The rhetorical or latent signified', says Barthes, discussing the ideology of fashion, is 'the essential paradox of connoted signification: it is, one might say, a signification that is *received* but not *read*.') This is an opportunity to look *at* rather than *through* the transvestite, in this case by regarding the unconscious of transvestism as a speaking symptom, a language of clothing which is, tacitly, both dress and address. Unlike professional female impersonators, or comedians who affect travesty for particular theatrical ends (Milton Berle, Flip Wilson as Geraldine, Dana Carvey as the Church Lady), these performers do not think of themselves as transvestites. But – as we will see – the way they are received and discussed in the media, and, increasingly, the way they emphasise their own trademark idiosyncrasies of dress in response to audience interest all suggest that the question of cross-dressing, whether overt or latent, is central to their success, and even to the very question of stardom.

My first example may strike you as a bit too obvious to be considered completely unmarked, but he is, I think, at the origin of a certain theatrical worrying of exactly that borderline. I refer, of course, to the figure 'known variously as Mr. Showmanship, the Candelabra Kid, Guru of Glitter, Mr Smiles, The King of Diamonds, and Mr Boxoffice', and described as 'undoubtedly America's most beloved entertainer':[11] Liberace.

Liberace, pianist, singer, tap dancer, and fashion plate, clearly regarded himself as a direct influence upon the pop stars of the eighties, citing Prince, Michael Jackson, Boy George, and Madonna as among those who had learned from him about 'escapism and fantasy'.[12] 'There was a time,' he reminisced, 'when one woman might say to another, "May I borrow your lipstick?" Now, it's not unusual for one male rocker to say to another, "May I borrow your eyeliner?" And practically no man is above borrowing his best friend's skin bronzer' (Liberace, p. 222). 'I was the first to create shock waves', he said. 'For me to wear a simple tuxedo onstage would be like asking Marlene Dietrich to wear a housedress. . . .'[13]

Liberace's mother, a great fan of the Latin lover [Rudolph Valentino], named her son Wladziu Valentino Liberace and, for good measure, also named his younger brother Rudolph. In many ways Liberace seems to have been haunted by the phantom of Valentino, 'my namesake', as he described him to reporters (Thomas, p. 100). He had some of Valentino's elaborate costumes copied for stage performance. He bought Valentino's bed and put it in one of his guest rooms; he collected and exhibited at the Liberace Museum a pair of silver goblets said to have been intended as wedding gifts to Valentino and Pola Negri.

Furthermore, Valentino appears as a major figure in Liberace's personal social history of crossover style: 'Years ago, both male and female movie legends influenced the fashion and cosmetic industries. All over the world, you could find copies of Dietrich's eyebrows, Joan Crawford's shoulder pads and shoes, Valentino's slave bracelet, as well as his slicked-back, glossy patent-leather hairstyle' (Liberace, p. 222). All of these, we might note, are cross-dressed or cross-gendered examples: a woman's shoulder pads, a man's bracelet, Dietrich's eyebrows. . . .

We have been looking at Rudolph Valentino as the unlikely role model for Liberace and as the equally unlikely object of what might be called 'transvestification'. But there is a third figure who stands in significant relation to these two, uncannily linked by circumstances that seem both bizarre and overdetermined, and that is the figure of Elvis Presley.

Liberace thought of himself as the precursor of glitter rock. But of all the show business 'copies' to which Liberace laid claim, the one he most insisted upon was Elvis Presley. In his testimony in a British court in 1959 he maintained that he had to 'dress better than the others who were copying me. One was a young man named Elvis Presley' (Thomas, p. 131). He made the same claim to the media on the occasion of his twenty-fifth anniversary in show business: 'Because of Elvis Presley and his imitators, I really have to exaggerate to look different and to top them.'[14] Elvis became a *cause* of feminine virile display.

There is a famous moment, a kind of sartorial primal scene, in which Elvis and Liberace themselves change clothes, become each other's changelings. In 1956 they met in Las Vegas, when Elvis appeared in the audience at Liberace's show. Liberace invited the young singer backstage, where, apparently at the suggestion of a press agent, Elvis put on Liberace's gold-sequinned tuxedo jacket, and Liberace donned Elvis's striped sport coat. They then swapped instruments, Liberace on guitar, Elvis on piano, and jammed together for twenty minutes on two of their signature tunes, 'Hound Dog' and 'I'll Be Seeing You'. 'Elvis and I may be characters', commented Liberace, 'me with my gold jackets and him with his sideburns – but we can afford to be' (Thomas, p. 117).

This crossover moment between two crossover stars (Liberace traversing the boundary between pop and classical, Elvis between 'white' and 'black' music) has important implications beyond those of local publicity. The *New York Times* obituary for Liberace says, succinctly, about his gold lamé jacket, 'Soon Elvis Presley was wearing a suit of gold lamé. Soon Elvis impersonators were wearing suits of gold lamé.'[15] (So that Elvis impersonators are really Liberace impersonators.[16])

Predictably, the keepers of the Elvis legend are less forthcoming about any Liberace connection.[17] The film *This is Elvis* shows a shot of Riviera Hotel marquee proclaiming 'Liberace' in large letters, presumably to show what kind of entertainment Las Vegas was used to before the arrival of the King. An off-screen narrator impersonating the voice of Elvis says, 'Liberace and his brother were one of the top acts of the time. I wasn't sure the place was ready for Elvis Presley.' The point is contrast, disruption, not continuity.

Thirteen years later Elvis returned to Las Vegas, heavier, in pancake makeup, wearing a white jumpsuit with an elaborate jewelled belt and cape, crooning pop songs to a microphone: in effect, he had become Liberace. Even his fans were now middle-aged matrons and blue-haired grandmothers, who praised him as a good son who loved his mother; Mother's Day became a special holiday for Elvis's fans as it was for Liberace's.

A 1980 videotape of *Liberace in Las Vegas* (made, therefore, three years after Elvis's death), opens with a lush videotour of his home, including a tour of his closet. This is surely in part a camp joke, but the racks and racks of sequins, rhinestones, and furs – all of which we will shortly see him model onstage – will be oddly but closely echoed in the 1981 Elvis retrospective film, *This Is Elvis*, in which – also quite early in the film – attendants are shown readying his wardrobe for the show. Once again there are racks of clothes, jumpsuits with spangles and rhinestones, a whole rolling rack of jewelled belts. Watching the two films in succession it is difficult to tell whose closet is whose.

But something else, even more uncanny, ties Elvis and Liberace together. Both of them, remarkably, were twins, each born with a twin brother who immediately died. Both, that is to say, were – in the sense in which I have been using the term – changelings, changeling boys, substitutes for or doubles of something that never was.

Elvis Aron and Jesse Garon. *The Rolling Stone Illustrated History of Rock & Roll* notes that 'His twin, Jesse Garon, died at birth, and he was always to be reminded of this absence ("They say when one twin dies, the other grows up with all the quality of the other, too . . . If I did, I'm lucky"), as if he were somehow incomplete, even down to his matching name,'[18] and almost all his biographers make some version of the same point.[19] Had Elvis's own child, Lisa Marie, been a boy, the parents intended to call him John Baron, continuing the rhyming line.

One biography of Liberace begins with a dramatisation of the entertainer's momentous birth:

> 'One of the babies was born under the veil,' said the midwife in a voice shaded with sadness. 'But the other one, my dear . . .' her voice suddenly joyful. 'A *big* baby boy!'
>
> How pitiful the dead infant looked, its tiny body almost a skeleton, a film of placenta over its shrivelled face like a cloth for burial . . .
>
> But the other baby – what a pulsing, squalling, robust piece of humanity. (Thomas, p. 1)

Uncannily enough, here is a *third* version of this changeling scenario, from the opening paragraphs of yet another biography.

> Just before the turn of the present century, two bouncing babies were born who were to bring untold happiness into the lives of men and women all over the world
>
> One was the fledgling cinema . . .
>
> The other was Rudolph Valentino . . .
>
> As the babes grew up together, it was tragically ordained that so they would die.[20]

Jesse Garon Presley, Liberace's unnamed twin, the silent movie: three ghosts that haunt, and perhaps shape, the very notion of contemporary stardom.

Furthermore, Elvis, like Liberace, was obsessed with Rudolph Valentino, to whose celebrity (and spectacular funeral) his own were inevitably compared. The son of his promoter in the early Memphis days remembers that Elvis 'aspired to be a second Rudolph Valentino' (Goldman, p. 129). Hence the sideburns, the 'sullen, sultry leer' (the adjectives are those of Albert Goldman, a highly unsympathetic biographer), the photo sessions from this period stripped to the waist, the claim to friends that he had Italian blood.[21]

But it is the delicacy and vulnerability of the two men's visual images, as much as their sheer sexual power, that binds them. The pout, the curled lip (about which Elvis would joke onstage in his later Las Vegas years, 'This lip used to curl easier'), the cool stare and contained sexuality, an auto-voyeurism incredibly provocative – all of these can be seen in Valentino's *Son of the Sheik*, an uncanny phantom of Elvis. Indeed Elvis made his own Sheik movie, *Harum Scarum* (1965), in which, dressed in 'Arab' robes and headdress, pursuing the Princess Shalimar (played by Miss America Mary Ann Mobley), he is clearly intended to evoke memories of Valentino. Even the antics of the midget Billy Barty – seemingly gratuitous to the plot – echo, as if for emphasis, the hapless dwarf in *Son of the Sheik*. In an earlier – and better – film, *Jailhouse Rock* (1957), Elvis is stripped to the waist and beaten, in another clear citation from the popular Valentino film. In fact, the example of Valentino is one reason why he chose a movie career, and thus missed out on the early great days of what he himself had started – the theatricalisation of rock and roll.

The comparison, explicit and implicit, is everywhere in the press. An article in *McCall's* (presumably a Bible for the matrons of fandom) described Elvis's bodyguards as 'on a scale not seen in Hollywood since the days of Valentino and Fairbanks'.[22] The *New York Times*, reporting on the hysterical scene at his funeral said, 'Those old enough to remember said there had been nothing like it since Rudolf [sic] Valentino.'[23] 'Not since Valentino has a showbiz death so touched the national spirit', reported *People*,[24] and a Tennessee professor of psychiatry linked Elvis's superstardom with the American propensity for cult figures, suggesting, 'Think of someone like Rudolph Valentino'.[25] In 1989 a retro film was released about teen love in the fifties, which begins with the young hero purchasing Elvis's trademark car, a pink Cadillac; both the car and the film were called *Valentino Returns* – another evocation of the phantom, for Elvis, as we will see, is the other revenant, the other always-expected visitor, too-early lost.

Elvis, like Valentino, seemed to take take the world by erotic surprise. Contrasted, again like Valentino, with a notion of the clean-cut all-

American boy (represented in his case by Pat Boone), Elvis seemed for a
time to stand as the personification of sex. But what does it mean to
personify sex? And which sex?

The famous Ed Sullivan story – of how the camera filmed Elvis only
from the waist up – has been told and retold, debunked as myth and
explained as titillating publicity, a displacement upward that increased
desire for a peek below. But what would that peek disclose?

'Is it a sausage? It is certainly smooth and damp-looking, but whoever
heard of a 172lb sausage 6ft. tall?' This is the beginning of *Time*
magazine's review of the film *Love Me Tender* in 1956. The referent, it soon
becomes clear, is Elvis himself, not – as one might think – only a part of
his anatomy. But Elvis as part-object, Elvis the Pelvis, became, not only a
fan's fantasy and fetish but also, perhaps inevitably, his own. 'The Pelvis'
– an anatomical region which seems at first specific, but is in fact both
remarkably vague and distinctly ungendered – became the site of
speculation and spectatorship.

Thus, for example, an admiring male rock critic writing in 1970 praised
Elvis as 'The master of the sexual simile, treating his guitar as both
phallus and girl. . . . rumor had it that into his skin-tight jeans was sewn
a lead bar to suggest a weapon of heroic proportions.'[26]

But a boyhood friend of Elvis's tells it somewhat differently, describing
a stage ploy from the singer's early career, around 1955: 'He would take
the cardboard cylinder out of a roll of toilet paper and put a string in one
end of it. Then, he'd tie that string around his waist. The other end, with
the cardboard roller, would hang down outside his drawers, so as when
he got onstage and reared back with that guitar in his hand, it would look
to the girls up front like he had one helluva thing there inside his pants.'[27]

Lead bar or toilet-paper cylinder, truth or rumour, this tale of Elvis
stuffing his own pants with a prosthesis presents the Presley phallus as
marionette, the uncanny as canny stage device, one that can manifest its
phallic power automatically, so to speak, with the tug of a string or the
backward push of the hips. Recall once more Lacan's paradox about virile
display. The more protest, the more suspicion of lack. For this is what the
phallus signifies: 'its reality as signifier of lack.' It is, as Stephen Heath
points out, 'the supreme signifier of an impossible identity'.[28]

Psychoanalytically, transvestism is a mechanism that functions *by
displacement* and *through fantasy* to enact a scenario of desire. In fetishistic
cross-dressing, particular objects of clothing take on a metonymic role,
displacing parts of the body, and especially the maternal phallus – that is,
the impossible and imagined phallus which would represent originary
wholeness.

What I am going to claim is that transvestism *on the stage*, and
particularly in the kind of entertainment culture that generates the
phenomenon known as 'stardom', is a symptom for the *culture*, rather

than the individual performer. In the context of popular culture these transvestic symptoms appear, so to speak, to gratify a social or cultural scenario of desire. The onstage transvestite is the fetishised part-object for the social or cultural script of the fan.

One of the hallmarks of transvestic display is the detachable part. Wig, false breasts, the codpiece that can conceal male or female parts, or both, or neither. In the Elvis story the detachable part is not only explicitly and repeatedly described as an artificial phallus but also as a trick, a stage device, and a sham. Not for the first time the phallus itself becomes an impersonator – and, moreover, a female impersonator, for only a female would lack the phallus and need a substitute.

Elvis as female impersonator? Let us look further.

Elvis's appearance at the Grand Ole Opry, at the very beginning of his career, provoked a double scandal. His music was too black, and he was wearing eyeshadow. He was not asked back. For Chet Atkins, soon to become the organiser of Elvis's recording sessions in Nashville, the one lingering memory of Elvis at the Opry was his eye-makeup. 'I couldn't get over that eye shadow he was wearing. It was like seein' a couple of guys kissin' in Key West.'[29] (Notice here once again the conflation of cross-dressing, theatricality, and homosexuality.)

Elvis's hair created even more of a furor. It was like a black man's (Little Richard's; James Brown's); it was like a hood's; it was like a woman's. Race, class, and gender: Elvis's appearance violated or disrupted them all. His created 'identity' as the boy who crossed over, who could take a song like 'Hound Dog' from Big Mama Thornton or the onstage raving – and the pompadour, mascara, and pink and black clothing – from Little Richard, made of Elvis, in the popular imagination, a cultural mulatto, the oxymoronic 'Hillbilly Cat', a living category crisis. Little Richard, defiantly gay, his conked pompadour teased up six inches above his head, his face and eyes brilliantly made-up, his clothes and capes glittering with sequins, appearing 'in one show dressed as the Queen of England and in the next as the pope',[30] was vestimentary crossover incarnate, not passing but trespassing. To put it another way, Elvis mimicking Little Richard is Elvis as female impersonator – or rather, as the *impersonator* of a female impersonator. And it is worth remembering that Richard attributes his adoption of bizarre costume in this period to *racial* crossover. 'We were breaking through the racial barrier. . . . We decided that my image should be crazy and way-out so that the adults would think I was harmless' (White, pp. 65–6). The year was 1956.

Elvis was the white 'boy' who could sing 'black', the music merchandiser's dream. And that crossover move was (perhaps inevitably) read as a crossover move in gender terms: a move from hypermale to hyperfemale, to, in fact, *hyperreal* female, female impersonator, transvestite.

It was in 1970, only two years after his much-heralded television 'Comeback' performance, that Elvis made a striking vestimentary crossover in Las Vegas:

> Not since Marlene Dietrich stunned the ringsiders with the sight of her celebrated legs encased from hip to ankle in a transparent gown had any performer so electrified Las Vegas with his mere physical appearance. Bill Belew [the costume designer], who had been very cautious up to this point about designing any costume that would make Elvis look effeminate, decided finally to kick out the jams. Now Elvis faced the house encased in a smashing white jumpsuit, slashed to the sternum and lovingly fitted around his broad shoulders, flat belly, narrow hips and tightly packed crotch. And then there were his pearls – loads of lustrous pearls, not sewn on the costume but worn unabashedly as body ornaments. (Goldman, p. 448)

'Not since Marlene Dietrich.' This – in the voice of Elvis debunker Goldman – is Elvis precisely as female impersonator. Critic after critic notices that his sexuality is subject to reassignment, consciously or unconsciously, though the paradox – male sex symbol as female impersonator – remains perplexing and unexamined. 'As for Elvis himself,' writes one biographer, 'he'll be gradually castrated into an everlasting pubescent boy. And as movie follows movie, each one worse than the last, he will actually start resembling a eunuch: a plump, jittery figure.'[31]

Elvis moves in the course of his career along a curious continuum from androgyne to transvestite. This male sex symbol is insistently and paradoxically read by the culture as a boy, a eunuch, or a 'woman' – as anything but a man.

His ex-wife Priscilla, the executive producer of the television series depicting Elvis's life, wanted in fact to repress, or expunge, the memory of his later years. 'The problem,' wrote one critic sympathetically, 'is that Elvis left in such bad shape: overweight, forgetting the words to his songs, wearing clownish rhinestone-covered jumpsuits. It's *that* Elvis – the one who keeps cropping up in books and TV-movies – that Priscilla wants to get out of people's minds.' And, 'if only Elvis had paid more attention to his image. Maybe he would have made it through the '70s, checked into the Betty Ford Center, turned on to aerobics. . . .'[32]

Overweight. Reviews and commentaries on Elvis in his last years speak frequently of him as having a 'weight problem', as looking fat, not being able to keep the weight off. Of which gender do we usually speak in these terms? We may think of Elizabeth Taylor and her constant battle with extra pounds: Liz fat, Liz thin, Liz in and out of the Betty Ford Center. This is the spirit in which Elvis watchers watched Elvis watching his weight, as if the eternal boy within could be disclosed by the shedding of pounds, the disappearance of a telltale paunch. The comparable corpulence of wonder-boys Orson Welles and Marlon Brando, though remarked by the press, is not feminised in this way.

Yet the feminisation and/or transgendering of Elvis begins much earlier than the Las Vegas jumpsuit days.[33] Whether through his mascara, his dyed hair, or his imitation of black music and style, Elvis was always already crossing over.

The 1990 debut of a weekly TV series on the life of Elvis Presley broke new ground for television programming, as John J. O'Connor noted in the *New York Times*. 'It is', he points out, 'the first weekly series built around the life of an actual entertainment personality'; 'a decided rarity – a half-hour format devoted not to a sitcom but to straightforward biography.' 'Can', he wondered in print, 'episodic biographies of Marilyn, Chaplin, Dean, et al., be far behind?'[34]

This list of celebrities to be compared to Elvis is instructive: Marilyn Monroe, Charlie Chaplin, James Dean. For all of them have been, like Elvis Presley, objects of imitation, repetition, replication – and re-gendering. (Think of Boy George's former boyfriend, the transvestite pop music figure Marilyn, with his long blond hair and hairy chest; of Lucille Ball's Chaplin [and Chaplin's own cross-dressing films[35]], of James Dean as lesbian butch idol, etc.) Andy Warhol, the master of pop replication, did multiple Elvises as well as Marilyns and James Deans, lots of them: a silkscreened print of Elvis's face reproduced 36 times (six across and six down); *Double* and *Triple Elvis*; *Red Elvis*, and a work called *Campbell's Elvis* – with Elvis's face superimposed over the label of a soup-can. Elvis was, in fact, the only pop figure Warhol carried over in his work from the fifties to the sixties. Critics have noted the affinities between the artist and the rock star: each 'opted for a blank and apparently superficial parody of earlier styles which surprisingly expanded, rather than alienated, their audience.' '[B]oth took repetition and superficiality to mask an obscure but vital aspect of their work: the desire for transcendence or annihilation without compromise, setting up a profound ambivalence on the part of both artist and audience as to whether the product was trash or tragedy.'[36]

Newsweek read Warhol's interest in Elvis as the recognition of 'an almost androgynous softness and passivity in his punk-hood persona',[37] and the claim to androgyny, as we have seen, is not infrequently made as an explanation of Elvis's powerful appeal to women and men. But one of the things Andy Warhol may have seen in Elvis was the perfection of his status as a pop icon in his condition as always already multiple and replicated. The phenomenon of 'Elvis impersonators', which began long *before* the singer's death, is one of the most startling effects of the Elvis cult.

What, then, is the relationship between transvestism and repetition? For one thing, both put in question the idea of an 'original', a stable starting point, a ground. For transvestism, like the copy or simulacrum, disrupts 'identity' and exposes it as figure. In one of the most famous of twentieth-century cultural analyses, Walter Benjamin noted the effect of mechanical reproduction on works of art like photography and film. 'The technique of reproduction', he wrote (and think of *Elvis* here),

> detaches the reproduced object from the domain of tradition. By making many reproductions it substitutes a plurality of copies for a unique existence. And in permitting the reproduction to meet the beholder or listener in his own particular situation, it reactivates the object reproduced.[38]

In the mystical anagram adopted by his followers, 'Elvis lives'. (Or, to cite the slogan employed by Elvis's long-time manager Colonel Parker after his 'boy's' death, 'Always Elvis'. That Colonel Parker deployed this slogan in the form of a rubber stamp says much about the reproduction of Elvis Presley. Had Colonel Parker known or cared anything about literary theory he might have had it read 'Always already Elvis.')

Elvis made his public debut as a performer in 1954. By 1956 – only two years later – the warm-up act for his show at the Louisiana Fair Grounds was performed by 'exact replicas of Elvis Presley, doing his songs with his gestures and dressed in his clothes'.[39] In Nashville one Wade Cummings, or 'Elvis Wade', as he called himself, was described as the 'first' or 'original imitation Elvis', complete with paunch and flashy costume slit to the waist. According to him, 'All Elvis impersonators are Elvis Wade impersonators.' (So, in his view at least, there *was* an original, an original impersonator.) But there are hundreds of others. Notice here the relationship of the 'impersonator' to Freud's 'uncanny'. The impersonator is something alive that seems almost like a machine. Is it possible that this is overdetermination through the dead brother, that all of these impersonators are some version of Jesse Garon Presley?

Most of these acts got their start *before* Elvis Presley's death; they were not only ghostly revisitations but also proliferations, multiplications. Some were even surgically reconstructed, like the man in Florida who had his nose, cheeks, and lip altered to look like the King. The surgeons 'gave a slight millimeter push to the left-hand corner of [his] lip', to approximate the famous sneer.[40]

Indeed, the impersonation of Elvis always seemed to verge on the multiple, the replicated, as if one could never be enough. Two hundred Elvis impersonators were scheduled to perform at the birthday party for the Statue of Liberty. (Only seventy-five showed up.) What was this insatiable desire that could never be gratified?

After his death the Elvis impersonators assumed the magnitude of a major cult. 'What, other than psychological transference', asked *People* magazine rhetorically one year later, 'can explain the hysteria over the 100 or so ersatz Elvises around the country who are putting on eerie shows – complete with drum rolls from *2001*, sweaty scarfs tossed to screaming women, karate chops, bodyguards, sneers and bathos?'

Time magazine noted the success in Saigon of one Elvis Phuong, who, 'complete with skintight pants and sneer, does Presley Vietnamese style'.[41] Two Elvis impersonators in London, one Chinese, the other an Indian Sikh who wears a turban, prompted a two-page feature on the front page of the 'Living Arts' section of the *New York Times* ('Honestly, not too many Chinese people do Elvis', Paul Chan confides to the *Times* reporter. 'I think I must be the first Chinese Elvis in the world.')[42] And a routine news item in the entertainment pages of the *Los Angeles Times* noted a casting call for Elvis impersonators, 'preferably overweight', for a 'small but fun role' in *Robocop II*. [43]

At the First Annual EP (for Elvis Presley) Impersonators International Association Convention held in Chicago in June 1990, dozens of impersonators put in an appearance, including a female Elvis from Hertfordshire, England, a 'Jordanian-American anesthesiologist Elvis' described by a Chicago newspaper as the 'Hindu Elvis', and a seven-year-old Elvis from Brooklyn. The event was coordinated by a group that eventually hopes to develop a 'Code of Ethics' for Elvis impersonators around the globe. 'If the actual Elvis was at the convention', one reporter commented, 'he might have been overlooked in the mob of look-alikes.'[44]

One of the most popular sessions at the EPIIA, 'How to Become an Elvis Impersonator', noted the three sartorial stages of Elvis's life as a performer: the fifties, or the Gold Lamé Period, the sixties, or the Black Leather period, and the seventies, or the Vegas Jumpsuit Phase, also known as the Aloha Years. Why do most impersonators choose the third phase, often believed to mark the decline of Elvis's career? This 'question that has plagued Elvologists' was answered by the session leader in two ways: on the one hand, the seventies were the most visually exciting of Elvis's career; on the other, the 'midlife demographics of the impersonator subculture' (largely over 40, largely working class) made the baritone, overweight Elvis an object of more ready – and more convincing – impersonation. As will be clear, I am suggesting a third reason for the appeal of the Vegas Jumpsuit Elvis, and also a link among the three vestimentary phases – a link for which 'unmarked transvestism' might be thought of as a common term.

Here once again, in a passage of typically purple prose, is Elvis biographer Albert Goldman on the subject of this phenomenon of impersonation:

What one saw after Elvis's death . . . was not just emulation but replication: the rite according to St. Xerox. Like those mythical soldiers sprung from dragon's teeth, there appeared overnight a new class of entertainers who were not so much mimics, impersonators or impressionists as Elvis clones. Some of these human effigies were so fantastically dedicated to their assumed identity that, like transsexuals, they submitted their bodies to plastic surgery so that their natural resemblance might be heightened to virtual indistinguishability. (Goldman, pp. 584–5)

We are very close here to Freud's notion of the uncanny repetition-compulsion, the *heimlich* transformed into the *unheimlich*, castration anxiety, the multiplication of doubles, 'something repressed which recurs'.[45] Meantime at Graceland, the Presley home (*Heim*?) and museum in Memphis, his costumes live, too, on mannequins (like Liberace's), for the delectation of the faithful. Elvis as ghost comes home to rejoin the ghostly twin brother whose grave has been moved to the Graceland memorial garden.

And these mechanisms of impersonation lead, with uncanny inevitability, to woman as Elvis impersonator. As Elvis's fame grew, and his looks became as famous as his sound, the hair and makeup began, fascinatingly, to cross back over gender lines. When his underage girlfriend Priscilla, later to become his wife, moved in with him in 1962, Elvis took charge of her appearance and turned her into a version of himself, insisting that she tease her hair up about twelve inches and dye it the same jet-black that his own hair was dyed. 'In fact,' writes biographer Goldman, 'some people began to insist that Elvis and Priscilla were coming to look alike, that they were becoming twins' (p. 355). Another set of uncanny twins: changelings.

As early as 1957 Little Richard toured Australia with a package of artists including Alis Lesley, billed as 'the female Elvis Presley', complete with pompadour and low-slung guitar (White, p. 91). At the 1984 American Grammy Awards Show pop singer Annie Lennox of the Eurythmics, known for her close-cropped orange hair and gender-bending style, made a startling appearance 'in full drag, as a convincing Elvis Presley'.[46] In Jim Jarmusch's film *Mystery Train* (1989) a young Japanese Elvis fan assembles a scrapbook by pairing pictures of Elvis with the Buddha and two women: the Statue of Liberty and Madonna. 'Elvis was even more influential than I thought', says her boyfriend. Canadian rockabilly star k.d. lang, who enjoys particular popularity with lesbian audiences, is famous for her short cropped hair and male attire. Often compared by critics to Elvis Presley, lang, whose lip in performance seems to curl, like Elvis's, of its own accord, did an Elvis impersonation on one of Pee Wee Herman's Christmas shows. And comedienne

Roseanne Barr, who has achieved stardom by playing a fat, lower-middle-class housewife on television, appeared in a one-woman show where she made jokes about her weight, 'handed out scarfs like Elvis', and 'closed the show singing "My Way" arm in arm with an Elvis impersonator'.[47]

So that Elvis is impersonated and evoked on the one hand by female pop and rock stars (Alis Lesley, Annie Lennox, Madonna, k.d. lang) and on the other hand by an overweight comic actress. What I want to suggest is that these particular impersonations, impersonations of Elvis by women, were not only apt but in fact inevitable.

It is almost as if the word 'impersonator', in contemporary popular culture, can be modified *either* by 'female' *or* by 'Elvis'.

Why should this be? Why is 'Elvis' like 'woman', that which can be impersonated?

From the beginning Elvis is produced and exhibited as parts of a body – detachable (and imitable) parts that have an uncanny life and movement of their own, seemingly independent of their 'owner': the curling lip, the pompadour, the hips, the pelvis.

Compare him, for example, with an All-American boy like Pat Boone, for whom the only detachable parts are his white bucks. The All-American boy doesn't have a body – or didn't until recently. Again it is useful to compare Elvis to Valentino, who replaced the All-American boy movie star with a model infinitely more dangerous and disturbing – because it had moving parts. Indeed, it could be said that a 'real male' cannot be embodied at all, that embodiment *itself* is a form of feminisation. If women, in the Western tradition, have been seen as the representatives of sex itself, then to personify sex on the stage must inevitably be to impersonate a woman.

Elvis is also – like a woman – not only a marked but a *marketed* body, exhibited and put on display, merchandised, not only by his manager Colonel Tom Parker, but also by Steve Binder, who invented the slick look of the 1968 TV 'Comeback Special', leather suit and all, and by David Wolper, who produced the posthumous film *This Is Elvis* and also staged the Statue of Liberty extravaganza.

'The woman of fashion', writes Roland Barthes in a passage we have already had occasion to note, is a 'collection of tiny, separate essences.' 'The paradox', he says, 'is a generality of accumulation, not of synthesis: in Fashion, the *person* is thus simultaneously impossible and yet entirely known' (Barthes, pp. 254–5.) Here Barthes says 'person', but, earlier, 'woman'. It is 'woman' whom fashion creates as this illusion of parts. And, 'woman' is what can be known, exhibited, disseminated, replicated – while at the same time remaining 'impossible'.

Elvis, too, is simultaneously impossible and entirely known. Much as he is exhibited, he is also withheld from view: in the army, in Hollywood, holed up at Graceland. At the end of every performance, while his fans screamed for more, an announcer would solemnly intone, 'Ladies and gentlemen, Elvis has left the building.' Like the changeling boy, Elvis is always absent or elsewhere. Indeed as always already absent, Elvis himself was the best, and the most poignant, of Elvis impersonators, staging a much-heralded 'comeback' in 1968 at the age of 30, and, in another comeback, revisiting his classic crossover rock songs of the fifties from the curious vantage point of Hawaii or Las Vegas in the middle seventies. Like a revenant, he just never stops coming back. (Here we might recall the story of the phantom hitchhiker in the film *Mystery Train* – who turns out, of course, to be the ghost of Elvis heading for Graceland.)

We have briefly noted the fact that Elvis in effect sat out the rock revolution that he himself had started. Instead of taking to the concert stage like the Beatles, he went to Hollywood to become a 'movie star', following the game plan of Colonel Parker, but also, presumably, his own dream of being a Valentino. Like Flaubert writing for the French theatre, he was a genre behind. He missed his own moment – the moment that he had engendered – and spent the rest of his career as he had spent the beginning, being always too early or too late to be the Elvis that he was.

Is it possible that this is the essence of stardom, of superstardom? To be simultaneously belated and replicated; not to be there, and to cover up that absence with representations?

In an essay on camp, Andrew Ross has suggested that 'in popular rock culture today, the most "masculine" images are signified by miles of coiffured hair, layers of gaudy make-up, and a complete range of fetishistic body accessories, while it is the clean-cut, close-cropped, fifties-style Europop crooners who are seen as lacking masculine legitimacy' (Ross, p. 164). As a cultural observation this is shrewd, yet it reinscribes the binary *within* the reassuring domain of the masculine. Ross underestimates the power of the transvestite as that spectral other who exists only in representation – not a representation of male or of female, but of, precisely, itself: its own phantom or ghost.

The argument from 'masquerade' tries to establish 'woman' as artifactual, gestural, a theatrical creature who can be taken apart and put back together. But what has become clearer and clearer is that 'man' – the male person – is at least as artifactual as 'woman'. Mechanical reproduction is the displacement into its opposite of the fear of artifactuality and dismemberment.

'Which is most macho'? The answer can come only from the impersonator. For by enacting on the stage – or the video screen – the disarticulation of parts, the repetition of images that is the breakdown of the image itself, it is only the impersonator who can theorise gender. Let me quote once again from Roland Barthes.

> As for the human body, Hegel had already suggested that it was in a relation of signification with clothing: as pure sentience the body cannot signify; clothing guarantees the passage from sentience to meaning; it is, we might say, the signified par excellence. But which body is the Fashion garment to signify? (Barthes, p. 258)

What are the choices? An article in the gay and lesbian journal *Out/Look* called attention to the power of 'The Drag Queen in The Age of Mechanical Reproduction', because the drag queen foregrounds illusion and falsehood as material reality: 'being a drag queen means the constant assertion of the body'.[48] But again, *which* body? The fashion garment of the drag queen signifies the absent or phantom body. Paradoxically, the body here is no body, and nobody, the clothes without the Emperor.

It is epistemologically intolerable to many people – including many literary and cultural critics – that the ground should be a figure. That gender exists only in representation. But this is the subversive secret of transvestism, that the body is not the ground, but the figure. Elvis Presley watching *his* figure, as his weight balloons up and down, Elvis deploying his lips and his hips to repeat by an act of will and artifice the 'natural' gestures that once made them seem to take on an uncanny, transgressive life of their own, Elvis Presley, male sex symbol as female impersonator, becomes the fascinating dramatisation of the transvestite effect that underlies representation itself.

14

Feminism and the Postmodern: Theory's Romance

Diane Elam

COMING TO KNOW: THEORY AND PLEASURE

Pure pleasure and pure reality are ideal limits, which is as much as to say fictions. The one is as destructive and mortal as the other.

Theory has one kind of textuality that upsets its claims to objectivity: an element of romance. Theory, as we all know but are afraid to admit, is sexy. Postmodernism is in part an admission of this fact, which I shall illustrate by focusing on two very disparate kinds of texts: Jacques Derrida's *The Post Card*, in which the acknowledged master of deconstruction finds his theory sexy and likes it, and the novels of Kathy Acker, in which the queen of postmodern S/M discovers that she likes her sex theoretical.

First, a brief word about Derrida. Derrida speaks of a friend presented with an 'apparently rigorously theoretical text . . . written such that it gave him an erection whenever he read it'.[1] Derrida links the demand of theoretical rigour, so often heard on the Left, with the masculinist discourse of penile tumescence. The very rigidity that would lend theoretical discourse its systematic objectivity is identified with a far from neutral machismo. And the persistent pun on *se bander*, meaning to get a hard on, and the *double bande* or double bind, which deconstruction tends to isolate in any theoretical discourse, marks this as a no-win situation for theoretical rigidity.

Kathy Acker's *In Memoriam to Identity*, on the other hand, marks the inseparability of sexual desire from its theorisation. The story of Airplane intermingles a discussion of sexuality between a female patient and a psychiatrist with a description of a live sex show. It is impossible to determine whether she is recounting the sex show as part of her therapy or whether a mock therapy session is part of the live sex show. After all, as Airplane muses, 'perhaps *come* equals *know*'.[2] Theoretical knowledge about sexual desire proves as erotic, if not more erotic, than the supposedly actual sexuality that is the object of knowledge. For Acker, sexual activity is pre-eminently fictional, in that pleasure is produced from the interplay of desire and fantasy, in a way that renders the fictions of the sex trade indistinguishable from those of the psychiatric theorist. This turns out to be inseparable from the concerns of feminism: it is a rape that causes Airplane to ask whether to come means to know, a phrase beneath which the question is posed of whether we can 'know' whether 'no' means no.

These postmodern texts fail to preserve a decent distance between theory and sexuality, confronting the theory of sexuality with the sexuality of theory. Modernist theory seeks to put an end to desire by offering instruction, the satisfaction of enlightenment: so that Marxism, for example, substitutes the determinate knowledge of social processes for the desire for social justice, a theory of historical materialism for utopian socialism. By contrast, Acker's *In Memoriam to Identity* asks us to remain suspicious of the role of enlightenment reason; as Acker puts it: 'What the fuck is *reason* in this life, a life of disease and sex show?'[3] Postmodernism, that is, reminds us that the one desire that knowledge cannot replace with a truth is the desire for knowledge itself: the seductions of theory.

Others have brought the question of seduction to our attention in relation to theory: most notably with regard to ideology.[4] Althusser's replacement of ideological falsification by the interpellation of an ideological subject is a step on this road, not least because in a sense what postmodernism refuses is the epistemological anonymity of the knowing subject. That particular situation of the subject, one which I would argue is modernist, is perhaps best typified by the work of Georg Lukács. Lukács identified Marx's notion of ideology as a system of lies, 'false consciousness' that needed only to be dispelled by correct analysis of the forces of material production at work under the cloudy veils of priestcraft.[5] Thus, if we were to apply Lukács's methods to the tradition of the British novel, we could accuse Jane Austen of suggesting that wealth and privilege proceed from birth rather than from the exploitation of workers. Her argument that merit rather than birth should be rewarded can thus be dismissed as a classical piece of bourgeois ideology. Since her novels tend to imply that aristocratic and middle-class prosperity is deserved and earned rather than stolen, injustice is merely the product of biological degeneracy. This notion of ideology has its appeals; I've always been tempted by the rallying cry, 'People on Wall Street don't make money, they steal it from the workers who really make it.' However, this statement implies that the subject is capable of breaking finally from ideological illusion, rendering itself anonymous as it passes an objective judgment on the real state of affairs. Althusser's contribution was to point out that no conspiracy theory of priestly drug dealers, offering the opium of the people at street prices, orchestrated the function of ideology. Rather, ideology consisted in the 'hailing' or 'interpellation' of the subject as a free and autonomous individual when s/he was, in fact, the product of determining material constrictions. Althusser thus introduces a double reserve. On the one hand, there is no simple true state of affairs which may be revealed by theoretical analysis. On the other hand, individuals' relation to their world is not simply determined as true or false; rather these relationships become a process and a performance to be measured in terms of their effectivity.[6]

Unfortunately, Althusser gives up on both these insights. In the first place, he introduces the notion of the epistemological break, which replays the old modernist paradigm through which knowledge of the system is freedom from it.[7] On the second count, the determinate goal of political revolution (or at least the programme of the French communist party in its latest manifesto) turns the analysis of effects back into a question of revealed truth, since effects are measured in terms of proximity to defined goals. So the subject is returned to objective anonymity, with its epistemological assurance, by means of an anthropomorphisation of the party.

Cultural studies has drawn many of its hermeneutic instruments from the notion of a subject constituted by the receipt of ideologically loaded messages: Laura Mulvey's account of visual pleasure and narrative cinema is a powerful text in this tradition.[8] However, the limitation of such an approach is that, if it speaks of falsification, hegemony, or violence as somehow 'bad things', it tends either to imply that a non-ideological, natural subjectivity can be located, or to invoke a notion of 'strategy' which still requires a teleological justification, an end. Either way, an attack on ideology *as such* is a problem, because it must imply a non-ideological origin or goal in opposition to which ideology can be justified. For the Marxist tradition this was no problem: we can understand the Althusserian paradigm shift as the refusal of any non-ideological origin in favour of an ultimately non-ideological goal of revolution, however long the lonely hour of the last instance might be in coming. Althusser's proclamation that there is no history to ideology is always underscored by the proviso that there must be a space outside ideology, even though it would be as yet unthinkable except as critical science.

For theory to think, or think in, its postmodernity, it would have to dispense with the notion of ideology, *if* ideology is in any way linked to falsification. For all his rejection of the notion of ideology as 'false consciousness', Althusser does have a teleological account of truth to oppose to ideology. In place of falsification, I want to think about seduction: which is to return ideology to its status as a kind of persuasion, as a *rhetorical* activity. The term seduction gets away from the truth/ falsehood opposition in a way that has a double valency for our juxtaposition of Acker and Derrida. With regard to deconstruction, the rhetorical overtones of 'seduction' allow us to recognise that the study of the problematic rhetorical status of textuality has a significant cultural and political import precisely in that it forces us to rethink culture and politics. With regard to feminism, the sexual overtones of 'seduction' introduce differences of gender and sexuality (which are also, but not 'ultimately', differences of power) to the supposed anonymity of cultural knowledge.

The addition of the term 'seduction' to our understanding of the situation of the knowing subject confronts knowledge with a sense of its own processes that it cannot finally know. That is to say, seduction does not imply the simple statement of a truth: there is always some rhetorical, persuasive play. On the other hand, seduction is not simply falsification and lying, ideological deceit. Thus, we might talk about the experience of watching TV or going to the movies as not simply one of being deceived, but of one of being seduced; for the analysis and correction of the many deceptions that we encounter in visual culture has proved singularly ineffective in dissuading its subjects. To take a hypothetical example, people flock out of eastern Europe to a land with 197 different kinds of shampoo, even if scientific analysis can tell us that they are all the same, in effect, and no more or less beneficial than, say, the one East German state brand. That ideology critique can unravel the web of deceit which causes us to buy these products (the cultural construction of femininity by which they are advertised, for instance) has little purchase on us. All of this is to say: knowledge will not put an end to desire.[9]

In speaking, then, of the seductions of theory, one is not simply concerned to issue a warning against sirens so much as to recognise, as Derrida does, that:

> I do nothing that does not have some interest in seducing you [*à te séduire*], in setting you astray from yourself in order to set you on the way toward me, uniquely – nevertheless you do not know who you are nor to whom precisely I am addressing myself. But there is only you in the world.[10]

This peculiar love letter, this anonymous, impersonal, and yet absolutely singular seduction, rewrites the notion of ideological interpellation outside of any simple process of falsification. The play of desire that grounds any exchange cannot be regulated in terms of an opposition of truth to falsehood. Knowledge cannot put an end to desire, since knowledge will always be set astray by the wandering of the desire for the pleasure of certainty. A *caveat* here is that desire will not put an end to knowledge either: I am not advocating an indifferent and general jouissance – as it is sometimes claimed that Barthes or Baudrillard do – a grand orgasm that will liberate us from a constricting rationality. To do so would be simply a parodic inversion of the modernist theoretical separation of knowledge from desire. To put it bluntly, we are not just lost in the funhouse. After all, I wouldn't vote for any man whose view of rape was simply 'relax and enjoy it'.[11]

Thus we can see that a concern with seduction is not merely a sign of either playful Parisian chic or an undifferentiated welcoming of late-capitalist commodity culture. Rather, it allows us a certain suspicion of the pretension of theory to survey objects from an indifferent point of view. In discussing the dislocation of metalinguistic mastery, I want to turn to the encounter between theoretical discourse and the generic concerns or romance. A peculiar rewriting of the romance genre is the most obvious affinity between Acker's novels and Derrida's *The Post Card*. And this is not coincidental, since it relates both to Acker's attempt to imagine a feminine sexuality and Derrida's stated aim in *Spurs* of philosophising from the position of a woman.[12] Romance is, after all, in some sense a 'women's genre'. In each of these cases, I shall focus on the way in which the seduction of theory by romance brings with it a dispersal of unified subjectivity. It will bear repeating that this dispersal is not merely a recent historical function – that the postmodern is not simply the contemporaneous. Rather, Derrida's concern with the economy of telecommunication in relation to the question of writing, and Acker's concern with a sexual economy in its relation to violence and pleasure, intersect with the romance genre in order to evoke the problematic subjectivity of the female: what both might call the 'non-name of woman'. My wider claim will be that postmodernism can in this sense be of vital importance to the feminist movement, in thinking around the modernist project of liberation through identity politics.

In suggesting the limitations of identity politics, it is necessary to proceed with a great deal of caution and respect for the efforts of those who pioneered feminist activism and the academic study of feminism under the banner of either 'women's experience' or 'women's identity'. It is all too easy to suggest that the sophistication of our notion of gender by psychoanalysis or the recognition of its dispersal in the postmodern reduce those struggles merely to past errors now superseded. If we have moved from the 'female imagination' to an exploration of *'écriture féminine'* it is because of rather than despite the efforts of scholars such as Sandra Gilbert, Susan Gubar, Kate Millett, Ellen Moers, and Elaine Showalter.[13] However, it would lack respect for our 'mothers' to remain merely slavish. In the space opened up by a series of modernist inquiries aimed at securing an identity and a proper place for women, difference between women (race, sexuality, and age perhaps are the most obvious examples here), the very differences that the patriarchal economy of exchange sought to level, have become apparent, most notably in the rise of a lesbian criticism which introduces a play of desire and danger as well as an atmosphere of nurture and support to relations among women. This example should suffice to make it clear that a suspicion of the notions of 'proper place' and 'identity' evident in attacks on feminism as a modernist project is not simply a question of revising 'theoretical' insufficiencies but necessary if our solidarity is to avoid being just as normalising as the stereotyped 'femininity' of 'The Donna Reed Show'. Romance allows each of these postmodern writers to imagine, invent, or experiment with the question of female gender and sexuality (which are not always the same thing, as anyone who has ever taught at a woman's college knows) in a way that may liberate women from the modernist account of women's liberation, which thinks freedom as a gain in identity and property.

INTERPRETATION AND GENDER

A correspondence: this is still to say too much, or too little.

In light of these concerns, I want to begin by tracing more precisely the ways in which Derrida and Acker turn to romance as a privileged genre in postmodern prose writing. The effect of romance, with its insistence on the problems that gender creates for realist assumptions, is to pose a difficulty for the interpretative tradition of Western thought. While Acker insists upon the interpretative problems raised by gender, what counts in Derrida's text is a relation between hermeneutics and the love letter. *The Post Card* returns Derrida's abiding concern with the system of communication and the supplementary relation of writing to that system (what we might summarise as the circuit of the letter) to the condition of epistolary novel. By far the largest part of this apparently theoretical book ('*Envois*') is taken up by a series of missives that detail a romance, which is both larded with philosophical allusions and with explicitly clichéd sentimentality in a manner not unlike *The Name of the Rose*. In calling attention to this, I want to argue that something more than either an inflated sense of the significance of his own personal life or an unavowable desire on Derrida's part to make himself a laughing stock seems to be at stake here. . . .

Romance introduces gender, which is never given in advance, to the givenness of Being. And Derrida gives the object of interpretation on a postcard, reminding us that the given is necessarily, even if only minimally, inscribed within a postal system so that the hermeneutic circle is exposed to the uncertain circuit of sending and delivery, a circuit that will not form a stable horizon. Thus, Derrida performs multiple interpretations of the 'one' postcard of Plato and Socrates, upon which his missives are inscribed. In this postmodern romance, depicted on a postcard found in the Bodleian library shop and printed in *The Post Card*, Socrates comes before Plato, writing at his desk while Plato looks over his shoulder. But for Derrida, Socrates comes before Plato in another sense, for Derrida also sees the story of a rather explicit romance between the two philosophers:

> For the moment, myself, I tell you that I see *Plato* getting an erection in *Socrates*' back and see the insane hubris of his prick, an interminable, disproportionate erection traversing Paris's head like a single idea and then the copyist's chair, before slowly sliding, still warm, under *Socrates*' right leg, in harmony or symphony with the movement of this phallus sheaf, the points, plumes, pens, fingers, nails and *grattoirs*, the very pencil boxes which address themselves in the same direction.[14]

An irreverent romance, carried out in the scene of writing, upsets the tradition of philosophical influence. No postscript will ensure that Plato comes before Socrates. Postmodern romance fails to send a message that would assure any one relationship – between Socrates and Plato, between sender and receiver. Plato and Socrates could even be 'two robed transvestites' carrying 'the name of the other above his head'.[15] The figure underneath the word 'Socrates' could be Plato, while the figure beneath 'Plato' could be Socrates. To put it grammatically, S is P. The identities of the figures are as uncertain as their genders in the endless seduction of the interpretation of their philosophical relationship of endless romance.

From sexy theory (the romance of Plato and Socrates) to theoretical sex: Acker's work combines allusions to popular romance and philosophical discourse. For instance, at the beginning of *My Death, My Life by Pier Paolo Pasolini*, we learn of Sally Gernhart's romance: 'Sally had her first boyfriend.'[16] Yet if this narrative detail, like the boyfriend's nickname 'Gype', would not be out of place in popular romance, we may find ourselves surprised to learn in the following paragraph that Gype's full name is Jack Lewis Habermas. Hermeneutics meets *First Love*.

Yet what is this reference doing here? What might Jürgen Habermas (staunch supporter of the incomplete project of modernity) have to do with Jack Habermas ('ex or H-addict'; consistently insubordinate, member of an LA gang called 'The Skulls')? And do we really need to care if 'the whole problem revolves around who Sally Gernhart really is'?[17] Acker lets us dangle – a hermeneutic activity as incomplete as modernity itself.

If interpretation does not come full circle, that the emphasis is on the female character and not on the philosophical allusion seems significant.

Whereas Acker's incomplete interpretative problem implicitly raises the question of gender relations and focuses our attention on the female character, Habermas's own incomplete project – modernity – only includes women as they figure as translators of his prose.[18] Seen in this way the situation is rather simple: Acker raises the question of gender for postmodernism; Habermas, like his fellow hermeneute Gadamer, doesn't find gender even a philosophical question.

Acker's engagement with romance, however, extends even further than this single passage from *My Death, My Life* can reveal. In *Don Quixote*, Acker's plagiarising of Borges's idea of the plagiarising of Cervantes ('Pierre Menard') twists Cervantes' own parody of courtly romance overtaken by modernity. Acker's romance is not Don Quixote's: her Don is a woman, her Sancho Panza a dog of indeterminate and multiple sexual identity. Here repressed romance returns in the guise of women's supermarket fiction and the uncomfortable slippage of gender identity in order to haunt modernist assumptions of authorial identity and propriety. As the dog narrates to Don Quixote:

> 'I want you.' I drew her (him) out of her (his) fantasy. 'I don't want just another affair, fantasy. All that romance, cause the mind always changes its thoughts, is peripheral. I want something beyond. I want you.'
> She (He) nodded her (his) head, slightly.
> 'But you're much younger than me. You probably don't want something like this: To settle down.'
> She (He) said as usual that she (he) wasn't worth anything.[19]

Acker makes clear from the beginning of this passage that 'genders were complex those days', to borrow her phrase from *Empire of the Senseless*.[20] And if one were to risk a plot summary of this section of *Don Quixote* it would perhaps read: He/She was the man/woman of his/her dreams.

Yet such disturbing gender slippage occurs only in the context of the persistence of romance clichés, which is also the work of seduction or drawing out (Lat. *seducere*), even as the drawing of him/her *out* of fantasy. Reality would be the product of a seduction away from fantasy, always already invested by desire. This multiply gendered dog/human recounts a scene that could be a modified passage from a Barbara Cartland novel, to use Umberto Eco's nemesis as an example. She/he utters the clichéd phrases of romantic encounters – 'I want you', 'I don't want just another affair' – and is concerned about whether his/her potential partner wants 'to settle down'.

Similarly, after a particularly graphic description of four women (or dogs) having sex with multiple dildos and discussing the relative merits of anal and vaginal penetration, we are told that Don Quixote 'felt sad because no man loved her'.[21] The structure of allusion has become indeterminate, as with Eco's intertwining of Barbara Cartland and the Song of Songs. Acker's texts differ, however, in that they contain an added effect of destabilisation: the dispersal of any possibility of psychological realism. Private emotion proves to be the product of a citation of uncertain origin. As Don Quixote puts it to St Simeon early in the novel, 'Of course I'm not interested in personal identity'.[22] Don Quixote's more pressing question is: 'what is it to be female?'.[23] Acker's point, whose importance cannot be overestimated, is that this question is *not* also a question of identity. Explorations of identity through the use of psychological realism prove insufficient to address what it is to be female.

It is at this moment, then, that we can begin to understand the important role that romance plays in Acker's work. If Cervantes' Don believes foolishly in ideas of justice and chivalry long since discarded by a world of hypocrites, Acker evokes romance as a means of calling attention to the difficulty of making sense of feminine experience when 'being born into and part of a male world, she had no speech of her own. All she could do was read male texts which weren't hers'.[24] Romance, that is, evokes a peculiar relation to the possibility of psychological, narrative realism. Rather than simply being opposed to realism (which is, after all, still fiction), romance writes a reality that is *invested by desire* – desire that cannot itself be given 'realist' expression, that remains alien to realism, since it is not simply the property of a speaking subject. As Acker says of realism: 'This is *realism*: the unification of my perceiving and what I perceive or a making of a mirror relation between my world and the world of the painting.'[25] For Acker, realism is ready-made reality: representation given to the viewer as unproblematically real. And she knows enough of Duchamp's 'ready-mades' to problematise this immediacy. The mirror relation, which characterises realism, only gives rise to an instantaneous, uncritical, reception, or as Acker puts it, 'I see what I see immediately; I don't rethink it'.[26]

That we are so unable to rethink the perception of representation is a result of education, an education that teaches children not to think. Such is one of the lessons that the dog dreams:

> In my dream, my teacher said to me: 'All the accepted forms of education in this country, rather than teaching the child to know who she is or to know, dictate to the child who she is. Thus obfuscate any act of knowledge. Since these educators train the mind rather than the body, we can start with the physical body, the place of shitting, eating, etc., to break through our opinions or false education.'[27]

Yet lest we are led to believe that we can come to understand the truth of the falsity of education (this would be Althusser's lesson about ideology),

Acker turns the dog's dream into a combination of repetitious realism and raunchy romance, which undercuts any such claim. The realistic dialogue of the Socratic method takes on the repetitious quality of a scratched record:

Delbène said: 'We must do what we consider crimes in order to break down our destructive education.'

'But *crimes* are evil because they're human acts by which humans hurt other humans.'

'But *crimes* are evil because they're human acts by which humans hurt other humans.'

'But *crimes* are evil because they're human acts by which humans hurt other humans.'

'A good reply,' answered my teacher, 'according to the world.'

'A good reply,' answered my teacher, 'according to the world.'

'A good reply,' answered my teacher, 'according to the world.'

'Wrong,' my teacher thundered, 'for any answer that seems to be the correct answer denies this world whose nature is chance and relativity. There is no correct answer.'

'Wrong,' my teacher thundered, 'for any answer that seems to be the correct answer denies this world whose nature is chance and relativity. There is no correct answer.'

'Wrong,' my teacher thundered, 'for any answer that seems to be the correct answer denies this world whose nature is chance and relativity. There is no correct answer.'

'Wrong,' my teacher thundered, 'for any answer that seems to be the correct answer denies this world whose nature is chance and relativity. There is no correct answer.'[28]

The point of this scene is probably best summed up by the dog's observation that 'you still don't know anything'.[29] Certainty is never certain in Acker's dream of pedagogy.

Nor can we be certain of the place or role of romance, for within the scene of education, seduction moves past the point of 'common decency.' As the dog explains:

Since the body is the first ground of knowledge, my teacher made me take off my clothes. A mouth touched and licked my ass. A finger stuck into my asshole. A dildo thrust into my asshole and a dildo thrust into my cunt. Both dildoes squirted liquid into me which I saw was white. I was so over-the-top excited, I came. The main thing for me was my body's uncontrolled reactions.[30]

The teacher tells the dog in the dog's dream that the physical body is the site of resistance to established education, opening an exploration of possibilities ('who she might be') against the hegemonic discourse of identity ('what she is'). The play of violence and eroticism in this passage, which as we have seen leads to the clichés of romance, seems immediately threatening and antifeminist in its implications. Given Acker's insistence on rape as a topos for female sexuality, one is disinclined to put this down to an effect of ignorance, accident, or ideological subjugation. . . . Acker refuses realism's conventions of decorum on the grounds that the 'good writing' taught in schools is 'a way of keeping you from writing what you want to'.[31]

I always get my sexual genders confused.

I would like to continue exploring the implications of Acker's statement and argue that, within both Acker's and Derrida's work, romance – which would be another name for 'bad writing' – stands to realism as postmodernism to modernism, as a counter-discourse on history and the real. Romance, that is to say, is not simply the negation of realism, postmodernism the negation of modernism; rather romance and postmodernism are not present in simple or stable states that might allow their apprehension by a knowing subject. Therefore, a feature of romance is that it is never 'pure fantasy'. Always impure, romance refuses the modern rationality that constructs reality by means of the exclusion of desire by a knowing subject. Thus, my use of the term romance as linked to the postmodern differs from 'Romanticism' in that this irrepressible desire cannot even be contained as the property of an individual subjective will, as in Nietzsche's assault on rationalism. That is to say, in its displacement of even an irrational subjective mastery, postmodern romance will not have been Romantic.

Indeed, the most obvious formal feature shared by Acker's and Derrida's romances is a persistent disruption of the identity of the speaking subject. Acker's novel *In Memoriam to Identity* foregrounds a process common to her entire oeuvre, by which 'each person has the possibilities of being simultaneously several beings, having several lives'.[32] Multiple voices speak schizophrenically from a single pronominal position, a single voice appears identified with a multiplicity of apparently different 'characters', in a heteroglossia that lacks even the coherence of the dialogic.

Derrida's interest in the multiple and contradictory nature of linguistic identity appears in the 'polylogue' for 'n + 1 female voices' entitled 'Restitutions' in *The Truth in Painting*, where the non-finite series of n + 1 refuses even the wholeness of an *infinite* dispersion.[33] 'Envois' in *The Post Card* explores this dissemination of subjective identity, not simply by formal insistence on the status of pronominal markers of identity as precisely that, as shifters by which gender, number, and position can be shuffled and multiplied:

> Although since the gender and number remain inaccessible for me I can always play on the plural. . . . You understand that whoever writes must indeed ask himself what it is asked of him to write, and then he writes under the dictation of some addressee, this is trivial. But 'some addressee', I always leave the gender or number indeterminate, must indeed be the object of a choice of object, and chosen and seduced.[34]

Here Derrida is not simply mirroring a 'postmodern condition' in which identities have become divided and multiple. Derrida's postmodernity is not, as Fredric Jameson would claim, an accidental schizophrenia resulting from the effects of late-capitalist commodity relations, a historical moment of crisis. Identity is not something that we have recently lost, or might recover. Rather, Derrida is concerned to insist upon the dispersion of subjectivity as a structural necessity that both constitutes and confounds communication:

> Who *will prove* that the sender is the same man, or woman? And the male or female addressee? Or that they are *not* identical? To themselves, male or female, first of all? That they do or do not form a couple? Or several couples? Or a crowd? Where would the principle of identification be? In the name? No, and then whoever wants to make a proof becomes a participant in our corpus. They would not prevent us from loving each other. And they would love us as one loves counterfeiters, impostors, *contrefacteurs* (this word has been looking for me for years).[35]

The postal system (Derrida's name for the circuit of communication) insists upon a structural deferral or *post*ponement inhabiting the very heart of the dream of telecommunications. The message that might fix the identity of the sender or addressee of a previous message is precisely that, another message, which the sender and addressee would require in turn to be established, and so on in non-finite series. And the *facteur* or postman goes on looking for the right person to whom to deliver a message. The *facteur* can only do so by entering the circuit of the letter, or post card (to give the material support of written communication its most etiolated form), by becoming him/herself a *contrefacteur*. In entering the circuit of the letter, the letter-carrier becomes an exchanger of letters, a *contre facteur*. But this is no gain in identity, since a *contrefacteur* is precisely a forger or counterfeiter. The postman keeps on looking, for years, postponed in the very attempt to overcome delay.

Far from being the accidental product of material circumstances, delay – and the hole that it opens in the identity both of and between sender and receiver – is structural to the postal system, even for its smallest imaginable unit, the postcard marked only by a date and a signature. The postcard hides nothing, enfolds nothing. The medium is the message, as it were. Here Derrida's interest is in showing how, even at the apex of telecommunicational efficiency, a deconstructive logic of differance splits and defers the possibility of identity. As Derrida puts it, 'letters are always post cards: neither legible nor illegible, open and radically unintelligible'.[36]

This disruption of identity is also carried out in relation to the status of the author/signature. In the writings of both Derrida and Acker, it is the very insistence of apparently direct interpolated autobiographical material that most marks the inability of the writer to 'be herself' (or himself or both, as the case may be), to achieve an identity. For instance, Acker writes of the travels and travails of 'Kathy' and even puts her photograph on the Grove editions of her novels. And in *The Post Card* Derrida drops a series of proper names (Hillis, Cynthia, Jonathan, and Paul, to name only a few) that invite the reader to read Derrida's text as if it were some kind of autobiographical *roman à cléf*. But this is not all. To add to the referential confusion, Derrida signs and re-signs in his text, continually punning on his name. Gregory Ulmer describes this condition well when he points out that 'what Derrida wishes to expose is the truth effect of the signature, of the "I" who appears to speak, by displacing the opposition between pre-text and text, life and art.'[37] The effect is one of dispersion, as the proper name falls into the very linguistic dissemination to which the common noun is prey. The name, which should mark an autonomous integrity for which language is a tool, instead becomes itself part of an anonymous work of language quite independent of any subjective presence.

Derrida summarises and enacts this problematic – one which he analysed earlier in 'Signature Event Context' and *Signéponge* – when he remarks that: 'The name is made to do without the life of the bearer, and is therefore always somewhat the name of someone dead'.[38] This disruption of the modernist logic of identity opens a space within knowledge analogous to the space that romance opens within the real. That space cannot itself be named, unless with the non-name of woman. As Acker puts it:

> Men told me they remembered whom they fucked: they brought out memories for display, notches cut into a belt, to name identity. Being female I didn't and don't have to prove that I don't exist.[39]

In Acker's novel the male sexual trophy parallels the effect of the signature in Derrida's analysis – the 'proof' of identity that marks its capacity to exist in the absence of the sender. Here, I would want to go so far as to say that as a postmodernist Acker asks what happens when desire is no longer the property of an individual subject. The importance of her work for feminism is that in some sense this has always been the situation of women, unable to call a desire their own, unable to have property in their own desire. Oversimplifying, I could say that Acker finds in the non-name of woman the kind of deconstructive trace effect that Derrida has tended to call 'writing'.

PLAGIARISM AND AUTHOR-ITY

Everything has been said. These lines are not my writing.

This connection is perhaps most clearly seen in Acker's own interest in writing as the illicit reproductive work of a signifier always in supplementary excess over the message it should convey. For Acker, the strong example of the trace-effect of writing is plagiarism, a concern which I raised earlier in the context of Acker's interrogation of gender. What was not evident in this earlier discussion, however, is the extent to which Acker's work persistently thematises plagiarism in order to call attention to a postmodern understanding of 'reproductive rights' (certainly a feminist concern). The disruption of the authoritative original in an insistence upon its preoriginary marking by reproduction is not simply a theoretical account of the sign, nor a critique of creativity (although it is both those things).[40] In the very widest sense, a sense that stretches from questions of philosophical influence to surrogate motherhood, it is an assault upon Western culture's privileging of abstraction, of the signifier over the signified, an assault on the legal fiction of paternity.

The obvious cases are two of Acker's titles: *Don Quixote* and *Great Expectations*.[41] Such overt plagiarism is enough to give any book-store clerk a moment's pause. But Acker 'borrows' more than titles. To name only a few examples: characters from Shakespeare's *Macbeth* and *Romeo and Juliet* and a section of Dickens's *Great Expectations* appear in *My Death, My Life*; *Florida* is an unacknowledged rewrite of the film *Key Largo*;[42] and Acker even repeats her own material in *Empire of the Senseless*. The significance of these multiple acts of plagiarism is best summed up in a letter Emily writes to Charlotte Brontë in Brussels in *My Death, My Life*: 'I can talk by plagiarizing other people's words that is real language, and then . . . then I make something'.[43] To say something different is not necessarily to say something original: it may be to plagiarise. Thus, for Acker, intertextual relations work to split apart the fusion of originality and identity that grounds the modernist notion of creative authority, or authorial subjectivity.[44]

Plagiarism is also, of course, a persistent concern of Derrida in *The Post Card*; as he puts it, 'I am citing, but as always rearranging a little. Guess the number of false citations in my publications'.[45] Every 'original' statement is doubly unauthentic, an inaccurate quotation in words that are only recognisable if they have already been used by others. And the reader, in the face of Derrida's taunts, can't with certainty sort out 'authentic' from 'false' citations – a condition reminiscent of the role anachronism plays in Eco's and Scott's romance. To put this another way, postmodern romance contains purloined letters – letters stolen and forged from the past – which may or may not reach their historical destinations. Redirected, these letters may end up as the anachronisms and false citations of postmodern romance.

What is important about the stolen and counterfeited letters of postmodern romance is that they provide for a freedom from tradition, including the restrictions of realism which so concerned Acker. Tradition could be said to exert its influence in much the same way as that of the stamp: in order to send a message via the post, the sender must purchase a stamp, must pay her/his debt to the post. Likewise, 'a master thinker emits postage stamps or post cards, he constructs highways with tolls'.[46] The bottom line is that one cannot send a message without attempting to pay one's debt to the past, and thus, 'the anxiety of influence is born' in the form of the postage stamp. Yet the possibility of purloined letters ensures that 'contrary to appearances, no one perceives or receives a thing';[47] the message is delayed, misdirected, lost.

In this postal context, postmodern romance is a way to loosen the tyranny of tradition, which exerts its control in the form of pre-occupations as mundane as chronological and alphabetical order – in texts as common or uncommon as phone books, street directories, and histories of philosophy. By contrast, the order of romance is not self-evident. For instance, in 'Envois' Derrida arranges his letters chronologically, and yet there is the single 'misplaced' letter on the back cover. Dated November 17, 1979, it begins by telling the reader that:

> You [*Tu*] were reading a somewhat retro loveletter, the last in history. But you have not yet received it. Yes, its lack or excess of address prepares it to fall into all hands: a post card, an open letter in which the secret appears, but indecipherably. You can take it or pass it off, for example, as a message from Socrates to Freud.

Does this letter come 'first,' in that the reader will read the back cover of the book first? Or do we hold dear the tyranny of chronological order and know to place it as the last in the series of letters – the concluding love letter of 'Envois,' the end of romance? As the contents of the letter suggest, however, no simple relationship between sender/receiver, origin/destination exists here. The last love letter in history has not yet been received; it is, one assumes, still purloined in the post. That romance does not provide an order for love letters, that it does not attempt to assure the receipt of its messages, would thus be the point that Derrida stresses when he provides us with his multiple versions of the romance between Plato and Socrates.

All of this is to say that postmodern romance should not be considered a genre that dictates aesthetic or historical order. In a sense, postmodern romance is a genreless genre because it is, impossibly, all genres. As Derrida puts it, 'I will have . . . loved according to every genre/gender [*genre*]'.[48] The future anterior of romance's love story invades all genres/genders and is limited by none.

That postmodern romance is not preceded by rules is a point that Acker's fiction stresses even more directly. The unanswerable question that she poses is: What might romance be? In *Great Expectations* this question takes shape in the second section, entitled 'The Beginnings of Romance', where the origin of romance is anything but clear. If the opening of the section could resemble a sordid version of Freud's family romance, in which the mother admits to not wanting her daughter and the father dies before ever appearing on the narrative scene, the remainder of the section strays further from any conventional understanding of romance. The narrator, for instance, understands her life in such a way that has nothing to do either with romance or with beginnings: 'I realize that all my life is endings,' she claims;[49] a subsequent subsection purports to cover 'Seattle Art Society', while going on to discuss 'historical examples'; and the concluding pages relate in dialogue format the complex relationship between Sarah, Clifford, She, and Portrait in Red. In each of these instances, no pattern emerges that would underscore the structure of postmodern romance. Propp or Genette would have a difficult time here.

This is not to suggest, however, that there is necessarily anything purely original about postmodern romance either. That the preceding section of *Great Expectations* is called 'Plagiarism' is significant. In some sense, we've heard it all before; 'everything has been said,' as Acker puts it.[50] The connection between plagiarism and the formlessness of postmodern romance becomes even clearer in *My Death, My Life*. Here Acker begins the section entitled 'Narrative Breakdown for Carla Harriman'[51] with what are effectively unacknowledged plot summaries of scenes from Pasolini's *The Decameron*. And after this gesture of plagiarism, Acker later adds a section that links the question of form with romance:

Accent her. Hand armors on wonder. Orphan forces war or instance of ovary. The manor of stove.

An instance of romance. Or form. Or form. Or form. Or form. Or form. Or form. Or form. Or form. Or form. Or form.

An land. An land. An land. An land. An land. An land. An land. An land. An land. An land. An land. An land. An land. An

And scape escape romance. And scape escape romance. And scape escape romance. And scape escape romance. And scape escape romance. And. . . .

2. Language breakdown.[52]

This then would be the message to Carla Harriman, that 'Ack' sent her ('Accent her'), with a signature that absents the sender even as it emphasises her. Without a present signatory, this 'orphan' sounds only like 'or form'. Just as 'instance of ovary' is reshuffled as 'manor of stove', the 'or' reverses to the 'ro' of 'romance'. The 'land' of 'An land' seems unable to join up with the 'scape' of 'And scape' to provide a recognisable landscape; instead we have merely the near homonym 'and scape'. In a strong sense, of course, this doesn't mean anything. Rather, the letters of romance and landscape are shuffled and hypogrammatised. The message plagiarises itself, consumes itself, from its apparent 'origin' in the words 'One. One and one . . .' repeated thirty-six times before it reaches 'one and two'. Language is generated almost mathematically in this missive, but it occurs as autocannibalism:

> Language is more important than meaning. Don't make anything out of broken-up syntax cause you're looking to make meaning where nonsense will. Of course nonsense isn't only nonsense. I'll say again that writing isn't just writing, it's a meeting of writing and living the way existence is the meeting of mental and material or language of idea and sign. It is how we live. We must take how we live.[53]

Like Derrida, Acker seems to be calling for a certain exhaustion of language, not a theory of romance in the modernist sense.[54] The broken syntax that brings together romance, form, and escape cannot be made to have 'meaning' in the sense that these words or signs do not correspond to previously understood significations.

Derrida confronts the problem of language by way of the postcard. If for Heidegger language is the house of Being, for Derrida language is a house of postcards. As Derrida puts it: 'Our entire library, our entire encyclopedia, our words, our pictures, our figures, our secrets, all an immense house of post cards'.[55] The fragility of a house of cards exposed to the postal system. In this way Derrida dissociates language from a Heideggerian notion of Being, stressing that 'Envois' will not have been a modernist theory of language, just as it will not have been a metahistory of the postal system, not outside the system but a postcard among postcards:

> By no longer treating the posts as a metaphor of the *envoi* of Being, one can account for what essentially and decisively occurs, everywhere, and including language, thought, science, and everything that conditions them, when the postal structure shifts, *Satz* if you will, and posits or posts itself otherwise. This is why this history of the posts, which I would like to write and to dedicate to you, cannot be a history of the posts: primarily because it concerns the very possibility of history, of all the concepts, too, of history, of tradition, of the transmission or interruptions, goings astray, etc. And then because such a 'history of the posts' would be but a miniscule *envoi* in a network that it allegedly would analyze (there is no metapostal), only a card lost in a bag, that a strike, or even a sorting accident, can always delay indefinitely, lose without return. This is why I will not write it, but I dedicate to you what remains of this impossible project.[56]

Herein lies the theoretical modesty of deconstruction, something which our critical academy has been inclined to miss. This theory will not claim to stand outside, to master, the textuality of which it speaks. As I remarked at the beginning of this chapter, this is theory in its postmodernity, whose 'post' marks a dependency upon the very modernity of the system that it deconstructs. This 'post' does not surpass; it 'remains'. 'Remains', not 'persists' or 'endures', with all the undertones of the incomplete, the 'left-over', the less-than-heroic. An original wound in modernism, a scar that remains, from the 'battle' declared in *Of Grammatology* between writing and logocentrism.[57] . . .

Deconstruction has become suspicious of theoretical purity, feminism of theoretical rigidity, the supposed gender-neutrality of knowledge. Our response should not be to promote alternatives, be they irrationalism or 'women's science'. There is no new identity for a knowing subject on the other side of the deconstruction or the feminist critique of theoretical metalanguages.

This long story about the seductions of theory and the dispersion of identities certainly tends to cast doubt on traditional claims about the goals of intellectual and political endeavour. I have said something about a suspicion of theory that is common to deconstruction and to feminism, though our institutional practices tend to cast both as kinds of theory. And in some sense, each can be said to have invited this description. Deconstruction has at times been thought of as merely a method of literary analysis, and feminist accounts of liberation have rested on notions of identity which, as necessarily normative, have functioned in exclusionary and oppressive ways. In ceasing to think about subjectivity in terms of identity, ideology in terms of falsification, we do not abandon critical discourse; rather, we shift away from a merely negative or reactive understanding of resistance as inherently oppositional. The interaction of feminism and deconstruction begins here(after), when attention to difference replaces oppositional identity, when solidarity displaces critical isolation. Their postmodern romance, however, is the matter of another work than this one. For romance's dispersion of identities includes that of the theorist, which perhaps precludes any conclusion. You can never have too much romance.

15

Women's Time

Julia Kristeva

TWO GENERATIONS

In its beginnings, the women's movement, as the struggle of suffragists and of existential feminists, aspired to gain a place in linear time as the time of project and history. In this sense, the movement, while immediately universalist, is also deeply rooted in the sociopolitical life of nations. The political demands of women; the struggles for equal pay for equal work, for taking power in social institutions on an equal footing with men; the rejection, when necessary, of the attributes traditionally considered feminine or maternal insofar as they are deemed incompatible with insertion in that history – all are part of the *logic of identification* with certain values: not with the ideological (these are combated, and rightly so, as reactionary) but, rather, with the logical and ontological values of a rationality dominant in the nation-state. Here it is unnecessary to enumerate the benefits which this logic of identification and the ensuing struggle have achieved and continue to achieve for women (abortion, contraception, equal pay, professional recognition, etc.): these have already had or will soon have effects even more important than those of the Industrial Revolution. Universalist in its approach, this current in feminism *globalises* the problems of women of different milieux, ages, civilisations, or simply of varying psychic structures, under the label 'Universal Woman'. A consideration of *generations* of women can only be conceived of in this global way as a succession, as a progression in the accomplishment of the initial programme mapped out by its founders.

In a second phase, linked, on the one hand, to the younger women who came to feminism after May 1968 and, on the other, to women who had an aesthetic or psychoanalytic experience, linear temporality has been almost totally refused, and as a consequence there has arisen an exacerbated distrust of the entire political dimension. If it is true that this more recent current of feminism refers to its predecessors and that the struggle for sociocultural recognition of women is necessarily its main concern, this current seems to think of itself as belonging to another generation – qualitatively different from the first one – in its conception of its own identity and, consequently, of temporality as such. Essentially interested in the specificity of female psychology and its symbolic realisations, these women seek to give a language to the intrasubjective and corporeal experiences left mute by culture in the past. Either as artists or writers, they have undertaken a veritable exploration of the *dynamic of signs*, an exploration which relates this tendency, at least at the level of its aspirations, to all major projects of aesthetic and religious upheaval. Ascribing this experience to a new generation does not only mean that other, more subtle problems have been added to the demands for sociopolitical identification made in the beginning. It also means that, by demanding recognition of an irreducible identity, without equal in the opposite sex and, as such, exploded, plural, fluid, in a certain way non-identical, this feminism situates itself outside the linear time of identities which communicate through projection and revindication. Such a feminism rejoins, on the one hand, the archaic (mythical) memory and, on the other, the cyclical or monumental temporality of marginal movements. It is certainly not by chance that the European and trans-European problematic has been posited as such at the same time as this new phase of feminism.

Finally, it is the mixture of the two attitudes – *insertion* into history and the radical *refusal* of the subjective limitations imposed by this history's time on an experiment carried out in the name of the irreducible difference – that seems to have broken loose over the past few years in European feminist movements, particularly in France and in Italy.

If we accept this meaning of the expression 'a new generation of women', two kinds of questions might then be posed. What sociopolitical processes or events have provoked this mutation? What are its problems: its contributions as well as dangers?

SOCIALISM AND FREUDIANISM

One could hypothesise that if this new generation of women shows itself to be more diffuse and perhaps less conscious in the United States and more massive in Western Europe, this is because of a veritable split in social relations and mentalities, a split produced by socialism and Freudianism. I mean by *socialism* that egalitarian doctrine which is increasingly broadly disseminated and accepted as based on common sense, as well as that social practice adopted by governments and political parties in democratic regimes which are forced to extend the zone of egalitarianism to include the distribution of goods as well as access to culture. By *Freudianism* I mean that lever, inside this egalitarian and socialising field, which once again poses the question of sexual difference and of the difference among subjects who themselves are not reducible one to the other.

Western socialism, shaken in its very beginnings by the egalitarian or differential demands of its women (e.g. Flora Tristan), quickly got rid of those women who aspired to recognition of a specificity of the female role in society and culture, only retaining from them, in the egalitarian and universalistic spirit of Enlightenment Humanism, the idea of a necessary identification between the two sexes as the only and unique means for liberating the 'second sex'. I shall not develop here the fact that this 'ideal' is far from being applied in practice by these socialist-inspired movements and parties and that it was in part from the revolt against this situation that the new generation of women in Western Europe was born after May 1968. Let us just say that in theory, and as put into practice in Eastern Europe, socialist ideology, based on a conception of the human being as determined by its place in *production* and the *relations of production*, did not take into consideration this same human being according to its place in *reproduction*, on the one hand, or in the *symbolic order*, on the other. Consequently, the specific character of women could only appear as non-essential or even non-existent to the totalising and even totalitarian spirit of this ideology.[1] We begin to see that this same egalitarian and in fact censuring treatment has been imposed, from Enlightenment Humanism through socialism, on religious specificities and, in particular, on Jews.[2]

What has been achieved by this attitude remains nonetheless of capital importance for women, and I shall take as an example the change in the destiny of women in the socialist countries of Eastern Europe. It could be said, with only slight exaggeration, that the demands of the suffragists and existential feminists have, to a great extent, been met in these countries, since three of the main egalitarian demands of early feminism have been or are now being implemented despite vagaries and blunders: economic, political, and professional equality. The fourth, sexual equality, which implies permissiveness in sexual relations (including homosexual relations), abortion, and contraception, remains stricken by taboo in Marxian ethics as well as for reasons of state. It is, then, this fourth equality which is the problem and which therefore appears *essential* in the struggle of a new generation. But simultaneously and as a consequence of these socialist accomplishments – which are in fact a total deception – the struggle is no longer concerned with the quest for equality but, rather, with difference and specificity. It is precisely at this point that the new generation encounters what might be called the *symbolic* question. Sexual difference – which is at once biological, physiological, and relative to reproduction – is translated by and translates a difference in the relationship of subjects to the symbolic contract which *is* the social contract: a difference, then, in the relationship to power, language, and meaning. The sharpest and most subtle point of feminist subversion brought about by the new generation will henceforth be situated on the terrain of the inseparable conjunction of the sexual and the symbolic, in order to try to discover, first, the specificity of the female, and then, in the end, that of each individual woman.

A certain saturation of socialist ideology, a certain exhaustion of its potential as a programme for a new social contract (it is obvious that the effective realisation of this programme is far from being accomplished, and I am here treating only its system of thought) makes way for . . . Freudianism. I am, of course, aware that this term and this practice are somewhat shocking to the American intellectual consciousness (which rightly reacts to a muddled and normalising form of psychoanalysis) and, above all, to the feminist consciousness. To restrict my remarks to the latter: Is it not true that Freud has been seen only as a denigrator or even an exploiter of women? as an irritating phallocrat in a Vienna which was at once Puritan and decadent – a man who fantasised women as sub-men, castrated men?

CASTRATED AND/OR SUBJECT TO LANGUAGE

Before going beyond Freud to propose a more just or more modern vision of women, let us try, first, to understand his notion of castration. It is, first of all, a question of an *anguish* or *fear* of castration, or of correlative penis *envy*; a question, therefore, of *imaginary* formations readily perceivable in the *discourse* of neurotics of both sexes, men and women. But, above all, a careful reading of Freud, going beyond his biologism and his mechanism, both characteristic of his time, brings out two things. First, as presupposition for the 'primal scene,' the castration fantasy and its correlative (penis envy) are hypotheses, a priori suppositions intrinsic to the theory itself, in the sense that these are not the ideological fantasies of their inventor but, rather, logical necessities to be placed at the 'origin' in order to explain what unceasingly functions in neurotic discourse. In other words, neurotic discourse, in man and woman, can only be understood in terms of its own logic when its fundamental causes are admitted as the fantasies of the primal scene and castration, even if (as may be the case) nothing renders them present in reality itself. Stated in still other terms, the reality of castration is no more real than the hypothesis of an explosion which, according to modern astrophysics, is at the origin of the universe: Nothing proves it, in a sense it is an article of faith, the only difference being that numerous phenomena of life in this 'big-bang' universe are explicable only through this initial hypothesis. But one is infinitely more jolted when this kind of intellectual method concerns inanimate matter than when it is applied to our own subjectivity and thus, perhaps, to the fundamental mechanism of our epistemophilic thought.

Moreover, certain texts written by Freud (*The Interpretation of Dreams*, but especially those of the second topic, in particular the *Metapsychology*) and their recent extensions (notably by Lacan), imply that castration is, in sum, the imaginary construction of a radical operation which constitutes the symbolic field and all beings inscribed therein. This operation constitutes signs and syntax: that is, language, as a *separation* from a presumed state of nature, of pleasure fused with nature so that the introduction of an articulated network of differences, which refers to objects henceforth and only in this way separated from a subject, may constitute *meaning*. This logical operation of separation (confirmed by all psycholinguistic and child psychology) which preconditions the binding of language which is already syntactical, is therefore the common destiny of the two sexes, men and women. That certain biofamilial conditions and relationships cause women (and notably hysterics) to deny this separation and the language which ensues from it, whereas men (notably obsessionals) magnify both and, terrified, attempt to master them – this is what Freud's discovery has to tell us on this issue.

The analytic situation indeed shows that it is the penis which, becoming the major referent in this operation of separation, gives full meaning to the *lack* or to the *desire* which constitutes the subject during his or her insertion into the order of language. I should only like to indicate here that, in order for this operation constitutive of the symbolic and the social to appear in its full truth and for it to be understood by both sexes, it would be just to emphasise its extension to all that is privation of fulfilment and of totality; exclusion of a pleasing, natural, and sound state: in short, the break indispensable to the advent of the symbolic.

It can now be seen how women, starting with this theoretical apparatus, might try to understand their sexual and symbolic difference in the framework of social, cultural, and professional realisation, in order to try, by seeing their position therein, either to fulfil their own experience to a maximum or – but always starting from this point – to go further and call into question the very apparatus itself.

LIVING THE SACRIFICE

In any case, and for women in Europe today, whether or not they are conscious of the various mutations (socialist and Freudian) which have produced or simply accompanied their coming into their own, the urgent question on our agenda might be formulated as follows: *What can be our place in the symbolic contract?* If the social contract, far from being that of equal men, is based on an essentially sacrificial relationship of separation and articulation of differences which in this way produces communicable meaning, what is our place in this order of sacrifice and/or of language?

No longer wishing to be excluded or no longer content with the function which has always been demanded of us (to maintain, arrange, and perpetuate this sociosymbolic contract as mothers, wives, nurses, doctors, teachers . . .), how can we reveal our place, first as it is bequeathed to us by tradition, and then as we want to transform it?

It is difficult to evaluate what in the relationship of women to the symbolic as it reveals itself now arises from a sociohistorical conjuncture (patriarchal ideology, whether Christian, humanist, socialist or so forth), and what arises from a structure. We can speak only about a structure observed in a sociohistorical context, which is that of Christian, Western civilisation and its lay ramifications. In this sense of psychosymbolic structure, women, 'we' (is it necessary to recall the warnings we issued at the beginning of this article concerning the totalising use of this plural?)[3] seem to feel that they are the casualties, that they have been left out of the sociosymbolic contract, of language as the fundamental social bond. They find no affect there, no more than they find the fluid and infinitesimal significations of their relationships with the nature of their own bodies, that of the child, another woman, or a man. This frustration, which to a certain extent belongs to men also, is being voiced today principally by women, to the point of becoming the essence of the new feminist ideology. A therefore difficult, if not impossible, identification with the sacrificial logic of separation and syntactical sequence at the foundation of language and the social code leads to the rejection of the symbolic – lived as the rejection of the paternal function and ultimately generating psychoses.

But this limit, rarely reached as such, produces two types of counter-investment of what we have termed the sociosymbolic contract. On the one hand, there are attempts to take hold of this contract, to possess it in order to enjoy it as such or to subvert it. How? The answer remains difficult to formulate (since, precisely, any formulation is deemed frustrating, mutilating, sacrificial) or else is in fact formulated using stereotypes taken from extremist and often deadly ideologies. On the other hand, another attitude is more lucid from the beginning, more self-analytical which – without refusing or sidestepping this sociosymbolic order – consists in trying to explore the constitution and functioning of this contract, starting less from the knowledge accumulated about it (anthropology, psychoanalysis, linguistics) than from the very personal effect experienced when facing it as subject and as a woman. This leads to the active research,[4] still rare, undoubtedly hesitant but always dissident, being carried out by women in the human sciences; particularly those attempts, in the wake of contemporary art, to break the code, to shatter language, to find a specific discourse closer to the body and emotions, to the unnameable repressed by the social contract. I am not speaking here of a 'woman's language', whose (at least syntactical) existence is highly problematical and whose apparent lexical specificity is perhaps more the product of a social marginality than of a sexual-symbolic difference.[5]

Nor am I speaking of the aesthetic quality of productions by women, most of which – with a few exceptions (but has this not always been the case with both sexes?) – are a reiteration of a more or less euphoric or depressed romanticism and always an explosion of an ego lacking narcissistic gratification.[6] What I should like to retain, nonetheless, as a mark of collective aspiration, as an undoubtedly vague and unimplemented intention, but one which is intense and which has been deeply revealing these past few years, is this: The new generation of women is showing that its major social concern has become the sociosymbolic contract as a sacrificial contract. If anthropologists and psychologists, for at least a century, have not stopped insisting on this in their attention to 'savage thought,' wars, the discourse of dreams, or writers, women are today affirming – and we consequently face a mass phenomenon – that they are forced to experience this sacrificial contract against their will.[7] Based on this, they are attempting a revolt which they see as a resurrection but which society as a whole understands as murder. This attempt can lead us to a not less and sometimes more deadly violence. Or to a cultural innovation. Probably to both at once. But that is precisely where the stakes are, and they are of epochal significance.

THE TERROR OF POWER OR THE POWER OF TERRORISM

First in socialist countries (such as the USSR and China) and increasingly in Western democracies, under pressure from feminist movements, women are being promoted to leadership positions in government, industry, and culture. Inequalities, devalorisations, under-estimations, even persecution of women at this level continue to hold sway in vain. The struggle against them is a struggle against archaisms. The cause has nonetheless been understood, the principle has been accepted. What remains is to break down the resistance to change. In this sense, this struggle, while still one of the main concerns of the new generation, is not, strictly speaking, *its* problem. In relationship to *power*, its problem might rather be summarised as follows: What happens when women come into power and identify with it? What happens when, on the contrary, they refuse power and create a parallel society, a counterpower which then takes on aspects ranging from a club of ideas to a group of terrorist commandos?

The assumption by women of executive, industrial, and cultural power has not, up to the present time, radically changed the nature of this power. This can be clearly seen in the East, where women promoted to decision-making positions suddenly obtain the economic as well as the narcissistic advantages refused them for thousands of years and become the pillars of the existing governments, guardians of the status quo, the most zealous protectors of the established order.[8] This identification by women with the very power structures previously considered as frustrating, oppressive, or inaccessible has often been used in modern times by totalitarian regimes: the German National-Socialists and the Chilean junta are examples of this.[9] The fact that this is a paranoid type of counterinvestment in an initially denied symbolic order can perhaps explain this troubling phenomenon; but an explanation does not prevent its massive propagation around the globe, perhaps in less dramatic forms than the totalitarian ones mentioned above, but all moving toward levelling, stabilisation, conformism, at the cost of crushing exceptions, experiments, chance occurrences.

Some will regret that the rise of a libertarian movement such as feminism ends, in some of its aspects, in the consolidation of conformism; others will rejoice and profit from this fact. Electoral campaigns, the very life of political parties, continue to bet on this latter tendency. Experience proves that too quickly even the protest or innovative initiatives on the part of women inhaled by power systems (when they do not submit to them right off) are soon credited to the system's account; and that the long-awaited democratisation of institutions as a result of the entry of women most often comes down to fabricating a few 'chiefs' among them. The difficulty presented by this logic of integrating the second sex into a value system experienced as foreign and therefore counterinvested is how to avoid the centralisation of power, how to detach women from it, and how then to proceed, through their critical, differential, and autonomous interventions, to render decision-making institutions more flexible.

Then there are the more radical feminist currents which, refusing homologation to any role of identification with existing power no matter what the power may be, make of the second sex a *countersociety*. A 'female society' is then constituted as a sort of alter ego of the official society, in which all real or fantasised possibilities for *jouissance* take refuge. Against the sociosymbolic contract, both sacrificial and frustrating, this countersociety is imagined as harmonious, without prohibitions, free and fulfilling. In our modern societies which have no hereafter or, at least, which are caught up in a transcendency either reduced to this side of the world (Protestantism) or crumbling (Catholicism and its current challenges), the countersociety remains the only refuge for fulfilment since it is precisely an a-topia, a place outside the law, utopia's floodgate.

As with any society, the countersociety is based on the expulsion of an excluded element, a scapegoat charged with the evil of which the community duly constituted can then purge itself; a purge which will finally exonerate that community of any future criticism. Modern protest movements have often reiterated this logic, locating the guilty one – in order to fend off criticism – in the foreign, in capital alone, in the other religion, in the other sex. Does not feminism become a kind of inverted sexism when this logic is followed to its conclusion? The various forms of marginalism – according to sex, age, religion, or ideology – represent in the modern world this refuge for *jouissance*, a sort of laicised transcendence. But with women, and insofar as the number of those feeling concerned by this problem has increased, although in less spectacular forms than a few years ago, the problem of the countersociety is becoming massive: It occupies no more and no less than 'half of the sky'.

It has, therefore, become clear, because of the particular radicalisation of the second generation, that these protest movements, including feminism, are not 'initially libertarian' movements which only later, through internal deviations or external chance manipulations, fall back into the old ruts of the initially combated archetypes. Rather, the very logic of counterpower and of countersociety necessarily generates, by its very structure, its essence as a simulacrum of the combated society or of power. In this sense and from a viewpoint undoubtedly too Hegelian, modern feminism has only been but a moment in the interminable process of coming to consciousness about the implacable violence (separation, castration, etc.) which constitutes any symbolic contract.

Thus the identification with power in order to consolidate it or the constitution of a fetishist counterpower – restorer of the crises of the self and provider of a *jouissance* which is always already a transgression – seem to be the two social forms which the face-off between the new generation of women and the social contract can take. That one also finds the problem of terrorism there is structurally related.

The large number of women in terrorist groups (Palestinian commandos, the Baader–Meinhoff Gang, Red Brigades, etc.) has already been pointed out, either violently or prudently according to the source of information. The exploitation of women is still too great and the traditional prejudices against them too violent for one to be able to envision this phenomenon with sufficient distance. It can, however, be said from now on that this is the inevitable product of what we have called a denial of the sociosymbolic contract and its counterinvestment as the only means of self-defence in the struggle to safeguard an identity. This paranoid-type mechanism is at the base of any political involvement. It may produce different civilising attitudes in the sense that these attitudes allow a more or less flexible reabsorption of violence and death. But when a subject is too brutally excluded from this sociosymbolic stratum; when, for example, a woman feels her effective life as a woman or her condition as a social being too brutally ignored by existing discourse or power (from her family to social institutions); she may, by counterinvesting the violence she has endured, make of herself a 'possessed' agent of this violence in order to combat what was experienced as frustration – with arms which may seem disproportional, but which are not so in comparison with the subjective or more precisely narcissistic suffering from which they originate. Necessarily opposed to the bourgeois democratic regimes in power, this terrorist violence offers as a programme of liberation an order which is even more oppressive, more sacrificial than those it combats. Strangely enough, it is not against totalitarian regimes that these terrorist groups with women participants unleash themselves but, rather, against liberal systems, whose essence is, of course, exploitative, but whose expanding democratic legality guarantees relative tolerance. Each time, the mobilisation takes place in the name of a nation, of an oppressed group, of a human essence imagined as good and sound; in the name, then, of a kind of fantasy of archaic fulfilment which an arbitrary, abstract, and thus even bad and ultimately discriminatory order has come to disrupt. While that order is accused of being oppressive, is it not actually being reproached with being too weak, with not measuring up to this pure and good, but henceforth lost, substance? Anthropology has shown that the social order is sacrificial, but sacrifice orders violence, binds it, tames it. Refusal of the social order exposes one to the risk that the so-called good substance, once it is unchained, will explode, without curbs, without law or right, to become an absolute arbitrariness.

Following the crisis of monotheism, the revolutions of the past two centuries, and more recently fascism and Stalinism, have tragically set in action this logic of the oppressed goodwill which leads to massacres. Are women more apt than other social categories, notably the exploited classes, to invest in this implacable machine of terrorism? No categorical response, either positive or negative, can currently be given to this question. It must be pointed out, however, that since the dawn of feminism, and certainly before, the political activity of exceptional women, and thus in a certain sense of liberated women, has taken the form of murder, conspiracy, and crime. Finally, there is also the connivance of the young girl with her mother, her greater difficulty than the boy in detaching herself from the mother in order to accede to the order of signs as invested by the absence and separation constitutive of the paternal function. A girl will never be able to re-establish this contact with her mother – a contact which the boy may possibly rediscover through his relationship with the opposite sex – except by becoming a mother herself, through a child, or through a homosexuality which is in itself extremely difficult and judged as suspect by society; and, what is more, why and in the name of what dubious symbolic benefit would she want to make this detachment so as to conform to a symbolic system which remains foreign to her? In sum, all of these considerations – her eternal debt to the woman-mother – make a woman more vulnerable within the symbolic order, more fragile when she suffers within it, more virulent when she protects herself from it. If the archetype of the belief in a good and pure substance, that of utopias, is the belief in the omnipotence of an archaic, full, total, englobing mother with no frustration, no separation, with no break-producing symbolism (with no castration, in other words), then it becomes evident that we will never be able to defuse the violences mobilised through the counterinvestment necessary to carrying out this phantasm, unless one challenges precisely this myth of the archaic mother. It is in this way that we can understand the warnings against the recent invasion of the women's movements by paranoia, as in Lacan's scandalous sentence 'There is no such thing as Woman'.[10] Indeed, she does *not* exist with a capital 'W', possessor of some mythical unity – a supreme power, on which is based the terror of power and terrorism as the desire for power. But what an unbelievable force for subversion in the modern world! And, at the same time, what playing with fire!

CREATURES AND CREATRESSES

The desire to be a mother, considered alienating and even reactionary by the preceding generation of feminists, has obviously not become a standard for the present generation. But we have seen in the past few years an increasing number of women who not only consider their maternity compatible with their professional life or their feminist involvement (certain improvements in the quality of life are also at the origin of this: an increase in the number of day-care centres and nursery schools, more active participation of men in child care and domestic life, etc.) but also find it indispensable to their discovery, not of the plenitude, but of the complexity of the female experience, with all that this complexity comprises in joy and pain. This tendency has its extreme: in the refusal of the paternal function by lesbian and single mothers can be seen one of the most violent forms taken by the rejection of the symbolic outlined above, as well as one of the most fervent divinisations of maternal power – all of which cannot help but trouble an entire legal and moral order without, however, proposing an alternative to it. Let us remember here that Hegel distinguished between female right (familial and religious) and male law (civil and political). If our societies know well the uses and abuses of male law, it must also be recognised that female right is designated, for the moment by a blank. And if these practices of maternity, among others, were to be generalised, women themselves would be responsible for elaborating the appropriate legislation to check the violence to which, otherwise, both their children and men would be subject. But are they capable of doing so? This is one of the important questions that the new generation of women encounters, especially when the members of this new generation refuse to ask those questions, seized by the same rage with which the dominant order originally victimised them.

Faced with this situation, it seems obvious – and feminist groups become more aware of this when they attempt to broaden their audience – that the refusal of maternity cannot be a mass policy and that the majority of women today see the possibility for fulfilment, if not entirely at least to a large degree, in bringing a child into the world. What does this desire for motherhood correspond to? This is one of the new questions for the new generation, a question the preceding generation had foreclosed. For want of an answer to this question, feminist ideology leaves the door open to the return of religion, whose discourse, tried and proved over thousands of years, provides the necessary ingredients for satisfying the anguish, the suffering, and the hopes of mothers. If Freud's affirmation – that the desire for a child is the desire for a penis and, in this sense, a substitute for phallic and symbolic dominion – can be only partially accepted, what modern women have to say about this experience should nonetheless be listened to attentively. Pregnancy seems to be experienced as the radical ordeal of the splitting of the subject: redoubling up of the body, separation and coexistence of the self and of an other, of nature and consciousness, of physiology and speech. This fundamental challenge to identity is then accompanied by a fantasy of totality – narcissistic completeness – a sort of instituted, socialised, natural psychosis. The arrival of the child, on the other hand, leads the mother into the labyrinths of an experience that, without the child, she would only rarely encounter: love for an other. Not for herself, nor for an identical being, and still less for another person with whom 'I' fuse (love or sexual passion). But the slow, difficult, and delightful apprenticeship in attentiveness, gentleness, forgetting oneself. The ability to succeed in this path without masochism and without annihilating one's affective, intellectual, and professional personality – such would seem to be the stakes to be won through guiltless maternity. It then becomes a creation in the strong sense of the term. For this moment, utopian?

On the other hand, it is in the aspiration toward artistic and, in particular, literary creation that woman's desire for affirmation now manifests itself. Why literature?

Is it because, faced with social norms, literature reveals a certain knowledge and sometimes the truth itself about an otherwise repressed, nocturnal, secret, and unconscious universe? Because it thus redoubles the social contract by exposing the unsaid, the uncanny? And because it makes a game, a space of fantasy and pleasure, out of the abstract and frustrating order of social signs, the words of everyday communication?

Flaubert said, 'Madame Bovary, c'est moi'. Today many women imagine, 'Flaubert, c'est moi'. This identification with the potency of the imaginary is not only an identification, an imaginary potency (a fetish, a belief in the maternal penis maintained at all costs), as a far too normative view of the social and symbolic relationship would have it. This identification also bears witness to women's desire to lift the weight of what is sacrificial in the social contract from their shoulders, to nourish our societies with a more flexible and free discourse, one able to name what has thus far never been an object of circulation in the community: the enigmas of the body, the dreams, secret joys, shames, hatreds of the second sex.

It is understandable from this that women's writing has lately attracted the maximum attention of both 'specialists' and the media.[11] The pitfalls encountered along the way, however, are not to be minimised: For example, does one not read there a relentless belittling of male writers whose books, nevertheless, often serve as 'models' for countless productions by women? Thanks to the feminist label, does one not sell numerous works whose naïve whining or market-place romanticism would otherwise have been rejected as anachronistic? And does one not find the pen of many a female writer being devoted to phantasmic attacks against Language and Sign as the ultimate supports of phallocratic power, in the name of a semi-aphonic corporality whose truth can only be found in that which is 'gestural' or 'tonal'?

And yet, no matter how dubious the results of these recent productions by women, the symptom is there - women are writing, and the air is heavy with expectation: What will they write that is new?

IN THE NAME OF THE FATHER, THE SON . . . AND THE WOMAN?

These few elements of the manifestations by the new generation of women in Europe seem to me to demonstrate that, beyond the sociopolitical level where it is generally inscribed (or inscribes itself), the women's movement – in its present stage, less aggressive but more artful – is situated within the very framework of the religious crisis of our civilisation.

I call 'religion' this phantasmic necessity on the part of speaking beings to provide themselves with a *representation* (animal, female, male, parental, etc.) in place of what constitutes them as such, in other words, symbolisation – the double articulation and syntactic sequence of language, as well as its preconditions or substitutes (thoughts, affects, etc.). The elements of the current practice of feminism that we have just brought to light seem precisely to constitute such a representation which makes up for the frustrations imposed on women by the anterior code (Christianity or its lay humanist variant). The fact that this new ideology has affinities, often revindicated by its creators, with so-called matriarchal beliefs (in other words, those beliefs characterising matrilinear societies) should not overshadow its radical novelty. This ideology seems to me to be part of the broader antisacrificial current which is animating our culture and which, in its protest against the constraints of the sociosymbolic contract, is no less exposed to the risks of violence and terrorism. At this level of radicalism, it is the very principle of sociality which is challenged.

Certain contemporary thinkers consider, as is well known, that modernity is characterised as the first epoch in human history in which human beings attempt to live without religion. In its present form, is not feminism in the process of becoming one?

Or is it, on the contrary and as avant-garde feminists hope, that having started with the idea of difference, feminism will be able to break free of its belief in Woman. Her power. Her writing, so as to channel this demand for difference into each and every element of the female whole, and, finally, to bring out the singularity of each woman, and beyond this, her multiplicities, her plural languages, beyond the horizon, beyond sight, beyond faith itself?

A factor for ultimate mobilisation? Or a factor for analysis?

Imaginary support in a technocratic era where all narcissism is frustrated? Or instruments fitted to these times in which the cosmos, atoms, and cells – our true contemporaries – call for the constitution of a fluid and free subjectivity?

The question has been posed. Is to pose it already to answer it?

ANOTHER GENERATION IS ANOTHER SPACE

If the preceding can be *said* – the question whether all this is *true* belongs to a different register – it is undoubtedly because it is now possible to gain some distance on these two preceding generations of women. This implies, of course, that a *third* generation is now forming, at least in Europe. I am not speaking of a new group of young women (though its importance should not be underestimated) or of another 'mass feminist movement' taking the torch passed on from the second generation. My usage of the word 'generation' implies less a chronology than a *signifying space*, a both corporeal and desiring mental space. So it can be argued that as of now a third attitude is possible, thus a third generation, which does not exclude – quite to the contrary – the *parallel* existence of all three in the same historical time, or even that they be interwoven one with the other.

In this third attitude, which I strongly advocate – which I imagine? – the very dichotomy man/woman as an opposition between two rival entities may be understood as belonging to *metaphysics*. What can 'identity', even 'sexual identity', mean in a new theoretical and scientific space where the very notion of identity is challenged? I am not simply suggesting a very hypothetical bisexuality which, even if it existed, would only, in fact, be the aspiration toward the totality of one of the sexes and thus an effacing of difference. What I mean is, first of all, the demassification of the problematic of *difference*, which would imply, in a first phase, an apparent de-dramatisation of the 'fight to the death' between rival groups and thus between the sexes. And this not in the name of some reconciliation – feminism has at least had the merit of showing what is irreducible and even deadly in the social contract – but in order that the struggle, the implacable difference, the violence be conceived in the very place where it operates with the maximum intransigence, in other words, in personal and sexual identity itself, so as to make it disintegrate in its very nucleus.

It necessarily follows that this involves risks not only for what we understand today as 'personal equilibrium' but also for social equilibrium itself, made up as it now is of the counterbalancing of aggressive and murderous forces massed in social, national, religious, and political groups. But is it not the insupportable situation of tension and explosive risk that the existing 'equilibrium' presupposes which leads some of those who suffer from it to divest it of its economy, to detach themselves from it, and to seek another means of regulating difference?

To restrict myself here to a personal level, as related to the question of women, I see arising, under the cover of a relative indifference toward the militance of the first and second generations, an attitude of retreat from sexism (male as well as female) and, gradually, from any kind of anthropomorphism. The fact that this might quickly become another form of spiritualism turning its back on social problems, or else a form of repression ready to support all status quos, should not hide the radicalness of the process. This process could be summarised as an *interiorisation of the founding separation of the sociosymbolic contract*, as an introduction of its cutting edge into the very interior of every identity whether subjective, sexual, ideological, or so forth. This in such a way that the habitual and increasingly explicit attempt to fabricate a scapegoat victim as foundress of a society or a countersociety may be replaced by the analysis of the potentialities of *victim/executioner* which characterise each identity, each subject, each sex.

What discourse, if not that of a religion, would be able to support this adventure which surfaces as a real possibility, after both the achievements and the impasses of the present ideological reworkings, in which feminism has participated? It seems to me that the role of what is usually called 'aesthetic practices' must increase not only to counterbalance the storage and uniformity of information by present-day mass media, data-bank systems, and, in particular, modern communications technology, but also to demystify the identity of the symbolic bond itself, to demystify, therefore, the *community* of language as a universal and unifying tool, one which totalises and equalises. In order to bring out – along with the *singularity* of each person and, even more, along with the multiplicity of every person's possible identifications (with atoms, e.g. stretching from the family to the stars) – the *relativity of his/her symbolic as well as biological existence*, according to the variation in his/her specific symbolic capacities. And in order to emphasise the *responsibility* which all will immediately face of putting this fluidity into play against the threats of death which are unavoidable whenever an inside and an outside, a self and an other, one group and another, are constituted. At this level of interiorisation with its social as well as individual stakes, what I have called 'aesthetic practices' are undoubtedly nothing other than the modern reply to the eternal question of morality. At least, this is how we might understand an ethics which, conscious of the fact that its order is sacrificial, reserves part of the burden for each of its adherents, therefore declaring them guilty while immediately affording them the possibility for *jouissance*, for various productions, for a life made up of both challenges and differences.

Spinoza's question can be taken up again here: Are women subject to ethics? If not to that ethics defined by classical philosophy – in relationship to which the ups and downs of feminist generations seem dangerously precarious – are women not already participating in the rapid dismantling that our age is experiencing at various levels (from wars to drugs to artificial insemination) and which poses the *demand* for a new ethics? The answer to Spinoza's question can be affirmative only at the cost of considering feminism as but a *moment* in the thought of that anthropomorphic identity which currently blocks the horizon of the discursive and scientific adventure of our species.

16

The Looking Glass, from the Other Side

Luce Irigaray

. . . she suddenly began again. 'Then it really *has* happened, after all!
And now, who am l? I *will* remember, if I can! I'm determined to do it!'
But being determined didn't help her much, and all she could say, after
a great deal of puzzling, was: 'L, I *know* it begins with L.'

Through the Looking-Glass

*Alice's eyes are blue. And red. She opened them while going through the mirror.
Except for that, she still seems to be exempt from violence. She lives alone,
in her house. She prefers it that way, her mother says. She only goes out
to play her role as mistress. School-mistress, naturally. Where unalterable
facts are written down whatever the weather. In white and black, or black and
white, depending on whether they're put on the blackboard or in the
notebook. Without colour changes, in any case. Those are saved for the times
when Alice is alone.* Behind the screen of representation. *In the house or
garden.*

*But just when it's time for the story to begin, begin again, 'it's autumn'. That
moment when things are still not completely congealed, dead. It ought to be
seized so that something can happen. But everything is forgotten: the 'measuring
instruments', the 'coat', the 'case', and especially the 'glasses'. How can anyone
live without all that?'* Up to now, that's what has controlled the limits of
properties, *distinguished outside from inside, differentiated what was looked on
with approval from what wasn't. Made it possible to appreciate, to recognise the
value of everything. To fit in with it, as needed.*

*There they are, all lost, without their familiar reference points. What's the
difference between a friend and no friend? A virgin and a whore? Your wife and
the woman you love? The one you desire and the one you make love with? One
woman and another woman? The one who owns the house and the one who uses
it for her pleasure, the one you meet there for pleasure? In which house and with
which woman does – did – will love happen? And when is it time for love,
anyway? Time for work? How can the stakes in love and work be sorted out?
Does 'surveying' have anything to do with desire, or not? Can pleasure be*

217

measured, bounded, triangulated, or not? Besides, 'it's autumn', the colours are changing. Turning red. Though not for long.

No doubt this is the moment Alice ought to seize. *Now is the time for her to come on stage herself. With her violet, violated eyes. Blue* and red. *Eyes that recognise the right side, the wrong side, and the other side: the blur of deformation; the black or white of a loss of identity. Eyes always expecting appearances to alter, expecting that one will turn into the other, is already the other. But Alice is at school. She'll come back for tea, which she always takes by herself. At least that's what her mother claims. And she's the only one who seems to know who Alice is.*

So at four o'clock sharp, the surveyor goes into her house. *And since a surveyor needs a pretext to go into someone's house, especially a lady's, he's carrying a basket of vegetables. From Lucien. Penetrating into 'her' place under cover of somebody else's name, clothes, love.* For the time being, *that doesn't seem to bother him. He opens the door, she's making a phone call. To her fiance'. Once again he slips in between them, the two of them. Into the breach that's bringing a woman and a man closer together, today at four o'clock. Since the relationship between Lucien and Alice lies in the zone of the 'not yet'. Or 'never'. Past and future both seem subject to quite a few risks. 'That's what love is, maybe?' And his intervention cuts back across some other in-betweens: mother-Alice, Lucien-Gladys, Alice–her friend ('She already has a friend, one's enough'), tall–short (surveyors). To mention only what we've already seen.*
Does his intervention succeed? *Or does he begin to harbour a vague suspicion that* she is not simply herself? *He looks for a light. To hide his confusion, fill in the ambiguity. Distract her by smoking. She doesn't see the lighter, even though it's right in front of her; instead she calls him into* the first bedroom *where there must be a light. His familiarity with the house dispels the anxiety. He goes upstairs. She invites him to enjoy her, as he likes. They separate in the garden. One of them has forgotten 'her' glasses by the telephone, the other 'his' cap on the bed. The 'light' has changed places.*

He goes back to the place where he works. She disappears into nature. *Is it Saturday or Sunday? Is it time for surveying or love? He's confused. There's only one thing to do: pick a fight with a 'cop'. The desire is compelling enough to make him leave at once.*

No more about cops, at least for the time being. *He finds himself (they find each other) near the garden. A man in love and a man in love with a woman who lives in the house. The first asks the second, or rather the second asks the first, if he can go (back) and see the woman he loves. He is beginning to be frightened, and begs to be allowed . . .* Afterward.
Good (common or proper) sense – any sense of propriety or property –

escapes Lucien. He gives things out, sets them in motion, without counting. Cap, vegetables, consent. Are they his? Do they belong to the others? To his wife? To somebody else's? As for what is his, it comes back to him in the dance. *Which does not prevent him from allowing others to take it. Elsewhere.*

So he comes (back) in. It's teatime. She . . . She? She who? Who's she? She (is) an other. . . looking for a light. Where's a light? Upstairs, in the bedroom, the surveyor, the tall one, points out cheerfully. Pleased at last to come across a specific, unquestionable, verifiable fact. Pleased that he can prove it (himself) using a + b, *or* 1 + 1, *that is, an element that repeats itself, one that stays the same and yet produces a displacement in the sum; pleased that it's a matter of a series, of a sequence. In short, of a* story. *Might as well say it's* true. *That he had already been there. That he . . . ? That she? Was? Wasn't? She.*

For the vegetables no longer prove anything. 'I must have eaten them.' 'I' who? Only the 'light' is left. But it isn't there to shore up the argument. And even if it were, no trace of what has happened would remain. As for attesting that the light has moved from here to there, or stating that its current whereabouts are known, or naming Alice's room as the only place it can be found, these are all just claims that depend on 'magic'.

Alice has never liked occultism. Not that the implausible surprises her. She knows more than anyone about fabulous, fantastic, unbelievable things . . . But she's always seen what she talks about. She's observed all the marvels first-hand. She's been 'in wonderland'. She hasn't simply imagined, 'intuited'. Induced, perhaps? Moreover, from a distance. And across partitions? Going through the looking glass, that's something else again.

Besides, there are no traces of such an adventure in that gentleman's eyes. It's a matter of nuances. So it's urgent for him to get out of the house at once. He won't? Then she's the one who'll leave, who'll desert it. The out-of-doors *is an extraordinary refuge. Especially in this season, with all its colours. He too goes into the garden. Right up close. So one no longer has the right to be alone? Where is one to go? If the house and garden are open to all comers. Omniscient surveyors, for example. It's imperative to hurry and invent a retreat they can't get to. Curl up somewhere protected from their scheming eyes, from their inquiries. From their penetration.* Where?

Lucien knows how to wait, even for quite a long time. His patience holds out indefinitely, at the edge of the vegetable garden. Installed outside the property, *he peels. Preferably beet stalks, which make little girls grow up. And lead them imperceptibly to marriage. From a long way off, very carefully, he's preparing a future. Improbable. That's not the only thing he's peeling. Perhaps that accounts for his arrival. Empty-handed. He doesn't even take the path, like everyone else. He comes across the grass. Always a little unseemly.*

Alice smiles. Lucien smiles. They smile at each other, complicitously. They are playing. *She makes him a gift of the cap. 'What will Gladys say?' That he has accepted a gift from Alice? That she has offered him that cap? A 'dragonfly' whose furtive flight volatises the giver's identity in the present moment. Who deserves more gratitude, the woman who duplicates the possibility of sexual pleasure or the woman who offers it a first time? And if one goes back and forth between them, how can one keep on telling them apart? How can one know where one is, where one stands? The confusion suits Lucien. He's delighted. Since this is the way things are, since everyone is giving up being simply 'myself', tearing down the fences of 'mine', 'yours', 'his', 'hers', he sheds all restraint. For although he looked as if he didn't care about anything, as if his prodigality were boundless, he was holding onto a little place for himself. A hiding-place, to be precise. A refuge, still private. For the day when everything goes wrong for everyone. For the time when troubles are too hard to bear. For a 'rainy day'. He's going to share that ultimate possession, that shred of property, with Alice. He's going to dissipate its private character. He takes her to a sort of cave. A concealed, hidden, protected place. A bit dark. Is this what Alice was trying to find? What he's looking for himself? And, since they've gotten to the point of telling secrets, they whisper in each other's ear. Just for fun, not to say anything. But Lucien realises that the cap has been forgotten on the 'bed'. That detail disturbs his stability. Leads him to act hastily. In an echo effect, he'll slip up again. Very softly, whispering, in confidential tones, he nevertheless imposes what is.*

Is? For him? For another? And who is he, to expose this way what might be? Alice is paralysed. Closed up. Frozen.

Since we've reached the point where we expound upon everyone's right to pleasure, let's go on to the lawyer's office. The meeting will take place outside. Inside, 'the woman eavesdrops', he says.

'I've made love with a girl, in a girl's house. What am I in for?'

'Nothing.' This outstrips anything one might imagine. All that for nothing. For free. Not even the shadow of a danger. Or penalty, or debt, or loss. Who can keep on surveying in the midst of such excesses? Yet there has to be a sequel. To the story.

Let's go on. 'So I've slept with a lady I don't know, in the house of another lady I don't know. What am I in for?'

'Four years.'

'Why?'

'Breaking and entering, cruelty. Two plus two make four, $2 \times 2 = 4$, $2^2 = 4$. Four years.'

'How can I get off?'

'That depends on the two of them. Separately and together. First you have to identify these two non-units. Then go on to their relationships.'

'I've identified one of them. The one to whom the coefficient "house" can be assigned.'

'Well?'

'I can't supply any other details, she's banned me from her property.'

'That's too bad. And the other one? The vagabond, the wanderer: the mobile unit?'

'She's disappeared into nature.'

'So . . .'

'Can you help me find her again?'

'My wife will be furious. I'll get dirty.'

'I'll take you. I'll get you there. I'm the one who'll carry the load; I'll do the dirty work.'

'O.K.'

But where in nature? *It's huge. Here? There? You have to stop somewhere. And if you put his feet on the ground a bit too abruptly, of course he'll realise that he's covered with mud. Which was absolutely not supposed to happen. 'What will my wife say?' What are we to think of a lawyer who gets his feet dirty? And* who, *after all, forbids dirtiness? The lawyer, or his wife? Why once again transfer to the other one the charge one refuses to address to one's own account? Because it might look a little disgusting. The gentleman's unattractive side. The one who claims he's a gentleman.*

Even though the surveyor came to get (back) on the right side of the law, he is revolted. If the numerical assessment gives him 'four years', he sets the lawyer's worth at 'zero'. He's going to have to start over again from that point.

Lucien has gone back to Gladys's house. He's sighing. Again. Too much precision makes him sad. Lost. Indefinitely, he contemplates the representation of the scene, behind a windowpane. That unseen glass whose existence punctures *his gaze. Rivets it, holds it* fast. *Gladys closes the door of the house. Lucien speaks. Finally. 'The scum, they've made love together.' 'Who's made love, Lucien? Who's one? Who's the other? And is she really the one you want her to be? The one you'd want?'* The ladies blur together, *virgin and/or whore. One blends into the other, imperceptibly.* Confusion *again* becomes legitimate. *The looking glass dissolves, already broken. Where are we? How far along? Everything is whirling. Everyone is dancing.*

Let's have some music, then, to accompany the rhythm, to carry it along. The orchestra is about to play. Somewhere else, of course. You've begun to notice that it is always in/on another stage *that things are brought to their conclusion. That the manifestation of things is saturated to the point where it exceeds plain evidence and certainty. Present visibility of the event. Incessant transferral: the complement of what is fomenting here moves over there – where? Moves from now to afterward – after the fact? From one to the other – who? And vice versa. Duplicating, doubling, dividing: of sequences, images, utterances, 'subjects'. Representation by the other of the projects of the one. Which he/she brings to light by displacing them.* Irreducible expropriation of desire occasioned by its impression in/on the other. *Matrix and support of the possibility of its repetition and reproduction. Same, and other.*

The duet being (re)produced at the moment has Alice's mother and her fiancé

*as interpreters. The instruments – let us be clear – are cellos. For the first time
the third party, one of the third parties, is a member of the party. Alice. Off to one
side, in a corner of the room –* a third bedroom *– she seems to be listening, or
looking. But is she really there? Or is she at least half absent? Also observing
what is going to happen. What has already happened.* Inside and outside.
*Without presuming to know what might define either once and for all. Difference
always in displacement. If 'she' is dreaming, 'I' must leave? The session
continues. Someone has disappeared. Someone else is going to fill in for this
missing subject. It's enough – just barely – to wait.*

*He reopens the door of the house. Listens, looks. But his role is really to
intervene. To subvert all the couples, by 'stepping between'. 'Houses, people,
feelings.' In order to sort them out, possibly to reconcile them. After he has passed
through, the surface has lost its other side. Perhaps its under side as well. But
'how can anyone live without that?' With a single side, a single face, a single
sense. On a single plane. Always on the same side of the looking glass. What is
cut cuts each one from its own other, which suddenly starts to look like any other.
Oddly unknown. Adverse, ill-omened. Frigidly other.*

   *'How can anyone live with that?' 'She's been cruel to me for five years!' 'Just
look at him: he always has a sinister look about him!' But when Eugene is
imitating the cat whose tail has been cut off, when he unburdens himself, on the
surveyor's person, of the only instrument whose intromission she allows into her
house, he is fierce. And if she sighs, frets, weeps, you'll understand that she's not
always cheerful. Moreover, just try to advise the one to leave since he is being
made to suffer; he'll leave his tool behind so he'll be sure to have to come back. Tell
the other that she doesn't love him, not any longer: she'll laugh. Even if she's sad.
And yet you were there – perhaps just for an instant – with eyes that know how
to look, at least at a certain aspect of the situation: they can't find each other this
time, they can no longer get back together. It's better for them to separate. At least
for today.* Anyway, they've never been united. *Each one has been putting up
with the other's other. While waiting.*

*Alice is alone. With the surveyor, the tall one. The one who made love with the
one who took over her house. It even happened on her bed. She knows, now. He
too has begun to understand the misunderstanding in the meantime. 'Do you
regret that mistake?' 'No.' 'Do you want us to clear up the confusion?' '. . . ?'
'Would you like to?' '. . . . ?'* How can they be differentiated in a single
attribution?

   *How can I be distinguished from her? Only if I keep on pushing through to the
other side, if I'm always* beyond, *because on this side of the screen of their
projections, on this* plane *of their representations, I can't live. I'm stuck,
paralysed by all those images, words, fantasies.* Frozen. *Transfixed, including by
their admiration, their praises, what they call their 'love'. Listen to them all
talking about Alice: my mother, Eugene, Lucien, Gladys . . . You've heard them*

dividing me up, in their own best interests. So either I don't have any 'self', or else I have a multitude of 'selves' appropriated by them, for them, according to their needs or desires. Yet this last one isn't saying what he wants – of me. I'm completely lost. In fact, I've always been lost, but I didn't feel it before. I was busy conforming to their wishes. But I was more than half absent. I was on the other side. *Well, I can say this much about my identity: I have my father's name, Taillefer. I've always lived in this house. First with my father and my mother. He's dead now. Since then, I've lived here alone. My mother lives next door. And then? . . .*

'What did she do next?' She is not I. *But I'd like to be 'she' for you. Taking a detour by way of her, perhaps I'll discover at last what 'I' could be. 'What did she do?'? 'She went upstairs to look for a light. She called me.' 'What's your name?' 'Leon . . .' So I go up, since that's the way she's acted. The only thing I do differently – on purpose? by mistake? – is that I call his name from a different bedroom.* The second. *He arrives, but it's the first room that he wants to go into. Is he mistaken again? Has he never been mistaken? For there to be a mistake, one of them has to be 'she', the other not.* Is it possible to tell who is 'she', or not? *What's important, no doubt, is that the scene is repeated. Almost the same way. From that point on, 'she' is* unique. *However the situation may be re-dressed.*

'What do I do now?' 'I don't know.' Alice was all alone when she was elsewhere. When she saw all sorts of wonders. While she was coming and going from one side to the other. On this side, she is only acquainted with contrived points of reference, artificial constraints. Those of school, in a way: nursery school, grade school. And there, in front of him, she doesn't feel she is mistress. But he doesn't know that. Either. He takes off his coat, as she had done. And then? . . .

'First do I take off what I have on top, then underneath? Or the other way around? Do I go from outside to inside? Or vice versa?' '. . . ?' And because she has always been secretive, she has always hidden everything, and because in this hiding place no one has discovered her, she thinks it will suffice simply to turn everything inside out. To expose herself in her nakedness so that she can be looked at, touched, taken, by someone, by him.

'Do you like me?' Does he know? What does that mean? How can the source of pleasure be named? Why part with it for her? *And who, what is that 'she' who is asking him,* scarcely a subject himself, *to assign her certain attributes, to grant her some distinctive characteristics? Apparently surveying isn't much use in love. At least not for loving her. How can anyone measure or define,* in truth, *what is* kept behind the plane of projections? *What goes beyond those/its limits? Still* proper ones. *No doubt he can take pleasure in what is produced there, in the person presented or represented. But how can he go beyond that horizon? How can he desire if he can't fix his line of sight? If he can't take aim at the other side of the looking glass?*

Outside, Alice, it's nighttime. You can't see a thing. You can't even walk straight, you can't stay upright, in the total darkness. You lose your balance. No more aplomb. At best, you're swaying. 'Someone's limping outside. I'll go see.'

The story *is coming to its end. Turning, and returning, in a closed space,* an enclosure *that is not to be violated, at least not while the story unfolds: the space of a few private properties. We are not going to cross a certain boundary line, we are not going above a certain peak. That would have forced us to find another style, a different procedure, for afterward. We would have needed,* at least, two genres. *And more. To bring them into articulation. Into conjunction. But at what moment?* In what place? *And won't this second one be just the* other side *of the first? Perhaps more often its complement. A more or less adequate complement, more or less apt to be joined by a copulative. We've never been dealing with more than one, after all. A unity divided in halves. More, or less. Identifiable, or not. Whose possibilities of pleasure have not even been exhausted. There are still remainders.* Left *behind. For another time.*

Because we're approaching the borders of its field, of its present frame, however, the affair is growing acrimonious. Subsequent events attest to an increasing exacerbation. But we can't be sure that it won't all end up in a sort of regression. With all parties retreating to their positions.

Since day has dawned, the surveyor, the tall one, *thinks it's fitting to take certain measures. Even if it's finally Sunday. Not daring to act alone, he phones* the short one *and asks him to go look for his coat, which he didn't forget at Alice's. To find out where things stand. To explain. To calculate the risks. Of an indictment . . . He takes him in his car up to the gate of the house. He's to wait for him in the bar, where he's meeting Lucien. Things are going rather badly between them. They've reached the point of insulting each other: 'asshole' on the part of you know who, 'rude' coming from the more timid one, who gets himself roundly scolded just the same for this insignificant outburst. It's because Leon doesn't joke around with rules; they're so necessary in his work. Alice doesn't have the coat, but she'll keep it. Because she wants to see him again. 'Why do you want to?' 'I just do.' 'Why?' 'To live on the right side.' But you can't understand what it's all about. You don't see anything at all. Or hardly anything. Well, it so happens that he has just noticed a detail that's crucial if we're to look the facts straight in the face: the glasses Ann forgot (?) by the telephone. She tries them on. Smiles. 'How can anyone live without these?' They absolutely have to be given back to Leon, to whom they don't belong. Because everyone – and especially Leon and Alice – ought to wear them when something really important happens. It would help them straighten out the situation,* or the opposite. *Then they could throw them away. That's undoubtedly what Ann did. Little Max hands Ann's glasses over to Leon, while Alice is phoning her to tell her to come get them at her house, because she's afraid she'll break them: all glass is fragile in her hands. Leon uncovers the riddle of Ann's disappearance. She couldn't live without that. He goes to the police station and confesses everything. As for the policeman, he doesn't understand a thing.* **Again,** it's a question of optics. *He doesn't see any reason for severity, doesn't see the cause for guilt, a* fortiori *doesn't see the possibility of reparations. But he's ready to turn his job over to a specialist. So Leon is not allowed to clear himself. Increasingly overwhelmed, he goes back to her house, the house belonging to one of them, whom he now appoints as his judge. Ann got there on her bicycle before he did.*

Still looking for her, Alice gets Ann to tell how it happened. She reassures her, of course, that it was the same for her. And to prove (to herself) that she is really 'her', Alice gets ahead of Ann in telling the rest of the story. She tells what happens when everything is already over. What happened to her the next day, which for her hasn't come yet. She says that love is fine once, but you mustn't ever start over again. Says that he may well be rather tiresome with his tendency to repeat everything.

Who spoke? In whose name? Filling in for her, it's not certain that she isn't trying also to replace her. **To be even more** (than) 'she'. *Hence the postscript that she adds to what was said to have taken place: 'He even wants to have a baby with me.' Then they fall silent, differently confused.*

That's the moment when the surveyor, of course, is going to intervene. **But how can he tell them apart?** *Who is she? And she? Since they are not the sum of two units, where can one pass between them?*

They get up, both of them, to answer him. But Ann can do it better. She's the one who'll tell him what they think. They? Or she? Which one? 'One, or the other, or both of us, or neither.' 'It's you!' 'It's I.' She's right there in front of me, as if nothing had ever happened. So I've invented everything that was supposed to have happened to her? Everything she was? 'I don't want to see you again.' That's too much. Just when she is finally present again, when that seeing-again could finally be confirmed, perhaps, by recognition, she claims to disappear then and there. 'And Alice?' 'Not her either.' Neither one nor the other. Neither one of the two. Nor the two, either, together or separately. How can she/they be allowed to escape that way? Behind. The door of the house, for example. 'You cunt(s), you'll see me again, you'll hear from me. I'll come back with big machines and I'll knock everything down, I'll flatten everything, I'll destroy it all. The house, the garden. Everything.'

Alice blinks her eyes. Slowly, several times. No doubt she's going to close them again. **Reverse** *them. But before her eyelids close, you'll have time to see that her eyes were* **red.**

And since it can't be simply a matter, here, of Michel Soutter's film,[1] nor simply of something else – except that 'she' never has a 'proper' name, that 'she' is at best 'from wonderland', even if 'she' has no right to a public existence except in the protective custody of the name of Mister X – then, so that she may be taken, or left, unnamed, forgotten without even having been identified, 'i' – who? – will remain uncapitalised. Let's say:

> *'Alice' underground*

Summaries and Notes

1. CATHERINE BELSEY AND JANE MOORE, INTRODUCTION: THE STORY SO FAR

1. She was long believed to have been the editor, but see Margaret Maison, 'Mary Wollstonecraft and Mr Cresswick', *Notes and Queries*, n.s. 34 (1987), pp. 467–8.
2. Kate Millett, *Sexual Politics* (London, 1971), p. xii.
3. Eva Figes, *Patriarchal Attitudes: Women in Society* (London, 1986), p. 15.
4. Dale Spender, *Man Made Language* (London, 1980), p. 101.
5. Jacqueline Rose, *Sexuality in the Field of Vision* (London, 1986), p. 91.
6. Elaine Showalter, 'Toward a Feminist Poetics', in Mary Jacobus (ed.), *Women Writing and Writing About Women* (London, 1979), pp. 22-41; reprinted in Elaine Showalter (ed.), *The New Feminist Criticism* (New York, 1985 and London, 1986), pp. 125–43.
7. Ellen Moers, *Literary Women* (London, 1977). See especially pp. 119, 170–2, 126.
8. Moers, *Literary Women*, p. 44.
9. Rosalind Coward, *Female Desire: Women's Sexuality Today* (London, 1984), p. 13.
10. Hélène Cixous, 'Sorties: Out and Out: Attacks/Ways Out/Forays', p. 92.
11. Mary Jacobus, 'The Difference of View', p. 72.
12. Jacobus, *Reading Woman: Essays in Feminist Criticism* (London, 1986), p. 109.
13. Bonnie Zimmerman, 'What Has Never Been: An Overview of Lesbian Feminist Criticism', in Gayle Green and Coppélia Kahn (eds.), *Making a Difference: Feminist Literary Criticism* (London, 1985), pp. 177–210, p. 198; also in Elaine Showalter (ed.), *The New Feminist Criticism* (New York, 1985 and London, 1986), pp. 200–24, p. 215.
14. Gayatri Chakravorty Spivak, *In Other Worlds: Essays in Cultural Politics* (new York and London, 1987), p. 150.

2. DALE SPENDER, 'WOMEN AND LITERARY HISTORY'
(From *Mothers of the Novel* (London, 1986), pp. 115-18 and 138-44.)

Summary

'Women and Literary History' raises questions concerning the disappearance of so much writing by women from the literary canon and literary history. How and why has woman's writing been excluded? Does it matter? The extract (from a book on eighteenth-century women writers) suggests that the suppression of women's writing entails the corresponding suppression not only of women's achievements but of women's meanings and values.

Notes

1 I have since checked the current course offerings of the English Department of
   Sydney University; in 1985, of twenty-five courses only *one* is devoted to a
   woman writer, and *only three include women writers*! What is more, the course
   entitled 'The Place of Women' gives pride of place to men, with three out of
   the four texts used being by male authors. I am indebted to Debra Adelaide
   for her assistance in gaining these figures and I deplore the fact that in twenty-
   five years and with the pressure of the contemporary women's movement, no
   progress has been made to give women recognition in this reputable
   university establishment.
2. Ian Watt, *The Rise of the Novel: Studies in Defoe, Richardson and Fielding* (London,
   1957), p. 296.
3. Ibid., p. 290.
4. Ibid., p. 298.
5. Germaine Greer, 'Flying Pigs and Double Standards', *Times Literary
   Supplement*, 26 July 1974, p. 784.
6. Matilda Joslyn Gage, *Woman, Church and State: the Original Exposé of Male
   Collaboration Against the Female Sex* (Chicago, 1873; reprinted Watertown, MA,
   1980).
7 Hilary Simpson, 'A Literary Trespasser: D. H. Lawrence's Use of Women's
   Writing', *Women's Studies International Quarterly*, 2 (1979), pp. 155–79.
8. Nancy Milford, *Zelda Fitzgerald* (London, 1975).
9. Marion Glastonbury, 'Holding the Pens', in Sarah Elbert and Marion
   Glastonbury, *Inspiration and Drudgery: Notes on Literature and Domestic Labour
   in the Nineteenth Century* (London, 1978), pp. 27–47.
10. Dora Russell, *The Religion of the Machine Age* (London, 1984); Elizabeth Robins,
    Ancilla's Share: an Indictment of Sex Antagonism (London, 1924); Kate Millett,
    Sexual Politics (London, 1971); Adrienne Rich, *On Lies, Secrets and Silence*
    (London, 1980).

3. ROSALIND COWARD, 'THE TRUE STORY OF HOW I BECAME MY OWN PERSON'
(From *Female Desire* (London, 1984), pp. 175-86.)

Summary

Focusing on women's novels, the essay traces a shift from the centrality of
marriage in the narrative structure of nineteenth-century fiction, towards the
prominence of sexual confession in novels of the late 1960s and early 1970s – a
period marked by the increasing influence of feminism and the so-called sexual
revolution. In this context questions are raised concerning the relation of women's
novels about sexuality to feminism. Are they automatically feminist novels? Do
they contribute to a more progressive understanding of female sexuality? The
essay suggests that fictional inscriptions of female sexuality construct historically-
specific subject positions for women which correspond to the structures of power
in society at large.

Notes

1. Samuel Richardson, *Pamela*, 1740–1; *Clarissa Harlowe*, 1746–7.

2. See Ian Watt, *The Rise of the Novel: Studies in Defoe, Richardson and Fielding* (London, 1957).
3. Maxine Hong Kingston, *The Woman Warrior* (London, 1981).
4. See, for example, 'Walter', *My Secret Life*, in Phyllis and Eberhard Kronhausen (eds), *Walter the English Casanova* (London, 1967).

4. TONI MORRISON, 'DISTURBING NURSES AND THE KINDNESS OF SHARKS'
(From *Playing in the Dark* (Cambridge, MA, 1992 and London, 1993), pp. 61–91.)

Summary

Morrison's essay examines the place of the white male hero in American literature. A reading of Ernest Hemingway's fiction brings out the degree to which the assumed autonomy of white masculinity is defined against and simultaneously threatened by the otherness of women and black men. By extension, it is argued that the white literary imagination is similarly constructed out of the marginalised African presence. The essay concludes that it is precisely the problem of how to respond to that presence which complicates fictional narratives, giving rise to a series of repetitions, disruptions, polarities, paradoxes and ambiguities, and resulting, finally, in literature itself.

Notes

1. James A. Snead, *Figures of Division: William Faulkner's Major Novels* (New York, 1986), pp. x–xi.
2. Ernest Hemingway, *To Have and Have Not* (London, 1970), p. 16.
3. Ibid.
4. Ibid., p. 19.
5. Ibid., pp. 12–13.
6. Ibid., pp. 72–3.
7. Ibid., p. 73.
8. Ibid., p. 78.
9. Ibid., p. 88.
10. Ibid., p. 73.
11. Ibid., p. 74.
12. Ibid., p. 73.
13. Ibid., p. 88.
14. Ibid., pp. 251–2.
15. Ibid., p. 252.
16. Ibid.
17. Ibid.
18. Ibid.
19. Ibid., p. 253.
20. Ibid.
21. Ibid.
22. Ernest Hemingway, 'The Killers', *The Short Stories of Ernest Hemingway* (New York, 1953), pp. 279–89, p. 286.
23. Hemingway, *To Have and Have Not*, p. 73.
24. Ernest Hemingway, 'The Short Happy Life of Francis Macomber', *The Short Stories of Ernest Hemingway*, pp. 3–37.

25. Ernest Hemingway, 'The Battler', *The Short Stories of Ernest Hemingway*, pp. 127–38.
26. Kenneth S. Lynn, *Hemingway* (New York, 1987), pp. 272–3.
27. Hemingway, 'The Battler', p. 133.
28. Ernest Hemingway, 'The Snows of Kilimanjaro', *The Short Stories of Ernest Hemingway*, pp. 52–77, p. 60.
29. Hemingway, *To Have and Have Not*, p. 114.
30. Ibid.
31. Ernest Hemingway, *The Garden of Eden* (New York, 1986), p. 30.
32. Ibid., pp. 177–8.
33. Ibid., p. 64.
34. Ibid., p. 29.
35. Hemingway, 'The Snows of Kilimanjaro', p. 60.

5. LINE POUCHARD, 'QUEER DESIRE IN *THE WELL OF LONELINESS*'

Summary

The essay addresses the possibility of re-constructing gender roles through a reading of queer, despite the naturalistic claims of early twentieth-century accounts of lesbianism, to which *The Well of Loneliness* is heavily indebted. Analysing a productive contradiction between the novel's advocacy of essentialist lesbian identities and its representation of multiple performances of queer desire, the essay questions the novel's assignation of identities within the single representational framework of sexual difference. The circulation of desire within the pair formed by the protagonist and her lover exposes the rigid, impermeable categories describing homo- and heterosexuality and reveals a parody of gender roles despite the novel's didactic project. On the one hand, the construction of Stephen Gordon's 'inversion' as inborn supports the plea for the socio-cultural acceptance of lesbians; on the other, her lover's femme performance points toward temporary sexual identifications which undermine the naturalisation of inversion. The figure of the mannish lesbian acquires its most complex significance when she is portrayed within pairs governed by an economy of desire made visible thanks to the critical agency of queer.

Notes

1. Radclyffe Hall, *The Well of Loneliness*, Virago Modern Classics (London, 1982), introduction by Alison Hennegan. Subsequent references are given in the text. I will abbreviate the novel's title as *The Well*.
2. For an analysis of the medical and social contexts in regard of lesbianism in which *The Well* was written, see Sonja Ruehl, 'Inverts and Experts: Radclyffe Hall and the Lesbian Identity' in Rosalind Brunt and Caroline Rowan (eds), *Feminism, Culture and Politics* (London, 1982).
3. Judith Butler, *Gender Trouble. Feminism and the Subversion of Identity* (London, 1990).
4. Michel Foucault (ed.), *Herculine Barbin, Being the Recently Discovered Memoirs of a Nineteenth-Century Hermaphrodite* (New York, 1980). For a discussion of Foucault's interpretation of the diaries, see Judith Butler, *Gender Trouble*, pp. 93–106.

5. For a critique of the metaphor of the body and its use in feminist criticism, see Domna C. Stanton, 'Difference on Trial: a Critique of the Maternal Metaphor in Cixous, Irigaray, and Kristeva', in Nancy Miller (ed.), *The Poetics of Gender* (New York, 1986), pp. 157–82.
6. Judith Butler, *Gender Trouble*, p. 132–4.
7. Ibid., p. 140.
8. Ibid., p. 138.
9. For discussions of queer, see *The Politics and Poetics of Camp*, ed. Moe Meyer (London, 1994), especially Moe Meyer's 'Introduction. Reclaiming the discourse of Camp', pp. 1–23.
10. Teresa De Lauretis, 'Sexual Indifference and Lesbian Representation', *Theatre Journal*, 40, 2 (May 1988), 155–77. Reprinted in Henry Abelove, Michele Aina-Barale, David Halperin (eds), *The Lesbian and Gay Studies Reader* (London, 1993).
11. Esther Newton, 'The Mythic Mannish Lesbian: Radclyffe Hall and the New Woman', *Signs*, 9, 4 (Summer 1984), 557–75.
12. Teresa De Lauretis, 'Sexual Indifference and Lesbian Representation', p. 177.
13. Sue-Ellen Case, 'Toward a Butch–Femme Aesthetic', *Discourse*, 11, 1 (Fall–Winter 1988–9), 55–73, reprinted in *The Lesbian and Gay Studies Reader*, p. 294.
14 Ibid., p. 299.

6. MARY JACOBUS, 'THE DIFFERENCE OF VIEW'
(From Mary Jacobus (ed.), *Women Writing and Writing About Women*
(London, 1979), pp. 10–21.)

Summary

'The Difference of View' poses the question of women's writing. How can we write and retain our difference, without reproducing the patriarchal differentiation which has either confined women to incoherence or silenced them altogether? On the one hand, in an effort to resist patriarchal meanings, French feminist writing has proposed inscribing the feminine as non-sense, but with the effect of denying to women the coherence of accepted definitions. On the other hand there is the problem that the production of (patriarchal) sense necessarily reproduces patriarchy itself. As a way out of this impasse the essay proposes an alternative way of reading women's texts. This involves the identification of moments in writing when structures are shaken, and when literary boundaries are transgressed as a result of the marginal being brought into focus. The effect is the disruption of familiar stabilities: the insistence of what is normally excluded throws into relief both the otherness of the transgressive material and the precariousness of the structures which usually hold it at bay.

Notes

1. Virginia Woolf, *Collected Essays*, vol. 1 (London, 1966), p. 204; my italics.
2. Ibid., vol. 1, p. 204.
3. See Elaine Marks, 'Women and Literature in France', *Signs: Journal of Women in Culture and Society*, 3 (1978), 833–42, for a discussion of the work of recent French feminist literary and psychoanalytic theorists, especially Hélène Cixous, *La Jeune née* (Paris, 1975; *The Newly Born Woman*, trans. Betsy Wing,

Minneapolis and Manchester, 1986), and 'Le Rire de la Méduse' ('The Laugh of the Medusa', trans. Keith and Paula Cohen, *Signs*, 1 (1976), 875-93); Luce Irigaray, *Speculum de l'autre femme* (Paris, 1974; *Speculum of the Other Woman*, trans. Gillian C. Gill, Ithaca, NY, 1985), and *Ce Sexe qui n'en est pas un* (Paris, 1977; *This Sex Which is Not One*, trans. Catherine Porter with Carolyn Burke, Ithaca, NY, 1985); Julia Kristeva, *La Révolution du language poétique* (Paris, 1974), *Polylogue* (Paris, 1977) and, from *La Révolution du language poétique*, 'Phonétique, phonologie et bases pulsionelles', translated as 'Phonetics, Phonology and Impulsional Bases' by Caren Greenberg, *Diacritics*, 4 (Fall 1974), 33–7. See also Michèle Montrelay, 'Inquiry into Femininity', trans. Parveen Adams, *m/f*, 1 (1978), 83–101, from *L'Ombre et le nom: sur la féminité* (Paris, 1977). The work of Luce Irigaray and Julia Kristeva is reviewed and compared by Josette Ferral, 'Antigone or *The Irony of the Tribe*', *Diacritics*, 8 (Fall 1978), 2–14. See also Stephen Heath, 'Difference', *Screen*, 19, 3 (1978), 51–112, especially 78–83 for a discussion of the theoretical implications raised by these writers.

4. See 'Study of Thomas Hardy', in E. D. Macdonald (ed.), *Phoenix: The Posthumous Papers of D. H. Lawrence* (London, 1967), p. 496.
5. Mary Wollstonecraft, *Mary, A Fiction and The Wrongs of Woman*, ed. Gary Kelly (London, 1976), pp. 83–4; my italics.
6. Virginia Woolf, *A Room of One's Own* (London, 1929), p. 104. (*Jane Eyre*, XII); my italics.
7. George Eliot, *Middlemarch* (4 vols, Edinburgh and London, 1871–2), vol. iv, pp. 369–70.
8. Woolf, *A Room of One's Own*, p. 7.
9. Ibid., p. 9.
10. Ibid., p. 146.
11. Ibid., p. 148.

7. GILLIAN BEER, 'REPRESENTING WOMEN: RE-PRESENTING THE PAST'
(First given at the Oxford English Limited conference on 'Re-thinking Literary History', May 1987.)

Summary

The essay addresses the problem of how to read or, more precisely, reread the past from the unavoidable perspective of present cultural influences and knowledges, without denying the specificity and difference of the past on the one hand or, on the other, pretending to have escaped the preconceptions of the present, which shape our readings of the past. To adopt the first of these alternatives is to succumb to what the essay calls 'presentism'. This is the belief that 'now' offers the only authoritative source of meaning, and that history is to be read for its relevance to present-day concerns. The problem with this approach is that it naturalises and fixes culturally constituted contemporary meanings of femininity; it also militates against seeing the past or the present as sites where meaning can change. The second way of thinking goes to the other extreme by attempting to ignore the present altogether. Yet in each case the effect is the same: the collapse of historical difference.

In place of these strategies, the essay proposes an alternative way of interpreting or re-presenting the past. This involves recognising difference – historical and sexual. For to emphasise the difference of past writings and past concerns from present-day beliefs and meanings is better to understand the historical processes of gender formation and gender change. Correspondingly, it is also to expose the present as unstable, not fixed, not timeless, a site of shifts in the meanings of femininity and masculinity. In practice, this means analysing writing by men alongside women's writing, in order first to recognise sexual difference and then to denaturalise it – to expose masculinity and femininity as historically and culturally specific.

Notes

1. Hélène Cixous, 'The Laugh of the Medusa', in Elaine Marks and Isabelle de Courtivron (eds), *New French Feminisms: An Anthology* (Brighton, 1981) pp. 245–64. Cixous retains the metaphoric contradiction: 'Even if phallic mystification has generally contaminated good relationships, a woman is never far from "mother" (I mean outside her role functions: the mother as non-name and as source of goods) . There is always within her at least a little of that good mother's milk. She writes in white ink.' (cf. p. 99 above.) Note the combination of mothering and trading metaphors here, which I discuss in relation to Moll Flanders.
2. Nancy Chodorow, *The Reproduction of Mothering: Psychoanalysis and the Sociology of Gender* (Berkeley, CA, 1978); Dorothy Dinnerstein, *The Rocking of the Cradle and the Ruling of the World* (London, 1978); Coppélia Kahn, 'The Hand that Rocks the Cradle: Recent Gender Theories and their Implications', in Shirley Nelson Garner et al. (eds), *The (M)other Tongue* (Ithaca, NY and London, 1985), pp. 72–88.
3. The descriptions and prescriptions concerning hysteria and menopause are cases in point.
4. Robert Halsband, 'Women and Literature in Eighteenth-Century England', in Paul Fritz and Richard Morton (eds), *Woman in the Eighteenth Century and Other Essays* (Toronto, 1976), pp. 55–71, p. 64.
5. Mary Hays, *Appeal to the Men of Great Britain in Behalf of Women* (London, 1798; reprinted New York and London, 1974), G. Luria (ed.), p. 50.
6. See Gillian Beer, *Darwin's Plots* (London, 1983); George Lakoff and Mark Johnson, *Metaphors We Live By* (Chicago, 1980).
7. Hélène Cixous, in Marks and de Courtivron (eds), *New French Feminisms*, p. 90. [See also pp. 91–2 below.]
8. The original sponsors of the paper were Lisa Jardine, Jill Mann, Gillian Beer, Stephen Heath, Tony Tanner.
9. Patrick Wright, *On Living in an Old County: the National Past in Contemporary Britain* (London, 1985); Simon Barker, 'Images of the Sixteenth and Seventeenth Centuries as a History of the Present', in Francis Barker et al. (eds), *Literature, Politics and Theory: Papers from the Essex Conference 1976–84* (London and New York, 1986), pp. 173–89.
10. For discussion of this question see Gillian Beer, *George Eliot* (Key Women Writers) (Brighton, 1986), pp. 17–20, 42–3.
11. See Peter Stallybrass and Allon White, *The Politics and Poetics of Transgression* (London, 1986).
12. For further discussion see Carolyn Merchant, *The Death of Nature: Women, Ecology and the Scientific Revolution* (London,1980); Ludmilla Jordanova (ed.), *Languages of Nature* (London, 1986); Evelyn Fox Keller, *Reflections on Gender and Science* (New Haven, CT and London, 1985), especially 'Baconian Science: The Arts of Mastery and Obedience', pp. 33–42.

13. Virginia Woolf, *A Room of One's Own* (London, 1929), p. 125.
14. Virginia Woolf, *Three Guineas* (London, 1938), pp. 252, 253.
15. Catherine Macaulay, *Letters on Education* (Dublin, 1790), pp. 127, 130.
16. Katharine Rogers, 'The Feminism of Daniel Defoe', in Fritz and Morton (eds), *Woman in the Eighteenth Century and Other Essays*, pp. 3–24 passim.
17. Luce Irigaray, *Ce sexe qui n'en est pas un* (Paris, 1977). See 'Le Marché des femmes', pp. 167–85 and 'Des Marchandises entre elles', pp. 189–93.
18. Quoted by Luce Irigaray, 'Le Marché des femmes', pp. 170–1.
19. Spiro Peterson (ed.), *The Counterfeit Lady Unveiled and Other Criminal Fiction of Seventeenth-Century England* (Garden City, NY, 1961), pp. 15, 97.
20. Juliet Mitchell (ed.), Daniel Defoe, *The Fortunes and Misfortunes of the Famous Moll Flanders* (Harmondsworth, 1978), pp. 315, 317.
21. Defoe, *Moll Flanders*, p. 262.
22. Ibid., p. 28.
23. In French, mother-earth is *'la terre-mère'*. In 'Le Marché des femmes' Irigaray asserts that the mother cannot become part of a mercantile system of circulation without undermining the social order: *'Valeur naturelle et valeur d'usage, la mère ne peut circuler sous forme de marchandise sous peine d'abolir l'ordre social'* (p. 180).
24. G. M. Trevelyan, *The History of England* (London, 1926). Woolf discusses Trevelyan's representation of women in history in *A Room of One's Own*, London, 1929; see especially pp. 63–73. I am grateful to Hazel Mills and the members of our seminar on women's history for making me realise how closely Trevelyan is linked to Orlando as well as to *A Room of One's Own*.
25. Virginia Woolf, *Orlando* (London, 1928), pp. 123–6.

8. HELENE CIXOUS, 'SORTIES: OUT AND OUT: ATTACKS/WAYS OUT/FORAYS'

(From *The Newly Born Woman*, trans. Betsy Wing (Minneapolis and Manchester, 1986), pp. 63–4, 83–8, 91–7. *The Newly Born Woman* was first published as *La Jeune née*, Paris, 1975.)

Summary

'Where is she?' To what place has the feminine been allocated in the history of Western patriarchal thought? How has sexual difference – the relation of women to men and of femininity to masculinity – been conceived? What is the association between gendered or culturally constituted sexual identities and anatomical sexuality? Can we distinguish between femaleness and femininity, maleness and masculinity? If we can, what are the consequences for the relationship between sexuality and textuality?

All of these questions relate to a recurrent concern of Cixous's work in general: namely, the connections between the female body and feminine writing or *écriture féminine*. In the following extracts from her long philosophical-poetical-autobiographical essay 'Sorties', these issues are channelled through an exploration of the possible 'ways out', or *sorties*, for women from their culturally marginal position.

The essay begins by investigating the hierarchical oppositions which have structured the history of Western philosophy – a history in which women have traditionally been placed on the side of negativity, passivity, powerlessness. The alienation of women from their bisexually charged bodily selves is identified as the most damaging effect of the subjection of the feminine to a masculine order, for what is also repressed is women's capacity for endless and boundless sexual pleasure, or *jouissance*, which is seen to arise from their recognition of the (masculine) other within themselves. 'Sorties' suggests that the way for women not only to break from but to undo their cultural repression is to begin writing their bodies, since it is in *écriture féminine* that women are at once able to reclaim the specificity of their sex, to affirm difference, and to challenge 'the discourse controlled by the phallus'.

Thus, feminine writing is identified as the liberatory act which resists patriarchal definitions of femininity as lack or negativity, and which will 'change the rules of the old game' by celebrating the affirmative power of a feminine sexual/textual aesthetic of difference. Although this aesthetic presently belongs to women writers, with the exception of some homosexual male writers such as Jean Genêt, or modernists like James Joyce, the essay envisages a utopian future in which the plurality and difference of each person's possible sexual/textual identities will be released.

Notes

1. Cixous, 'Les Comtes de Hoffmann' ('Tales of Hoffmann'), in *Prénoms de personne* (*Nobody's First Names*) (Paris, 1974), p. 112ff.
2. See 'Bisexualité et difference des sexes', *Nouvelle Revue de Psychoanalyse*, 7 (Spring 1973).

9. TORIL MOI, 'FEMINIST, FEMALE, FEMININE'
(Edited extracts from 'Feminist Literary Criticism', in Ann Jefferson and David Robey (eds), *Modern Literary Theory* (London, 1986), pp. 204–21.)

Summary

The title of 'Feminist, Female, Feminine' alludes silently to the three categories of nineteenth-century women's writing identified in Elaine Showalter's *A Literature of Their Own*. Moi redefines the terms and then uses them as the basis of a (mild) critique of Showalter's own theoretical position.

In the extract reprinted here it is argued that 'feminist' is a political term, 'female' a biological one, and 'feminine' a cultural definition. The essay calls into question the belief that female experience is the basis of feminism, or in other words that politics is a direct effect of biology. Meanwhile, if 'feminine' specifies a cultural rather than a biological difference, to oppose 'feminine' to 'masculine' in an absolute binary opposition is ultimately to reaffirm an essentialist and patriarchal distinction. It follows that to privilege 'feminine writing' (the *écriture féminine* of French feminism) is to be in perpetual danger of falling into yet another form of biological essentialism.

The essay goes on to develop the argument that 'the feminine' is not an essence but a culturally produced position of marginality in relation to patriarchal society. As a relational position rather than a fact of nature, it is a place from which to conduct a feminist politics committed to change.

Notes

1. Kate Millett, *Sexual Politics* (London, 1971), p. 25.
2. Dale Spender, *Women of Ideas and What Men Have Done to Them* (London, 1982).
3. Sandra M. Gilbert and Susan Gubar, *The Madwoman in the Attic: the Woman Writer and the Nineteenth-Century Literary Imagination* (New Haven, CT, 1979).
4. Rosalind Coward, 'Are Women's Novels Feminist Novels?', in Elaine Showalter (ed.), *The New Feminist Criticism* (London, 1986), p. 230.
5. For a discussion of such political differences within American feminism, see Hester Eisenstein, *Contemporary Feminist Thought* (London, 1984).
6. Coward, 'Are Women's Novels Feminist Novels?', p. 237.
7. Mary Ellmann, *Thinking About Women* (New York, 1968); Penny Boumelha, *Thomas Hardy and Women: Sexual Ideology and Narrative Form* (Brighton, 1982).
8. Hélène Cixous and Catherine Clément, *The Newly Born Woman*, trans. Betsy Wing (Minneapolis and Manchester, 1986), p. 64.
9. Verena Andermatt Conley, in her book on Cixous, would certainly disagree: see *Hélène Cixous: Writing the Feminine* (Lincoln, NE and London, 1984).For a discussion of some of her views, see also Toril Moi, *Sexual/Textual Politics: Feminist Literary Theory* (London, 1985), pp. 123–6.
10. Meaning in Derrida's theory is always plural, unfixed, in 'play'.
11. Julia Kristeva, *Revolution in Poetic Language* (New York, 1984). For Lacan and the symbolic order, see Elizabeth Wright, *Psychoanalytic Criticism: Theory in Practice* (London, 1984); Moi, *Sexual/Textual Politics*; and Terry Eagleton, *Literary Theory: An Introduction* (Oxford, 1983); as well as Anika Lemaire, *Jacques Lacan* (London, 1977), which for me remains the most serious and wide-ranging introduction to Lacan. [See also the Glossary. Eds]
12. For a necessary critique of the political implications of Kristeva's theories at this point, see Moi, *Sexual/Textual Politics*, pp. 150–73.
13. Elaine Showalter, *A Literature of Their Own: British Women Novelists from Brontë to Lessing* (Princeton, NJ, 1977).

10. SHOSHANA FELMAN, 'WOMAN AND MADNESS: THE CRITICAL PHALLACY'
(From *Diacritics*, 5 (1975), pp. 2–10.)

Summary

Felman's essay was originally written as a review of three books, *Women and Madness* by Phyllis Chesler, Luce Irigaray's *Speculum de l'autre femme* and a new edition of Balzac's short story, *Adieu*. Chesler treats women's madness as either an effect or a refusal of the role allotted to women in our culture. Chesler's book reproduces the voices of women. Irigaray is also critical of the place of silence allocated to women, but she undertakes to speak *for* women in her own voice, and so casts doubt on her own undertaking. Chesler, without a theory, leaves women in the position of victims: Irigaray, on the other hand, offers a theoretical analysis, but fails to analyse the position from which she herself speaks. *Adieu*, meanwhile, is a story about a woman, madness and silence. Just as the institution of literary criticism systematically omits women from its concerns, silences them, so the modern commentators on *Adieu* excise the role of the woman in the story. Balzac's 'realism' is thus seen to concern itself with men and with reason: women and madness are located outside or beyond the 'real' world. Felman goes on to offer an alternative, feminist reading of *Adieu*. For the heroine reason and 'femininity' prove to be synonymous, in that what constitutes sanity is the recognition of man, of her lover, giving him back his identity, his own reflection, his interpretation of the world. But the restoration of her reason brings about the death of both the woman and her lover, and the end of the story. The fiction thus both depicts and aligns itself with a realm beyond 'realism', beyond both reason and masculinity, and beyond the limits of representation.

Notes

1. Phyllis Chesler, *Women and Madness* (New York, 1973), p. xxii.
2. Ibid., pp. 68–9.
3. Ibid., p. 138.
4. Ibid., p. 56.
5. Ibid., p. xxiii.
6. Luce Irigaray, *Speculum de l'autre femme* (Paris 1974).
7. Freud has thus pronounced his famous verdict on women: 'Anatomy is destiny'. But this is precisely the focus of the feminist contestation.
8. Honoré de Balzac, *Adieu [Colonel Chabert, suivi de El Verdugo, Adieu, et du Requisitionnaire]*. Edited and annotated by Philippe Berthier. Preface by Pierre Gascan (Paris, 1974).
9. Balzac, *Adieu*, p. 9. Quotations from the *Préface*, the 'Notice' and from Balzac's text are my translations; in all quoted passages, italics mine unless otherwise indicated.
10. Ibid., pp. 10–11.
11. Ibid., p. 12.
12. Ibid., p. 266.
13. Ibid., p. 265.
14. Ibid., pp. 11–12.
15. Ibid., pp. 14–17.
16. Ibid., p. 17.
17. Ibid., p. 16.
18. Louis Althusser, *Lire le Capital*, 1 (Paris, 1968), pp. 26–8 (translation mine; Althusser's italics).
19. Balzac, *Adieu*, pp. 148, 156, 159, 164.
20. Ibid., p. 164.
21. Ibid., p. 196.
22. Ibid., p. 150.
23. Ibid., pp. 208–9.
24. Ibid., pp. 147, 151.
25. Ibid., p. 157.
26. Ibid., p. 202.
27. Ibid., p. 208.
28. Ibid., p. 159.
29. Ibid., p. 180.
30. Ibid., p. 197.
31. Michel Foucault, *Histoire de la folie à l'âge classique* (Paris, 1972), p. 540 (translation mine).
32. Balzac, *Adieu*, pp. 200–1.
33. Ibid., p. 201.
34. Ibid., p. 207.
35. Ibid., p. 163.
36. Ibid., p. 200.

37. Ibid., pp. 209–10.
38. This suicidal murder is, in fact, a repetition, not only of Philippe's military logic and his attitude throughout the war scene, but also of a specific previous moment in his relationship with Stéphanie. Well before the story's end, Philippe had already been on the point of killing Stéphanie, and himself with her, having, in a moment of despair, given up the hope of her ever recognising him. The doctor, seeing through Philippe's intentions, had then saved his niece with a perspicacious lie, playing precisely on the specular illusion of her proper name: '"You do not know then," went on the doctor coldly, hiding his horror, "that last night in her sleep she said, 'Philippe!'". "She named me," cried the baron, letting his pistols drop' (Balzac, *Adieu*, p. 206).
39. Here again, the ambiguous logic of the 'saviour', in its tragic and heroic narcissism, is prefigured by the war scene. Convinced of his good reason, Philippe, characteristically, *imposes* it, by force, on others, so as to 'save' them; but ironically and paradoxically, he always saves them *in spite of* themselves: '"Let us save her in spite of herself!" cried Philippe, sweeping up the countess' (Balzac, *Adieu*, p. 182).
40. Balzac, *Adieu*, p. 8.

11. JANE MOORE, 'PROMISES, PROMISES: THE FICTIONAL PHILOSOPHY IN MARY WOLLSTONECRAFT'S *VINDICATION OF THE RIGHTS OF WOMAN*'
(First given at the Cardiff Critical Theory Seminar, November 1987.)

Summary

Do contemporary theories of language and subjectivity help or hinder the feminist reader of past texts? That is, does reading from the inescapable perspective of the twentieth century necessarily impose present-day theoretical presuppositions on to a different past, thereby eliminating historical difference? In the light of these questions the essay explores the consequences of using a deconstructive methodology to analyse Mary Wollstonecraft's *Vindication of the Rights of Woman*.

The essay locates oppositions of genre and, correspondingly, of gender at work in the *Vindication*: the literary is associated with the feminine, while reason and a plain-speaking philosophical prose is aligned with masculinity. Deconstruction, it is argued, enables the reader to undo these oppositions and to reveal their radical instability. On the other hand the essay suggests that if the radical edge of the *Vindication's* project to persuade women to speak a 'male' language of reason is to be brought fully into view, then the twentieth-century deconstructive reader needs to employ simultaneously another focus: this is history.

To situate an eighteenth-century taxonomy of genre and gender in its difference from twentieth-century conceptions of the relationship between sex and text, the essay suggests, is not to fix past meanings and past oppositions, which would reinvest them with the authority that deconstruction usefully denies; nor is it to give way to the indefinite sliding of meanings beyond all historical and cultural limits, as deconstruction proposes. Rather, it is to expose the historical instability and cultural constitution of genre and gender categories, without simultaneously collapsing past and present. It is in consequence to reveal the past and the present as moments in a continuous history of change.

Notes

1. Gillian Beer, 'Representing Women: Re-presenting the Past', pp. 77–90 above.
2. Ibid., p. 80 above.
3. Colin MacCabe, 'Foreword' to Gayatri Chakravorty Spivak, *In Other Worlds: Essays in Cultural Politics* (New York and London, 1987), p. xi; Christopher Norris, *Deconstruction: Theory and Practice* (London and New York, 1982), p. 92.
4. Norris, *Deconstruction*, p. 98.
5. Hélène Cixous, 'Sorties: Out and Out: Attacks/Ways Out/Forays', p. 91 above.
6. Cixous, 'Sorties', p. 91 above. Cixous not only identifies the binarism structuring Western patriarchal thought: she actively challenges it. 'Sorties' argues that the movement which makes oppositions possible also undoes them: 'the movement whereby each opposition is set up to make sense is the movement through which the couple is destroyed. A universal battlefield. Each time, a war is let loose. Death is always at work', p. 92 above. What Cixous locates here is the textual movement of differance. That is, differance as distinct from difference: unlike difference, differance invokes both difference and deferral. As such it introduces the possibility that meanings are not static, their binarism is not fixed. Rather, each term belonging to an opposition ceaselessly invades the other so that the moment in which the different meanings of words is made possible is also the moment in which that difference is unmade: difference slides into differance.

   Cixous's work at this point is much influenced by Jacques Derrida's critique of the static logic of binary thought, as well as by his argument that meanings are produced not in the field of difference but on the textual battleground of differance. The implications that the notion of differance has for how we understand the production of genre difference are discussed in Derrida's essay 'The Law of Genre', *Glyph* 7 (1980), pp. 202–32. This essay argues that the system of generic classification, like all seemingly self-evident closed systems, is opened out by the impossibility of the classifying mark that makes generic taxonomy possible. On another level the problem of the impossibility of generic taxonomy becomes one of metaphor, or more precisely, one of metaphor in philosophy. This problematic is addressed by Derrida's essay 'The White Mythology', in *Margins of Philosophy*, trans. Alan Bass (Brighton, 1982), pp. 207–29. Here it is argued, as Michael Ryan puts it, that 'because all language is metaphoric (a sign substituted for a thing), no metametaphoric description of language is possible that escapes infinite regress.' (*Marxism and Deconstruction: A Critical Articulation* (Baltimore and London, 1982), p. 20.) One of the implications of the infinite regress of metaphor is that it is no longer possible to believe in the separate existence of literary and philosophical modes of language. In Cixous's 'Sorties', however, this deconstructive line of thought is not maintained. Philosophical and literary modes are not collapsed; on the contrary their difference is maintained in a metaphor of sexual difference: each discursive mode is associated respectively with masculine and feminine forms of writing.
7. Hélène Cixous and Catherine Clément, *The Newly Born Woman*, trans. Betsy Wing (Minneapolis and Manchester, 1986), p. 65.
8. Cixous, 'Sorties', p. 98 above.
9. Mary Wollstonecraft, *Vindication of the Rights of Woman* (London, 1792; Miriam Brody (ed.), Harmondsworth, 1986). Parenthetical notation refers to page numbers in this edition.
10. Mary Jacobus, 'The Difference of View', p. 70 above.

11. John Locke, *Essay Concerning Human Understanding* (London, 1690; reprinted London and New York, 1961), pp. 105–6. Cited in Paul de Man, 'The Epistemology of Metaphor', *Critical Inquiry*, 5 (1978), 13–30, p. 15.
12. Jean-Jacques Rousseau; cited in Wollstonecraft's *Vindication*, p. 183.
13. For more information about male and female reformers of women's education during the eighteenth century see Alice Browne, *The Eighteenth Century Feminist Mind* (Brighton, 1987); especially pp. 102–21.
14. John Bennett, *Letters to a Young Lady*, 2nd edn, 2 vols (London, 1795), vol. 1, pp. 168–9. Cited in Browne, *The Eighteenth Century Feminist Mind*, pp. 123–4.
15. See Browne, *The Eighteenth Century Feminist Mind*, p. 105.
16. Sarah Scott, *Millenium Hall* (London, 1762; reprinted London, 1986).
17. Mary Hays, *Memoirs of Emma Courtney* (London, 1796; reprinted London, 1987); Mrs Opie, *Adeline Mowbray: or, The Mother and Daughter* (London, 1804; reprinted London, 1986).
18. I have drawn here on an observation made by Kelvin Everest in his reading of William Godwin's *Enquiry Concerning Political Justice*. See Kelvin Everest and Gavin Edwards, ' William Godwin's *"Caleb Williams"*: Truth and *"Things As They Are"*', in Francis Barker et al. (eds), *1789: Reading Writing Revolution: Proceedings of the Essex Conference on the Sociology of Literature* (Colchester, 1982), pp. 129–59, p. 134.
19. Miriam Brody, 'Introduction' to Wollstonecraft's *Vindication*, p. 41.
20. I have placed the terms 'philosophy' and 'literature' within cautionary brackets and inverted commas in order to draw attention to the impossibility of fixing their meanings. I wish to stress that, like all categories of knowledge which pretend to be self-enclosed, they cannot avoid the deconstructive operations of differance; but I want also to demarcate philosophy from literature so as to retain the historical specificity of their (separate) meanings. I do not continue the practice of framing the terms philosophy and literature in inverted commas, except where it seems me that it may be useful to (re)emphasise that these terms are always under erasure, although, of course, not fully erased.
21. Kelvin Everest has argued that late eighteenth-century radicals invoked the notion of 'truth' from the perspective of becoming, rather than of being: thus the emphasis is not on what is, but on what might be. See Everest and Edwards, 'William Godwin's *"Caleb Williams"*: Truth and *"Things As They Are"* ', pp. 134–5. In the light of Everest's observations it should be remarked that it may well be possible to produce a non-contradictory reading of the *Vindication*'s inscription of reason-as-truth in the future tense.
22. Quoted in Mary Wilson Carpenter, 'Sibylline Apocalyptics: Mary Wollstonecraft's *Vindication of the Rights of Woman* and Job's Mother's Womb', *Literature and History*, 12 (1986), 215–28, p. 227, n. 9.
23. Miriam Brody, 'Introduction' to Wollstonecraft's *Vindication*, p. 41. For counter-readings of the *Vindication* which, unlike Brody's and Wardle's, do not suggest that a rationalist philosophy is that text's only discourse, see Mary Wilson Carpenter, 'Sibylline Apocalyptics'. This essay focuses on the *Vindication*'s 'prophetic' discourses and suggests that the text's (re)inscription of the *Book of Job* invokes a 'suppressed female plot of origin', p. 22. See also Cora Kaplan, 'Wild Nights: Pleasure/Sexuality/Feminism', in *Sea Changes: Essays on Culture and Feminism* (London, 1986), pp. 31–56. Kaplan suggests that rather than silencing female sexuality, as it aims to do, the *Vindication* is suffused with and proliferates the sexual. Finally, it is another woman, Mary Poovey, who has noted that the language of the *Vindication* becomes increasingly obscure, even 'purposefully vague', when Wollstonecraft

confronts women's sexuality. See Poovey, *The Proper Lady and the Woman Writer: Ideology as Style in the Works of Mary Wollstonecraft, Mary Shelley, and Jane Austen* (Chicago, 1984), pp. 77–80.

24. Mary Wollstonecraft, *The Wrongs of Woman: or, Maria* (London, 1789); reprinted together with *Mary, A Fiction*, ed. Gary Kelly (Oxford, 1984). All references are to page numbers in this edition.

Another edition of *The Wrongs of Woman* which is commonly cited is *Maria: or, The Wrongs of Woman*, ed. Moira Ferguson (New York, 1975). It is interesting to note that the American and British editions have differently ordered titles. The insertion of 'Maria' in front of 'The Wrongs of Woman' in the title of the American edition could, perhaps, be seen to bear out an American concern for the politics of the individual over those of the collective. Furthermore, it might be said that privileging the individual 'Maria' over the 'Wrongs' that women suffer correspondingly prioritises the text's 'literary' content, and thus subordinates its 'philosophical' concerns. All of these reversals contradict what the text itself stresses: namely, that 'Woman' refers to the female sex in general: '. . . the history ought rather to be considered, as of woman, than of an individual', 'Author's Preface', p. 73.

25. Wollstonecraft, *The Wrongs of Woman*, p. 73.
26. Ryan, *Marxism and Deconstruction*, p. 83.
27. 'Negative affirmation': the phrase is Michael Ryan's.
28. Marilyn Butler, *Romantics, Rebels and Reactionaries: English Literature and its Background 1760–1830* (Oxford, 1981), p. 55.
29. Mary Robinson, *The False Friend*, 4 vols '(London, 1799), vol. 2, p. 77. Quoted in Alice Browne, *The Eighteenth Century Feminist Mind*, p. 154.
30. Horace Walpole is said to have called Mary Wollstonecraft 'a hyena in petticoats'. This compound metaphor, signifying animality, sexuality and femininity, constructs Wollstonecraft not as a rational being, who has the power to name animals, but as the animal who is named; this is interesting not least because it seems to correspond to Romanticism's desire to fix a tamed and sensuous, rather than sensual, meaning of femininity.
31. Maria Edgeworth, *Belinda* (London, 1801; reprinted London, 1986).
32. This is the argument of Everest's essay, 'William Godwin's "*Caleb Williams*": Truth and "*Things As They Are*"'.

12. GAYATRI CHAKRAVORTY SPIVAK, 'THREE WOMEN'S TEXTS AND A CRITIQUE OF IMPERIALISM'
(From *Critical Inquiry*, 12 (1985), 243–7, 247–51, 252–61.)

Summary

'Three Women's Texts' raises questions concerning the politics of interpreting nineteenth-century British literature from the perspective of the twentieth century. What has been the impact of feminism on twentieth-century readings of *Jane Eyre*? And is it possible, through attending to the imperialist values in circulation at the moment of textual production, to produce an alternative to previous feminist interpretations of that text – a reading which shows British Imperialism as the price paid for nineteenth-century female individualism? The essay suggests that it is and proposes that only by being historically specific is it possible to recognise the full extent to which nineteenth-century British literature is caught within the history of imperialism, as well as the impossibility in these texts of a fully realised cultural identity for subjects from the Third World.

Notes

1. My notion of the 'wording of a world' upon what must be assumed to be uninscribed earth is a vulgarisation of Martin Heidegger's idea; see 'The Origin of the Work of Art', in *Poetry, Language, Thought*, trans. Albert Hofstadter (New York, 1977), pp. 17–87.
2. See Charlotte Brontë, *Jane Eyre* (New York, 1960); all further references to this work, abbreviated *JE*, will be included in the text.
3. See Jean Rhys, *Wide Sargasso Sea* (Harmondsworth, 1966); all further references to this work, abbreviated *WSS*, will be included in the text. And see Mary Shelley, *Frankenstein; or, The Modern Prometheus* (New York, 1965); all further references to this work, abbreviated *F*, will be included in the text.
4. I have tried to do this in my essay 'Unmaking and Making in *To the Lighthouse*', in Gayatri Chakravorty Spivak, *In Other Worlds: Essays in Cultural Politics* (New York and London, 1987), pp. 30–45.
5. As always, I take my formula from Louis Althusser, 'Ideology and Ideological State Apparatuses (Notes towards an Investigation)', in *'Lenin and Philosophy' and Other Essays*, trans. Ben Brewster (New York, 1971), pp. 127–86. For an acute differentiation between the individual and individualism, see V. N. Vološinov, *Marxism and the Philosophy of Language*, trans. Ladislav Matejka and I. R. Titunik, Studies in Language, 1 (New York, 1973), pp. 93–4, 152–3. For a 'straight' analysis of the roots and ramifications of English 'individualism', see C. B. MacPherson, *The Political Theory of Possessive Individualism: Hobbes to Locke* (Oxford, 1962). I am grateful to Jonathan Rée for bringing this book to my attention and for giving a careful reading of all but the very end of the present essay.
6. I am constructing an analogy with Homi Bhabha's powerful notion of 'not-quite/not-white' in his 'Of Mimicry and Man: The Ambiguity of Colonial Discourse', *October*, 28 (Spring 1984), 132. I should also add that I use the word 'native' here in reaction to the term 'Third World Woman'. It cannot, of course, apply with equal historical justice to both the West Indian and the Indian contexts nor to contexts of imperialism by transportation.
7. See Roberto Fernández Retamar, 'Caliban: Notes towards a Discussion of Culture in Our America', trans. Lynn Garafola, David Arthur McMurray, and Robert Márquez, *Massachusetts Review*, 15 (Winter–Spring 1974), 7–72; all further references to this work, abbreviated 'C', will be included in the text.
8. See José Enrique Rodó, *Ariel*, ed. Gordon Brotherston (Cambridge, 1967).
9. For an elaboration of 'an inaccessible blankness circumscribed by an interpretable text', see my 'Can the Subaltern Speak?', in Cary Nelson and Lawrence Grossberg (eds), *Marxism and the Interpretation of Culture* (Urbana, IL, 1988) pp. 271–313.
10. See Elizabeth Fox-Genovese, 'Placing Women's History in History', *New Left Review*, 133 (May–June 1982), 5–29.
11. Rudolph Ackermann, *The Repository of Arts, Literature, Commerce, Manufactures, Fashions, and Politics* (London, 1823), p. 310.
12. See Terry Eagleton, *Myths of Power: A Marxist Study of the Brontës* (London, 1975); this is one of the general presuppositions of his book.
13. See Sandra M. Gilbert and Susan Gubar, *The Madwoman in the Attic: The Woman Writer and the Nineteenth-Century Literary Imagination* (New Haven, CT, 1979), pp. 360–2.

14. Immanuel Kant, *Critique of Practical Reason*, in *The Critique of Pure Reason, The Critique of Practical Reason and Other Ethical Treatises, The Critique of Judgement*, trans. J. M. D. Meiklejohn et al. (Chicago, 1952), pp. 326, 328.
15. I have tried to justify the reduction of sociohistorical problems to formulas or propositions in my essay 'Can the Subaltern Speak?' The 'travesty' I speak of does not befall the Kantian ethic in its purity as an accident but rather exists within its lineaments as a possible supplement. On the register of the human being as child rather than heathen, my formula can be found, for example, in 'What is Enlightenment?' in Kant, *Foundations of the Metaphysics of Morals, What is Enlightenment? and a Passage from The Metaphysics of Morals*, trans. and ed. Lewis White Beck (Chicago, 1950). I have profited from discussing Kant with Jonathan Rée.
16. Jean Rhys, in an interview with Elizabeth Vreeland, quoted in Nancy Harrison, *Jean Rhys and the Novel as Women's Text* (Chapel Hill, NC, 1988). This is an excellent study of Rhys.
17. See Louise Vinge, *The Narcissus Theme in Western European Literature up to the Early Nineteenth Century*, trans. Robert Dewsnap et al. (Lund, 1967), ch. 5.
18. For a detailed study of this text, see John Brenkman, 'Narcissus in the Text', *Georgia Review*, 30 (Summer 1976), 293–327.
19. This is the main argument of my 'Can the Subaltern Speak?'.
20. See Barbara Johnson, 'My Monster/My Self', *Diacritics*, 12 (Summer 1982), 2–10.
21. See George Levine, *The Realistic Imagination: English Fiction from Frankenstein to Lady Chatterly* (Chicago, 1981), pp. 23–35.
22. Consult the publications of the Feminist International Network for the best overview of the current debate on reproductive technology.
23. For the male fetish, see Sigmund Freud, 'Fetishism', *The Standard Edition of the Complete Psychological Works of Sigmund Freud*, ed. and trans. James Strachey et al., 24 vols (London, 1953–74), 21, pp. 152–7. For a more 'serious' Freudian study of *Frankenstein*, see Mary Jacobus, 'Is There a Woman in This Text?', *New Literary History*, 14 (Autumn 1982), 117–41. My 'fantasy' would of course be disproved by the 'fact' that it is more difficult for a woman to assume the position of fetishist than for a man; see Mary Ann Doane, 'Film and the Masquerade: Theorising the Female Spectator', *Screen*, 23, 3–4 (1982), 74–87.
24. Kant, *Critique of Judgement*, trans. J. H. Bernard (New York, 1951), p. 39.
25. See [Constantin François de Volney], *The Ruins: or, Meditations on the Revolution of Empires* (trans. pub., London, 1811). Johannes Fabian has shown us the manipulation of time in 'new' secular histories of a similar kind; see *Time and the Other: How Anthropology Makes Its Object* (New York 1983). See also Eric R. Wolf, *Europe and the People without History* (Berkeley and Los Angeles, 1982), and Peter Worsley, *The Third World*, 2nd edn (Chicago, 1973); I am grateful to Dennis Dworkin for bringing the latter book to my attention. The most striking ignoring of the monster's education through Volney is in Gilbert's otherwise brilliant 'Horror's Twin: Mary Shelley's Monstrous Eve', *Feminist Studies*, 4 (June 1980), 48–73. Gilbert's essay reflects the absence of race-determinations in a certain sort of feminism. Her present work has most convincingly filled in this gap; see, for example, her recent piece on H. Rider Haggard's *She* ('Rider Haggard's Heart of Darkness', *Partisan Review*, 50 [1983], 444–53).
26. 'A letter is always and a priori intercepted, . . . the "subjects" are neither the senders nor the receivers of messages . . . The letter is constituted by its interception' (Jacques Derrida, 'Discussion', after Claude Rabant, 'Il n'a aucine chance de l'entendre', in René Major (ed.), *Affranchissement: Du*

transfert et de la lettre (Paris, 1981), p. 106; my translation). Margaret Saville is not made to appropriate the reader's 'subject' into the signature of her own 'individuality'.

27. The most striking 'internal evidence' is the admission in the 'Author's Introduction' that, after dreaming of the yet-unnamed Victor Frankenstein figure and being terrified (through, yet not quite through, him) by the monster in a scene that she later reproduced in Frankenstein's story, Shelley began her tale 'on the morrow . . . with the words "It was on a dreary night of November"' (F, p. xi). Those are the opening words of chapter 5 of the finished book, where Frankenstein begins to recount the actual making of his monster (see F, p. 56).

13. MARJORIE GARBER, 'CROSS-DRESSING, GENDER AND REPRESENTATION: ELVIS PRESLEY'
(From *Vested Interests: Cross-dressing and Cultural Anxiety* (New York, 1992), pp. 353–7, 359, 363–74.)

Summary

Drawing on Joan Riviere's essay, 'Womanliness as a Masquerade', Marjorie Garber calls into question the contrast between female impersonators ('marked transvestites') and 'real' women. She goes on, however, to consider three 'unmarked' cross-dressers, Liberace, Rudolph Valentino and Elvis Presley. (We have reluctantly omitted her detailed accounts of the first two.) Dress as display, as representation, stands in, the essay argues, for what is not there, what is 'lost' when people enter into the Symbolic, the order of language and culture. Elvis, endlessly impersonated, was also the impersonator of an identity which existed only as performance, 'crossing' between black and white in his music, and between masculine and feminine in his appearance. The absence of a single, originating essence, Garber proposes, veiled by representation, is the cause of the audience's desire, and the defining characteristic of the superstar. Elvis Presley's masculinity, no less a masquerade than womanliness is, implies that gender has no place beyond representation, and that representation itself has no origin elsewhere.

Notes

1. *George Michael: Music, Money, Love, Faith* (MTV Networks, 1988). I am grateful to Nancy Vickers for this reference.
2. *San Francisco Chronicle*, 9 May 1990: E1.
3. Mablen Jones, *Getting It On: The Clothing of Rock 'n' Roll* (New York, 1987), p. 129.
4. Andrew Ross, 'Uses of Camp', in *No Respect: Intellectuals and Popular Culture* (New York, 1989) p. 165.
5. Mablen Jones, *Getting It On*, p. 44.
6. Kris Kirk and Ed Heath, *Men in Frocks* (London, 1984), p. 58.
7. Joan Riviere, 'Womanliness as a Masquerade', in *Formations of Fantasy*, ed. Victor Burgin, James Donald and Cora Kaplan (London, 1986), p. 38.
8. Jacques Lacan, 'The Signification of the Phallus', in *Ecrits: A Selection*, trans. Alan Sheridan (New York, 1977), p. 291.
9. Eugénie Lemoine-Luccioni, *La Robe* (Paris, 1983), p. 124.

10. Roland Barthes, *The Fashion System*, trans. Matthew Ward and Richard Howard (New York, 1983), pp. 231–2.
11. Dustjacket copy for *The Wonderful Private World of Liberace*, by Liberace (New York, 1986).
12. Liberace, *The Wonderful Private World of Liberace*, p. 171.
13. Bob Thomas, *Liberace* (New York, 1987), p. 243.
14. *Time*, the *New York Times*, and the *Los Angeles Times* all carried articles on him. Thomas, *Liberace*, p. 173.
15. James Barron, 'Liberace, Flamboyant Pianist, Is Dead', *New York Times*, 5 February 1987: B6.
16. There have, in fact, been numerous Liberace imitators, as Dick Alexander notes in the *San Francisco Examiner*, 22 July 1990: T4.
17. Although at least one, Jac L. Tharpe, points it out in passing. Tharpe, 'Will the Real Elvis Presley . . . ', in Tharpe, *Elvis: Images and Fancies* (Jackson, MS, 1979), p. 4.
18. Peter Guralnick, *The Rolling Stone Illustrated History of Rock & Roll*, ed. Jim Miller (New York, 1980), p. 21.
19. Nik Cohn's novel, *King Death* (1975), speculates on what would have happened had Jesse lived. Albert Goldman comments that 'This spirit brother is one of the most important characters in the life of Elvis Presley'. Albert Goldman, *Elvis* (New York, 1981), p. 65.
20. Norman A. Mackenzie, *The Magic of Rudolph Valentino* (London, 1974), p. 11.
21. 'This surprising identification with the film idol of the silent era, a man who was dead before Elvis was born', writes Albert Goldman, 'is the first unmistakable sign that Elvis had discovered the essence of his appeal and was starting to cultivate a corresponding image. It is also a sign of prescience, for nothing better defines Elvis' future role than the formula: teen Valentino. If you add to the basic image of the sultry Latin lover the further garnishings of an erotic style of music and dance, the tango for the twenties, rock 'n' role for the fifties, the parallel is perfect. Soon Elvis would even have crow-black hair' (Goldman, *Elvis*, p. 129).
22. Vernon Scott, 'Elvis Ten Million Dollars Later', *McCalls*, February 1963, p. 124.
23. Molly Ivins, 'Presley Fans Mourn in Memphis . . .', *New York Times*, 18 August 1977: C18.
24. 'The King Is Dead, But Long Lives the King in a Showbiz Bonanza', *People*, 8, 15 (10 October 1977), p. 29.
25. Werner T. Mays, in John Edgerton, 'Elvis Lives!' *The Progressive*, 43, 3 (March 1979), 23.
26. George Melly, *Revolt into Style* (Harmondsworth, 1970), pp. 36–7.
27. David Houston. Goldman, *Elvis*, p. 157.
28. Stephen Heath, 'Joan Riviere and the Masquerade', in *Formations of Fantasy*, p. 53.
29. Goldman, *Elvis*, p. 122. Patsy Guy Hammontree, *Elvis Presley, A Bio-Bibliography* (Westport, CT, 1985), p.13.
30. Charles White, *The Life and Times of Little Richard* (New York, 1984), pp. 66, 69.
31. William Allen Harbinson, *The Illustrated Elvis* (New York, 1977), p. 93.
32. J. David Stern, 'The King Is Back', *TV Guide*, 38, 7 (17 February 1990), pp. 6–7.
33. Albert Goldman, whose view of Elvis often borders on the vitriolic, puts the turning point at his army experience, which was traditionally supposed to make a man of him: 'The Elvis who had appeared on the Dorsey, Berle, and Sullivan shows, who had starred in *Loving You* and *Jailhouse Rock*, was butch. He had a chunky, clunky aura. . . . After the army, Elvis appears very delicate and vulnerable. . . . With his preposterous Little Richard conk, his limp wrist,

girlish grin, and wobbly knees, which now turn out instead of in, he looks
outrageously gay' (Goldman, *Elvis*, pp. 329–30). Goldman targets, especially,
what he describes as 'his queer showing on *Frank Sinatra's Welcome Home
Party for Elvis Presley*' 'When he confronts the much smaller but more
masculine Sinatra, Elvis's body language flashes, "I surrender, dear".'

Goldman's hostility toward (and fascination with) his subject is clear, as is
his desire to pop-psychoanalyse and re-gender him. Thus he describes the 21-
year-old Elvis's 'Girlish boudoir', full of Teddy bears (picture caption,
Goldman, pp. 337) and claims that he was so sensitive about his
uncircumcised state that 'instead of pissing in a urinal . . . he would always go
inside, like a woman' (Goldman, p. 339). When it comes to accounting for the
singer's popularity, Goldman has recourse again to gender and to a kind of
instant cultural criticism. 'Much of Elvis's power over young girls came not
just from the fact that he embodied their erotic fantasies but that he likewise
projected frankly feminine traits with which they could identify. This AC/DC
quality became in time characteristic of rock stars in general, commencing
with Mick Jagger and the Beatles (who had such ravishingly girlish falsettos)
and going on to include Jim Morrison, David Bowie, Elton John and many
figures of the punk pantheon' (Goldman, p. 345).

34. John J. O'Connor, '"Elvis" The Series: Poor Boy Makes Good', *New York Times*,
    6 February 1990: B1.
35. *The Masquerader*, 1914; *The Woman*, 1915. Of *The Masquerader*, *Bioscope* wrote,
    'Mr. Chaplin gives a really remarkable female impersonation. The makeup is
    no less successful than the characterisation, and is further proof of Mr.
    Chaplin's versatility.' *The Films of Charlie Chaplin*, ed. Gerald D. McDonald,
    Michael Conway, and Mark Ricci (Secauscus, NJ, 1971), p. 62.
36. John Carlin, *The Iconography of Elvis*, as quoted in Victor Bockris, *The Life and
    Death of Andy Warhol* (New York, 1989), pp. 124–5.
37. *Newsweek*, 29 August 1977. Cited in Tharpe, *Elvis: Images*, p. 4.
38. Walter Benjamin,'The Work of Art in the Age of Mechanical Reproduction',
    Illuminations, trans. Harry Zohn (New York, 1969), p. 221.
39. Goldman, *Elvis*, p. 229.
40. 'Elvis Presley Imitations in Spirit and Flesh', *Rolling Stone*, 261 (23 March
    1978).
41. *Time*, 9 April 1990, p. 38.
42. Sheila Rule, 'The Men Who Would Be Elvis', *New York Times*, 26 June 1990: B1.
43. 'Beauty Pageant's "Roger & Me" Lesson', 'Outtakes' column, reprinted from
    the *Los Angeles Times*, *San Francisco Chronicle*, 12 February 1990: F3.
44. Alice Kahn, 'A Whole Lotta Elvis Going On', *San Francisco Chronicle*, 11 June
    1900: B3.
45. Sigmund Freud, 'The Uncanny' (1919) *SE* 17, p. 241.
46. Simon Frith, 'Confessions of a Rock Critic', in *Music for Pleasure: Essays in the
    Sociology of Pop* (New York, 1988), p. 193.
47. *San Francisco Chronicle*, 22 February 1990.
48. Mark Leger, 'The Drag Queen in The Age of Mechanical Reproduction',
    Out/Look, 6 (Fall 1989), 29.

14. DIANE ELAM, 'FEMINISM AND THE POSTMODERN: THEORY'S ROMANCE'
(Edited extracts from *Romancing the Postmodern* (London and New York, 1992), pp. 143–9, 153–66, 174.)

Summary

The extract reprinted here from Elam's book *Romancing the Postmodern* argues for a rereading of romance as a postmodern genre. Maintaining that the seductive rhetoric of romance is postmodern in so far as it exceeds any essentialist notion of sexual or historical truth, Elam goes on to show how Kathy Acker's and Jacques Derrida's postmodern romances subvert the Enlightenment project of arresting the play of the signifier and mastering the truth of sexual difference.

Notes

1. Jacques Derrida, *The Post Card: From Socrates to Freud and Beyond*, trans. Alan Bass (Chicago, 1987), p. 175.
2. Kathy Acker, *In Memoriam to Identity* (New York, 1990), p. 141.
3. Ibid., p. 133.
4. Other considerations of the relationship between theory and seduction include: Jean Baudrillard, *De la séduction* (Paris, 1979); Jane Gallop, 'French Theory and the Seduction of Feminism', in Alice Jardine and Paul Smith (eds), *Men in Feminism* (New York and London, 1987); Ellen Rooney, *Seductive Reasoning: Pluralism as the Problematic of Contemporary Literary Theory* (Ithaca, NY, 1989).
5. See especially Georg Lukács, *History and Class Consciousness: Studies in Marxist Dialectics*, trans. Rodney Livingstone (Cambridge, MA, 1985); and *The Historical Novel*, trans. Hannah and Stanley Mitchell (Lincoln, NE, and London, 1983).
6. See Louis Althusser, 'Ideology and State Apparatuses (Notes Towards an Investigation)', *Lenin and Philosophy*, trans. Ben Brewster (New York and London, 1971); and Louis Althusser and Etienne Balibar, *Reading Capital*, trans. Ben Brewster (London, 1977).
7. An ideological break occurs when ideology reaches critical self-knowledge, so that ideological subjects become scientists capable of symptomatic readings. The prime example for Althusser is the later Marx, the Marx of *Capital*, who provides a theory of historical materialism that allows the critical reader to overcome the limitations of Marx's own historically determined perspective with the aid of principles drawn from *Capital* itself. Thus, the empirical inadequacies of *Capital* are transcended by the theoretical second or symptomatic reading which the text proposes for itself.
8. The impact of Mulvey's 'Visual Pleasure and Narrative Cinema' is perhaps best attested to by the frequency with which it has been anthologised since its first appearance in *Screen*,16, no. 3 (Autumn 1975).
9. The resistance of haircare to revolutionary Marxist analysis appears also in the apocryphal story of Lenin in Geneva prior to the Russian Revolution, when he supposedly spent as much time chasing a cure for baldness around the pharmacies as in the library studying Marx.
10. Derrida, *The Post Card*, p. 69.
11. My reference here is to the 1990 Texas gubernatorial candidate, Clayton Williams, who in a press conference remarked that Texas weather is like rape:

'If it's inevitable, just relax and enjoy it.' That Williams lost the election to Ann Richards bears remembering. Her victory slogan read: 'A woman's place is in the Dome.' For a fuller account of the incident, see Jan Jarboe, 'Clayton Williams: Onward to the Past', *Texas Monthly*, October 1990.

12. See Jacques Derrida, *Spurs: Nietzsche's Styles/Eperons: Les Styles de Nietzsche*, trans. Barbara Harlow (Chicago, 1979). Along these lines, John Caputo also claims that for Derrida 'woman spells the end of hermeneutics', *Radical Hermeneutics* (Bloomington, IN, 1987), p. 157.

13. See for instance: Sandra M. Gilbert and Susan Gubar, *The Madwoman in the Attic: The Woman Writer and the Nineteenth-Century Literary Imagination* (New Haven, CT, 1979); Kate Millet, *Sexual Politics* (London, 1977); Ellen Moers, *Literary Women: The Great Writers* (New York, 1977); Elaine Showalter, *A Literature of Their Own: British Women Novelists from Brontë to Lessing* (Princeton, NJ, 1977). For an extended discussion of the relationships between Anglo-American feminist criticism and French feminist theory, see Toril Moi, *Sexual/Textual Politics: Feminist Literary Theory* (New York and London, 1985).

14. Derrida, *The Post Card*, p. 18.

15. Ibid., p. 121.

16. Kathy Acker, *My Death, My Life By Pier Paolo Pasolini, Literal Madness* (1984) (New York, 1989), p. 180.

17. Ibid., p. 180.

18. I am referring here, of course, to Habermas's essay 'Modernity – An Incomplete Project', in Hal Foster (ed.), *The Anti-Aesthetic* (Seattle, WA, 1983), pp. 3–15. In the course of this extended discussion of modernity and its relationship to postmodernism, Habermas never mentions a single female author, nor does he consider gender an issue for either modernity or postmodernism. The question of gender is left to the signature of the female translator (Seyla Ben-Habib), which appears at the end of the essay.

19. Kathy Acker, *Don Quixote* (New York, 1986), p. 134.

20. Kathy Acker, *Empire of the Senseless* (New York, 1988), pp. 179–80.

21. Acker, *Don Quixote* p. 178.

22. Ibid., p. 29.

23. Ibid.

24. Ibid., p. 40.

25. Kathy Acker, 'Realism for the Cause of Future Revolution', in Brian Wallis (ed.), *Art After Modernism: Rethinking Representation* (Boston, 1984), p. 33.

26. Ibid.

27. Acker, *Don Quixote*, pp. 165–6.

28. Ibid., pp. 166–7.

29. Ibid., p. 167.

30. Ibid., p. 168.

31. Acker, *My Death, My Life By Pier Paolo Passolini, Literal Madness*, p. 246.

32. Acker, *In Memoriam to Identity*, p. 92.

33. Jacques Derrida, 'Restitutions of the truth in pointing [*pointure*]', *The Truth in Painting* (1978), trans. Geoff Bennington and Ian McLeod (Chicago, 1987), p. 256.

34. Derrida, *The Post Card*, p. 143. Another example of Derrida's insistence on the multiplicity of gendered positions would be his remarks to Christie V. McDonald in what is now a widely cited interview: 'Choreographies', *Diacritics*, 12, no. 2 (Summer 1982). This rather brief attempt to explain the complexity of the effect of 'polysexual signatures' has been dismissed by some critics as simply utopian. I would argue that Derrida's more extended discussion in 'Envois' makes such a dismissal much more difficult.

35. Derrida, *The Post Card*, p. 234.
36. Ibid., p. 79.
37. Gregory L. Ulmer, *Applied Grammatology: Post(e)-Pedagogy from Jacques Derrida to Joseph Beuys* (Baltimore and London, 1985), pp. 131–2.
38. Derrida, *The Post Card*, p. 39.
39. Acker, *In Memoriam to Identity*, pp. 203–4.
40. For a general account of the philosophical problems of reproducibility for the thought of original creation, see Rosalind Krauss, 'The Originality of the Avant-Garde: A Postmodern Repetition', in Brian Wallis (ed.), *Art After Modernism* (Boston, 1984), pp. 13–30. On surrogate motherhood, see Katha Pollitt, 'When Is A Mother Not a Mother?', *The Nation*, 252, no. 23 (23 December 1990).
41. Kathy Acker, *Great Expectations* (New York, 1982).
42. Kathy Acker, *Florida. Literal Madness* (New York, 1989).
43. Acker, *My Death, My Life By Pier Paolo Passolini, Literal Madness*, pp. 289–90.
44. Glenn A. Harper makes a similar point when he argues that the result of Acker's plagiarism is 'the breakup of the illusory self-centeredness of language and, as in feminist appropriation, the refusal of the rules of art-as-commodity' ('The Subversive Power of Sexual Difference in the Work of Kathy Acker', *SubStance*, 54, no. 3 (1987), 47). Larry McCaffery takes a somewhat different line on Acker's style, comparing it to punk music ('Kathy Acker and "Punk" Aesthetics', in Ellen Friedman and Miriam Fuchs (eds), *Breaking the Sequence: Women's Experimental Fiction* (Princeton, NJ, 1989), pp. 215–30).
45. Derrida, *The Post Card*, p. 89.
46. Ibid., p. 200.
47. Ibid.
48. Ibid., p. 109.
49. Acker, *Great Expectations*, p. 64.
50. Ibid., p. 123.
51. Acker, *My Death, My Life By Pier Paolo Passolini, Literal Madness*, p. 234.
52. Ibid., p. 244.
53. Ibid., p. 246.
54. In making this connection between Acker and Derrida, here I think particularly of Derrida's remark in 'Envois': 'What counts then is that it is still up to us to exhaust language' (*The Post Card*, p. 56).
55. Derrida, *The Post Card*, p. 53.
56. Ibid., pp. 66–7.
57. Derrida argues for eighteenth-century modernity as the moment in the history of metaphysics when the defence of logocentrism is most explicitly carried forward against the threat of an awareness of the materiality of writing:

> What threatens indeed is writing. It is not an accidental and haphazard threat; it reconciles within a single historical system the projects of *pasigraphy*, the discovery of non-European scripts, or at any rate the massive progress of techniques of *deciphering*, and finally the idea of a *general science of language and writing*. Against all these pressures a battle is then declared. 'Hegelianism' will be its finest scar. (*Of Grammatology*, trans. Gayatri Chakravorty Spivak (Baltimore, 1976) p. 99).

15. JULIA KRISTEVA, 'WOMEN'S TIME'
(Extract from 'Women's Time', *Signs*, 7 (1981), pp. 13–35,
trans. Alice Jardine and Harry Blake.)

Summary

'Women's Time' begins by arguing that people can be thought of as belonging to national units on the one hand, or to transnational or international groupings on the other (young people, for instance, or women). These distinct ways of classifying people correspond to two ways of thinking about time, one historical and linear, and the other cyclical (repetitive, according to the rhythms of nature) or monumental (eternal, time-less, mythic). The second of these ways of thinking, the cyclical or monumental, has been associated specifically with women, but this association, common to many cultures and especially to mystical ones, is not fundamentally incompatible with masculine values.

The extract reprinted here begins by differentiating between the traditional form of feminism, which seeks a place and rights for women within the nation and linear history, and a more recent phase which locates the feminist struggle primarily within sexual relations. This second phase emphasises the difference between men and women, and draws on psychoanalysis as the main existing theory of sexual difference. But Kristeva's own version of Freud is profoundly modified by Lacan, so that the fear of castration is precisely symbolic – the fear of the loss of presence, totality, pleasure, which is consequent upon the acquisition of language as separation from nature. This separation, the entry into the symbolic order, a world of difference and so of power and meaning, is the sociosymbolic contract which is the basis of identity, and it is common to both women and men.

But its implications have been different for each. The place in the symbolic order allotted to women has been an unequal, frustrating one, their task merely to perpetuate the contract by transmitting it to the next generation. One reaction to this is the construction of a revolutionary countersociety, but the essay draws attention to the dangers which ensue when power changes hands without changing its nature. Another reaction has been the quest for creativity through the idealisation of the experience of motherhood, or through the production of a specifically women's writing, *écriture féminine*. The essay identifies both these reactions as 'religious', a mythologising of Woman. In their place it proposes a third phase for feminism: instead of stressing the single difference between men and women, we might affirm the sociosymbolic internalisation of difference itself as the foundation of identity. The affirmation of difference as the basis of subjectivity would release at once the individuality and the multiplicity of each person's possible identities.

Notes

1. See D. Desanti, 'L'Autre Sexe des bolcheviks', *Tel quel*, 76 (1978); Julia Kristeva, *On Chinese Women*, trans. Anita Barrows (New York, 1977).
2. See Arthur Hertzberg, *The French Enlightenment and the Jews* (New York, 1968); B. Blumenkranz and A. Seboul (eds), *Les Juifs et la révolution française* (Paris, 1976).
3. In a section of the article which precedes the extract reprinted here Kristeva says: 'I think that the apparent coherence which the term "woman" assumes in contemporary ideology, apart from its "mass" or "shock" effect for activist purposes, essentially has the negative effect of effacing the differences among

the diverse functions or structures which operate beneath this word.' (Signs, 7 (1981), 18.)

4. This work is periodically published in various academic women's journals, one of the most prestigious being *Signs: Journal of Women in Culture and Society*, University of Chicago Press. Also of note are the special issues: 'Ecriture, fémininité, féminisme', *La Revue des sciences humaines*, Lille III (1977), 4; and 'Les Femmes et la philosophie', *Le Doctrinal de sapience*, Editions Solin 3 (1977).

5. See linguistic research on 'female language': Robin Lakoff, *Language and Women's Place* (New York, 1974); Mary R. Key, *Male/Female Language* (Metuchen, NJ, 1973); A. M. Houdebine, 'Les Femmes et la langue', *Tel quel*, 74 (1977), 84–95. The contrast between these 'empirical' investigations of women's 'speech acts' and much of the research in France on the conceptual bases for a 'female language' must be emphasised here. It is somewhat helpful, if ultimately inaccurate, to think of the former as an 'external' study of language and the latter as an 'internal' exploration of the process of signification. For further contrast, see e.g. 'Part II: Contemporary Feminist Thought in France: Translating Difference' in Hester Eissenstein and Alice Jardine (eds), *The Future of Difference* (1980); the 'Introductions' to *New French Feminisms*, ed. Elaine Marks and Isabelle de Courtivron (Brighton, 1981); and for a very helpful overview of the problem of 'difference and language' in France, see Stephen Heath, 'Difference', *Screen*, 19, 3 (1978), 51–112. – AJ.

6. This is one of the more explicit references to the mass marketing of *'écriture féminine'* in Paris over the last ten years. – AJ.

7. The expression *à leur corps défendant* translates as 'against their will,' but here the emphasis is on women's bodies: literally, 'against their bodies'. I have retained the former expression in English, partly because of its obvious intertextuality with Susan Brownmiller's *Against Our Will* (New York, 1975). Women are increasingly describing their experience of the violence of the symbolic contract as a form of rape. – AJ.

8. See *On Chinese Women*.

9. See M. A. Macciocchi, *Elements pour une analyse du fascisme* (Paris, 1976); Michèle Mattelart, 'Le Coup d'état au féminin', *Les Temps modernes* (January (1975).

10. See Jacques Lacan, 'Dieu et la jouissance de la femme' in *Encore*, Paris (1975), pp. 61–71, especially p. 68. This seminar has remained a primary critical and polemical focus for multiple tendencies in the French women's movement. For a brief discussion of the seminar in English, see Heath, 'Difference'. – AJ.

11. Again a reference to *écriture féminine* as generically labelled in France over the past few years and not to women's writing in general. – AJ.

16. LUCE IRIGARAY, 'THE LOOKING GLASS, FROM THE OTHER SIDE'
(From *This Sex Which Is Not One* (Ithaca, NY, 1985), pp. 9–22.
First published as 'Le Miroir, de l'autre côté' in *Critique*, 309, February 1973.)

Summary

Invoking Lewis Carroll's Alice and Michel Soutter's film, *The Surveyors*, Luce Irigaray here breaks with the conventions of the theoretical essay to pose the question of woman's identity. A fragmented narrative recounts how Alice, paralysed by her existence in the mirror where her multiple selves are no more than images reflected for others, goes behind the screen of representation and baffles the gaze of the male surveyor. But what is she there? Not a true self, the text indicates, in a world where, outside the order of representation, there can be no distinctions, no proprieties, no property, no names. Who, then? Part of the resistance . . .

Notes

1. *The Surveyors*. The story goes like this: Alice lives alone in her childhood home, after her father's death. Her mother lives next door. Lucien and Gladys live in the same small village. There is also Ann, about whom we know nothing except that she makes love. And Eugene, Alice's friend, who only plays the cello. A highway is to cut through the village. So two surveyors arrive – Leon and Max. But surveying means 'striding back and forth between houses, people and feelings'.

Glossary

Note: Words or phrases given in italics are also defined in their alphabetical place in the Glossary.

Althusser, Louis   French structuralist Marxist whose work on *ideology* challenges the humanist assumption that the *individual* is the *author* and guarantor of his or her meanings. A seminal essay is his 'Ideology and Ideological State Apparatuses (Notes towards an Investigation)', in *Lenin and Philosophy and Other Essays*, trans. Ben Brewster (London, 1971), pp. 127–86. For a critical, accessible introduction to his work in the light of subsequent theories of ideology and *discourse* see Diane Macdonell, *Theories of Discourse: An Introduction* (Oxford, 1986).

author   See *individual*

binary opposition(s)   A binary opposition comprises two terms which are classified hierarchically so that the second term is assumed to be derivative from and exterior to the first. For example, nature/culture, logos/pathos, man/woman.

bisexuality   The 'bi' of bisexuality invokes the binary numerology of two. Correspondingly, an oppositional mode of sexual difference is produced. This has the effect of fixing a polarised structure of sexual difference in which the sexes are always-already and forever locked in antithesis.

deconstruction   The uncovering of the trace of otherness within what seems single and self-identical. Deconstruction undoes the hierarchic *binary oppositions* which are no more than an effect of linguistic *difference*.

Derrida, Jacques   Influential French philosopher whose work challenges the basis of the Western philosophical tradition. Derrida's account of language is available in relatively accessible form in *Positions*, trans. Alan Bass (London, 1987).

desire   See *lack*.

differance   The term differance is a development by *Jacques Derrida* of *Ferdinand de Saussure*'s account of language as a system of differences. Spelt with an 'a' to distinguish it virtually from *difference*, differance signifies not only 'difference' but also 'deferral'. The idea of deferral resists the closure of meanings which might appear to be the effect of difference, for it involves the belief that signification always delays or displaces pure intelligibility. Differences of meaning are therefore not anchored in concepts: rather those differences slide constantly within the infinite *displacement* and relegation of meaning. In other words, meaning is constructed only by the process of referring to other (absent) meanings, with the consequence that the relatively stable structure of difference slides into and is destabilised by differance.

difference   *Ferdinand de Saussure* proposed that words have no inherent meaning but take on meaning from their difference from other words.

discourse   In the work of *Michel Foucault* a discourse is a knowledge (physics,

253

psychoanalysis, for example) inscribed in a specific vocabulary and sometimes a specific syntax. A particular discourse may be identified by the institution and interests it serves as well as by the *subject* positions it constructs.

displacement   Invoked by Freud and later *Lacan* as a practice of the unconscious, displacement is a term, like *supplement* and *differance*, deployed as a means of preventing the conceptual closure of meaning and fixing of *binary oppositions*.

'*Dora*'   From the feminist point of view, Dora is perhaps the most famous of Freud's case histories. In 1900, when she was eighteen, Dora was treated by Freud for hysteria. She left before he had completed his analysis. Her rebellious refusal to continue treatment and the diagnosis of hysteria have been of more than passing interest to feminist theory, especially French feminism.

écriture féminine   Feminine (female) writing. French has only one adjective from *femme* (woman), and that is *féminin*. Consequently, in French the distinction between female (a matter of nature) and feminine (an effect of cultural construction) is a difficult one to make. *Ecriture féminine* is written by/from the (female) body.

Foucault, Michel   French philosopher and historian of ideas. Foucault's recurrent concern is the relation between knowledge and power. See for example *Discipline and Punish: The Birth of the Prison*, trans. Alan Sheridan (London, 1977) and *The History of Sexuality*, vol. 1, trans. Robert Hurley (London, 1979).

ideology   Ideologies are the beliefs, meanings and practices which shape our thoughts and actions. In the work of *Althusser*, from which most of the essays in this volume derive their use of the term, ideology not only defines our understanding of the world, and our position in it, but is the condition of our experience. Althusser's treatment of ideology differs from the common definition of ideology as a set of external doctrines that *individuals* knowingly choose or reject, such as a 'Conservative' ideology; instead, it is central to his thesis that all *subjects* are *interpellated* by ideology: there is no escaping ideological subjection. Unlike classical Marxism, which approaches ideology as an expression of the determining economic base, thereby suggesting that ideologies are formulated as abstract ideas in the individual's consciousness or mind, Althusser asserts that ideology has a material existence in the State apparatuses (the Church, the family, educational institutions, etc.). These apparatuses constitute the social formation and have ideological effects. Althusser stresses that all ideologies are produced out of struggle. Thus, a dominant ideology, though it may present its beliefs as self-evident, natural and true, is always the result of a struggle with antagonistic ideologies.

imaginary   In the work of *Jacques Lacan* the imaginary is a condition of illusory unity, mastery and plenitude. It is beyond *difference*, and therefore outside (differentiated from) the *symbolic order*.

individual   The concept of the individual (woman, man, child) derives from humanist, commonsense assumptions that the source and guarantor of meaning is the autonomous mind of an individual. In this context the belief that individuals are the authors of meaning, thus consciously controlling and authorising the meanings they produce, has been challenged by post-structuralism, which has called into question the concepts of 'origin', 'truth' and 'individuality'. Roland Barthes, in particular, has proclaimed the death of the author, in so far as the literary institution treats the author as the explanation of the text.

interpellation   Interpellation by *ideology* is the universal mechanism by which *individuals* recognise themselves and are recognised as *subjects*. *Althusser* argues that it is only in ideology that individuals are constituted as subjects: the process of interpellation by ideology addresses individuals as unique subjects, conferring on them an identity which appears 'obvious'. But this 'obviousness' is itself an ideological effect, 'the elementary ideological effect'. The result is that individuals accept their subject position in the social formation as 'freely chosen', so that they 'work by themselves'.

jouissance   Ecstasy (sexual); coming. Also enjoyment (of rights, property, etc.).

Lacan, Jacques   French psychoanalyst and theorist who reread Freud in the light of *Saussure*'s theory of language. Jane Gallop, *Reading Lacan* (Ithaca, NY, 1985), is excellent but is not addressed to beginners. For an introduction to Lacanian theory see Malcolm Bowie, 'Jacques Lacan', in John Sturrock (ed.), *Structuralism and Since: From Lévi-Strauss to Derrida* (Oxford, 1979), pp. 116–53.

lack   The *subject*, which comes into existence only with the entry into the *symbolic order*, can never be the origin of meaning, but only its (unstable) effect. Meanwhile its loss, as a signifying subject, of an illusory organic wholeness is the cause of the lack in being which initiates desire.

logocentrism   According to *Jacques Derrida*, logocentrism gives independent existence to concepts, which are no more than an effect of linguistic *difference*. Logocentrism makes ideas the origin of language, and finds the guarantee of truth outside language – in the mind of God or, more recently, in the subjectivity of the *individual*.

metaphysics   From the point of view of *Jacques Derrida*, any claim to truth which resides outside or beyond language is metaphysical. The effort to fix meaning, to arrest its play, depends on the metaphysics of presence, a faith in an essential truth made present in the sign.

Name of the Father (nom du père)   For *Lacan* the primary Other is the symbolic father, whose name guarantees and makes possible the process of signification within the *symbolic order*.

Other   The subject is constituted in the Other, the order of language and culture. In consequence the subject is always other than itself.

phallocentrism   The order of the masculine and the *symbolic*, where masculine sexuality is both privileged and reproduced by a belief in the phallus as primary signifier. Thus, the feminine is subordinated to a masculine order, and woman is placed on the side of negativity and *lack* (of the phallus).

phallogocentrism   This term brings together the notions of *phallocentrism* and *logocentrism*. Both these terms have been associated, especially by French feminism, with the organisation of sexual difference and language in Western patriarchal cultures.

power   In the work of *Michel Foucault* power is defined as a relation. Power is exercised in *discourses* and institutions; it structures the relations of *difference* (of control, or lack of it) between competing discourses and the *subjects* constituted by them. For a useful and accessible analysis of discourse, power and resistance from the perspective of feminist poststructuralism see Chris Weedon, *Feminist Practice and Poststructuralist Theory* (Oxford, 1987), especially chapter 5, pp. 107–35.

problematic   Theoretical framework, complete with its own set of problems (and solutions).

real   The real in Lacanian theory is part of the triad '*imaginary/symbolic/real*'. The real both breaks the dualism of the *imaginary* and the *symbolic* and introduces the notion of a world of objects and things whose existence precedes and exceeds the *subject*. The only way for the subject to realise this world is from its position in the symbolic order, which gives it the means of naming (of creating the world of things in words). But this task can never be completed, precisely because the real can be known only in language, which always takes its place.

Saussure, Ferdinand de   Swiss linguist who developed the science of signs in his pioneering *Course in General Linguistics*, published in 1916. Saussure's theory of language is revolutionary in its insistence that language is not a way of labelling things which already exist outside language, but a system of differences with no positive terms, out of which meaning arises.

selfsame   In Betsy Wing's translation of Hélène Cixous's 'Sorties', the selfsame is taken from the French word *'propre'* which corresponds to 'ownself'. This suggests property and appropriation as well as proper, appropriate and clean.

semiotic   In Julia Kristeva's writing the semiotic is a domain which precedes the *subject*'s entry into the *symbolic order*. It is pre-oedipal, pre-*imaginary*, and characterised by a rhythmic babble, that is, a language which introduces difference but is unformulated in terms of the rules of the symbolic. Although the semiotic is cited as the place of a repressed femininity, it is not inherently female: it is also present in, and challenges, the symbolic. This is evident in moments when language becomes unstable and meanings are ruptured.

sociosymbolic   See *symbolic order*.

subject   That which acts and speaks, which says 'I'. Because the subject is not the origin but the effect of the meanings it speaks, it can never be fully present to itself in its own utterance. It is thus inevitably split, unfixed, in process.

supplement   A supplement is something 'added on', seemingly self-consciously, to a prior term in order to make good an omission within it. Thus, the supplement appears to be exterior and secondary to the primary term it supplements. *Jacques Derrida*, however, has argued against the *metaphysical* logic which fixes the supplement in a subordinate position to a prior term: he suggests that if the supplement is necessary to compensate for the absence it reveals in a prior term, then it is not so much an external extra as a necessary constituent of the term it supplements. See, for example, Derrida's critique of Rousseau's insistence that writing is inferior to and at the same time a supplement to speech, in *Of Grammatology*, trans. Gayatri Chakravorty Spivak (Baltimore, 1976), pp. 141–64, 165–268.

symbolic order   The order of language and culture. It is also the location of *difference*. In *Jacques Lacan's* reading of Freud, the fear of castration is parallel to the recognition of difference, as the child enters the symbolic order.

Suggestions for Further Reading

ACCESSIBLE

Armstrong, Isobel (ed.), *New Feminist Discourses: Critical Essays on Theories and Texts* (London and New York, 1992). Representative collection of essays on literature, theory, art and psychoanalysis by feminist critics working in Britain.

Beauvoir, Simone de, *The Second Sex* (1949), trans H.M. Parshley (London, 1972). Influential account of the social construction of woman.

Belsey, Catherine, *Desire: Love Stories in Western Culture* (Oxford and Cambridge, MA, 1994). A critique of Family Values.

Bowlby, Rachel, *Just Looking: Consumer Culture in Dreiser. Gissing and Zola* (New York and London, 1985). Sees department stores as sites for the construction of female desire in the nineteenth century.

Carby, Hazel, *Reconstructing Womanhood: The F.mergence of the Afro-American Woman Novelist* (Oxford, 1990). Black cultural history.

Christian, Barbara, *Black Women Novelists: The Development of a Tradition. 1892–1976* (Westport, CT, 1980). Charts the history of black women's writing.

Coward, Rosalind, *Female Desire: Women's Sexuality Today* (London, 1984). Analysis of women in popular culture. Wears its theoretical sophistication lightly.

Davis, Angela, *Women, Race and Class* (New York, 1981). Powerful social history of racism and sexism in America.

Donaldson, Laura E., *Decolonizing Feminisms: Race, Gender and Empire-Building* (London, 1992). Investigates the relationship between postcolonial and poststructuralist theories.

Elam, Diane and Robyn Wiegman (eds), *Feminism Beside Itself* (New York and London, 1995). Innovative anthology exploring feminism's troubled relation to itself.

Ellmann, Maud, *The Hunger Artists: Starving, Writing and Imprisonment* (London, 1993). Witty and compelling poststructuralist analysis of the meanings of the body, writing and hunger in Western culture.

Haraway, Donna, 'A Manifesto for Cyborgs' (1985), in *Feminism/Postmodernism*, ed Linda Nicholson (New York and London, 1990), pp. 190–233. Influential account of the cyborg as figurative postmodern subject.

Heath, Stephen, *The Sexual Fix* (London, 1982). Uses psychoanalysis and poststructuralism to challenge the myth of a natural sexuality.

hooks, bell, *Yearning: Race. Gender and Cultural Politics* (London, 1991). Postmodern black feminist critique of identity politics.

Jacobus, Mary (ed.), *Women Writing and Writing About Women* (London, 1979). Essays in feminist criticism by Gillian Beer, Elaine Showalter, Cora Kaplan and others.

Jordan, Glenn and Chris Weedon, *Cultural Politics: Class, Gender, Race and the*

Postmodern World (Oxford and Cambridge, MA, 1994). Clear, focused introduction to the politics of cultural difference, as well as feminism.

Kaplan, Cora, *Sea Changes: Essays on Culture and Feminism* (London, 1986). Uses Marxism and psychoanalysis to interpret canonical and popular texts.

Mohanty, Chandra Talpade, Ann Russo and Lourdes Torres (eds), *Third World Women and the Politics of Feminism* (Bloomington, IN, 1991). Problematises the relationship between woman and the colonised.

Moi, Toril, *Sexual/Textual Politics* (London and New York, 1985). Critical account of differences in feminist criticism.

Morrison, Toni, *Playing in the Dark: Whiteness and the Literary Imagination* (Cambridge, MA, 1992 and London, 1993). Compelling analysis of racism in American fiction.

Nead, Lynda, *The Female Nude: Art, Obscenity, Sexuality* (London, 1992). Lucid and clever poststructuralist examination of the philosophy and politics of the nude.

Newton, Judith and Deborah Rosenfelt (eds), *Feminist Criticism and Social Change: Sex, Class and Race in Literature and Culture* (New York and London, 1985). Materialist-feminist essays by British and American women.

Rich, Adrienne, 'Compulsory Heterosexuality and Lesbian Existence' (*Signs* 5, 1980), *Blood, Bread and Poetry: Selected Prose 1979–1985* (London, 1987), pp. 23–75. Influential redefinition of lesbianism that challenges the dominance of heterosexuality.

Riviere, Joan, 'Womanliness as a Masquerade' (1929), in Victor Burgin, James Donald and Cora Kaplan (eds), *Formations of Fantasy* (London, 1986), pp. 35–44. An early challenge to the essential feminine.

Robinson, Lilian S., *Sex, Class and Culture* (Bloomington, IN, 1978 and New York, 1986). Pioneering analysis of a range of cultural signifying practices.

Sharpe, Jenny, *Allegories of Empire: The Figure of Woman in the Colonial Text* (Minneapolis and London, 1993). Uses contemporary feminist theory to explore the theme of rape in nineteenth-century British and Anglo-Indian fiction.

Smith, Barbara, 'Toward a Black Feminist Criticism' (1977), in Elaine Showalter (ed.), *The New Feminist Criticism* (New York, 1985 and London, 1986), pp. 168–85. Early call for the construction of a black women's canon.

Spender, Dale, *Man Made Language* (London, 1980). How patriarchy silences women.

Weedon, Chris, *Feminist Practice and Poststructuralist Theory* (second edition, Oxford, 1996). Clear and convincing case for the feminist appropriation of theory.

Woolf, Virginia, *A Room of One's Own* (1929) (London, 1977). Still full of crucial insights.

MORE DIFFICULT, BUT WORTH IT

Braidotti, Rosi, *Patterns of Dissonance: A Study of Women in Contemporary Philosophy*, trans. Elizabeth Guild (Oxford and Cambridge, MA, 1991). Critical feminist analysis of the work of Foucault, Derrida, Deleuze and Lyotard.

Bronfen, Elisabeth, *Over Her Dead Body: Death, Femininity and the Aesthetic* (Manchester, 1992). Lacanian analysis of Western culture's fascination with dead female bodies.

Butler, Judith, *Gender Trouble: Feminism and the Subversion of Identity* (New York and London, 1990). The case for gender as performance.

Cixous, Hélène and Catherine Clément, *The Newly Born Woman*, trans. Betsy

Wing (Minneapolis and Manchester, 1986). Together and separately, Cixous and Clément pose the question of a specifically feminine language.

Conley, Verena Andermatt and William V. Spanos (eds), 'On Feminine Writing: A *Boundary 2* Symposium', *Boundary 2*, xii, 2 (1984). Includes fictional and non-fictional work by Cixous, as well as an interview with Derrida about the (non-)place of woman.

De Lauretis, Teresa, *Alice Doesn't: Feminism, Semiotics, Cinema* (Bloomington, IN, 1984). Sophisticated and elegant poststructuralist analysis.

——, *The Practice of Love: Lesbian Sexuality and Perverse Desire* (Bloomington, IN, 1994). Critical use of psychoanalysis.

Derrida, Jacques, *Spurs: Nietzsche's Styles*, trans. Barbara Harlow (Chicago, 1979). Derrida's proposition that women baffle the knowing, mastering male gaze has provoked controversy between feminists.

Diacritics: A Review of Contemporary Criticism, 25 (Summer, 1995). Special issue reviewing twenty-five years of *Diacritics*. Bears witness to the influence of feminism on contemporary theory.

Elam, Diane, *Feminism and Deconstruction: Ms. en Abyme* (London and New York, 1994). Poststructuralist account of the relationship between ethical concerns, American feminism and deconstruction.

Felman, Shoshana, *What Does a Woman Want? Reading and Sexual Difference* (Baltimore, 1993). Skilled and nuanced exploration of how psychoanalysis and literature construct the sexual difference.

Gallop, Jane, *Feminism and Psychoanalysis: The Daughter's Seduction* (London, 1982). Lacanian discussion of sexual difference, desire and language.

Garber, Marjorie, *Vested Interests: Cross-Dressing and Cultural Anxiety* (New York and London, 1992; Harmondsworth, 1993). Transvestism throws into relief the relativity of gender codes.

——, *Vice Versa: Bisexuality and the Eroticism of Everyday Life* (New York, 1995; London, 1996). Problematises the idea of sexual identity.

Jacobus, Mary, *Reading Woman: Essays in Feminist Criticism* (London and New York), 1986. Literary criticism which brings the insights of psychoanalysis to bear on feminism, while at the same time bringing a feminist critique to bear on psychoanalysis.

Jardine, Alice, *Gynesis: Configurations of Woman and Modernity* (Ithaca, NY, 1985). The relationship between (French) feminism and (American) postmodernism.

Jardine, Alice and Paul Smith (eds), *Men in Feminism* (New York and London, 1987). Debates the sexual politics of poststructuralism.

Johnson, Barbara, *A World of Difference* (Baltimore, 1987). Elegant poststructuralist literary criticism.

Kofman, Sarah, *The Enigma of Woman: Woman in Freud's Writings*, trans. Catherine Porter (Ithaca, NY, 1985). Psychoanalytic reading of Freud's anti-feminism.

Marks, Elaine and Isabelle de Courtivron (eds), *New French Feminisms: An Anthology* (Brighton, 1981). Contains writing by more than twenty French feminists.

Mitchell, Juliet and Jacqueline Rose, *Feminine Sexuality: Jacques Lacan and the Ecole Freudienne* (New York, 1985 and London, 1986). Assembles Lacan's controversial pronouncements on women.

Moi, Toril (ed.), *The Kristeva Reader* (Oxford, 1986). Indispensable for students of Julia Kristeva.

——, (ed.) *French Feminist Thought: a Reader* (Oxford, 1987). Valuable collection of essays by Julia Kristeva, Luce Irigaray, Michèle Montrelay and others.

Rose, Jacqueline, *Sexuality in the Field of Vision* (London, 1986). The case for psychoanalysis in theory and critical practice.

Spivak, Gayatri Chakravorty, *In Other Worlds: Essays in Cultural Politics* (New York and London, 1987). Skilled and precise analyses of literature and cultural difference, invoking Marxism, feminism, deconstruction and psychoanalysis.
——, *The Post-colonial Critic: Interviews, Strategies, Dialogues*, ed. Sarah Hasym (New York and London, 1990). Sophisticated application of theory.

Notes on Contributors

Gillian Beer is King Edward VII Professor of English Literature at the University of Cambridge and President of Clare Hall. Her books include *Darwin's Plots* (1983), *George Eliot* (1986) and *Open Fields: Science in Cultural Encounter* (1996).

Catherine Belsey chairs the Centre for Critical and Cultural Theory at the University of Wales, Cardiff. Her books include *Critical Practice* (1980), *The Subject of Tragedy: Identity and Difference in Renaissance Drama* (1985) and *Desire: Love Stories in Western Culture* (1994).

Hélène Cixous is Director of the *Centre d'Etudes Féminines* at the University of Paris VIII. She has published more than thirty works of poetical fiction, as well as plays and collections of critical work. Her books in English translation include *The Newly Born Woman* (1986), *'Coming to Writing' and Other Essays* (1991), *Three Steps on the Ladder of Writing* (1993), *Manna* (1994) and *First Days of the Year* (1996).

Rosalind Coward teaches Media Studies at Reading University and is a Senior Research Fellow at Nene College, Northampton. She is author of *Language and Materialism* (with John Ellis, 1977), *Patriarchal Precedents* (1983), *Female Desire* (1984), and *Our Treacherous Hearts: Why Women Let Men Get Their Way* (1992). She also writes as a columnist for the *Guardian*.

Diane Elam is Professor of English at the University of Wales, Cardiff. She is author of *Romancing the Postmodern* (1992) and *Feminism and Deconstruction* (1994), as well as co-editor with Robyn Wiegman of *Feminism Beside Itself* (1995).

Shoshana Felman is the Thomas E. Donnelley Professor of French and Comparative Literature at Yale University. She is the editor of *Literature and Psychoanalysis: the Question of Reading: Otherwise* (1982) and author of *Writing and Madness: Literature/Philosophy/Psychoanalysis* (1985), *Jacques Lacan and the Adventure of Insight: Psychoanalysis in Contemporary Culture* (1987), *Testimony: Crises of Witnessing in Literature, Psychoanalysis and History* (1992) and *What Does a Woman Want? Reading and Sexual Difference* (1993).

Marjorie Garber is Director of the Center for Literary and Cultural Studies at Harvard University. Her publications include three books on Shakespeare, several volumes of essays on cultural studies, *Vested Interests: Cross-Dressing and Cultural Anxiety* (1992) and *Vice Versa: Bisexuality and the Eroticism of Everyday Life* (1995).

Luce Irigaray is Director of Research at the *Centre National de Recherche Scientifique*, Paris. Her books in English include *Speculum of the Other Woman* (1985) and *This Sex Which Is Not One* (1985). *The Irigaray Reader* was published in 1991.

Mary Jacobus is Professor of English and Women's Studies at Cornell University. She is author of *Reading Woman: Essays in Feminist Criticism* (1986), *Romanticism,*

Writing and Sexual Difference: Essays on The Prelude (1989) and *First Things: The Maternal Imaginary in Literature, Art, and Psychoanalysis* (1995), as well as editor of *Women Writing and Writing About Women* (1979) and co-editor of *Body/Politics: Women and the Discourses of Science* (1990).

Julia Kristeva is a practising psychoanalyst and also teaches at the University of Paris VII. Her books include two novels, as well as *Desire in Language* (1980), *Powers of Horror* (1982), *Revolution in Poetic Language* (1984), *Tales of Love* (1987) and *Strangers to Ourselves* (1991).

Toril Moi is Professor of Literature and Romance Studies at Duke University. She is editor of *The Kristeva Reader* (1986) and *French Feminist Thought* (1987), as well as author of *Sexual/Textual Politics* (1985) and *Simone de Beauvoir: The Making of an Intellectual Woman* (1994).

Jane Moore lectures in the Centre for Critical and Cultural Theory at the University of Wales, Cardiff. She has published a number of articles on feminism and theory. Her current research projects include a book on Mary Wollstonecraft.

Toni Morrison's fiction includes *The Bluest Eye* (1970), *Sula* (1973), *Song of Solomon* (1978), *Tar Baby* (1981) and *Jazz* (1992). Her *Beloved* was awarded the Pulitzer Prize in 1988.

Line Pouchard is currently working at the University of Tennessee at Knoxville. Her publications include 'Louise Labé in Dialogue with her Lute: Silence Constructs a Poetic Subject' (1995).

Dale Spender's publications include *Man Made Language* (1980 and 1985), *Women of Ideas and What Men Have Done to Them* (1982), *Feminist Theorists* (1983), *There's Always Been a Women's Movement* (1985), *Mothers of the Novel* (1986), and *Writing a New World: Two Centuries of Australian Women Writers* (1988).

Gayatri Chakravorty Spivak is Avalon Foundation Professor in Humanities at Columbia University. She has published a translation of Derrida's *Of Grammatology* (1976), as well as *Imaginary Maps* (1994), a critical translation of Mahasweta Devi's fiction. Her own books include *In Other Worlds* (1987), *The Postcolonial Critic* (1988) and *Outside in the Teaching Machine* (1994).

Index